SCOTLAND IN THE
TWENTIETH CENTURY

SCOTLAND IN THE TWENTIETH CENTURY

edited by T.M. Devine and R.J. Finlay

EDINBURGH UNIVERSITY PRESS

© Edinburgh University Press 1996
22 George Square, Edinburgh EH8 9LF

Reprinted 1997, 2000, 2002, 2003

Typeset in Monotype Bembo
by Nene Phototypesetters, Northampton, and
printed and bound in Great Britain
at the University Press, Cambridge

A CIP record for this book is available from the British Library

ISBN 0 7486 0751 X (hardback)
ISBN 0 7486 0839 7 (paperback)

The Publisher acknowledges subsidy from

THE SCOTTISH ARTS COUNCIL

towards the publication of this volume.

CONTENTS

LIST OF CONTRIBUTORS

Professor T.M. Devine
Professor of Scottish History, Director of the Research Centre in Scottish History and Deputy Principal, University of Strathclyde

Professor P.L. Payne
Professor Emeritus of Economic History, University of Aberdeen

Dr I.G.C. Hutchison
Senior Lecturer in History, University of Stirling

Dr R.J. Finlay
Lecturer in Scottish History, Assistant Director, Research Centre in Scottish History, University of Strathclyde

Dr J. Mitchell
Senior Lecturer, Department of Government, Director, Territorial Politics Research Centre, University of Strathclyde

Dr D. McCrone
Reader in Sociology, University of Edinburgh

Dr R. Rodger
Senior Lecturer in Economic and Social History, University of Leicester

Dr E. Cameron
Lecturer in Scottish History, University of Edinburgh

Mr G. Sprott
Curator, Scottish Agricultural Museum

Dr A. McIvor
Senior Lecturer in History, University of Strathclyde

Dr C. Brown
Senior Lecturer in History, University of Strathclyde

Professor L. Paterson
Professor of Education, Moray House Institute of Education,
Heriot-Watt University

Dr G. Walker
Reader in Politics, Queen's University of Belfast

Dr I. Maver
Lecturer in Scottish History, University of Glasgow

Professor R. Watson
Professor of Scottish Literature, University of Stirling

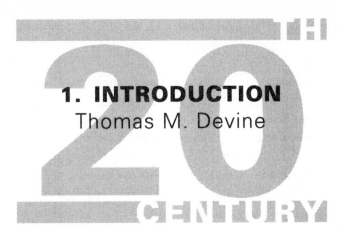

1. INTRODUCTION
Thomas M. Devine

The reader interested in trying to understand the historical development of Scotland in the twentieth century is certainly not spoilt for material. The relatively small number of general books which have appeared in recent years often provide adequate coverage of some themes and topics but rarely aim for comprehensiveness. There are interesting and useful works on political, economic and social history which cover at least part of the century but, as yet, no single-volume study exists which attempts to give an overview of the whole Scottish experience from 1900 to the threshold of the new millennium. The last effort, Christopher Harvie's *No Gods and Precious Few Heroes: Scotland 1914–1980* (1984), concentrated mainly on the first five decades and inevitably could not take into account the important new research on twentieth-century Scotland which has appeared over the last ten years.

It was in large part because of this major gap in the literature that an ambitious two-year seminar was established in the Research Centre in Scottish History at the University of Strathclyde in sessions 1993–4 and 1994–5 on the theme of Scotland in the Twentieth Century. The chapters in this volume are based on the papers given at that seminar and are written by scholars who are acknowledged leaders in their respective fields. The book is a collective and, it is hoped, a coherent attempt to understand and describe the experience of Scotland during a century of unprecedented political, economic, social and cultural change. The study has an inter-disciplinary approach – the authors represent a range of academic subjects including history, economic history, literature, sociology, educational studies and politics. All the chapters provide an overview of existing knowledge but at the same time include, whenever possible, new research and fresh analytical perspectives. The book is about Scotland but in order to bring out what was distinctive in the country's development comparative references to other societies in the UK and in Europe run through the analysis.

One of the key features of the Scottish culture revival of the last three decades has been an enormous increase in the quality and quantity of Scottish historical research. However, a good deal of that work has concentrated on the early modern period and the eighteenth and nineteenth centuries. The more recent past has been comparatively neglected. It would be probably true to say that scholars know more about the period of the Enlightenment and the Industrial Revolution than they do about our own century. It is hoped that this book will help to begin to correct that imbalance by encouraging more systematic research on the nation's recent past. But this is not a volume intended only for academics: its main purpose is to appeal widely to all who are interested in Scotland and wish to understand the modern nation better through a more informed appreciation of its recent history. The sections which follow summarise some of the main themes of the book.

THE ECONOMY

At the beginning of the twentieth century Scotland by any measure was one of the great manufacturing centres of the world. On the eve of World War I the Clyde built nearly a fifth of the world's total output of ships; by 1885 around forty per cent of the British-make of Siemens steel was produced in Scotland; the extraordinary integrated complex in the western Lowlands combining coal, engineering, shipbuilding and metal manufacture and processing sent products to all parts of the globe. The great fact of Scottish economic history in the twentieth century was the erosion and then the elimination of that heavy industrial structure.

Yet, as Peter Payne demonstrates in his chapter on the economy, the staple industries remained intact for most of the period. Only from the 1970s did their disintegration accelerate until by the early 1990s, with the closure of Ravenscraig, the process was complete. An economic system based on coal, iron, steel and heavy engineering which developed in central Scotland from the 1830s and was dominant especially from the 1880s to the 1960s had gone in the space of a couple of decades. What is surprising perhaps is that the structure survived so long. With hindsight it can be seen to have been very vulnerable. The series of heavy industries were all committed directly or indirectly to the fickle, uncertain and competitive overseas markets. The complex of activities was highly integrated, which helped to provide critical mass but also ensured that one sector could not easily remain insulated from the difficulties of another. The Scottish specialisation was normally in the production of simple capital goods which could easily be imitated by overseas competitors. Even shipbuilding, the dynamo of the whole system, was a vast assembly industry which was eventually easily adapted by European and Asian countries. The Scottish economy of the early twentieth century seemed dangerously over-committed to a narrow range of industries all dependent on foreign markets. The problem was compounded by the virtual absence of any significant growth in the newer 'light' industries mainly concerned with servicing the needs of the domestic consumer market. The basic weakness here was that the Scottish market was not only small in population terms, but that Scottish incomes were also relatively low compared to those parts of England – the Midlands and the South – where many of these lighter industries, producing cars, consumer durables and furnishings, were developing rapidly.

Yet, despite the inherent insecurities of the system and the savage impact of the inter-war depression, the economic structure of Scotland c.1960 was not significantly different from that of the early years of the twentieth century. The analysis in this volume suggests that four factors might help to explain resilience. First, the 'decline' of the heavy industries might be apparent now but it was by no means so obvious at the time. Many firms in these sectors continued to achieve profit in several years and it could therefore be plausibly argued that improved organisation and better working practices might bring a more prosperous future. Second, World War II perpetuated the old order by once again creating massive demand for ships, iron, steel and munitions. Third, company structure was often crucial. Many of the key businesses were private limited companies dominated by families. Despite difficulties and persistent losses they often clung on for the sake of the dependent families when public organisations might have more prudently decided to accept the inevitability of voluntary liquidation. Fourth, and particularly in the 1950s and 1960s, the development of regional policy helped to provide support for several of these industries for political and social reasons.

Indeed, one reason for the frightening speed of collapse in the 1970s and 1980s was the withdrawal by the state of 'the life-support system of public ownership', thus exposing the heavy industries to the relentless impact of market forces. More fundamentally, the impact of foreign competition and the fuller integration of Scotland with the British and the international economy unleashed major pressures for change. Painfully, a new economic order emerged in the last quarter of the twentieth century. It was a traumatic process resulting in the decimation of several traditional industries within the space of a few years and the service sector in Scotland, although expanding, did not grow rapidly enough to absorb the redundant labour.

The main features of the Scottish economy which have emerged from this period differ fundamentally from those of the early years of the century. Electronics, financial and other services and tourism dominate. The economic structure has converged to resemble that of Great Britain as a whole. In 1914 Scotland was a global economic power; yet by the 1990s the country's key industries were predominantly foreign-owned. In the early 1970s nearly sixty per cent of manufacturing employment was in plants whose ownership lay outside Scotland. Even more significantly only fourteen per cent of the five fastest growing sectors were Scottish-controlled. Inward investment from large multi-national conglomerates, a relatively low start-up rate of indigenous enterprises and the transfer of Scottish ownership in the merger boom of the late 1960s and early 1970s were all important influences on this.

But in Payne's analysis in this volume a striking continuity with the past also emerges. Standards of living in the later twentieth century are substantially higher than in earlier decades but the vulnerability of the Scottish economy remains. Payne detects 'an alarming fragility' about the manufacturing sector of the economy despite its apparent success. North Sea oil has had limited impact on the industrial base. The much vaunted electronics sector has brought much needed employment but has yet to develop strengths in product design, development and integration which would provide a more secure future. Even more threatening is the possibility of major closures as the larger companies might migrate to lower-cost locations in eastern Europe or higher-skilled areas of the Pacific Rim. The economic future of Scotland remains uncertain. Major challenges exist for business, government, education and the institutions.

GOVERNMENT AND THE CONSTITUTIONAL QUESTION

A universal trend among all developed societies in the twentieth century has been a vast increase in the role and influence of government. In his chapter on government Iain Hutchison argues that there is reason to believe that in a UK context government, especially after 1945, has had an even greater impact than in England and Wales. The Scots tended to put more emphasis on public housing and education than their counterparts elsewhere. For much of the century Scottish unemployment rates were higher and per capita income lower, thus encouraging more reliance on the social security and health systems. For these and other reasons, not least the attempts to prop up the decaying heavy industry complex in the 1950s and

1960s through state support, public expenditure has normally been at higher levels than in England and Wales. All this from one perspective might have been expected to increase the loyalty of the Scots to the British state. After all they were manifestly benefiting from the union relationship. Moreover, several government initiatives were of specific and particular value. Ewen Cameron, in his discussion of the Highlands, demonstrates the vital importance of the North of Scotland Electric Board and suggests it 'can be regarded as one of the outstanding achievements of any public service body in post-war Britain and certainly the most fundamental contribution from any direction in twentieth century Highland history'. While government may have been seen to neglect Scotland in the period between the wars, the balance from the later 1950s swings decisively in the country's favour. In 1960–1 Regional Grant assistance to Scotland stood at £2 million, whereas by 1980–1 it had climbed to £3.2 million. At the same time there were several pressures for greater assimilation of Scotland within the United Kingdom. These included the expansion of the post-1945 Welfare State and the development of modern communications which might in theory have been expected to consolidate a British identity with, as James Mitchell indicates, 'the same news and entertainment being beamed into homes the length and breadth of the country'.

Yet all this did not produce satisfaction with the British state. Increasingly in the last quarter of the century a majority of the Scottish population demanded a change in the constitutional relationship. Whatever the range of opinion on the extent of that change there seems to be a consensus that the status quo is no longer acceptable. The appeal of Britain has declined since the war with the end of the Empire and relative economic decline. In the 1940s, 1950s and 1960s the state was rightly seen as a source of welfare and a support of employment. But the trauma of Scottish deindustrialisation was accompanied by the end of large-scale state economic intervention during the Thatcher years. The social miseries of the later 1970s and 1980s could be blamed more easily on the government, which was seen to have abdicated its responsibilities precisely at the time when they were most needed. The Welfare State, a key element in binding the Scots to the Union, was perceived to be at risk. Britain no longer seemed to be delivering the social and material benefits of the post-war years and nationalist and devolutionist programmes gained wider appeal.

HOME RULE

Home Rule for Scotland within the United Kingdom is an idea with a long lineage. In the later nineteenth century it was part of a wider political

strategy for dealing with the vexed question of Ireland. From 1888 until
the outbreak of World War I several Home Rule bills were presented to
Parliament with one in August 1914 passing its second reading in the House
of Commons before being abandoned at the outbreak of war.

Home Rule had first emerged as a Liberal concept but a striking feature
of the emergence and development of the Labour Party in the 1920s was
its commitment to the idea. Virtually all the twenty-nine Labour MPs
elected in Scotland in 1922 were committed to a parliament in Edinburgh.
Some argued that the extent of the social and health problems in the Scottish cities in the immediate post-war years were so serious that they necessitated a Scottish legislature. The Westminster Parliament, it was suggested,
would not have the time necessary to devote to such urgent matters in one
part of the UK. Yet if Home Rule is an old idea it is also one with a very
tortuous history. The Government of Scotland Bill of 1927, backed by the
Scottish Home Rule Association, failed because it was not given sufficient
parliamentary time. From the early 1930s Home Rule became less of a
priority for the Labour Party and in subsequent decades ceased to be an
important area of policy. In 1950, for the first time, Labour went into a
General Election without a manifesto commitment to Scottish Home
Rule. It is true that between the 1920s and 1940s Scottish nationalism in a
formal organisational sense flourished as never before. The National Party
of Scotland was formed in 1928 and merged with the Scottish Party in 1934
as the Scottish National Party. The foundation of the National Trust for
Scotland and the Saltire Society in the same decade indicated that concern
with Scotland's interests was not confined to the political sphere.

Yet too much should not be made of the apparent resurgence of nationalist politics in these years. In part it reflected the indifference now shown to
the Home Rule agenda by the Labour Party. In the 1935 General Election
the Scottish National Party achieved only derisory results, except in the
Western Isles where it achieved twenty-eight per cent of the vote. In 1945
at Motherwell, the party, now firmly committed to independence, won a
parliamentary election but then lost it soon afterwards at the general election of that year. Indeed, in the immediate post-war years the SNP had very
limited political impact. Even the famous National Covenant needs to be
seen in perspective. At one level it clearly demonstrated the political and
cultural reality of a strong sense of Scottish identity among the population
of the country and a desire for a form of Home Rule. Those who signed
the Covenant, it was stated, 'pledge ourselves in all loyalty to the Crown
and within the framework of the United Kingdom, to do everything in
our power to secure for Scotland a Parliament with adequate legislative

authority in Scottish affairs'. It eventually attracted a remarkable two million names and illustrated the resilience of Scottish patriotism. Yet, there were at least two problems with the Covenant. Neither of the two major parties showed any interest. Both Labour and Conservative gave no sign of a wish to satisfy Scottish aspirations for Home Rule. Second, the Covenant itself was not a real test of the Scottish desire for Home Rule. It merely showed that many thought the concept attractive but there was no evidence that it could be regarded as an essential political aspiration to which people were strongly committed.

Indeed, the truth was that for most of the 1930s, 1940s and 1950s Home Rule was in the political doldrums. The Labour Party which alone could have achieved it, lost interest. Even the Scottish Trades Union Congress, a fervent supporter in the inter-war period, became mainly antagonistic by the 1950s. Constitutional issues seemed less important during the great economic crisis of the 1930s. During World War II a greater sense of 'Britishness' developed and the remarkable success of administrative devolution through the Scottish Office under Tom Johnstone between 1940 and 1945 might be seen as an excellent practical substitute for political devolution. Post-war economic planning and the development of the Welfare State were both based on a centralist strategy and, at least in the short run, were widely perceived as promising a better future for Scotland in the second half of the twentieth century than the nation had experienced for much of the first half. Home Rule seemed irrelevant to this set of expectations and it was therefore no surprise when, in 1956, the Labour leader Hugh Gaitskell committed his party to the preservation of the Union and opposition to Scottish Home Rule. Three years later the party's Scottish conference followed suit. It is remarkable to look back to those days from today's perspective. According to a survey conducted for the *Sunday Times Scotland* (August, 1995), there is support of forty-six per cent for a Scottish parliament, thirty per cent for independence and twenty-one per cent for the status quo. Even among Conservative voters substantial support for constitutional change was recorded with thirty-one per cent in favour of devolution and seven per cent for independence. Home Rule for Scotland had not only moved back on to the agenda over the last three decades but, in the 1990s, alongside the issue of independence, has become a central element in the Scottish political debate at the end of this century. In the chapters by James Mitchell, Iain Hutchison and David McCrone the detailed context of this political transformation are described. Below, some of the major influences which might explain it are briefly examined.

The Scottish electorate had become quickly disillusioned with the

Labour government of Harold Wilson and its failure to produce economic growth in the 1960s. It was this which triggered the first successes of the SNP at that time and, in particular, Winnie Ewing's stunning victory in Hamilton in 1967 (winning 18,399 votes, compared with 16,598 for Labour and 4,986 for the Conservatives). Both Labour and Conservative parties reacted swiftly to the nationalist threat. Almost immediately there was a *volte-face* by Labour. Devolution was once again seen as a good thing, although its readoption by the party was widely regarded as opportunistic and rooted in an attempt to stop the SNP bandwagon. This was no easy task because, as McCrone shows below, the rise of the SNP in this period was not only caused by short-term material and political factors but reflected deeper changes in Scotland's social and economic structures. The SNP was given a further boost with the discovery of North Sea oil in 1970. The famous slogan, 'It's Scotland's Oil', was designed to answer the attack that an independent Scotland would be a poorer Scotland. The continued vigour of the SNP and the threat that nationalism posed to the UK at a time when oil off the Scottish coast was deemed vital to the British economy, ensured that both Labour and Tories would view some form of Home Rule as a vital response.

Even the debacle of 1979, when Labour's devolutionary Scotland Bill failed to achieve the necessary forty per cent of the vote, did not kill off the Home Rule movement. Indeed if anything it seemed to develop even greater political momentum in the following decade. The main reason for this was the electoral dominance of the Conservative Party throughout the 1980s and 1990s in Britain and the impact on Scotland of the set of ideas which became known as 'Thatcherism'. In simple terms, Scotland has voted consistently for left-of-centre parties but has had to accept a series of right-wing governments. In addition, the Conservative governments of these years have mounted a radical assault on the public sector, have withdrawn from large-scale public intervention in support of industry and carried through a number of measures, above all the notorious poll tax, which have stimulated open hostility in Scotland. The irony is that much of this new Tory agenda, including council-house purchase and parental choice in school placements, has been popular. But on the whole, the policies were perceived as alien impositions, a reaction which demonstrated the differences in political culture between Scotland and England. The number of Tory MPs in Scotland plummeted from twenty-two in 1979 to a rump of eleven in 1992. At the same time a coherent strategy of Home Rule and, for an increasing and substantial minority of Scots, full independence, became even more attractive.

SOCIAL TRENDS

The enormous changes in the structure of the Scottish economy in the last four decades of this century had inevitable effects on occupations. As with other advanced societies Scotland has experienced the transition from manufacturing employment to service jobs. In 1911 services absorbed nineteen per cent of the employed population; by 1981 they accounted for forty-three per cent of the labour force. In addition while 'services' normally meant domestic employment in the early twentieth century, by the latter half they included the vast range of state and other public employments which mushroomed after 1945 and ranged from education to social work.

Deindustrialisation has had other significant effects on social structure and it is important to note that these are shared with the rest of the UK. If Scotland had a distinctive social order in earlier decades, the second half of the twentieth century saw convergence with a British norm. White-collar work expanded while manual workers declined in importance as the heavy industries began to experience terminal decline. Nevertheless, it is important to realise that the convergence was not complete in the 1980s. Scotland still had a higher share of manual workers and a lower share of non-manual workers than the rest of the UK.

Too often historians and social scientists concentrate virtually exclusively on urban and industrial Scotland and neglect rural society in the twentieth century. Yet, as Gavin Sprott explains in his chapter on lowland country life, the countryside experienced a social transformation in this century to equal anything which was taking place in the towns and cities. This occurred in two stages. First, in the inter-war period, and particularly in the 1920s, the collapse in land prices produced a huge turnover in estate ownership. An estimated two-fifths of the land changed hands. The principal buyers were the sitting tenants and there was a remarkable expansion in owner-occupation. The traditional social order, recognised from time immemorial, of landlord, rent-paying tenant and farm servant/labourer disintegrated over the space of a few years. In the late 1880s, ninety per cent of farms consisted of rent-paying tenancies; a century later, in 1991, two-thirds of farms were owner-occupied. When the total is examined in more detail, Sprott concludes, 'The number of farms which are tenancies within estates with the old-fashioned tenant and laird relationship is comparatively small'.

The second stage was the demographic effects of mechanisation and, in particular, the impact of the tractor and the combine harvester. The old farming, even given the technical innovations of the later nineteenth and early twentieth centuries, was highly labour-intensive. The adoption of the Ferguson tractor and the combine harvester reduced labour requirements to a revolutionary extent. Again, it is the sheer speed of change which is noteworthy. The old regime of horses and men still prominent in the 1940s had virtually gone by the early 1960s. Migration from the land accelerated. The exodus of people had been a constant feature for many generations, but this was something new: the end of a social and economic order structured round horse-work and the disappearance of a way of life that had characterised rural Scotland since the Agricultural Revolution of the later eighteenth century.

However, since the middle decades of the nineteenth century the Scots have predominantly been a nation of city and town dwellers. No other society in western Europe had experienced a faster rate of urban growth during the Industrial Revolution. By 1911 Scotland had become the most urbanised country in the world after England with sixty per cent of the population living in towns of more than 5,000 inhabitants. Yet, as Richard Rodger argues below, even this explosive expansion pales somewhat in relation to the twentieth-century experience. It was not that the pace of growth accelerated further after 1914. On the contrary, such was the scale and speed of nineteenth-century urbanisation that it could not be sustained at the same momentum. The Scottish urban population continued to increase but at a slower rate. In addition, however, as the traditional industrial structure crumbled from the 1950s so the rate of urban expansion declined, especially in the western lowlands.

Rather, what distinguished twentieth- from nineteenth-century urban development was the transformation in physical form, the radical changes in housing ownership and control and the fundamental impact of planning, technology and transportation on the way of life of those who lived in Scottish towns and cities. As Rodger notes (p. 123):

> Physically, the Scottish townscape at the end of the twentieth
> century is in certain fundamentals radically different from that at
> the beginning of the century. Cobblestones have been replaced by
> tarmac, electric lighting has replaced gas lights and mantles indoors
> and on the pavements, traffic lights and street signs abound where
> none existed, advertising hoardings have been replaced by neon
> signs and corporate logos, and brick, glass and plastics have
> overwhelmed traditional materials of stone and slate.

The structure of housing authority and ownership has also been revolutionised. By the second half of the twentieth century the dominance of public over private ownership was complete. While the private landlord was responsible for about ninety per cent of all dwellings in 1900, by 1990 this had shrunk to six per cent. This was yet another illustration of the growth in the role and powers of the local and national state which is such a key theme in the history of Scotland in the twentieth century. Yet in few other areas of society was the influence of the public sector more pervasive than in urban housing. In fifty Scottish local authorities in 1981 seventy per cent of all dwellings were council houses. Over time the influence of private landlords was also eroded by the growth of owner-occupation which had started to become more significant during the inter-war period and helped to promote the proliferation of colonies of 'bungalow belts' around the great urban conurbations which remain such a striking feature of the Scottish urban townscape to the present day.

But for the majority of city dwellers it was the decisions of local authorities, governments and urban planners which were to have a fundamental impact on their way of life in the twentieth century. Before 1914, four- and five-storey tenement blocks in the centre of towns were the common dwellings of most urban working-class Scots. This started to be replaced during the inter-war period by two- and three-storey tenements on new land on the fringes of the cities of which the best examples in Glasgow were the estates of Mosspark and Knightswood. Residents had the novel experience of possessing their own front door, small gardens and improved domestic amenities such as hot and cold running water and inside toilets.

But the record of public provision was not all positive, especially in the second half of the twentieth century. Local authorities attracted bitter criticism in the 1970s and 1980s for destroying neighbourhoods by wholesale redevelopment, decanting families into sterile housing estates virtually bereft of social amenity and denying residents any significant say in the physical planning of their own communities. In the 1960s and 1970s in some Scottish towns and cities there was an extraordinary mania for remoulding the urban landscape in a radical way, of which the best-known example was Glasgow's programme of rapid and intensive building of high-density tower blocks. Partly in reaction to these excesses more responsive agencies for urban housing development, such as tenants' associations, have grown up from the 1980s to permit a more measured and sensitive management of housing issues in the Scottish city. In this, as in so many other areas surveyed in this book, it is too early to say whether a new equilibrium will emerge.

This brief overview of some of the key changes in Scottish society in this century has concentrated on economy, politics, government and on the transformation of rural and urban life. The chapters which follow provide a much richer and broader perspective with new insights into class, popular culture, women in society, Catholicism, Protestantism and literature. Together they represent the most ambitious academic study of Scotland in the twentieth century ever published in one volume. Yet this period in Scottish history remains remarkably understudied, and all the authors here view their conclusions as interim judgements, as stimuli to further research rather than as definitive pronouncements.

We are already planning a new and more comprehensive edition of this work for the Millennium and are aware that not only will the areas presently covered or outlined change in the light of on-going analysis but that there are some topics such as demography, law and environmental issues which are hardly touched on here. We would welcome comments and suggestions towards an even fuller volume which will be published in due course.

2. THE ECONOMY
Peter L. Payne

During the twentieth century, the Scottish economy has undergone a massive structural transformation but, like the earlier industrial revolution, it has been characterised by slow motion. Only recently has the process become conspicuously rapid. It is the purpose of this chapter to outline and to speculate upon this metamorphosis (see Table 1).

I

Whatever doubts recent econometric analysis has cast upon the accuracy of earlier conceptions of the British economy during the nineteenth century, they have so far done little to weaken the belief – held by contemporaries and economic historians alike – in the vitality exhibited by the Scottish economy on the eve of World War I, and perhaps best symbolised, as Roy Campbell has observed, in Glasgow's City Chambers, opened by Queen Victoria in 1888.[1]

No one at this time could have failed to be aware of the declining importance of the spinning and weaving of cotton, but the remainder of the textile industry together with clothing manufacture still accounted for one in eight jobs in Scotland in 1911, and the proportion was much higher in the Borders and Tayside, where a third of the labour force were so employed.[2] The differing experiences of the various branches of textiles may be regarded as a sign of adaptability to changing market conditions. These encompassed cyclical swings in fashion, arbitrarily imposed barriers to international trade, particularly in the form of tariffs, and long-term changes in both regional and international comparative advantage. While cotton and flax spinning contracted and jute's period of 'wonderful prosperity' had already come to an end, family firms engaged in the manufacture of thread, linoleum, Axminster carpets, worsted yarns and knitwear

TABLE 1
The Structure of the Scottish Economy, by distribution of Employment by Sector (percentages)

Employment categories	1901	1911	1921	1931	1951	1961	1971	1981	1990
1. Agriculture, Forestry, Fishing	12.0	11.0	9.9	8.9	7.4	5.8	4.1	2.2	1.5
2. Energy and Water Supply	6.8	7.9	9.0	7.3	5.7	5.3	3.0	3.7	3.1
3. Metals, Minerals and Chemicals	3.6	4.4	5.6	4.9	5.6	5.4	4.8	3.3	2.4
4. Metal Goods, Engineering, Vehicles	8.0	9.3	13.0	9.6	12.6	12.6	13.0	10.6	8.5
5. Other Manufacturing	21.7	20.4	19.0	18.6	16.9	14.4	14.3	11.3	10.3
6. Construction	7.4	5.6	3.1	4.5	6.9	7.9	8.2	7.0	6.0
7. Distribution, Hotels, Catering	7.7	8.0	12.0	14.9	12.4	14.4	12.8	19.3	19.4
8. Transport/Communication	7.7	8.8	7.2	8.0	8.2	7.9	6.7	6.3	5.8
9. Banking, Finance, Insurance, Business Services, Leasing	0.9	1.1	1.4	1.5	1.5	1.9	2.9	6.5	9.0
10. Public Administration and other services	17.0	17.0	19.7	20.3	22.6	24.2	29.8	29.7	34.1
11. Not Classified	7.3	6.4	–	1.5	0.1	0.2	0.4	–	–

Source: 1901–71, calculated from data provided by C.H. Lee, *British Regional Employment Statistics,
1847–1971*; 1981, 1990, calculated from CSO, *Regional Trends* (1991), pp. 152–3.

continued to thrive. They did so by moving up market; by correctly anticipating or even moulding consumer demand; by the adoption of collusive
tactics, often facilitated by the prior creation of trade association; and
sometimes by sheer manufacturing and marketing efficiency. On the eve of
World War I, Scottish textiles displayed the entire spectrum of firm sizes,
from very small units in the Border Knitwear industry producing 'a
bewildering variety of styles, sizes and classes of garments',[3] to those which
dominated their respective branches of trade: the United Turkey Red
Company of the Vale of Leven in dyeing, Cox Brothers of Dundee in jute,
Templetons – whose Glasgow factory almost equalled the flamboyance of
the City Chambers – in carpets, and, greatest of all, J. & P. Coats, whose
capitalisation of over £10 million made it one of the largest of all British
industrial companies and which, in addition to its huge factories at Paisley,
was in 1913 manufacturing thread in ten European countries, in the United
States and Canada, Brazil, Mexico and Japan.

   In the closing years of the nineteenth century textiles and garment
manufacture retained an importance in the Scottish economy that tends to
be inadequately recognised. This is because some historians, mesmerised by
the decline in the central processes of cotton manufacture, were seduced
by the spectacular developments in coal, iron and steel, engineering and
shipbuilding. Focusing on these industries does lend credence to the belief
that the late Victorian Scottish economy possessed a singular dynamism,
engendering among contemporaries an optimism that made the acute

disappointments of the inter-war period all the harder to bear. Scottish coal mining, the most concentrated in Britain, recorded the highest average output per man-hour (the best measure of productivity) in the United Kingdom in the early years of the twentieth century, testimony to the relatively heavy capital investment and systematic adoption of new technology by its managers since the 1850s.[4] It is significant that by the late 1880s the largest Scottish colliery proprietors were all iron masters who, having ruthlessly exploited the native blackbank ores, responded to the incipient exhaustion of this natural resource by converting their family partnerships into limited companies, transferring the conduct of their enterprises to a new breed of professional managers and permitting them to integrate backwards into coal rather than forward into the infinitely more risky business of steel production.[5] This left the field free for thrusting newcomers, several of whom had established themselves in making malleable iron, to go in for steel-melting to such effect that by 1885 nearly a quarter of a million tons, or some forty per cent of the British make of Siemens steel, was being produced by Scottish firms. By 1913 their output had risen to 1.5 million tons, some twenty per cent of the British total, no less than three quarters of which was destined for what was indisputably the most buoyant of all Scottish industries: shipbuilding.

On the eve of World War I the Clyde built not only one third of British shipping tonnage but almost a fifth of the world's total output. Yet, for all the growing complexity and rapidly rising value of its products, the industry remained dominated by small-scale independent family firms, perhaps because of the modesty of its fixed capital needs. The volatility of demand for ships acted as a disincentive to investment and confirmed the rationality of labour-intensive techniques. These enabled the shipbuilders to minimise overhead costs and to transfer many of the financial burdens associated with downswings in the cycle to the 50,000-strong labour force, the majority of whom could readily be laid off. Yet, 'in the great days', as George Blake's fictional hero, Leslie Pagan, told his son in *The Shipbuilders*, 'there was not one of [the] yards but had two or three big ships a-building, so that up and down the River the bows of vessels unlaunched towered over the tenement buildings of the workers and people passing could hardly hear themselves speak for the danger of metal upon metal that filled the valley from Old Kilpatrick up to Govan'.[6] And through the yard gates there flowed a stream of steel plates, castings and rivets – the basic items of construction – and all manner of fittings ranging from delicate navigational instruments, clocks, pressure gauges, and brass mouldings, to anchors, fathoms of heavy chains, engines, boilers, pumps and auxiliary machines, such as Howden's system of forced-draught. Many of these components were made locally by firms whose very existence was rooted in catering to the needs of what was in many ways a huge assembly industry.[7]

In addition, from a multitude of engineering works there poured machine tools, locomotives and rolling stock, bridges and piers, architectural iron work and sanitary appliances, the apparatus required for mining and for the production, storage and distribution of gas, textile machinery, and equipment for sugar-crushing and refining.[8] Thus, by 1913 there had grown up in Scotland a collection of interrelated activities employing over a third of a million men, or a quarter of the total labour force: some 150,000 in coal, 100,000 in metal manufacture, 75,000 in mechanical engineering and 50,000 in shipbuilding, whose future prospects were dependent upon the vagaries of the export market and the course of international trade, particularly within the Empire. The fortunes of the eastern coalfields relied heavily on sales to northern Europe; those of the complex of steel and shipbuilding on the demands of the shipowners (whose orders were governed by the course of freight rates and, towards the eve of international conflict, increasingly influenced by the requirements of the Admiralty) and much of that part of the engineering industry unrelated to shipbuilding, on the prosperity of countries whose purchasing power was determined by the level of primary product prices and whose orders were increasingly subject to capricious political decisions.

Although Clive Lee has rescued services from neglect and has convincingly demonstrated that they were by no means 'simply derivative from the stimulus of industrial development',[9] it is undeniable that the general well-being of the entire Scottish economy between, say, 1870 and 1950 was largely determined by the health of these basic heavy industries, to which Scotland was more heavily committed than any other region of the United Kingdom.[10]

II

This over-commitment was sustained, even strengthened by the exigencies of war, the policies pursued by the Ministry of Munitions and the expectations implicit in the sharp, feverish post-war boom. By 1921 the proportion of Scotland's labour force engaged in mining and the heavy industries had risen even further despite the fact that the flaws in these sectors, dimly perceptible before 1913, had become more obvious. The imbalance between smelting and steel-melting had worsened. The coal measures of Lanarkshire had become progressively more exhausted and the markets of the eastern coal fields, adversely affected by government controls, were rendered increasingly vulnerable to German and Polish competition. And shipbuilding, having assumed what was to prove the encumbrance of a sorely afflicted steel industry, was suddenly to be transformed from being the most buoyant force within the Scottish economy to its greatest incubus. Meanwhile, what was left of the car industry after the failure of the Argyll Company in 1907, was to be dragged down by the collapse of the bloated Beardmore empire. The two most progressive cotton spinners, the Clyde Spinning Company and the Glasgow Cotton Spinning Co., had been liquidated by disappointed English speculators who had taken them over in the post-war boom, and jute was shortly to be brought down by tumbling prices and declining demand. Even J. & P. Coats, still the largest single employer in Scotland, threatened to disintegrate from centrifugal tensions following the abandonment of the highly centralised system of functional control created by Otto Philippi, who had died in 1917.

It is unnecessary to rehearse the travails of the Scottish economy in the inter-war period.[11] It is enough to try to answer one fundamental question. Given Scotland's over-commitment to industries that were declining or stagnant, why did resources not move more readily to activities that possessed greater potential for growth? The answer is necessarily complex and certainly subjective. First, the heavy industries clung tenaciously to their resources. With the benefit of hindsight, it is clear that coal, iron and steel, shipbuilding and heavy engineering were to decline, but this was by no means apparent at the time. Given continued investment and improved marketing arrangements, there was no reason to believe that the Scottish coal industry did not have a prosperous future. Would not the high and sustained productivity of labour in Scotland – higher than any other district in Britain with the one exception of Yorkshire – offset the lower selling prices of the major grades of Scottish coal? In the 1930s it was plausible to think so, especially with the inauguration of regional schemes to regulate competition. The ability of the iron and steel industry collectively to remedy its deep-rooted problems may have been paralysed in the 1920s by the deep recession and profound conflicts of interest stemming from the industry's multi-layered ownership,[12] but once the productive strength and the managerial and technical skills of Colvilles had been brought together with the financial power of the Lithgows, it was possible for the Colville group to gain control of over eighty per cent of Scottish steel-making capacity and to provide Sir Andrew McCance with sufficient resources to secure significantly lowered conversion costs and impressive productivity gains. The accuracy of the belief expressed by the consulting engineers, H.A. Brassert of Chicago, in 1929 that *only* a fully integrated iron and steel-making plant with the most modern ore dock facilities on tidewater would permit the rehabilitation and long-term survival of Scotland's iron and steel industry is now obvious. But, at that time, Brassert's case failed to convince those who would have had to finance and implement this radical scheme, and thus McCance's brilliant improvisations in the following decade proved to be – as Kenneth Warren has since emphasised[13] – a case of the better being the enemy of the best.

It was essentially the same in shipbuilding. Despite the fact that by the mid-1920s there were patently more shipyards than would be needed in the foreseeable future, few were eliminated by market forces. 'Shipbuilders die hard', one of them observed. 'They hang on in the hope that competitors may go under and that things will get better. ... Some of these men would prefer to fight on and go down fighting rather than surrender. Intense individualism is in their blood.'[14] Thus, as Tony Slaven has shown, although National Shipbuilders Security was able to sterilise about a third of Scotland's total tonnage capacity, it did little to rationalise the industry;[15] nor did the surviving employers attempt to redesign the productive process and 'deskill' the workforce.[16] The fragmented structure and working practices that the industry had inherited from the nineteenth century endured throughout the inter-war years, and perhaps the only real opportunity that was to occur for the introduction of the radical changes necessary for long-term survival was missed.

What is interesting about these industries, and induced so many of their constituent firms to cling on in the teeth of demoralising lack of profitability, was the nature of their ownership. Public companies might have gone into voluntary liquidation; private limited companies had the family to think of – not merely those who were active in the various businesses, but the pensioners whose incomes were derived from the trusts established in more prosperous times. The votes of the trustees may have kept firms alive but they also inhibited, even prevented, the adoption of policies calculated to re-invigorate them.[17] Collusion too may have had a retardative effect on the pace of changes in the structure of the Scottish economy. This was particularly so after the introduction of the General Tariff on iron and steel in 1932, when manufacturers of specific finished products – for example, rails, tubes and tin plates – eagerly participated in their respective cartels, not merely to negotiate with, and force concession from their international competitors but more comprehensively to 'regulate' the newly protected domestic market.[18] The iron and steel industry had long been notorious for its 'terminable agreements or associations of various kinds, whether for controlling output, fixing prices or otherwise regulating the conditions of production or trade'. After 1932, these 'arrangements' were legitimised and by giving a new lease of life to firms which might otherwise have abandoned the struggle, inhibited structural change.

Similar consequences flowed from the activities of the Shipbuilders Conference, in that the schemes that this body evolved in co-operating with the National Shipbuilders Society to purchase and close down blatantly obsolete yards, served mainly to reduce the potential for reckless price cutting. It was the same in various branches of textiles, in coal and engineering. Hargrave's verdict on the firms involved in providing railway equipment has a more general applicability: 'established firms, set in their ways, were more interested in dividing the cake than in baking a new larger one',[19] and they found in trade associations, collusion and work-pooling arrangements a means of tempering competition and ensuring survival, even regular dividends. Hargrave has labelled such tactics 'Micawberism' – 'hoping that something would turn up (but making little effort to find that something)' – and he believes that this 'may be altogether more typical of British industry than we might wish were the case'.[20]

In the event, something did turn up: World War II, which fastened the heavy industries even more securely on to the Scottish economy.

> Rearmament made a major contribution to recovery from 1935–6 onwards. The upturn in the steel industry was so pronounced that by 1934 it [was] the main engine of growth … and it was defence orders that sustained the industry during the severe recession of 1937–8. However, rearmament and the growing demand from shipbuilding were also responsible for the fact that the industry shifted to only a limited extent towards new products and new technologies.[21]

In this context, equally important was the fact that during the 1940s the trade associations became established in Whitehall and cartels – with their new respectability – 'formed the ready-made intermediaries between manufacturers [and the government agencies] for apportioning scarce materials [and] orders'. Nothing could be more calculated to freeze the structure of the Scottish economy in its early twentieth-century mould: the composition of the labour force continued to reflect comparative advantages that had long since disappeared.

And if the foregoing discussion goes some way to explaining why labour, management and capital were retained in coal and the heavy industries, the relative weakness of the service industries in Scotland accounts for their inability to attract such resources away from the declining Scottish staples in which during most of the inter-war years they were under-employed. But why were services so poorly represented in the Scottish economy? Clive Lee has emphasised the deficiency in demand for services stemming from the low level of Scottish incomes. Estimates of per capita income in real terms indicate that the Scottish figure stood at only ninety-three per cent of the British average in 1924 and thereafter declined even further: to ninety per cent in 1932 and eighty-nine per cent in 1938.[22] There were regional differences, of course. It is probable, Lee believes, that the regional income for Lothian was well above either the British or Scottish average, but in terms of its share of Scotland's total population, Lothian – with its concentration of professional occupations, in banking, commerce, government and education – was of insufficient weight to compensate for the overall national deficiency, influenced, above all, by Strathclyde.[23]

But between the dominant heavy industries and the service trades, were there no opportunities for new light industries to establish themselves or for the relatively few firms already in this sector to expand their activities? This question was addressed by the Scottish Economic Committee and the inquiries commissioned by this body make depressing reading.[24] It is evident that the growth of new industries was inhibited by an inability to obtain raw materials, semi-finished goods and electricity at low cost, and that supplies of appropriately skilled labour were scarce. Added to these supply-side problems were those encountered in marketing the product, not least being the distance from the major markets in the south of England. In several activities there was no tradition of aggressive selling. In furniture, Edgar Lythe found that all too many manufacturers were unwilling to advertise or 'go out into the market to seek custom. In the good old days, and not so very old either, his customers had to come and seek him – and did [so]. He made good stuff, and left it to sell itself.'[25] Although a fair proportion of existing furniture-makers made use of 'trade names', these were virtually unknown to the general public for there was a reluctance to advertise: it constituted too great a drain on scarce capital.

In the hosiery industry, the efforts of Scottish manufacturers were discouraged by the refusal of the Glasgow engineering firms to make flat knitting machines because, it was inferred, they believed the market to be too narrow and already dominated by Germany.[26] In the provision of ventilating apparatus, it was found that 'the English industry had an advantage over that in Scotland by being earlier in the field, and by reason of the greater scope available for its activities ... most of the ventilation work done in Scotland was carried out according to rule-of-thumb methods, and the small demand afforded but little opportunity to firms and operatives of becoming conversant with ... more modern systems and appliances'.[27] And in leather boots and shoes, by 1930 no Scottish firm had 'developed large scale production catering for the open wholesale market'.[28]

Among the Colville records, there exists a small collection of papers relating to Sir John Craig's attempts to establish the Clyde Blade Company. In what was apparently a private venture with his elder son Thomas and his close colleague, Dr Andrew McCance, Craig tried to break into the razor-blade market. Commercially, it was an utter failure, and few business archives better illustrate the problems of industrial diversification than the picture they conjure up of these three giants of the Scottish steel industry examining in bewilderment why they were unable to sell more than a few hundred gross packets of razor blades a month between 1935 and 1939.[29]

All these difficulties, real or imagined, conspired to stultify indigenous initiative. It is possible to believe that given time, institutional support and government encouragement, many of the problems might have been overcome, but the inter-war period spanned merely twenty years, too short a period effectively to achieve significant structural change.[30] And if this argument goes some way to explaining the apparent apathy of Scottish enterprise, the sheer depth of the Depression gave little or no incentive for thriving English concerns to establish branch plants in Scotland: more than sufficient labour and space for expansion was available to them locally.[31] Moreover, such was the organisational immaturity of the major British firms in the 1930s that the proliferation of branch plants – so characteristic of the post-World War II period – was never seriously contemplated.[32] Certainly, the data assembled by Carol Heim reveal the negligible attractive power exercised by Scottish locations on British manufacturers during the 1930s when competitive conditions made industrial diversification particularly difficult in the depressed areas. As she observed, '[these] areas had no significant cost advantages to offset barriers to entry'.[33]

III

It should occasion little surprise, therefore, that on the eve of World War II the structure of the Scottish economy was not dissimilar from that which had evolved before World War I, and the nature of the demands placed upon Scottish industry during the years of global conflict and post-war reconstruction conspired to preserve its essential characteristics for at least another decade. When change did become inevitable, through the exhaustion of indigenous geological resources in the case of coal, the unreliability of matching (far less undercutting) the costs of huge integrated plants on

tidewater sites in the case of steel, and the financial and technical impossi-
bility of small, cluttered Clyde yards producing the pre-fabricated, mass
produced, monster tankers and bulk carriers that were soon to be the staple
carriers of international commerce in shipbuilding, this painful process was
artificially prolonged by politicians who, doubtless socially motivated, kept
the industries going. The state-owned electricity industry was forced to
consume deep-mined coal, the steel industry was propped up by cross-
subsidisation and the absorption of losses by the taxpayer, and shipbuilding
received massive grants and loans and Admiralty contracts.

It is not the purpose of this chapter to make political points, nor to
defend the manifestly erroneous decisions made by the owners and managers – or even the labour force – of many enterprises. Its object is simply
to try briefly to explain the glacial slowness of structural change in the Scottish economy during the first five or six decades of the present century.
When change did come, it came suddenly. It came as a result of renewed,
if occasionally misconceived government initiatives; it came as a consequence of the fuller assimilation of the Scottish economy into first the
British and then the international economy; and it came fortuitously as
a by-product of the discovery of North Sea oil. But, above all, it came
because the state decided to turn off the life-support system of public
ownership. Once exposed to the cruel accountancy of market forces, either
directly or as part of the preparation thought necessary for the return to
private enterprise, Scottish heavy industries were found wanting and
allowed to die. Even Ravenscraig, having in its final years been sweated
down to its essentials and at last apparently capable of making a profit, was
sacrificed by British Steel in order more effectively to load the mills at
Llanwern and Port Talbot.[34] An industry which less than twenty years
earlier had directly employed some 15,000 men (1977) had been ex-
tinguished, partly brought down by the prior collapse of its major customer,
shipbuilding and marine engineering, whose own labour force contracted
between 1951 and 1991 from 77,000 to 14,000. Similarly, since 1971 coal-
mining has shed 15,000 men: only the few miners turned owners at Monk-
tonhall and the men of Longannet saved by contractual arrangements
entered into by Scottish Power, are still working underground.

With such a 'shake-out' – to employ a weasel word designed to blind us
to private miseries – the structure of Scottish industry (as measured by
employment) *had* to alter, if for no other reason than that the decimation
of several manufacturing categories automatically raised the relative proportions of other sectors. There were numerous rearguard actions intended
to preserve traditional activities by diversifying them, but the most dramatic

of these ended in failure: the strip mill at Ravenscraig, motor manufacture at Bathgate and Linwood, the aluminium smelter at Invergordon, and Wiggins Teape's pulp mill at Corpach, Fort William. Elsewhere in Great Britain, employment in the services grew rapidly, soaking up – even attracting labour from – declining manufacturing activity. In Scotland, this movement was for many years inhibited by the persistently low level of per capita incomes. Not until recently have average real incomes risen sufficiently to begin to close the gap, thereby giving a remarkable boost to Scotland's service sector.

Although the Scottish service sector as a whole (distribution, hotels and catering; transport and communications; tourism, financial and business services; public administration and defence, and education and health) has grown, financial and business services have been by far the most dynamic sub-sector. Contributing between five and six per cent of Scotland's GDP in the early 1970s (compared with between seven and eight per cent in the UK), by the late 1980s its share had risen to some 15 per cent (compared with some seventeen per cent in the UK).[35] The Scottish experience has not been unique – during the 1980s the service sectors of all the OECD countries experienced high rates of growth – but the fact that Scotland was *not falling* behind may be regarded as a minor triumph. Certainly, the dynamism displayed by financial services reveals a remarkable ability to exploit the profound changes implicit in deregulation, the opportunities inherent in the 'coming of oil' (see below), and the increasing use made of business and financial consultants by manufacturing enterprises subjected to fierce competition pressures.

In effect, since 1945 the Scottish financial sector has successfully built upon a nineteenth-century legacy centred upon the Bank of Scotland, numerous investment trusts and several large and powerful insurance companies such as Standard Life, Scottish Amicable and Scottish Widows.[36] Although by 1960 all the Scottish clearing banks had strong external links, the Clydesdale being fully owned by the Midland Bank until it was sold to the North Australia Banking Group in 1987, while a substantial proportion of the shares of the Bank of Scotland and the Royal Bank were held by Barclays and Lloyds respectively,[37] many of the insurance companies have retained their independence.[38] One of them, Standard Life, is the largest mutual insurance company in Europe; another, General Accident, is among the largest British composite insurance companies.[39] Ranked by turnover, no fewer than ten of the largest fifteen Scottish companies in 1993–4 were in the financial sector,[40] and the funds under management by Scottish life offices and independent fund managers exceeded £100 billion, representing a threefold increase in seven years and placing Scotland 'fourth in the European league, after London, Frankfurt and Paris'.[41] And around the core functions of banking, insurance and fund management, there clustered accountants, actuaries, corporate lawyers, stockbrokers, private and merchant bankers, economic consultants, designers and firms specialising in public relations. No fewer than 220,000 were engaged in financial services in Scotland in 1992, or some eleven per cent of the total labour force.[42]

IV

In the last three decades, Scotland's industrial structure has come to re-semble that of Great Britain as a whole (see Table 2). To a considerable extent this belated transformation has been dependent upon foreign capi-tal and enterprise, and nowhere has greater success been achieved than in electronics. But how deeply rooted is this industry in the Scottish econ-omy? A brief examination reveals not only disquieting features but illustrates the future necessity of far faster adaptation to change. In 1935 electrical engineering and the manufacture of radio and allied electronic equipment were virtually unrepresented in Scotland.[43] The dispersal of factories brought several firms, including Ferranti, north during the war, and by its end it is estimated that there were in Scotland some three thou-sand employees engaged in the manufacture of products recognisably of an electronic nature. The creation of branch factories by major American multinationals seeking to exploit the potentially large European market and to circumvent high European tariffs gave a major boost to such employ-ment in the 1950s, when IBM, NCR, Burroughs and Honeywell estab-lished manufacturing facilities. Their example was followed in the 1960s by other British and American companies – including National Semiconduc-tor, Motorola and Hewlett Packard – so that by the end of the decade, total employment in the industry in Scotland had risen to about thirty thousand. The *rate* of growth, measured in terms of the number of employees, then slackened, though the increase in the number of firms did not. By 1983 there were nearly three hundred companies engaged in the manufacture of industrial products, information systems (including computers), defence-related products and avionics, and electronic components. Indeed, in this last and perhaps most important sector of the industry, Scotland's four US-owned plants constituted Europe's largest group of producers, accounting in 1983 for seventy-nine per cent of the UK's and twenty-one per cent of Western Europe's output of integrated circuits.[44] The overall picture is given in Table 3.

TABLE 2

The Structure of the Scottish Economy, by the contributions of broad industrial sectors to Gross Domestic Product, 1963–88

		Percentage Share to Total GDP of			
	Agriculture	Manufacturing	Services	Energy and Water	Construction
1963	5.34	30.63	50.00	3.13	7.63
1973	5.07	30.61	50.90	5.03	8.38
1979	3.35	28.53	54.60	5.55	7.99
1988	2.69	21.93	62.70	5.09	7.57
	(1.44)★	(21.97)★	(64.48)★	(5.27)★	(6.85)★

		Change in Share of Total GDP, by percentage points, of			
	Agriculture	Manufacturing	Services	Energy and Water	Construction
1963–1973	−0.27	−0.02	0.90	1.90	0.75
1973–1979	−1.72	−2.08	3.70	0.52	−0.39
1979–1988	−0.66	−6.60	8.10	−0.46	−0.42
1963–1988	−2.65	−8.70	12.70	1.96	−0.06

Note: ★ The figures in brackets for 1988 are comparable proportions of GDP for the United Kingdom as a whole, though their compilation may not be entirely consistent with that employed for Scotland.

Sources: F.A. Shera and G.B. Robertson, 'Structural Change in the Scottish Economy', *Scottish Economic Bulletin*, No. 43 (June 1991), 16; UK figures: calculated from Table 2.1, CSO, *UK National Accounts*, 1990.

TABLE 3

Scottish electronics industry by main product area, 1983

	No. of companies	No. of employees	Average size of company	Share of total electronics employment
Industrial products	82	8984	109.6	21.1
Information systems	24	8880	370.0	20.9
Defence and avionics	9	7739	859.9	18.2
Electronic components	52	7406	142.4	17.4
Telecommunications	14	3961	282.9	9.3
Electronic sub-contracting	46	2507	54.5	5.9
Consumer products	11	2048	186.2	4.8
Design and services	17	596	35.1	1.4
Medical electronics	14	402	28.7	1.0
Total electronics	269	42523	158.1	100.0

Note: The product classifications are based on the categories employed by Booz, Allen & Hamilton in their surveys of the Scottish electronics industry. Companies are allocated to a category on the basis of their major product, although many are multi-product firms.

Source: J. Firn & D. Roberts, 'High Technology Industries', in Hood & Young, *Industry, Policy and the Scottish Economy*, p. 299, based upon a survey by the Scottish Development Agency, June 1983.

During the following decade, 1983–93, electronics appeared to consolidate its position in the Scottish economy. Gross output increased four-fold in the 1980s, representing a compound rate of growth of fourteen per cent over a period during which the remainder of the manufacturing sector dwindled, and by 1990 the sector provided forty-two per cent of Scotland's manufactured exports.[45] Moreover, the Japanese had arrived, a sure sign of British industrial rejuvenation: NEC at Livingston, Mitsubishi at Hadding-ton, Glenrothes and Livingston, Oki at Cumbernauld, JVC at East Kilbride and Terasaki at Clydebank. The estimated share of electronics employment (42,700) in total manufacturing employment first rose above ten per cent in 1983 and although this proportion has remained virtually unchanged in the last ten years, the number employed has edged fractionally and irregu-larly upward to reach 45,300 by 1993.[46]

Electronics constitutes the crown jewel of Scottish industry. Its growth and importance has justified the sustained and costly efforts to secure its transplantation in Scotland's traditional industrial belt bounded by Edin-burgh, Dundee, Greenock and Ayr. The pioneering American multi-nationals – to whom speed of entry was of great importance – were induced to settle in East Kilbride, Glenrothes, Cumbernauld and Livingston. Moti-vated primarily by a desire to exploit market and cost factor advantages, they were influenced in their choice of specific locations by the govern-ment's regional policy, the most powerful elements of which appear to have been locational restrictions, generous financial assistance, the blandishments of local government agencies and the ready availability of new or even custom-built facilities for immediate occupation in New Towns. Their plants were primarily manufacturing establishments. Significantly, in choosing to locate in Scotland they were unconcerned by the availability or absence of local pools of research or developmental skills. Not until the late 1960s was this factor accorded any real importance and then, it may be assumed, only because it constituted one of a number of attractions which *together* permitted the central belt of Scotland to achieve the 'critical mass' necessary to ensure further development. By the late 1970s Silicon Glen's cluster of electronic firms had generated concentration economies which enhanced the area's magnetism for high-technology companies.[47]

Such a cluster has the capacity to induce regional economic growth. This is because the demands of incoming multinationals for components and services create market opportunities for the formation of new indigenous businesses which, with the transfer of technology and expertise, become specialist suppliers, themselves able to exploit alternative markets at home and overseas. 'Corporations get deeply embedded in the local economy through the creation of a network of sophisticated, interdependent link-ages, which support the expansion of local firms and generate [the] self-sustaining growth of the cluster as a whole'.[48] Such is the more optimistic, *developmental* scenario; but it is legitimate to visualise a less happy outcome, in which local clusters become the unwitting pawns of powerful multi-nationals whose global policies expose local economies to volatile world markets and render them vulnerable to the forces of international competition. In this *dependent* scenario, 'the motives for multinationals extending local linkages are driven more by cost-cutting than by a desire to add value through the exchange of technology and information. Linkages with suppliers are hierarchical and the relationships adversarial rather than co-operative. Consideration of price or short-term convenience are uppermost. Proximate suppliers save corporations labour costs, capital investment and overheads at times of increased competition and falling profits. Suppliers do not participate in the development and technical evolution of the product'.[49]

Turok's careful analysis makes it plain that the Scottish electronics industry conforms more closely to the dependent model than to the developmental. Currently, there are very real fears for its future. The spectacular recent growth in the industry's gross output (in effect, its sales) is misleading. The annual figures for value-added (the aggregate value of the output of the firms in the industry less the cost of materials and services brought in) have risen far more slowly. For the period 1983–9 the comparable compound rate of growth figures were gross output, 16 per cent per annum; value added, 7.1 per cent. This would not cause anxiety had Scottish-based firms, many of them called into existence to serve the needs of the American-owned branch plants, captured a large share of the market for such inputs. In fact, they have not done so. Of the annual purchases by the foreign-owned electronics firms in Silicon Glen, Scottish companies appear to have provided only about 12 per cent during the late 1980s.[50] Moreover, foreign firms, which were experiencing a higher rate of growth than companies that were Scottish-owned or UK subsidiaries, were importing well over half of their material inputs from abroad. Even more ominously, of the products brought in by the leading foreign firms those in which local sources have secured a significant share (keyboards, plastic components, cables, sheet metal, and packaging and printing materials) are easy to manufacture, 'using standard machinery or labour-intensive methods'.[51] These local suppliers, including such companies as Fullerton Fabrication, Mimtec and TFC, are 'simple sub-contractors without their own technology and products'. Of the few local companies to have broken into the markets for more sophisticated, higher-value components, such as disk drives and power supplies, Rodime enjoyed spectacular success before going bankrupt in 1991 and Domain Power was taken over by an

American company and subsequently sold to a Japanese concern.[52]

Indigenous firms appear to be restricted mainly to making relatively straightforward products, lacking technological content. Thus, the demands of Motorola – a major player in the industry employing 3,600 people making semiconductors at East Kilbride and cellular telephones at Bathgate – benefit few local suppliers and, of these, even fewer are under local ownership and control. They are simply not equipped to meet Motorola's quality appraisal schemes. Mitsubishi procure forty per cent of their imports in Europe, of which one quarter are from Scottish sources, only because, it must be presumed, it is obliged to do so by EC regulations. Even in that branch of electronics in which indigenous firms have been most successful – the manufacture of printed circuit boards – the great majority of the ever more sophisticated products are specified and designed by the purchasers, for all that the two largest firms, Exacta Circuits of Selkirk and Prestwick Holdings, are apparently being bought increasingly 'into partnership with their major customers'.[53]

Facts such as these have forced Turok to conclude that 'the prospects for self-sustaining, internally generated growth of the Scottish electronics industry cannot yet be described as promising'.[54] The accuracy of this depressing conclusion has recently been strengthened by a report commissioned by Scottish Enterprise. Prepared by the Boston-based Monitor consultancy, this report predicts the possibility of major closures as multinational companies migrate to lower-cost locations in Eastern Europe and, increasingly, better-skilled locations in Asia.[55] Not the least of the reasons for expecting such a future migration is that 'the cycle of innovations' – the very factor that might reduce the inherent mobility of the multinationals – is 'very weak and poorly integrated' in Scotland. Of the world's electronic centres, Scotland is strongest in areas of limited importance to long–term competitiveness.[56] Unless this serious weakness is quickly rectified, it is expected that employment in electronics will fall to about 17,500 by 1997, plants will close, and inward investment will cease. Even if this fate is avoided, there seems to be little doubt that the 9,500-strong workforce in the military and telecommunications sectors will experience a substantial diminution, and productivity improvements in computers, peripherals and active components will reduce the labour force by about five per cent per annum over the next five years.

What action is required to enable Scotland to avoid a shrinkage in its most buoyant manufacturing activity? The Monitor report makes it clear that Scotland's current concentration on hardware (fifty-five per cent of output compared with sixteen per cent globally) is 'severely misaligned'.

'To reduce its vulnerability, Scotland needs to develop capability in product design, development, integration and marketing, in addition to software', which accounts for just seven per cent of output, compared with
forty-four per cent globally. This will not be easy.[57] The Scottish Electronics
Forum, which might be expected to implement the report's recommendations, consists of the very same multinational companies whose policies
have, in effect, denied local enterprise either the motivation or the opportunity to acquire the expertise necessary to overcome its weaknesses. Scotland's inability to add more value has produced what John Ward, resident
Scottish director, has called 'a jobbing shop mentality'. The irony of this
observation is that in the past, Ward's own company, IBM, has shown little
inclination to do more than employ simple sub-contractors willing and able
to handle discrete orders at short notice. Nevertheless, his prescription for
strengthening Scotland's electronics is indisputable: 'We must try to bring
more original design work ... to Scotland so that we are literally designing-
in the local suppliers – creating the products with their participation'.[58]

Whether or not this is achieved depends on whether it will ever be in
the interests of the major multinationals domiciled in Scotland to source
products with indigenous technological content[59] and, perhaps just as
important, whether the Scottish education system is capable of creating the
skilled manpower required by the industry. Only if it is will a sound, long-
term foundation be secured for Silicon Glen.

The other factor that seemed to many to possess the potential of re-
generating the Scottish economy was the discovery of North Sea oil in
1969. It was hoped that major benefits would accrue to those branches of
manufacturing industry that seized the opportunities created by the manifold demands of the giant multinational companies who would search for,
discover and exploit the riches that lay beneath the grey North Sea. These
exceptions have been realised only to a disappointingly limited degree.
William Pike has calculated that of the orders, totalling some £13.5 billion
in value, placed and executed to construct, equip and install Scottish North
Sea platforms between 1972 and 1989, the Scottish content was between
twenty-two and twenty-three per cent. This proportion 'represented to
many a failure of the Scottish economy to take its rightful place in the
development and production of North Sea oil'.[60] Certainly, Scottish industry has not been transformed by 'the coming of oil'. There has been no
development of a large and powerful indigenous oil-related sector ready to
export its products and exploit its expertise overseas when the oil runs out.

What is the explanation of this apparent failure? Could the Scottish content have been higher in the palmy days before the oil crisis of 1986? What

chance did Scottish industry have in participating more fully in the great North Sea oil boom which ended with Saudi Arabia's abandonment of the quota system in June 1985? Answers to these questions can only be speculative. Indeed, perhaps the questions themselves stem from the false premise that a Scottish content of twenty-three per cent *was* low. To Pike, whose thesis is informed by a knowledge derived from many years of practical experience in the industry, it is plausible that this figure is as much – or almost as much – as could reasonably have been expected given contemporary circumstances. In this context it is impossible to do justice to his multi-faceted argument, but an attempt to summarise its salient points may illuminate several important facets of the recent development of the Scottish, indeed the British, economy.

It is important to recognise that over the past century the international oil and gas industry has come to be dominated by a group of major companies who have developed a system of *de facto* contractual relationship with their specialised suppliers of material and labour. In the absence of government intervention, such as that exercised by the OPEC countries, these close working relationships have seldom been ruptured. In the case of the North Sea – such was the rapidity of its development – there was little real chance that any newly-created major Scottish-owned companies would be able to compete effectively with the multinational oil and gas operators, suppliers and contractors, for the former did not possess the required technical expertise, the skilled labour and the immense financial resources to do so. If to this incapacity be added the initial lack of conviction that oil existed in commercially exploitable quantities in the forbiddingly hostile environment of the United Kingdom Continental Shelf, it may readily be understood why the international companies gained a foothold in the North Sea that gave them insuperable long-term advantages.[61]

By the time that Scottish enterprise was mobilised, it was confronted by all but insurmountable barriers to entry to the oil industry. In 1987 the price of oil plunged to a level ($6.00–$8.00 a barrel) which, had it existed ten years earlier, might well have stifled the infant oil province at birth.[62] 'It had been a narrow window of opportunity for Scottish industry, an opportunity for which Scottish industry was ill prepared, but for which the international oil industry was not'.[63] Telling examples of this are to be found in iron and steel and heavy engineering, both activities which would appear to have been well placed to benefit from the development of North Sea oil and gas. That they did not – at least to any great extent – was due to the fact that 'the methods utilised, and the goods produced, by these industries were of different specifications from those required by the oil and gas industry'.[64] For both platform construction and tubular pipelines the steel required was of a totally different character from that which the Scottish mills were capable of producing, nor did the plant exist to supply the necessary 36-inch diameter pipe.[65] Likewise, although the Clyde shipyards appeared to offer a perfect venue for the construction of the massive off-shore platform jackets, they too proved to be unadaptable. Ships are built primarily of welded steel plate. Platform jackets, by contrast, are constructed from rolled and tubular steel, connected by cast or welded anodes, a technique requiring specialised rolling machines and automatic welding techniques quite alien to the technology of shipbuilding. Furthermore, not only did existing yards usually lack sufficient space for the construction of broad-based jackets, but the Clyde was too narrow for their ready transportation and too remote from their intended destinations to compete with jackets built in Norway or the east coast of Scotland, both of which locations involved a shorter, less expensive and much less dangerous tow. It is for reasons such as these that Pike was able to assert:

> Scottish industry simply did not understand the oil and gas industry or its requirements until the opportunity presented by the North Sea had already been lost and foreign companies were firmly entrenched. ... Nor can the oil and gas companies be faulted for utilising their traditional international infrastructure to exploit the discoveries in the North Sea. In the volatile international market, they simply could not afford the luxury of waiting for a suitable infrastructure to develop in Scotland.[66]

The question of speed is of critical importance in understanding the extent of indigenous participation in the North Sea. The oil companies' desire rapidly to replace declining or nationalised production and regain their international leadership from OPEC was given added momentum by the anxiety of successive British governments, beginning with that of Harold Wilson, to exploit the United Kingdom's offshore oil and gas as quickly as possible in order to solve the problems arising from the nation's seemingly intractable and worsening balance of trade.[67] By offering generous licensing terms, instigating programmes for the express accommodation of the multinationals, and insisting on rapid development, British governments 'forfeited the chance to mandate greater British and greater Scottish, investment in North Sea development'.[68]

Other difficulties for British companies stemmed from their relative lack of technological knowledge and expertise, much of it beyond ready access because of patent protection.[69] Moreover, there was no tradition in

Scottish firms of research and development in this field that might have reduced the severity of this initial disability. It is apparent that Scottish firms *could not* immediately compete with the incoming multinationals in their core activities. Even the most adventurous could expect only to break into the periphery of the potential market within the period that ended with the collapse of the boom in 1986.[70]

After a hesitant start Scottish firms *did* enter the industry. Of these, only a handful have been conspicuously successful. From a medium-sized firm engaged principally in fishing and ship-repairing, the Wood Group of companies has created a multi-million pound presence in the Scottish oil and gas industry supplying onshore and offshore logistic, engineering and drilling services, some of them embodying high technology. In 1981 Ian Wood explained how his firm had overcome its initial lack of relevant knowledge by a three-pronged strategy: buying the necessary expertise by employing a number of 'highly experienced, offshore oil managers to provide ... the technology and ... the basic training for the traditional management and staff'; by joint ventures with companies already possessing 'the technological experience and know-how'; and by the acquisition of one or two small specialist companies, particularly those with really good managements.[71]

Other Scottish firms who have established themselves include Ramco, Rigblast plc and Ferguson Seacabs of Inverurie, along with many more, but each is essentially confined to activities in which an inability to gain immediate access to technology did not constitute a major barrier to entry. Yet the birth of a large *number* of firms, overwhelmingly located in and around Aberdeen,[72] gave rise to 'a strong belief [sedulously fostered by government spokesmen] that UK industry has done well in the development of North Sea oil'. Ian Wood, speaking in 1981, felt this to be 'a dangerous myth':

> Far too many of the successful North Sea performers are incoming
> international companies who are simply operating a local UK base
> to cater for North Sea oil – they are not building up genuine UK
> technology and know-how to be applied in further expansion
> overseas. Such was our Government's haste to get the oil out of the
> ground as quickly as possible that far too little attention was paid to
> the build-up of genuine UK oil technology and manufacturing
> know-how to provide an important new indigenous addition to the
> UK's falling industrial base. The Government's initial impetus
> through the Offshore Supplies Office to try and ensure that UK
> industry did play a meaningful part in this new industrial revolution
> has now substantially waned. As a result, any present realistic

assessment of the number of UK companies who have the know-how, technology and manufacturing skills to expand into the offshore industry, world-wide, would provide a pitifully small number, nowhere near the level of presence and influence that should have been achieved from our privileged frontier starting position.[73]

And if this was so on the eve of the oil-price crisis during which oil companies' revenues fell by over fifty per cent in the space of a year, how much worse so was it thereafter? Between 1985 and 1987 activity in the drilling sector dropped precipitously, many ambitious development plans were shelved and expenditures were reduced in construction, equipping, installation, transportation (pipeline and floating transfer facilities), terminal construction, and a whole host of supplementary and ancillary activities. The construction yards at Ardesier, Nigg, Dundee, Stornoway, and particularly Loch Kishorn, all suffered massive redundancies. Only the production sector was little affected, largely because it was so costly and complicated to close down existing operations.[74]

Among the consequences of this recession was a considerable fall in oil-related employment, particularly in the Grampian region,[75] and perhaps more significantly, the failure of dozens of indigenous ventures spawned during the preceding boom. But whereas 'smaller Scottish companies simply disappeared, [the] larger international companies pooled resources, negotiated take-overs and subsumed themselves with larger entities'.[76] By 1987 three dominant conglomerates had emerged: Baker Hughes, Halliburton and Schlumberger. By 1989 these companies provided at least eighty per cent of the drilling and production services in the Scottish sector of the North Sea.[77] The post-boom industry may have been 'leaner and fitter' than it had been but it was even less Scottish than before. Such is the current excess capacity in the world oil industry that it is unlikely that activity on the scale that marked the 1970s and early 1980s will ever re-occur. If so few Scottish firms failed to put down the roots necessary for future survival and growth in an international market then, it seems improbable that they will do so in the future.[78] The great North Sea oil bonanza has come and gone without making any significant impression on the structure of the Scottish economy.[79]

V

Not the least interesting feature of these two brief discussions is the anxiety expressed by many of those on whose researches they rest concerning the character of the indigenous firms that have been spawned by the advent of electronics and the coming of oil. The long-term development and success of the Scottish economy depends not merely upon the formation of new firms in sufficient number to provide employment, profits and sustained growth, but upon the nature of those firms with respect to their owner-ship, products, services and potential markets. Were sheer numbers of firms enough to secure the future, the ululations of economists, planners and many businessmen would be greatly muted, if not entirely stilled. Is it not reassuring that having been decimated during the oil-price crisis of 1986–7, the number of oil-related firms in Grampian region had rebounded to about 1,500 by July 1992?[80] Is it not a reason for confidence that of the 232 firms in Silicon Glen in 1991 about seventy per cent are British concerns?[81] In both cases the answers are ambiguous. In oil, indigenous firms are main-ly concerned with 'rope and dope', unlikely long to survive the exhaustion of the reservoirs of oil and gas; in electronics, the products of all too many Scottish firms, engaged, as currently they are, in the provision of low-value added components and services, cannot realistically be expected to follow the global wanderings of their footloose customers.

For all its apparent recent successes, there is an alarming fragility about the manufacturing sector of the Scottish economy. The old certainties associated with coal, iron and steel and shipbuilding, even with textiles, are gone. The produce cycle is ever shortening: only the distillation of whisky seems to have achieved any real immunity from its lethal influence on business longevity.[82] Is a solution to be found in increasing the business birthrate, hoping that sufficient infant enterprises survive to maturity to permit sustained economic growth and long-term employment prospects? Many think so. 'If Scotland could equal the new business birthrate of the rest of the UK it would mean a 50 per cent increase in [Scotland's] current annual crop of new-starts. Between [1993] and the end of the century, an additional 25,000 businesses would be created. This is the target which Scottish Enterprise is ... setting itself.'[83]

Why is it that Scotland persistently fails to create new business on the scale achieved by other parts of the United Kingdom and many competi-tor nations? A study undertaken by Scottish Enterprise in 1992 identified three major reasons for Scotland's comparatively poor performance. Of these, the cost of and access to finance was believed to be 'far and away the most critical factor in restraining the formation and early development of new businesses in Scotland'.[84] The banks – which are said 'to have estab-lished such "utter dominance" as to be regarded as near-monopolists in a market where effective competition from other lenders like building societies is "partial at best"' – are condemned for their extreme caution in seeking high levels of owners' capital and security and low levels of risk; the venture capitalists are criticised for their reluctance to fund start ups; and the potentially valuable contribution by private individuals – commonly known in financial circles as 'business angels' – has been inhibited by a lack of accurate information and promising prospects: 'networking is often ineffective in Scotland, which can make it difficult both for angels trying to find investment opportunities and for entrepreneurs seeking angels'.[85]

Other factors which were found to explain Scotland's low business birthrate were essentially cultural. Through surveys conducted for Scottish Enterprise by MORI at home and abroad, it was apparent that 'as an occupation, Scots view the contribution of entrepreneurs to society less positively than the population of England and Wales – and much less positively than the population of Germany and the United States'.[86]

If to these factors calculated to depress the entrepreneurial spirit be added those consequent upon Scotland's skewed distribution of personal wealth (evidence for which is provided by the much lower proportion of Scots who are home owners, fifty-one per cent compared with sixty-eight per cent in Britain as a whole), the relatively high liquidity preference of Scottish savers,[87] and the possible reduction of the pool of managerial advice and talent resulting from the external take-over of so many Scottish companies, it will readily be apparent why Scotland's business birthrate lags behind that of the south of England.[88]

For all that, the doubt persists that a simple increase in the number of business births is an inadequate solution to Scotland's economic malaise. A survey of 200 firms formed in West Lothian in the 1980s revealed that their:

> undistinguished growth record and orientation towards local
> markets mean that they have probably not generated much
> additional local income. ... They also appear to have done little
> to alter the structure of the local economy and improve its
> competitiveness. The new firms generally seem to be imitative
> rather than innovative in terms of their products and processes, and
> are not the dynamic forms of organisation that some have claimed.
> ... There does not seem to be much reason to believe that they will
> generate sustained growth in the future.[89]

The findings of a broader study which looked at the performance of 2,600 new firms which started in Scotland between 1980 and 1982 and which were still in existence in 1987, while distinctly more encouraging, also cast doubt on the more optimistic claims made by those who seek to increase the business birthrate. In Scotland the creation of jobs per firm compared

unfavourably with the south-east of England and, while there was strong
representation in textiles and food processing, the proportion of new high
technology firms in Scotland was very low (50 firms out of 2,600). Of these
less than twenty per cent could be described as 'high fliers' (those which by
1987 had reached a turnover of £3.5 million or employed at least fifty
people) and not one of them was in the critical areas of pharmaceuticals,
telecommunications, computer services and R & D.[90]

The implications of these and similar studies are that perhaps too much
emphasis has been given since the 1960s on increasing the *number* of business start-ups. Sustained economic growth demands more carefully targeted
programmes and services. This much is now recognised by the institutional
midwives such as Scottish Enterprise, who are seeking to solve the endemic
problems of Scotland's relatively sluggish business birthrate. But the conception and birth of a high-tech company is not in itself sufficient to ensure
long-term survival. The evidence suggests that high tech firms grow very
slowly. They need to be carefully nursed by the provision of long-term
support: 'a longer than normal view needs to be taken of [their] funding
needs',[91] not least because Scottish firms have to move into export markets
relatively early in their life cycles to maintain their initial rates of growth.

Perhaps this constitutes a major clue to the aetiology of the fundamental
problem of the Scottish economy? Again and again, Clive Lee has emphasised the importance of consumer spending levels in explaining regional
differences in economic growth. Estimates of per capita wealth show Scotland averaging some ten per cent below the United Kingdom level in the
1980s. Paradoxically this lower level of wealth is combined with a relatively
high per capita level of personal savings, thus reducing effective demand
even further. But whereas this characteristic of household financial behaviour might imply an easing in the financial constraints confronting those
seeking to create or expand firms, it apparently does no such thing. Investigations devoted to explaining the high rate of savings in Scotland suggest
that it is inspired by a desire for liquidity. This is perhaps rooted in past
experience: the corrosive effects of the inter-war depression, relatively high
unemployment and, more recently, the virtual extinction of the old staple
trades, has bred an uncertainty concerning future economic prospects. The
Scots really do 'save for a rainy day' and divert their savings into assets which
possess high liquidity: cash, bank accounts, government securities and listed
securities. Even small firms are wary of seeking public-share capital and
unwilling to engage in highly geared financing in order to minimise
financial exposure.[92]

This combination of powerful retardative influences on both the supply and demand of business enterprise goes some way to elucidating not only Scotland's low company birthrate but the vulnerability of the Scottish economy to inward investment and the disappointing take up of potential opportunities generated by the activities of incoming multinationals. Without going into further details, we have seen – albeit only by partial illustration – that in the 1960s and 1970s the new industries that were instrumental in restructuring the Scottish economy did at last come, but overwhelmingly they came from England, in the form of branch factories of established concerns, and from the United States, as subsidiaries of American multinationals. By the early 1970s nearly sixty per cent of manufacturing employment was in plants whose ultimate ownership lay outside the Scottish economy, and this proportion seemed destined to rise.[93] Firn's analysis of data collected by the Scottish Council (Development and Industry) revealed, inter alia, that the faster growing the economic sector (e.g. the high technology industries), the lower the amount of Scottish participation. The five fastest-growing sectors had less than 14 per cent indigenous control.[94] In electrical engineering the proportion was only 7.8 per cent, and in vehicles and chemicals, only 9.8 per cent and 11.8 per cent respectively. By contrast, among the sectors that remained largely in Scottish hands (measured by employment figures) were the manufactures of leather and timber products.

At the time of Firn's inquiries, a high proportion of the externally controlled activity was conducted in new 'greenfield' production faculties, particularly by the American companies who employed about fifteen per cent of Scotland's manufacturing labour force in plant whose average size was over five times that of indigenous concerns.[95] Since the mid 1970s such conspicuous investment has markedly declined in both absolute and relative terms, to be largely superseded by inward acquisition. Because this has frequently involved the external take-over of small and medium-sized companies, this phase in the erosion of indigenous ownership of Scottish industry has been much more insidious, especially when the bidder's acquisitive moves were either welcomed or, at least, uncontested. Ashcroft and his fellow researchers believed that, initially at least, the transfer of ownership of many Scottish companies in the course of the merger boom of the late 1960s and early 1970s was 'virtually unnoticed'. Only when a take-over bid involved a major Scottish company, whose potential loss was thought so to weaken the Scottish economy that the public interest would be violated, was sufficient national anxiety aroused to warrant reference being made to the Monopolies and Mergers Commission.[96]

But how much does external take-over really matter in the context of the evolution of the Scottish economy? Have the periodic outbursts of complaint that Scottish businessmen are 'selling out to foreigners' any more significance than simple cries of wounded national pride? To answer this question is extremely difficult, not least because, as Peacock and Bannock recently observed, its solution depends not solely on measuring the performance of an acquired company before and after acquisition but on a comparison 'with some "counterfactual" position representing what would otherwise have happened … if take-over had not occurred'.[97] Only one thing is certain: any change in ownership and control invariably involves changes in the objectives which a company is expected to achieve, with consequential changes in its organisation and working methods and in the pattern of its links with both customers and suppliers. It may realistically be assumed that such changes will not always be congruent with the growth and development of a regional economy, particularly when the acquiring company is a powerful multinational.[98] This is not to argue that external take-overs have conferred no benefits on the Scottish economy. It is conceivable that in their absence, numerous Scottish firms would simply have disappeared, victims of the competitive pressures that induced their previous owners to seek a purchaser.[99] In such cases a manufacturing presence has been preserved and the loss of employment limited to that dictated by the acquiring group's subsequent internal rationalisation. In other cases, acquired companies have greatly benefited by gaining access to capital resources, the relative paucity of which was sometimes the very factor that rendered them vulnerable to take-over in the first place. Where such firms have been seen by the acquiring multinational group as a means of entry to British or European markets, the short-term effect on the target company – and hence the Scottish economy – has undoubtedly proved beneficial.

Emphasis has been given to the short-term effect because there is a growing body of evidence to support the belief that unless certain marketing and management functions, particularly research and development, are retained within the target firm, the long-term effect of external acquisition is often a stultification of growth, the direct consequence of the conversion of an autonomous concern into a mere branch plant.[100] Certainly, this is what might be expected, but Richardson and Turok's painstaking examination of the experience of thirty-two Scottish firms acquired during the 1980s revealed such a diversity of post-acquisition outcomes that generalisation on the effects of take-overs proved to be difficult, if not impossible. Nevertheless, the fear persists that by diluting the skills and capacity needed to build and develop growing businesses and by weakening the links with local providers of professional services, external take-overs 'are bound to diminish the capacity of the Scottish economy to generate and sustain growth'.[101]

VI

In the inter-war period and in the years immediately following World War II, it seemed imperative that the attainment of sustained economic growth and improved social welfare necessitated a structurally better balanced Scottish economy. No one would disagree that this did constitute a valid and desirable objective as long as the Scottish economy continued to possess an autonomous or at least semi-autonomous character. As this character-istic has been eroded by assimilation first into the British economy and then into a European or even international economy, these earlier historically determined aspirations to achieve balance have become increasingly un-realistic and incapable of realisation. In future, it is possible that the Scottish economy will be forced to shed entire fields or sections of activity; only those in which Scotland possesses some degree of comparative advantage will survive. One of these might be tourism; another, the provision of higher education; and a third, if Silicon Glen does prove able to move into software, electronics.[102]

NOTES AND REFERENCES

1. R.H. Campbell, 'A precarious prosperity', *The Story of Scotland*, Vol. 4, Part 41 (Glasgow, 1987–8), p. 1125.
2. More precisely, the proportion of the Scottish labour force in textiles, clothing and footwear was 13.2 per cent; in Strathclyde the proportion was 12 per cent, in the Borders, 28.9 per cent, and in Tayside, 33 per cent. The data are from C.H. Lee, *British Regional Employment Statistics* (Cambridge, 1979). Subsequently cited as *Statistics*.
3. C. Gulvin, *The Scottish Hosiery and Knitwear Industry* (Edinburgh, 1984), p. 67.
4. The basic statistical data are provided by R. Church, *The History of the British Industry*, Vol. 3: 1830–1913 (Oxford, 1986), pp. 347, 400–1, 474–94.
5. See P.L. Payne, *Colvilles and the Scottish Steel Industry* (Oxford, 1979), pp. 47–54.
6. G. Blake, *The Shipbuilders* (London, 1935), p. 72.
7. It has been estimated that early in the twentieth century locally-made components constituted well over half the value of a ship. See report by the Shipbuilding Working Group, *Strathclyde built in the 1990s* (Strathclyde Regional Council, May 1987).
8. For a detailed survey of these and other activities see M.S. Moss and J.R. Hume, *Workshop of the British Empire* (London, 1977).
9. C.H. Lee, 'Modern Economic Growth and Structural Change in Scotland: the Service Sector Reconsidered', *Scottish Economic & Social History*, Vol. 3, No. 3 (1983).
10. This point has often been made; for brief, clear discussions, see C.E.V. Leser, 'Manufacturing Industry' in A.K. Cairncross (ed.), *The Scottish Economy* (Cambridge, 1954), pp. 118–32, and N.K. Buxton, 'Economic Growth in Scotland between the Wars: The Role of Production Structure and Rationalisation', *Economic History Review*, second series, xxiii (1980), pp. 538–55. John Butt has emphasised the 'very narrowness of [Scotland's] industrial structure'. S.G.E. Lythe and J. Butt, *An Economic History of Scotland, 1100–1939* (Glasgow and London, 1975), p. 217.
11. For a brief survey, see P.L. Payne, *Growth and Contraction, Scottish Industry c.1860–1990*

(Glasgow: Economic & Social History Society of Scotland, 1992), pp. 25–35. See also N.K. Buxton, 'Economic Growth in Scotland between the Wars'.

12. On this question, the finest discussion is that by S. Tolliday, *Business, Banking and Politics. The Case of British Steel, 1918–1939* (Cambridge, 1987), pp. 82–123.

13. K. Warren, 'Locational Problems of the Scottish Iron and Steel Industry', *Scottish Geographical Magazine*, LXXXI (1965), pp. 87–8.

14. P. Pagnamenta & R. Overy, *All our Working Lives* (London, 1984), p. 134.

15. A. Slaven, 'Self-Liquidation: the National Shipbuilders Security Ltd. and British Shipbuilding in the 1930s', in S. Palmer and G. Williams (eds), *Chartered and Unchartered Waters* (London, 1981), pp. 125–47.

16. See A. McKinlay, 'Employers and skilled workers in the inter-war depression: engineering and shipbuilding on Clydeside, 1919–1939', unpublished D.Phil. thesis, University of Oxford, 1986.

17. My own detailed knowledge of these matters is limited to iron and steel, but I suspect that more widespread inquiry could reveal the stultifying influence of family trusts on much of Scottish industry.

18. See C. Wurm, *Business, Politics and International Relations* (Cambridge, 1993), pp. 83, 89.

19. J.F. Hargrave, 'Competition and collusion in the British railway track fittings industry: the case of the Anderson Foundry, 1800–1960', unpublished Ph.D. thesis, University of Durham, 1991, p. 175.

20. ibid., p. 421.

21. Wurm, *Business Politics*, p. 134.

22. A.D. Campbell, 'Income', in A.K. Cairncross (ed.), *The Scottish Economy* (Cambridge, 1954), p. 58.

23. Lee, 'The Service Sector Reconsidered', p. 26; see also J. Foreman-Peck, 'Seedcorn or Chaff? New firm formation and the performance of the inter-war economy', *Economic History Review*, second series, XXXVIII, pp. 402–22.

24. Scottish Economic Committee, *Light Industries in Scotland. A Case for Development* (1938).

25. S.C.E. Lythe, 'Report on the Furniture Industry in Scotland', ibid., p. 32.

26. W. Davis, 'Report on the Hosiery Industry in Scotland', ibid., p. 63.

27. J.M. Hay, 'Report on the manufacture of Heating, Ventilating and Refrigerating Apparatus in Scotland', ibid., pp. 82–3.

28. A.G. Buchanan, 'Report on the Boot and Shoe Industry … in Scotland', ibid., p. 191.

29. Papers relating to Clyde Blades Ltd, 1935–39, among Sir John Craig's private papers. A report, dated 22 April 1939, recorded the sales manager's endeavour to create 'an ordered system out of something which seemed chaotic'.

30. A point emphasised by Ronald Weir, 'Structural Change and the Scottish Economy, 1918–1939', *Refresh*, Vol. 19 (Autumn, 1994), pp. 5–8.

31. C.E. Heim, 'Industrial Organization and Regional Development in Inter-War Britain', *Journal of Economic History*, XLIII (1983), p. 934.

32. A point discussed by J. Foreman-Peck, 'Seedcorn or Chaff?', p. 413.

33. Heim, '*Industrial Organisation and Regional Development*', p. 944.

34. P.L. Payne, 'The End of Steelmaking in Scotland, c.1967–1993', *Scottish Economic & Social History*, p. 15, 1995.

35. Calculations based upon data provided by F.A. Shera and G.B. Robertson, 'Structural Change in the Scottish Economy', *Scottish Economic Bulletin*, No. 43 (June, 1991), p. 22 and C.C. Moncur, 'Regional Accounts: Scottish Trends 1971–1980', *Scottish Economic Bulletin*, No. 25 (Summer 1982), p. 9.

36. J. Scott and M. Hughes, *The Anatomy of Scottish Capital* (1980), pp. 93, 143.

37. In 1981 the Royal Bank Group sought to merge with the Standard Charter Bank and contested a take-over bid from the Hong Kong and Shanghai Banking Corporation. Following a report of the Monopolies and Mergers Commission which recommended that neither merger should be permitted, these proposals were abandoned. A.D. Bain and R.G. Reid, 'The Finance Sector' in N. Hood and S. Young (eds), *Industry, Policy and the Scottish Economy* (Edinburgh, 1984), p. 388. See also the 'Memorandum to the Monopolies and Mergers Commission' in *Quarterly Economic Commentary of the Fraser of Allander Institute* (July 1981), pp. 38–53.

38. Scottish Equitable, the fourth largest Scottish life insurance firm (and among the ten largest

Scottish companies) was taken over by the Dutch-based Aegon insurance group in 1993. *Quarterly Economic Commentary of the Fraser of Allander Institute*, 18, No. 4 (1993), pp. 20–1.

39. J. Scott, 'The Role of the Scottish Financial Sector', *Quarterly Economic Commentary of the Fraser of Allander Institute*, 18, No. 4 (1993), p. 53.
40. *Scottish Business Insider*, 12, No. 1 (January 1995), p. 59.
41. J. Scott, 'Scottish Financial Sector', p. 53.
42. ibid., cf. 75,800 or 3.7 per cent of the total labour force, generating about 5.5 per cent of Scottish GDP in 1976. Bain and Reid, 'The Finance Sector', p. 366.
43. R. Saville, 'The Industrial background', in R. Saville (ed.), *The Economic Development of Modern Scotland, 1950–1980* (Edinburgh, 1985), p. 34. One of the reasons given to the Scottish Economic Committee in 1938 for 'the lack of development of the radio industry in Scotland' was 'the growth of combines … of wireless manufacturers and … battery makers, valve manufacturers, etc., and in particular the strength of the E.M.I. combine (H.M.V., Columbia and Marconi)', J.A. Cowan, 'Report on the Manufacture of Electrical Appliances and Equipment in Scotland', in Scottish Economic Committee, *Light Industries in Scotland*, pp. 211, 214–16. See also J.C. Logan, 'Electricity supply, electrical engineering and the Scottish economy in the inter-war years', in A.J.G. Cummings and T.M. Devine (eds), *Industry, Business and Society in Scotland since 1700* (Edinburgh, 1994), pp. 115–19.
44. This, and much of the previous paragraph, rests on J.R. Firn and D. Roberts, 'High-Technology Industries', in N. Hood & S. Young (eds), *Industry, Policy and the Scottish Economy* (Edinburgh, 1984), pp. 297–9. For Ferranti, see ibid., pp. 317–21.
45. I. Turok, 'Inward Investment and Local Linkages: How deeply embedded is "Silicon Glen"?', *Regional Studies*, Vol. 27, No. 5 (1993), p. 403.
46. For the gains and losses in the electronics industry in Scotland during the 1980s, see S. Young, E. Peters and N. Hood, 'Performance and employment change in overseas-owned manufacturing industry in Scotland', *Scottish Economic Bulletin*, No. 47 (Summer 1993), pp. 34–5.
47. This paragraph is based upon P. Haug, 'US High Technology Multinationals and Silicon Glen', *Regional Studies*, Vol. 20, No. 2 (1986), pp. 106–9.
48. Turok, 'Inward Investment', pp. 402–3.
49. ibid.
50. ibid., pp. 403–5; and see J. McCalman, 'What's wrong with Scottish firms? Local sourcing in Scottish Electronics', *Scottish Economic Bulletin*, No. 32 (December 1985).
51. Turok, 'Inward Investment', p. 407.
52. For Rodine of Glenrothes, see Turok, 'Inward Investment', p. 408; Firn & Roberts, 'High-Technology Industries', p. 306; and the *Quarterly Economic Commentary of the Fraser of Allander Institute*, Vol. 17, No. 1 (1991), p. 24. Domain Power, based in Greenock, was taken over by Switchcraft Inc. of Chicago in the summer of 1990 and sold to the Japanese company, Mineba, early in 1992. *Pointer* (July 1990, February 1992).
53. I. Turok, 'The Growth of an indigenous electronics industry: Scottish printed circuit boards', *Environment and Planning A*, Vol. 25 (1993), pp. 1780–1813.
54. Turok, 'Inward Investment', p. 415.
55. The report itself has never been published and is currently time barred, but its essence has been extensively leaked and a summary presented in the *Scottish Business Insider*, Vol. 10, No. 12 (December 1993), pp. 4–7; see also *The Sunday Times Scotland*, 30 January 1994. I have, however, had the opportunity of discussing some parts of the report with Mr Ron Botham of Scottish Enterprise, to whom I am greatly indebted. Some critics have argued that the report is too pessimistic – 'a "worse case scenario" which no one seriously expects to happen' (Terry Murden in *The Sunday Times*, 30 January 1994) – but it is noteworthy that its completion coincided with the decision by the Californian company, Conner Peripherals, to abandon its £50 million disk drive plant at Irvine only three years after its establishment with assistance from Locate in Scotland, and shortly after the American electronics corporation Unisys closed its Livingston plant with the loss of 686 jobs in October 1991. Of the latter closure, the chairman of the Livingston Development Corporation said, 'It is serious because this is a successful operation … with its own research and development organisation and manufacturing plant, everything that is supposed to make a factory less vulnerable. It has nothing to do with

the recession in Scotland but everything to do with decisions made thousands of miles away in the United States'. *The Times*, 9 October 1991.

56. In discussing the prospects for multi-media technology in Scotland, Douglas MacKenzie of the consultants DMC is pessimistic: 'There is virtually no private sector infrastructure. *Silicon Glen is not Silicon Valley*. We are hampered by the lack of our indigenous computer industry. We have concentrated on importing hardware manufacturers – assembly-line jobs. It would be different if we had a Microsoft nearby or one of the other big software producers. They encourage people with ideas; but that does not happen here'. [Emphasis supplied.] *Scottish Business Insider*, Vol. 12, No. 2 (February 1995), p. 51. Multi-media represents the integration of the separate technologies used for human/machine interaction, namely high-fidelity audio, full-motion video and computers.

57. See the discussion by J. McCalman, 'The Japanisation of Silicon Glen. Implications for spin-off and Supplier Linkages'. *Fraser of Allander Quarterly Economic Commentary*, Vol. 17, No. 1 (1991), pp. 56–63. McCalman concludes, inter alia, that Japanese firms are more likely to create opportunities for indigenous spin-offs than American multinationals.

58. *Scottish Business Insider*, Vol. 10, No. 12 (1993), p. 7: cf. Turok, 'Inward Investment', p. 413 and see the article by J. McClelland, 'Why IBM spared Greenock', in *The Sunday Times Scotland*, 30 January 1994.

59. Some observers have detected a recent trend among the multinationals in the industry to devolve greater responsibility to their regional managers, giving them more power to instigate policies. Discussion with Mr Ron Botham of Scottish Enterprise. Cf. the stark findings of S. Young, N. Hood and J. Hamill, *Foreign Multinationals and the British Economy* (London, 1988), p. 251, that foreign MNEs 'never have been and never will be anything other than a modest palliative for the British economy'. Indeed, their very presence has hampered and delayed efforts to make Britain's indigenous enterprises more competitive.

60. W. Pike, 'The construction and installation of offshore petroleum structures: the Scottish experience 1972–1989', unpublished paper delivered to the Economic History Society, 1990; W. Pike, 'The Impact of North Sea Oil on the Scottish Economy', unpublished Ph.D. thesis, University of Aberdeen, 1993 (hereafter, '*Thesis*'), p. 269. It will be observed that Pike's figures are much lower than those published by the government. Several informed commentators have emphasised that the official figures exaggerate the share of oil supply work won by British/Scottish-owned companies. See, for example, the discussion in A.H. Harris, M.G. Lloyd and D.A. Newlands, *The Impact of Oil on the Aberdeen Economy* (Aldershot, 1988), pp. 24–8.

61. For example, the Weir Group, sharing the belief of the Scottish engineering industry in the late 1960s and early 1970s that the North Sea was but a 'temporary market', was so slow in responding to the 'opportunity' that they found their potential market for pumps already captured by the American firms Baker Oil Tools, Cameron and Vetco. T. MacKay, 'The Oil and Oil Related Sector', in N. Hood and S. Young (eds), *Industry, Policy and the Scottish Economy* (Edinburgh, 1984), p. 357. See also C. Harvie, *Fool's Gold. The Story of North Sea Oil* (London, 1994), passim, but especially pp. 80–5. As late as December 1972 the report commissioned by the Department of Trade and Industry from the consultants International Management and Engineering Group, entitled *Potential Benefits to British Industry from Offshore Oil and Gas Developments* observed that 'British industry generally remains extremely unsure of the facts about offshore requirements'.

62. The price of oil, about $14 a barrel in 1977–8, had risen sharply to peak in 1981 at about $37 a barrel. See Harris et al., *Impact of Oil*, p. 18.

63. Pike, *Thesis*, pp. 277–8.

64. ibid., p. 279.

65. Harvie, *Fool's Gold*, p. 81.

66. Pike, *Thesis*, p. 283.

67. C. Robinson, 'Oil depletion policy in the United Kingdom', *Three Banks Review*, No. 135, September 1982, pp. 3–8.

68. Pike believes that 'a policy of slower, more closely controlled development, similar to that adopted by Norway, could have boosted Scottish content significantly'. *Thesis*, pp. 284, 286. See also Harris et al., *Impact of Oil*, pp. 29, 67–8, 120.

69. See P. Hallwood, *The offshore oil supply industry in Aberdeen: the affiliates – their characteristics and importance.* North Sea Study Occasional Paper No. 23 (Department of Political Economy, University of Aberdeen, 1986).

70. See J.A. Cairns, A.H. Harris and H.C. Williams, *Barriers to entry in the North Sea offshore oil supply industry.* North Sea Study Occasional Paper, No. 24 (Department of Economics, University of Aberdeen, 1987).

71. I. Wood, 'Offshore Oil – problems and opportunities for local industry', paper presented at the SSRC North Sea Oil Panel Seminar in 1981, quoted T. MacKay, 'Oil and Oil Related Sector', in N. Hood and S. Young (eds), *Industry, Policy and the Scottish Economy* (Edinburgh, 1984), pp. 351–2. For the early development of the Wood Group, see ibid., pp. 353–6. In 1993 it was reported that 'to avoid over dependence on the North Sea', over the previous three years the Wood Group had acquired major interests in (or taken over) numerous companies in the United States, France, Italy and Abu Dhabi. The report was occasioned by the Group's purchase of a forty-seven per cent interest in ERC Inc. of Houston, a company which manufactures and maintains wellhead equipment and valves. [Aberdeen] *Press and Journal* (20 January 1993).

72. Of the 1,100 firms in Scotland involved with offshore oil and gas in c.1984, 80 per cent were new starts as far as Scotland was concerned and about 800 were located in the Aberdeen area. Of the 64,000 employed in the oil industry in 1983, almost three quarters were in the Grampian Region. MacKay, 'Oil and Oil Related Sector', pp. 351–2; Harvie, *Fool's Gold*, p. 219.

73. Ian Wood, quoted MacKay, 'Oil and Oil Related Sector', p. 359. For the role of the Offshore Supplies Office, see ibid., pp. 346–50. It was estimated in 1984 that the long-term oil-related employment which might survive the exhaustion of the North Sea province was unlikely to exceed 5,000 jobs. See S. McDowall, in Saville, (ed.), *The Economic Development*, p. 306, and see Harris et al., *Impact of Oil*, pp. 115-18.

74. W. Pike, 'The oil price crisis and its impact on Scottish North Sea development, 1986–1988', *Scottish Economic and Social History*, Vol. 13 (1993), p. 65. See also Harris et al., *Impact of Oil*, p. 104.

75. From a peak of 52,500 in mid-1985 oil related employment fell to 41,000 in mid-1987. A. Campbell, 'Oil and Grampian: the first 22 years' (Aberdeen, Economic Development and Planning Department, Regional Council, September 1991), p. 7.

76. Pike, 'The oil price crisis', p. 67.

77. ibid., p. 68. Baker Hughes and Halliburton are American companies; Schlumberger, nominally French, conducts most of its activities in, and is essentially managed from, the United States.

78. Harris, et al., addressing this point in 1988, observed that 'after North Sea production runs down … [it is likely] that the vast majority of firms currently based in Aberdeen will leave … with a corresponding devastating effect upon the local economy'.

79. In 1994 the Offshore Supplies Office was reorganised as the Oil and Gas Projects and Supplies Office to encompass the downstream refining and petrochemical sector and onshore production operations, and it was suggested the British companies were winning work worth at least £2 billion a year in a world offshore market valued at more than £50 million (*The Times*, 16 February 1995). It is apparent that considerable opportunities for UK firms do exist in the former Soviet republics, the Far East and Latin America. What is less clear is how far these markets will be exploited. There are signs that the share accruing to Scottish firms is increasing gradually. In the North Sea the oil companies are permitting contractors to take over management functions previously handled by their own personnel, but the greater risk involved in these 'new deals' may well breed even greater hesitancy, particularly among the smaller firms characteristic of the Grampian region.

80. Grampian Regional Council, Economic Development and Planning Department, *Oil and Gas Prospects, 1992 Update* (Aberdeen, 1992), p. 2.

81. Figures derived from data provided by I. Turok, 'Inward Investment', p. 416 and S. Young, E. Peters and N. Hood, 'Performance and Employment Change in Overseas-owned manufacturing industry in Scotland', *Scottish Economic Bulletin*, No. 47 (Summer 1993), p. 34. See also Industry Department Scotland, Statistical Bulletin No. C1.2, *The Electronics Industry in Scotland* (February 1988), p. 3.

82. The whisky industry, as Ronald Weir has emphasised, is unusual in that, unlike the old staples its market has been declining since 1900. This means that it has had more time to adjust capacity to demand. Furthermore, the industry was dominated by one company, the Distillers Company, led by an individual unconstrained by family interests who developed the concept of 'organised competition' which allowed the industry to be regulated from a much earlier date than other Scottish industries. For all that, Distillers found diversification to be extremely difficult and risky. See R. Weir, 'Rationalization and diversification in the Scotch Whisky industry, 1900–39', *Economic History Review*, second series, XLII (1989), pp. 375–95; R. Weir, 'Structural Change and the Scottish Economy, 1918–1939', *Refresh*, 19 (Autumn, 1994), p. 8; R.B. Weir, *The History of the Malt Distillers' Association of Scotland* (Elgin, 1974). The industry is the subject of useful discussions by D.B. Small and L.D. Smith in Hood and Young (eds), *Industry, Policy and the Scottish Economy*, pp. 187–210, and B. Ashcroft and J.H. Love, *Takeovers, Mergers and the Regional Economy* (Edinburgh, 1993), pp. 114–41.

83. S. Berry, 'Wanted: more business babies', *Scottish Business Insider*, Vol. 10, No. 11 (November 1993), p. 72.

84. 'The Neutered Scot Syndrome', *Scottish Business Insider*, Vol. 9, No. 11 (November 1992), p. 10.

85. ibid. The last point was apparently made in a report by KPMG.

86. The Scots apparently regard teachers as the greatest contributors to society, but rank entrepreneurs fifth out of eight occupations in this respect, after bus drivers and plumbers but ahead of lawyers and churchmen! ibid., p. 13. See also D.J. Storey and S. Johnston, 'Regional variations in entrepreneurship in the U.K.', *Scottish Journal of Political Economy*, 34 (1987), pp. 161–73, and B. Ashcroft, J.H. Love and E. Malloy, 'New firm formation in the British counties with special references to Scotland', *Regional Studies*, 25 (1991), pp. 395–409.

87. See S. Dow, 'The Regional Financial Sector: A Scottish case study', *Regional Studies*, Vol. 26, No. 7, p. 629; and see below.

88. See ibid., p. 11; S. Boyle, M. Burns et al., *Scotland's Economy: Claiming the Future* (London, 1989), p. 34.

89. I. Turok and R. Richardson, 'New Firms and Local Economic Development: Evidence from West Lothian', *Regional Studies*, Vol. 25, No. 1 (1991), pp. 81–2.

90. C. Gallacher and P. Miller, 'The performance of new firms in Scotland and the South West, 1980–87', *Royal Bank of Scotland Review*, 170 (June 1991), pp. 38, 41, 46–7.

91. ibid., p. 50.

92. The underlying data for these speculations are provided by the important paper by Dow, 'The Regional Financial Sector', pp. 627–9; see also C.C. Moncur, 'Regional Accounts: Scottish Trends, 1971–80', *Scottish Economic Bulletin*, 25 (Summer 1982), pp. 13–14, and D.N.F. Bell and V.G. Bulmer Thomas, 'Household Savings in Scotland', Fraser of Allander Institute, *Discussion Paper* 12 (1978).

93. J.R. Firn, 'External control and regional development: the case of Scotland', *Environment and Planning A*, 7 (1975), pp. 393–414.

94. That is, the level of Scottish control in the five fastest-growing sectors was a mere 13.5 per cent of total employment in these sectors in Scotland. ibid., p. 405.

95. See the discussion by B.K. Ashcroft, J.H. Love and J. Scoulter, *The Economic Effects of the Inward Acquisition of Scottish Manufacturing Companies 1965 to 1980*. ESU Research Papers No. 11, (Industry Department, Scottish Office, Edinburgh, 1987).

96. Four key cases are reviewed by Ashcroft and Love, *Takeovers*, pp. 150–64.

97. A Peacock and G. Bannock, *Corporate Take-overs and the Public Interest* (Aberdeen, 1991), p. 67.

98. The possible consequences of the concentration of the textile industry on Scottish textiles are briefly discussed by P.L. Payne, *Growth and Contraction*, pp. 40–5.

99. It must be recognised that many acquired Scottish firms were not the hapless victims of predators but actively sought a purchaser as a solution to what might have been terminal problems. See Ashcroft et al., *Economic Effects*, pp. 2, 59, 62–6. Of a sample of thirty-two Scottish firms taken over in the 1980s, a quarter of the takeovers were initiated by the acquired firms. R. Richardson and I. Turok, *Scotland for Sale: The Impact of External Take-overs in the 1980s*, Strathclyde Papers on Planning No. 15, (Glasgow, University of Strathclyde, 1990).

100. Ashcroft, et al., *Economic Effects*, p. 7, provide a very useful table of the hypothesised positive and negative effects of external control.

101. Richardson and Turok, *Scotland for Sale?*, p. 41; cf. B. Ashcroft, 'External Take-overs in Scottish Manufacturing: the effect on local linkages and corporate functions', *Scottish Journal of Political Economy*, 35 (1988), pp. 129–48; J.H. Love, 'External take-overs and regional linkage adjustment: the case of Scotch whisky', *Environment and Planning A*, 22 (1990), pp. 101–18; I. Turok and R. Richardson, 'External take-overs of Scottish companies in the 1980s', *Area*, 23 (1991), pp. 73–81.

102. Despite the undoubted recent success of financial services, it is difficult to believe that this sub-sector of the service industries will continue to experience growth at the rate achieved during the last two decades. As the chief executive of the Clydesdale Bank observed in November 1994, 'We have a situation in banking and financial services which is over-capacitised, competition is very intense and margins are being squeezed', *Scottish Business Insider*, 12, No. 1 (January 1995), p. 36.

3. GOVERNMENT
Iain G.C. Hutchison

State involvement in many aspects of British life has grown throughout most of the twentieth century. It is, however, arguable that the role of government has been markedly more evident in Scotland than in England and Wales, and while it is difficult to measure this accurately for the period before World War II, the indicators for the post-1945 era are significant.

The heavy dependence of the Scots on the state for employment is one obvious element. The programme of nationalisation carried out by the Attlee governments of 1945–51 had major implications for the Scottish economy, with its over-concentration this century on the basic heavy staple sector – notably coal-mining, iron and steel and transport. In addition, the role of the Scots as greater consumers of the public sector tended to mean more people were employed providing these needs – in local government, in health and education. One of the most striking contrasts with the rest of Britain in this context is in housing tenure. In 1981, public-sector housing represented thirty-two per cent of the total British stock, but fifty-five per cent of the Scottish total.[1] This is probably the largest share of housing in state hands in an advanced economy outside the former eastern block countries.

Similarly, the greater tendency of Scots to use public-sector education is marked. Unlike in England and Wales, parents from virtually every social stratum send their children to be educated in state schools, with the use of private schools restricted to a very few; in England and Wales the figure is much more significant. It should be borne in mind, moreover, that a sizeable proportion of those attending private schools are the children of Scots expatriates. Thus the actual resident Scots availing themselves of non-state schooling is even smaller. In addition, the proportion of Scots attending university has throughout this century (and before) far exceeded that of England and Wales.

More sombrely, the consistently higher unemployment rates obtaining in Scotland since World War I, along with the lower Scottish income per capita, has meant that the social security system has had proportionally more users in Scotland. These indicators of poorer living standards are mirrored by poorer health than in England and Wales, so Scots have used the National Health Service to a greater degree.

The upshot of all of these (and other) factors is that identifiable public expenditure on Scotland has been at higher levels than in England or Wales. While the exact calculations are the subject of intense academic and political debate, it seems that the balance of opinion inclines to the view that Scotland has usually not been disadvantaged. In 1976–7 identifiable public expenditure per head in Scotland was twenty-two per cent above that in England, and even after taking into account relative needs, Scotland was still eleven per cent higher.[2] In part this may reflect the perpetuation until the mid-1970s of the late Victorian Goschen formula (which laid down that Scotland would receive 11/80ths of the total British figure for appropriate government spending) long after the demographic element behind this calculation had shifted, with Scotland's share of Britain's population declining throughout the post-1918 period.

At first sight, this enlarged role of the state in the twentieth century appears paradoxical. Scotland, after all, as Margaret Thatcher never tired of remarking, had been the birthplace of the formulation of the principles of laissez-faire and a minimal state presence. These concepts had been enthusiastically sustained through the nineteenth century, notably in Scotland's fervent espousal of economic liberalism and free trade, and in a harsher application of social policy as embodied in the poor law. In Scotland the conditions for receipt of poor relief were less generous than in England, most notably in the denial of benefit to able-bodied unemployed men. But to accept this impression at face value is to adopt a superficial interpretation of the legacy, and to imply, by extension, that the acceptance of an enhanced government role in this century arose from a cynical exploitative pragmatism is also misleading.

It is worth noting that in the nineteenth century an alternative vision of public involvement ran parallel with the philosophy of Adam Smith. At one level it can be seen in the application of a gospel of municipal socialism in the later nineteenth century in places like Glasgow. Here the city authorities pursued a policy of municipal ownership and enterprise that far outstripped Joseph Chamberlain's socialistic endeavours in Birmingham, making Glasgow the cynosure of American urban reformers in the 1890s and 1900s.[3] Another instance is the acceptance in nineteenth-century Scotland of the principle of state financial support for education, itself the continuance of a long tradition. Thus in the late years of the nineteenth century, the Scottish universities launched a sustained campaign to be put on a firmer financial footing through the injection of public funds. This was not merely special pleading by academics: government ministers for Scottish affairs insisted to sceptical colleagues that there was widespread middle-class backing for this demand. Treasury ministers and officials alike, coming as they did from the Oxbridge approach of private financing of universities, found these arguments both incomprehensible and reprehensible.[4]

In this century, acceptance by the Scottish business community of the desirability of a measure of state intervention in industry has also been notable. In the 1930s the case was argued by the Scottish Council (Development and Industry) (SCDI), a predominantly business organisation, long before employers in England. Prominent capitalists in Scotland were well to the fore in seeking active state intervention to sort out industrial difficulties. The names of such Scottish entrepreneurs as Lord Weir, Sir James Lithgow, Sir Andrew Duncan, Lord Bilsland and Sir William McLintock litter the pages of studies of the process of increasing government involvement in managing economic change.[5] Indeed, it is noticeable that during the depression of the 1930s, the Scottish Office pushed vigorously for a more active state participation in economic development. Largely, this was due to the concerns of Scottish business, many of whom were dependent on government orders, especially in the shipbuilding industry. The reaction of Whitehall to these suggestions was frosty in the extreme.[6] Similarly after 1945, the SCDI pushed this line further: the Council played a crucial part in prompting the Scottish Office to secure the arrival of IBM in Greenock in the early 1950s. A more significant landmark was the Council's sponsoring of the highly influential Toothill Report of 1961.[7] Toothill, himself the managing director of a large manufacturing concern, advocated that the government adopt a radical new strategy to stimulate economic growth in Scotland, but a strategy which envisaged more, not less, state contribution.

Agriculture also represents an area of growing state presence this century. The state became a large landowner, more so than in England, partly through the acquisition of parts of estates to set up smallholdings, especially after World War I.[8] In addition the Forestry Commission increasingly located a disproportionate share of its activities in Scotland, where by the 1970s about three quarters of all new work took place. The regulation of the crofting system, begun with the Crofters Act of 1886 and added to thereafter, also represented a presence not replicated in the rest of Britain. In the 1930s the British government embarked on a programme of greater assistance to agriculture organised on quasi-corporatist lines. It may be relevant that the minister responsible for launching this new departure was a Scot, Walter Elliot. The first important by-product of this policy as far as Scottish farming was concerned was the Scottish Milk Marketing Board, set up in 1933. Another major initiative was the Agricultural Executive Committee, formed in 1940. Similar trends were occurring in the fishing industry with, for instance, the creation of the White Fish Authority. Because a higher proportion of the Scottish workforce was engaged in farming and fishing than elsewhere in Britain, this further underscored the prominence of the state in Scotland.

At the heart of the expansion of the role of the state in Scotland was the Scottish Office.[9] The general trends of its development were an increasing responsibility for Scottish administration, a greater physical presence in Scotland and the professionalisation of the business of the Office. Before World War I the Scottish Secretary had no place within the Cabinet and the Scottish Office, located in Dover House in London, was responsible for overseeing the limited functions of government in Scotland. Most of the Scottish central administration was carried out by boards in Scotland which dealt with a wide range of matters including lunacy, prisons, law and order and agriculture. The boards were autonomous and not legally answerable to the Scottish Office. The staff were usually made up from local dignitaries rather than professional civil servants and the appointments often had strong overtones of political patronage.[10]

In 1926 the Scottish Secretary was raised to a Secretary of State, although the concomitant salary rise was delayed for a decade. An additional minister was appointed in 1919. Following critical enquiries into the boards, they were transformed in 1928 into departments of state, but still retained a quasi-independent standing. The breakthrough came with the publication of the Gilmour Report in 1937, whose conclusions were legislated for immediately. The departments were placed firmly under the control of the Secretary of State, and proper professional civil service standards and modes of operation were implemented. As a physical symbol of the enlarged scope of the Scottish Office and its new centrality in Scottish life, the civil servants were moved up to Edinburgh and housed in the recently built (1939) St Andrews House.[11]

After World War II, the Scottish Office grew apace in line with the increased demands of government in Britain as a result of the expansion of the corporate economy and the Welfare State. Its existing functions expanded, in particular, in health, housing and economic development. Furthermore, the Balfour Report of 1953 argued that wherever practicable, the Scottish Office should handle Scottish matters and many additional functions were placed at the doorstep of St Andrews House – notably aspects of transport and energy administration. Three more ministers were added to the team, and three Commons committees were created to augment the Scottish Grand Committee in scrutinising Scottish business. The number of civil servants employed by the Scottish Office mushroomed from around 2,400 in 1937 (itself a substantial advance on the handful before 1914) to 8,300 in 1970. It is, however, worth nothing that the bulk of non-industrial civil servants working in Scotland are not under the Scottish Office's control. In 1981, of the 68,710 civil service staff employed in Scotland, 10,910 worked for the Scottish Office, and a further 2,800 for other 'Scottish' agencies. The remainder worked for British departments. Nevertheless it is important to stress that virtually all of the personnel in the administrative class, the élite cadre, were in the Scottish Office.[12]

The Scottish Office as a bureaucratic system needs some discussion, for it is not a mirror-image of Whitehall, although frequently described as such. First, it is important to note that there is no direct Treasury presence in Edinburgh. This may well make a difference to the mood and approach of the Scottish Office, for in Whitehall the Treasury is the central, overarching department whose influence and power extends everywhere. Significantly, too, because, as is shown later, the Scottish Office élite are composed of largely home-grown products, the Treasury has been less successful in carrying out its policy of positioning individuals drawn from that department in key posts at the head of other departments. In this way the British civil service has had a 'Treasury culture' instilled into all departments, so imposing a cash-conscious mentality. It is possible that this may account in good part for the Scottish Office's less guarded approach to public spending. Certainly the Treasury from at least the 1930s tended to see the Scottish Office as eager to spend. Indeed, it was claimed that once, when the Treasury heard that a deputation from the Scottish Office was due to arrive, the cat's milk was taken in.[13] The Treasury refused to sanction extra funding for the Scottish universities in the 1930s, despite Scottish Office backing, arguing that the Scots should follow their English institutions and raise money from non-state sources.[14]

Another deviation from the Whitehall model is that the relative importance of departments within St Andrews House may not be the same as their British equivalents. Thus the Scottish Education Department (SED) has tended to be a very weighty player in the Scottish Office. The Department

of Education in Whitehall, on the other hand, has historically been regarded as a rather low-level ministry with relatively little clout. The SED's
influences had several sources. In part this was because it had been set up
before several other departments. More importantly, its role as the guardian
of the only aspect of Scottish national identity over which the state has a
direct influence gave it greater prominence. Linked to this was the great
pride in the alleged superiority of Scottish over English education, which
provided a useful lever for the SED to deploy within the civil service. The
significance of the department was reinforced by its control of key functions which the British Education Department did not possess. Inspectors
of Schools south of the border were employed by and answerable to local
education authorities. In Scotland, they were officials of the SED. Similarly
the SED controlled the Central Institutions, but their English counterparts
– the Colleges of Advanced Technology (many later becoming polytech-
nics) – were again under the aegis of local government. Lastly, teacher training in England and Wales remained beyond the direct administration of
central government, but in Scotland this was managed from the centre. The
SED was run by a succession of confident, dynamic heads, such as Sir John
Struthers, whose personality stamped itself on the department and on Scottish education in the first quarter of the century.[15] This was an aggressive,
confident department which was prepared to throw its weight about. It
resisted, for instance, attempts in the 1950s by the established universities
to prise all teaching of advanced engineering away from its prized protégé,
the Central Institutions.[16]

Agriculture is also a relatively insignificant department in Whitehall, but
in Scotland it exercises more influence. It is revealing that the department
was able to induce the Secretary of State to reject the advice of the Alness
Committee in 1945 when it recommended the closure of certain Scottish
university departments of agriculture. In England the University Grants
Committee's (UGC) call for similar reductions in the number of departments was accepted without resistance. The UGC was quite shaken by the
disregard of expert opinion shown by the Department of Agriculture for
Scotland.[17]

These episodes naturally raise the question of the distribution of power
within the Scottish Office, not so much between departments, but between
officials and ministers, and reflect a much wider debate about the influence
of civil servants in policy formulation in Britain.[18] There are two aspects
which require examination: relations between ministers and civil servants,
and relations between the Scottish Office and Whitehall.

It is widely accepted that British ministers have a struggle to control their departmental civil servants, but Scottish Office ministers labour under an additional burden. It is often very hard for politicians, who have to spend much of the week in Westminster, to maintain supervision over administrators 400 miles away in Edinburgh. In addition, because civil servants in the Scottish Office are often long-serving in their section, as noted earlier, they are steeped in departmental values, which means they tend to follow very closely the departmental brief. This is perhaps most obviously the case in the SED, where there is on the one hand a very strong departmental ethos, while on the other, many of the ministers handling the subject have not been themselves products of the system. Most Conservative and Liberal ministers this century have been part of that tiny percentage of Scots educated outwith the state sector.[19]

However, the ability of civil servants to manipulate decisions in the direction they desired has never been guaranteed. For instance the ambition of many in the late 1920s and early 1930s to effect substantial reforms to the organisation of government in Scotland was not begun until 1937 following the Gilmour Report. The catalyst for action was political, not the machinations of officials: the rise of Scottish nationalist opinion in the middle 1930s rang alarm bells among the National Government ministers, and a degree of administrative devolution, it was hoped, would placate Home Rule sentiment.[20] Likewise the opportunity for officials to lead was dependent on the passivity of the decision-makers. The history of two reports on the funding of universities is illuminating. The first, chaired in 1937–8 by a former Scottish Secretary, Lord Alness, followed the civil service line, which was to be rather negative towards the claims of the Scottish universities to additional funding. Nearly a decade later another committee looked into the same matter. Its chairman was Lord Cooper, a former MP and now a law lord. Cooper clearly swept the civil service brief aside and produced a report which pugnaciously asserted the entitlement of the universities to improved funding.[21]

It is also useful to reflect that politicians are not always more astute than their officials. A careful examination of the much vaunted Council of State suggests caution. The Council of State was created by Tom Johnston in 1941 as one of the conditions he laid down before accepting the offer of the Secretaryship of State from Churchill. The Council consisted of all the living former Scottish Secretaries and Secretaries of State for Scotland. Its purpose was to consider the economic and social requirements of Scotland and to report on how these should be tackled. In fact, it appears that the Council was a windy talking-shop with little grasp of economic and social realities, and possessed no great vision. Too preoccupied with immediate issues, its overall impact was ineffective and irrelevant to the long-term restructuring of the Scottish economy. Indeed, it has been contended that the Scottish Office bureaucrats working on similar problems at the end of the previous decade showed a better understanding of the possibilities for action.[22]

In their contacts with the British civil service in Whitehall, the Scottish Office personnel seemed to be regarded, or to regard themselves, as inferior and less influential. For example, in 1937, an official in the UGC administration (who was seconded from the mainstream civil service) wrote to a senior member of staff at the Scottish Office with a revealing *obiter dicta*: 'They have been fairly prudent to the point of being almost Scrooge-like, to refer to a famous character of Dickens, in the conduct of their affairs'.[23] It is very difficult to believe that such a condescending aside would have been made in addressing a Whitehall equivalent. This may well stem from the differing backgrounds of the upper echelons of the two civil services. The Scottish Office élite were drawn very heavily from Scottish-born graduates of Scottish universities, while – at least until the 1970s – the Whitehall mandarinate were predominantly products of Oxbridge. Even in 1980, only eleven per cent of Scottish Office personnel of principal and higher rank were Oxbridge products, compared to thirty per cent for Britain.[24] There was, moreover, very little traffic between the two: from 1945 to 1970 only twenty-three Whitehall top officials moved north to pursue their careers, and a mere twenty-five Scottish Office individuals of equivalent standing switched to London-based departments.

The second factor in accounting for the limited influence of the Scottish Office in initiating policy was that the Scottish departments had only a few individuals running their affairs, whereas the British department would have a large number of staff, each of whom would possess very detailed knowledge of the minutiae of their specialist area. When representatives from the two met to deal with matters of common interest, it was invariably the Whitehall side who led the proceedings and who provided the expertise. As a result many decisions affecting Scotland emanated from Whitehall. The reminiscences of a senior Scottish administrator show that this happened on innumerable occasions in the 1950s and 1960s in the establishment of health policy.[25] Elsewhere, the raising of the school-leaving age, the introduction of comprehensive schools, the fixing of agricultural price support levels, were primarily initiated outside Scotland.

Knowing this background, one can better understand the failure of the Scottish Office to elicit a positive response in Whitehall to, for instance, arguments in the 1930s for a forward policy on attacking unemployment.

Scottish civil servants had, however, a useful extra weapon in their battery, which was the political dimension. Ministers for the Scottish Office were always aware of the need to defend Scottish interests in order to avert hostile public opinion in Scotland. Their civil servants could thus use their masters to help overcome Whitehall resistance. So, when there was little response from fellow bureaucrats to SED appeals in the 1950s to grant Central Institutions a protected status against the universities, intensive briefings of the Scottish ministers helped sway the decision. When the Secretary of State was either exceptionally dynamic, or where he had particular influence, or where a particular conjunction of circumstances conspired, policy could be affected. An example of the first is Hector MacNeil's lobbying of the Board of Trade, which was instrumental in winning the siting of IBM in Greenock (incidentally, MacNeil's own constituency) away from Whitehall's preferred location of St Helens.

In the second category, perhaps, comes James Stuart's particularly close relationship with Churchill. During World War II he was his Chief Whip and personal confidant. Stuart seems to have played on this to get Cabinet approval for the building of the Forth Road Bridge at a time of economic difficulty. These links may also explain why Stuart won Cabinet approval in 1953 for the construction of Cumbernauld New Town projects despite the strenuous opposition of the Housing minister, Harold Macmillan, to any additional New Towns being embarked on. In the third class may be placed John MacLay's exploitation of his party's electoral unpopularity in Scotland to tilt the Cabinet into endorsing massive developments such as the building of Ravenscraig strip-mill. More generally, the Scottish Secretary in Cabinet frequently formed alliances with other spending departments to try to loosen the Treasury purse-strings for projects of mutual interest. The Crossman and Castle diaries reveal Willie Ross pursuing this strategy again and again in the Wilson governments of the 1960s and 1970s.[26]

The effect of this growth in central government activity may be explored by looking at the record in two areas: the economy and housing. The former is significant because it has grown to be the central preoccupation of the Scottish Office. Before World War II, the role of government was not very positive. Indeed, it has been claimed that the uneven economic development characteristic of Britain prior to the war meant that state action militated against Scottish interests. This was especially the case in industrial growth associated with new defence needs. The bulk of establishments concerned with air warfare, for instance, were sited well away from Scotland, while the Admiralty conducted naval research in the south and east of England, despite the Clyde's long record of warship-building.[27] At the same time, Whitehall strenuously opposed any calls for industrial diversification into depressed areas.

During and after World War II, however, the attention of the Scottish Office became more centrally focused on the economy. This interest intensified after the later 1950s with a flurry of legislation to promote government action. This was accompanied by the creation of a stream of agencies to implement the broad objectives enunciated by ministers – the Highlands and Islands Development Board and the Scottish Development Agency being perhaps the most important. In addition, internal reorganisations of the machinery of government at St Andrews House led to the formation of a department with specific responsibilities for promoting economic development – the Scottish Development Department. This snowstorm of bureaucratic activity was reinforced by considerable amounts of state funding being channelled towards the Scottish economy. Whatever the complaints about neglect by government between the wars, the balance now shifted to Scotland's benefit. In the period after 1945, about thirty per cent of government grants for the whole of Britain were allocated to Scotland. In 1980–1 Regional Grant assistance to Scotland reached £200 million, whereas in 1960–1 it was £3.2 million.[28]

Verdicts on government economy strategy suggest a mixed degree of success. It is accepted that Scotland's GDP drew closer to British levels, rising from 88 to 97 (against a British norm of 100) in the 1970s, while earnings rose over the same period from 92 to 99. Expenditure under the Regional Policy scheme created around 67,000 jobs and supported many firms. But there were drawbacks: unemployment was four times higher in 1979 than in 1960, and it would have required the creation of 230,000 new jobs (against the 678,000 actually created) to soak up the increase. Other complaints are that too much emphasis was put on attracting non-Scottish firms to settle in the country, so creating a branch economy which could disappear in harsher times. It has been stressed that more should have been done to foster indigenous enterprise as this would have been a better prospect for permanence and for genuine research and development activities.[29]

The quality of some of the larger decisions was also increasingly criticised. Some influential voices argued that there was lack of realism behind some of the major ventures. Cooler appraisal at the outset, this opinion went, would have realised the fragility of projects like Ravenscraig, Linwood, Bathgate and Invergordon.[30] Allied to this was a feeling that too much government energy and state money had gone into propping up nationalised industries whose long-term survival in their existing form was highly questionable. Again, it was contended that seeking new areas of economic activity would have offered a more secure outlook in the long run.

In housing, the second sphere where government has been especially prominent, the result of intervention is also ambiguous. It is unquestionably the case that housing standards have risen over the period of intense central government commitment. The seemingly endless slums and the widespread overcrowding which disfigured late Victorian towns and shocked visitors have been virtually abolished. Yet the replacements have not always been greeted with approval. The poor quality of building standards applied to public-sector housing, the depressing environment in which so many schemes are set and the high degree of social deprivation and alienation to be found in a great number of estates is often attributed to lack of forethought and the absence of a broader vision on the part of the Scottish Office, which had the ultimate responsibility for overseeing the state housing programme.[31]

The reasons for this variable balance are complex. A variety of factors may be at play in explaining the economic aspect. One simple point is that the state may not always be the best judge of what constitutes a viable development at the micro-level. One instance which some would certainly point to in this context was the decision to finance the construction of the Ravenscraig strip-mill. This was imposed by government against the commercial instincts and judgement of the steel company concerned, Colvilles. Colvilles' reluctance was based on their analysis that the site was inappropriate for modern steel production, and the firm would rather have opted for a coastal location. Moreover, the commercial assumptions were worrying for Colvilles. A capacity of three million tons per annum would be created in Scotland with Ravenscraig, yet the maximum demand for steel in Scotland did not exceed two million tons. Thus, in order to be profitable, Ravenscraig would have to sell one-third of its output elsewhere – i.e., in England. Yet this was a fiercely competitive market, especially with the government funding the construction of rival steel works in Wales and England, and additional transport costs from Motherwell would inevitably place Colvilles in a weak position. The result of the insistence that the mill go ahead was almost catastrophic for Colvilles, which came close to collapse in the period after Ravenscraig opened.[32]

Another obstacle facing Scottish ministers and civil servants was structural. Scottish economic development was inextricably linked with British economic priorities. Most obviously, national decisions on fiscal policy and government spending levels had direct, and usually dire, implications for Scotland. It is no surprise to find in cabinet discussions in the 1960s and 1970s the Scottish Secretary resisting Treasury demands for fiscal rectitude. Other decisions worked negatively on Scotland: adverse changes in energy pricing policy imposed by the national government helped to render the pulp mill at Fort William and the Invergordon smelter unprofitable. A further difficulty was wrangling between government departments over the distribution of government support and assistance. Until the SDA was set up in 1975, both the Treasury and the Department of Trade and Industry were actively involved in Scottish industrial and economic issues, often indeed colliding with the Scottish Office. Not unnaturally, these departments tended to take a British perspective, in which the needs of Scotland might not loom so large as when viewed from St Andrews House. The hairsbreadth by which MacNeil won IBM against Whitehall pressure shows how slender the margin could be.

The resistance encountered by the Scottish Office in effecting reforms in social matters such as housing, health and education, came largely from local government. So, a determined bid initiated by central government in the 1930s to establish an effective co-ordinated hospital service was defeated by the refusal of local authorities to go along with the proposals.[33] Again, one of the reasons advocated within the SED for declining to accede to a request made in 1937 by the Scottish universities for additional state funding was the likely opposition which councillors would show. The finance sought by the universities was to come from the Education (Scotland) Fund, and so would be taken from monies otherwise destined for councils. The point was made by the civil servants that the SED needed to be on good relations with local government as a number of major educational innovations were due to be launched, and without the full co-operation of burgh and county education authorities, progress would be limited.[34]

Perhaps the more substantial conflicts came in questions of housing. Sometimes councils could be mulishly awkward and slow, thus thwarting central government's desire to proceed apace with improvements. Thomas Kennedy recounts an episode in the Labour ministry of 1929–31 when Midlothian County Council dragged their feet very effectively against attempts by the Scottish Office, prompted by Willie Adamson, the Secretary of State, to have positive action taken in a case of seriously substandard housing. Finally, Kennedy relates, Adamson convened a meeting with council officials and representatives of the trade union which had raised the case. The meeting was set up in order that Adamson could reveal to the complainants his impotence in the face of council obstructionism.[35]

A more serious instance of local authority intransigence over housing centred on a major effort by the Scottish Office to initiate a more dynamic approach. Walter Elliot, somewhat exasperated at the slow response of councils to the continuing housing crisis, established the Scottish Special Housing Association (SSHA) in 1937. The intention was that the SSHA would pioneer new building materials, techniques and designs which would then be adopted by local authorities, after seeing the results in their own areas. Towards the end of the war, the association was given a target by the Labour Scottish Secretary, Tom Johnston, to construct half of the new stock in the next decade: about 100,000 units. In the event, corporations like Glasgow froze the SSHA out of any significant building activity within their territorial fiefs. A grand total of only 400 SSHA houses were put up in Glasgow, the core of the problem. Instead the SSHA was driven to marginal works: providing accommodation for Forestry Commission and lighthouse workers became a main staple. The association did do a degree of building for miners, especially with the relocation of pitworkers from declining to expanding areas in the decade and a half after 1945. So successful was the resistance of local councils that by 1955 the SSHA had built only 30,000 houses, well below the target.

The motives for this successful campaign of obstruction by local authorities appear to be manifold. Partly there was a sense of wounded civic *amour propre*, as councillors resented outside agencies moving in on their patch with the apparent intention of teaching them their job. Equally important were more practical considerations. The loss of jobs directly controlled by the council and an erosion of the important patronage powers wielded by councillors in allocating houses to tenants were unacceptable consequences of an active SSHA presence. Implicit in these threats was a challenge to the political control of the local authority by the political party in power, by now usually Labour. The outcome was that there were delays in introducing new building methods, so fewer people were accommodated, designs were uniform and drab, so many tenants felt disaffected, and management styles remained rigid, so tenants' needs were not responded to.[36]

A similar fate befell one of the most imaginative attempts in the twentieth century to tackle the social problems of the Glasgow area. The Clyde Valley Regional Plan was drawn up at the end of World War II by Patrick Abercrombie. The plan proposed that the population of Glasgow should be drastically reduced – from around one million to about 600,000. The population should be relocated in four specially constructed New Towns, with the highest standards of housing and social amenities. The New Towns would be a focus for attracting new industries such as car manufacturing, so lessening the region's dependence on declining heavy staples.

The city fathers resisted these proposals bitterly. There was a suspicion, although not usually openly articulated, that the enthusiasm with which the Conservatives took up the New Towns idea in the 1950s had a political motive, namely to weaken Labour's electoral base by reducing the parliamentary representation of Glasgow and 'Red Clydeside'. Certainly James Stuart, Scottish Secretary from 1951 to 1957, seems to have harboured this thought. The Tories, moreover, believed that once transferred to New Towns, Labour identification among voters would decline, and in the 1960s a special Conservative committee was set up to consider ways of wooing New Town voters. The councillors argued that the removal of large swathes of the population would have serious effects. It was likely that the wealthier, fully employed ratepayers would be siphoned off to the desirable New Towns. The corporation would have to deal with the remainder, which would inevitably contain many socially disadvantaged people, and yet there would be a substantially reduced financial base with which to attack their problems. Accordingly, the city fought a sustained campaign against the building of East Kilbride, while Cumbernauld was subject to a three-year delay by an unseemly squabble over the allocation of costs between Glasgow Corporation and the government.[37]

On the publication of the Clyde Valley Plan, Glasgow Corporation claimed that there was no need for the population to be removed on the scale proposed. The city's chief engineer contended that it could rehouse all of its population quite satisfactorily within its existing boundaries. This argument was deployed to justify the sabotaging of the Clyde Valley Plan, but by the early 1950s Glasgow had to acknowledge that in reality it could not build sufficient houses within the city limit to satisfy its housing needs. This acceptance was hastened by the publication of evidence in the mid-1950s which indicated that the slum problem in Glasgow was still very acute and required an urgent and massive response. The city, however, still declined to accept the solution offered by more New Towns, especially as they were very costly and slow to mature; Cumbernauld took ten years from conception to construction. Instead it negotiated overspill agreements with sympathetic councils: by 1964, 57 arrangements had been made. But with overspill, the corporation felt that it had more control over the process and it was less costly than building New Towns.[38] As a result of the delays and disputes consequent upon the publication of the plan, many Glaswegians languished in substandard conditions for longer than might have been the case. Local authorities had shown a lack of broader vision and could not adopt a regional planning perspective, preferring instead to fight for their own corners.

This lack of power by the Scottish Office against local government is, on the surface, rather surprising. For various reasons, councils in Scotland received more of their funding from central government than those in England, so the exercise of influence should have been considerable. A number of reasons may be adduced for the persistence of local council independence. One may be that of personnel. This has two angles. Firstly, a large number of MPs began their political careers on councils. This was especially true of Labour members, and particularly applied to those taking their seats in the thirty or so years after 1945. Almost all Labour MPs representing urban West of Scotland constituencies had a record of service on the council behind them. This of course gave councils a strong voice in parliament when their interests were threatened and may have impeded the Scottish Office from trampling over them. Secondly, as local government was reformed, the calibre both of councillors and officials improved greatly. The reform of 1929, which swept away many small units of local government and transferred their responsibilities to county and burgh councils had a dramatic impact in professionalising the system. On the one hand, local government officials were less often part-time and were instead highly qualified and competent to argue on a more level footing with central government representatives. With the growth of political competition and better party management and organisation, the quality of local councillors was pushed up as the selection of local candidates became more rigorous. Furthermore, intensely local vested interests, who had dominated parish and education authorities with a narrow and penny-pinching outlook, were removed. With increased responsibilities and better back-up staff, council leaders approached the Scottish Office with more confidence.

The most spectacular evidence of this came with the reorganisation of local government in 1974–5, the core of which was the setting up of regional councils, with very large population and geographical bases. These had been formed after the investigations of the Wheatley Commission. This had been prompted by the unease felt in the Scottish Office at the perceived lack of a broader perspective shown, as discussed earlier, during the New Towns dispute and reinforced by problems encountered in securing local authority co-operation in developing and resourcing large-scale projects like the motor plants at Linwood and Bathgate. Paradoxically, these changes created authorities even more capable of facing central government. Strathclyde in particular, with its huge resources and led by councillors who had a sweeping mandate from the electorate (indeed by the 1980s they could claim to represent public opinion more faithfully than the ministers with whom they were locked in combat), was a formidable foe. Immediately upon its establishment, Strathclyde announced its rejection of Scottish Office plans to build a further New Town at Stonehouse.[39] The region's hostility was not the only factor in this rejection. Similarly, in the early 1990s Strathclyde's campaign against water privatisation probably played a decisive part in the abandonment of that proposal in Scotland. It may be significant that in England, where local government power was less concentrated, the councils could not resist water privatisation. Strathclyde's establishment of an office in Brussels to secure direct communication with the EEC, in full competition with the Scottish Office's own bureau there, summed up the confidence and resilience of local government in relation to the centre.

To many the resistance offered by local government was a badly needed contribution to the balance of democratic forces within the Scottish political context. The steady accretion of responsibilities in the hands of Scottish central government over the century, and especially in the post-1945 period gave rise to unrest about an over-concentration of power in the Scottish Office. To some extent the need for democratic scrutiny of the executive lay behind the clamour for legislative devolution from the late 1960s. In part this arose from a sense of MPs' inability to function effectively as watchdogs over the St Andrews House bureaucrats. Despite the existence of the Scottish Grand Committee, initially formed in 1907, along with two Scottish Standing Committees, set up in 1955 and 1963, and a Scottish Select Committee dating from 1969, there was a strong feeling that little real restraint was exercised by Westminster-based parliamentarians. Scottish backbench MPs, as a recent survey has argued, lacked the interest to tackle the Scottish Office on a broad synoptic front. On most policy issues backbenchers are charged with failing to take the initiative or to devise a Scottish perspective as distinct from holding to a narrow partisan stance. Instead they have pursued their local constituency issues to the exclusion of all else.[40] A whiff of the general relationship between the two pillars of the constitution can be gleaned from the memoirs of a senior Scottish Office administrator, J. Hume. He recalls that MPs used the room in which the Grand Committee met as a personal office, dealing with pressing constituency business without taking any part in the deliberations of the committee. The feeling of contempt for the MPs in this account is almost tangible.[41]

In many ways the development of government in Scotland has been dependent on a coalition of competing interests; local government, civil servants at the Scottish Office, British central government, local MPs and political parties, all of whom have promoted state intervention, not only for the benefit of the nation as a whole, but also to promote their own interests. It is within this framework of competing priorities and interests that the evolution of the role of government in twentieth-century Scotland is best understood.

NOTES AND REFERENCES

1. A. Midwinter, M. Keating and J. Mitchell, *Politics and Public Policy in Scotland* (1991), p. 18.
2. J.G. Kellas and P. Madgwick, 'The Territorial Ministries: the Scottish and Welsh Offices', in P. Madgwick and R. Rose, *The Territorial Dimension in British Politics* (1982), pp. 21–7.
3. B. Aspinwall, *A Portable Utopia: Glasgow and the United States, 1820–1920* (Aberdeen, 1984), pp. 151–84 is the fullest account.
4. See I.G.C. Hutchison, *The University and the State: The Case of Aberdeen* (Aberdeen, 1993), pp. 138–42 for a discussion of this. Also D.J. Withrington, 'The Idea of a national University in Scotland, 1820–1870' in J.J. Carter and D.J. Withrington (eds), *Scottish Universities: Distinctiveness and Diversity* (Edinburgh, 1992), pp. 40–55 for a related theme.
5. K. Middlemas, *Politics in Industrial Society* (London, 1979), is the locus classicus for this trend. The names listed in the text contain some of the largest entries in the index.
6. R.H. Campbell, 'The Scottish Office and the Special Areas in the 1930s', *Historical Journal*, 22 (1979), pp. 167–83.
7. J.N. Toothill, *Inquiry into the Scottish Economy* (Edinburgh, 1961).
8. L. Leneman, *Fit For Heroes? Land Settlement in Scotland After World War One* (Aberdeen, 1989), pp. 20–53.
9. J.S. Gibson, *The Thistle and the Crown: a History of the Scottish Office* (Edinburgh, 1985); H.J. Hanham, 'The Development of the Scottish Office', in J.N. Wolfe (ed.), *Government and Nationalism in Scotland: An Enquiry by Members of the University of Edinburgh* (Edinburgh, 1969), pp. 51–70 and J. Mitchell, 'The Gilmour Report on Scottish Central Administration', *Juridical Review* (1989), pp. 173–88.
10. L. Paterson, *The Autonomy of Modern Scotland* (Edinburgh, 1994).
11. J. Mitchell, 'The Gilmour Report'.
12. J.G. Kellas, *The Scottish Political System* (4th edn, Cambridge, 1989), pp. 62–6.
13. T. Johnston, *Memories* (n.d.), p. 102.
14. I.G.C. Hutchison, 'The Scottish Office and the Scottish Universities', in Carter and Withrington (eds), *Scottish Universities*, pp. 55–6.
15. R. Munro, *Looking Back: Fugitive Writings and Sayings* (n.d.), pp. 144–7 for a revealing, because not overtly stated, portrayal of Struthers' character. Also see W. Humes, *The Leadership Class in Scottish Education* (Edinburgh, 1986), pp. 26–82.
16. Hutchison, 'Scottish Office and the Universities', pp. 61–4.
17. Hutchison, *University and the State*, pp. 93, 123–4.
18. P. Hennesy, *Whitehall* (1989).
19. J. Hume, *Mandarin Grade 3* (Edinburgh, 1993), pp. 138–42.
20. J. Mitchell, 'The Gilmour Report', pp. 173–8 and Gibson, *The Thistle and the Crown*, pp. 73–6, 80–1.
21. Hutchison, 'Scottish Office and the Universities', pp. 57–61.
22. R.H. Campbell, 'The Committee of Ex-Secretaries of State for Scotland and Industrial Policy', *Scottish Industrial History*, 2 (1979), pp. 3–11.
23. Scottish Record Office, ED 26/291, J. Beresford (UGC) to G. Stewart (Scottish Office), cited in Hutchison, *University and the State*, p. 59.
24. P. Kellner, *The Civil Servants: An Enquiry into the British Ruling Class* (Oxford, 1980).
25. Hume, *Mandarin*, pp. 39–42.
26. R.H.S. Crossman, *The Diaries of a Cabinet Minister: Housing Minister, 1964–1966* (1975), pp. 54, 59.

27. S.V. Ward, *The Geography of Inter-War Britain: The State and Uneven Development* (1988), pp. 84–99.

28. N.K. Buxton, 'The Scottish Economy, 1945–79: Performance, Structure and Problems', in R. Saville (ed.), *The Economic Development of Modern Scotland* (Edinburgh, 1985), Table 9, p. 72.

29. Buxton, 'Scottish Economy', pp. 69–76 and N. Hood and S. Young, *Industrial Policy and the Scottish Economy* (Edinburgh, 1984), pp. 38–56.

30. See Peter Payne's chapter in this volume.

31. A. Gibb and D. MacKinnon, 'Policy and Process in Scottish Housing, 1950–80', in Saville (ed.), *The Economic Development of Modern Scotland*, pp. 270–91 and Richard Rodger's chapter in this volume.

32. P. Payne, *Colvilles* (Oxford, 1979), pp. 321–411; P. Payne, 'The Decline of the Scottish Heavy Industries, 1945–80' in Saville (ed.), *The Economic Development of Modern Scotland*, pp. 93–101 and Payne's essay in this volume.

33. G. MacLachlan, *Improving the Common Weal: Aspects of the Scottish Health Service, 1900–84* (Edinburgh, 1987), pp. 72–7, 231–3.

34. Hutchison, 'The Scottish Office and the Universities', pp. 55–61.

35. T. Kennedy, *The Scottish Socialists: A Gallery of Contemporary Portraits* (n.d.), pp. 110–17.

36. T. Begg, *Fifty Special Years: A Study in Scottish Housing* (1987); R. Roger and H. Al-Qadoo, 'The Scottish Special Housing Association and the Implementation of Scottish Housing Policy' in R. Roger (ed.), *Scottish Housing in the Twentieth Century* (Leicester, 1989), pp. 184–213.

37. R. Smith, 'The Origins of the Scottish New Towns Policy and the Founding of East Kilbride', *Public Administration*, 52 (1974), pp. 143–60 and R. Smith, 'The Politics of Overspill Policy: Glasgow, Cumbernauld and the Housing of the New Town Development (Scotland) Act', *Public Administration*, 55 (1977), pp. 79–85.

38. Smith, 'The Politics of Overspill', pp. 88–94.

39. R. Ferguson, *Geoff: The Life of the Rev. Geoffrey M. Shaw* (Gartocharn, 1979), pp. 211–69 for the early years of Strathclyde Regional Council.

40. J. Brand, *British Parliamentary Parties: Policies and Power* (Oxford, 1992), pp. 210–48.

41. Hume, *Mandarin*, pp. 27–9.

4. CONTINUITY AND CHANGE: SCOTTISH POLITICS 1900–45
Richard J. Finlay

The object of this chapter is to review the main developments in Scottish political life from the turn of the century to the close of World War II. As well as looking at the fundamental changes which altered the Scottish political landscape in this period, it will also focus on important lines of continuity, so that the dramatic turning points of Scottish political history can be put in a context that encompasses the evolution of Scottish politics.

The Khaki election of 1900 was a triumph for the Conservative Party throughout Britain as the party fought and won a landslide in the general election. This forced Scottish politicians to reassess their rather complacent notions of Scottish political culture. The widely-held belief that Scotland was an impregnable bastion of liberal principles, impervious to the baser tendencies of the 'lower Saxon mentality', was shattered when the Scots appeared to reject their traditional Gladstonian moral individualism in favour of Tory jingoism and the desire to punish the Boers. The Conservative Party and its ally, the Liberal Unionists, were able to win more than half of the parliamentary seats in Scotland, which was an unprecedented result.[1] The new century seemed to be a radical departure from the political certainties of Victorian Scotland. The Liberals had their hegemony smashed and the Conservatives, for the first time, were able to emerge from the shadows of aristocratic privilege and reactionary landlordism to proclaim themselves as a genuine mass party with popular support. Conservative claims of a new era in Scottish politics, however, were premature. The 1900 general election in Scotland was a freak and although the result occasioned a dramatic change in party fortunes, a number of factors militated against any long-term political realignment.[2]

First, it has to be borne in mind that the Liberals had been under pressure since the split with the Liberal Unionists in 1886, and 1900 marked the culminating point in a process of short-term decline that started with the general election of 1895. What made the election of 1900 so important was the psychological effect of the Liberal Party's failure to attain more than half the Scottish seats, something it had consistently achieved since 1832. Second, the Liberal vote did not collapse and the party was still able to secure over half of the total votes cast. On closer analysis, the expected Liberal wipe-out did not happen and the party's misfortunes were due more to the vagaries of the first-past-the-post electoral system which saw the loss of five seats on a 1.5 per cent swing to the Conservatives and the Liberal Unionists. The electoral damage was more apparent than real. A third factor working against any realignment was the ambiguous relationship of the Liberal Unionists with the Conservative Party. Although both parties would merge in 1912, this was not necessarily apparent in 1900 and many Liberal Unionist candidates stressed their Liberal credentials, believing that too strong an identification with the Conservative Party would lose them support.[3]

Finally, the election was fought in unusual circumstances. It came at a bad time for the Liberal Party, which was divided on the issue of the war in South Africa. Furthermore, the party was prone to 'faddism', with different sections espousing their own particular interest such as church dis-establishment, educational reform, temperance and other minority interests. This meant that the Liberal Party lacked the coherence necessary to make it electorally credible and, in any case, it was known before the election that victory was unlikely because in over one hundred and fifty constituencies there was no Liberal challenge.[4] All of this, understandably, combined to produce a lacklustre Liberal campaign. The Conservatives and Liberal Unionists, on the other hand were able to unite around the banner of British patriotism and imperialism – the Scots were just as enthusiastic in their British imperial patriotism as other parts of the United Kingdom. While anti-war radicals have attracted the historian's attention, it must be remembered that these groups were formed in *response* to the overwhelming support the war received among the Scottish public.[5]

The real long-term effect of the Khaki election was that it forced the major parties to rethink their political strategies. The election brought home the realities of mass politics and the need to cater to it. For the Conservatives and Liberal Unionists the lesson to be learned was that British patriotism was a powerful electoral tool which could dislodge traditional Liberal values, particularly in west central Scotland.[6] It comes as no surprise to find, therefore, that British imperial patriotism became the central tenet of the Conservative and Unionist faith in the period before 1914 and it was put to strident use, particularly over the controversy about Irish Home Rule in the years after 1910.[7] While the Conservatives and Liberal Unionists always had imperialist leanings, the rationale for its use in political propaganda and electioneering was that it had paid dividends in 1900 and there was the belief that it would do so in the future.[8]

The process of readapting was more drawn out in the Liberal Party. Electoral defeat and widespread jingoism in Scotland led many radicals to conclude that the party had been complacent in its Scottish policy. In 1900, the Young Scots Society was set up to inculcate 'Liberal principles' in Scottish society and its first meeting to protest about the South African war brought down a barrage of popular imperialist wrath.[9] The society soldiered on in its effort to 'revive Liberal ideas at a time when liberal ideals have been forgotten' and the slogan 'Back to Gladstone' reveals their yearning for the halcyon days of Scottish Liberalism.[10] By 1903 much progress had been made and the society had over three thousand members in thirty branches, and this would rise to over ten thousand members in fifty branches by the eve of World War I.[11] While the Young Scots had set themselves the target of revitalising Scottish liberal culture, in essence they sought to recapture a 'golden age', and their methods would do a great deal to modernise and transform Scottish Liberalism by adapting its strategy and ideology to the demands of a new era.

The initial impact of the Young Scots on the Liberal Party was in the field of organisation. Run-down constituency caucuses were berated and harangued into action: 'The Young Scots Society condemns the liberals in West Edinburgh for not pulling their weight. [We] have done a considerable power of work in the constituency, theoretically in conjunction with the Liberals, but practically without their aid or support. They are conspicuous by their absence at meetings … It is nothing less than a disgrace.'[12] Commitment, enthusiasm and hard graft were the new watch words for electoral campaigning:

> There must be no doubt about it. In every constituency where our influence extends we must throw ourselves into the fight, heart and soul … If we really want to win 'Scotland for Liberalism' we must fight a brain to brawn fight for the cross of every voter.[13]

Not only were the radicals determined that the style of campaigning should be invigorated, they also decided that the quality of Liberal candidates had to be improved and, wherever possible, that this be done by selecting one of their own: 'We must influence the selection of candidates and get rid of the present haphazard and helpless political nonentities who pose as

Scottish candidates.'[14] Vacant seats were targeted and as early as the beginning of 1904 the society had eight of its men placed as prospective candidates with another seven being secured during the year. Furthermore, sixteen Scottish Liberal MPs publicly endorsed the activities of the Young Scots, including the leader of the party, Campbell Bannerman. In the period 1905 to 1914, the Young Scots would see about thirty of its members elected to parliament.[15]

The Young Scots were also to change the ideological outlook of the Liberal Party by promoting radical and progressive candidates. Strategic reasons played a part in this as it was recognised that the votes of the skilled working class were essential to future Liberal success. It was believed that this section of the community was most vulnerable to the twin dangers of socialism and jingoism and, consequently, an attractive programme had to be constructed to appeal to the working class. Issues such as housing, poverty, education reform and work legislation took up an increasing amount of radical Liberal time.[16] It was accepted that the working class had legitimate grievances and that these would have to be addressed in order to thwart the advance of socialism.

Undoubtedly the espousal of social reform did much to dent the prospects of the Labour Party in Scotland before 1914 and indeed, the radicals were keen to pacify working-class agitation.[17] The Young Scots held many debates with the Fabians and the Independent Labour Party and some even went as far as to endorse the Labour candidate, George Barnes, for the Blackfriars seat in Glasgow because of his moderate espousal of the principles of progressivism.[18] Many radicals felt that there was not a world of difference between themselves and the labour movement. The combination of effective campaigning directed at the working class with the old Liberal staple of Free Trade was to secure massive dividends at the general election of 1906.

In many ways the result of the general election of 1906 was a foregone conclusion. The Conservative and Liberal Unionist government had effectively and comprehensively destroyed any prospect of re-election. The Education Act of 1902 had alienated the non-conformist middle class in England and Wales, the handling of the military campaign in South Africa had been disastrous, there was scandal over the use of 'Chinese slave labour' in South African mines, the working class were outraged at the Taff Vale judgement which crippled trade union rights and finally, and perhaps most importantly, there was Joseph Chamberlain's second unauthorised programme which called for tariff protection on imports which would be used to fund social legislation.[19] This had the effect of splitting the Conservative and Liberal Unionist parties between free traders and protectionists and reduced the government to a chaotic shambles after 1903.[20]

In Scotland these divisions were glaringly exposed with the Scottish Secretary, Balfour of Burleigh, dissenting from the official protectionist programme.[21] Some Liberal Unionists likewise found the protectionist programme too much to stomach and desperately tried to scuttle back to the old Liberal fold. They were ruthlessly exposed and gunned down by the radicals.[22] The Free Trade issue was a very welcome window of opportunity for the Liberal Party in Scotland and even before the election of 1906 it was used to good effect in by-elections, allowing the Liberals to win every vacated Tory seat in Scotland. Protectionism was not popular with the working class because of fears that it would lead to increases in the price of food. Liberal campaigners capitalised on such fears using the slogan 'big loaf or little loaf' and for good measure claimed that the real motivation for protectionism was to tax the working class so as to augment the income of the despised land owners.[23] Well before the election, the Young Scots set to work promoting the free trade gospel. An Autumn tour in 1903 addressed over 60,000 people and distributed over a million leaflets.[24] Prominent figures such as Leonard McCourtney and Winston Churchill were brought north to add weight to the campaign. Extensive use was made of populist propaganda, with cartoons depicting a sinister Joseph Chamberlain, complete with monocle and black cape, as the Svengalli of British politics.[25] The campaign became the blueprint for the offensive in 1906:

> One could not but be materially impressed by the hostility of the working man to Mr Chamberlain's proposals. Throughout our long tour, on only one occasion was an amendment moved. ... Our tour took us through the enemy's country (we purposely chose Tory counties) and we are strongly convinced that if candidates could be secured who could arouse the industrial portions of the constituencies there would be no doubt that the Liberal could even sweep the Tory west.[26]

This proved to be correct and the Liberals won fifty-eight seats, the Liberal Unionists and the Conservatives won twelve and Labour notched up its first two Scottish seats.

The 1906 Liberal landslide in Scotland was not based on free trade alone. Although the 1906 Liberal government embarked on a series of social reforms, few historians believe that this was a significant factor in shaping the result of the election in England. Party literature south of the border made little reference to social policy and there was little political debate on the issue.[27] This was not the case in Scotland. The *Edinburgh Evening News* and the *Scottish Review* in their election specials stated that social reform would dominate the contest. Other newspapers such as the *Glasgow Herald* and *The Scotsman* likewise gave extensive coverage to social questions. Many radicals had been actively pressing social reform as the main tenet of the new Liberal political philosophy: 'In view of the general election, we are, as a party, preparing to appeal to the country on a programme of social reform. This is as it should be.'[28] The 'new' liberalism was enthusiastically embraced north of the border because it would secure the party's electoral support among the working class and would see off any potential challenge from the Labour Party:

> The fact is that old liberalism is doomed. It is in vain that the fossils
> and doctrinaires connected with the party protest against the
> advance of socialism. They have stultified themselves by their
> acquiescence in Irish legislation and the Scottish Crofters Act.
> The conditions that justified these measures for the country would
> equally excuse similar interference with the social circumstances of
> our cities. One sees with regret the riven ranks of the progressive
> party, but the breach can only be healed by a frank acceptance of
> these responsibilities on the part of liberalism. ... One can seldom
> give more than a modified adhesion to any principle. It is one
> thing, however, to admit that socialism is only capable of a limited
> application, and quite another to condemn, as certain Liberals do,
> the principle itself – to recognise the political and ignore the social
> problem. If this policy persists, one may with perfect confidence
> predict the imminent revolt from Liberalism of the working
> classes. ... I look to the Young Scots to guide the party in the
> more excellent way of what has been called the New Liberalism.
> A country resting on a starved and ignorant proletariat must
> inevitably confess its impotency and become a despotism ... it
> is among the elect of our working class and those in intimate
> relationship with them that we can still happily find the brawn
> and heart of our nation.[29]

Election literature reflected this concern with social problems, while the espousal of progressivism or the new liberalism, together with trumpeting the baleful effects of protectionism, effectively ensured the Liberal Party the support of the working class and electoral dominance of Scotland in 1906.[30]

The 1906 election set the benchmark for the subsequent development of pre-1914 Scottish politics. The Conservatives and Liberal Unionists were awestruck by the totality of their defeat and set to work emulating the activities of the Young Scots by setting up their own organisation, the Junior Imperial League, without much success.[31] The radical edge of Scottish liberalism was reinforced by electoral success and the intake of new Young Scots MPs. Debates about social reform continued and occupied the core of organisational activity until 1910.[32] Radical demands were further fuelled by the persistent meddling of the Conservative-dominated House of Lords with Liberal legislation, and calls for the reform of the Upper Chamber became more vocal after 1908.[33]

Another issue which became increasingly prominent after 1908 in radical circles was Scottish Home Rule.[34] Scottish nationalism with a small 'n' had always been part and parcel of the Scottish radical tradition and Liberal MPs had been putting forward Scottish Home Rule bills in Parliament from the 1890s. Most of these bills had been adjuncts to Irish Home Rule and had little thought or momentum behind them.[35] A Scottish parliament only became a serious policy option when the issue of social reform gained wider political currency. This happened for four reasons. First, there was the practical difficulty of legislating specific reform for Scotland. According to the MP for Aberdeen North, D.V. Pirie, the social issues of temperance, education and land reform had to be framed to fit the Scottish legal system and the six hours of parliamentary time allocated to Scottish legislation was unable to do justice to these complex issues.[36] Second, the Scots had already seen the important reforms such as the 1908 Children's Act mangled and deformed to fit Scottish law because of a lack of parliamentary time, which raised serious questions as to the ability of Westminster to deliver appropriate and specific Scottish legislation. Third, many Scottish Liberals believed that social reform in Scotland was being delayed by English conservatism. It was repeatedly claimed that 'there is not one single item in the whole programme of Radicalism or social reform today, which, if Scotland had powers to pass laws, would not have been carried out a quarter of a century ago'.[37] And finally, given that social reform was the core radical objective and that the Westminster parliament was believed to be ineffective in realising such aspirations, the obvious conclusion for many was to create a Scottish parliament that would deal with domestic legislation.

The January and December general elections of 1910 in Scotland were fought on predominantly British issues, the first on reform of the House of Lords and the second on Irish Home Rule. The Liberals consolidated and marginally improved their position in Scotland by winning an extra seat from the Unionists, in contrast to the situation in England where the

Conservatives recovered their position, leaving the two parties almost equal. The Liberals were only able to continue in government due to the support of the Irish Nationalists. Undoubtedly the party machine played a major part in the Liberal success north of the border. The same aggressive campaigning techniques which had brought success in 1906 were used to good effect in 1910. Marginal seats were targeted, speaking tours arranged, open-air demonstrations against the House of Lords were held and over a million propaganda leaflets distributed. Even the Conservatives were forced to admit that they were powerless in the face of the 'radical machine'.[38]

For the radicals, the House of Lord's obstruction of social and land reform formed the crux of the campaign. Vehement class rhetoric was used against the unelected and idle rich who opposed the will of the people.[39] The Liberals were able to capitalise on a century of Scottish resentment against the landowning class who were pilloried for their 'unearned income', causing evictions and emigration in the past, and their unjust and undemocratic use of patronage. The Conservative and Unionist camp, on the other hand, conducted a rather lacklustre campaign focusing on the danger to property from the 'People's Budget', imperial defence, protection against local vetoes on the drink trade, and vague promises were made on holding a referendum before tariff reform was introduced.[40] In essence, there was little to distinguish it from the campaign south of the border. The reform of the House of Lords after the Parliament Bill, however, not only opened up the possibility of more social legislation, it also removed the most reliable brake on Irish Home Rule and this prospect galvanised the Unionist camp into action in the December election of 1910. '80 Irish votes, the price of home rule' thundered the Liberal Unionist manifesto which accused the Asquith government of bartering British unity and security for the support of the 'Irish revolutionary party'. Appeals were made to loyal Protestants not to forsake their fellow countrymen in Ulster and 'fight as never before for the maintenance of the Union'.[41] British patriotism formed the main component of the Conservative and Liberal Unionist campaign and it was hoped that this would pay electoral dividends. It did not. Although the Unionist vote went up marginally from 39.6 to 42.6 per cent, both parties failed to take any more seats. The Liberals continued with the same themes of the earlier campaign, although Scottish Home Rule was placed higher on the agenda by the radicals.[42] The December election was fought by all sides in a spirit of exhaustion and the turnout was lower than in January.[43]

In the period from 1910 to the eve of World War I, Scottish politics was dominated by Irish and Scottish Home Rule. The radicals made Scottish

Home Rule their priority. It was formally adopted as part of the Young Scots constitution and it was held to be the key to all further social reform.[44] Campaigns were undertaken to promote the cause throughout the country, pledges from all Scottish candidates in support of a Scottish parliament were sought and nominations from English candidates for Scottish seats were blocked.[45] All this gave the issue an unprecedented momentum which the Conservative and Unionist Party was forced to acknowledge.[46] At this point, it is important to stress that Scottish Home Rule had built up its own dynamic independent of Irish Home Rule.[47] The notion that Scottish Home Rule was simply promoted in order to make Irish Home Rule more palatable to the Scottish electorate and/or act as a delaying tactic is not borne out by the evidence. First, Home Rule, both Irish and Scottish, would not have been supported simply to please Catholic Irish constituents in Scotland because the vast majority of them did not have the vote. In any case, the most vociferous supporters of Irish Home Rule in Scotland represented constituencies with little or no Catholic population, the one exception being Dundee. Second, too much attention has focused on Churchill's Dundee speech of 1911 (which was in favour of political devolution throughout the United Kingdom) and not enough on the activities of the rank and file who time and time again referred to the popularity of Scottish Home Rule on the platform. Churchill did not create support for Home Rule all across Scotland, rather he was reacting to a groundswell of opinion that already existed. Third, Scottish home rulers were ambivalent in their attitudes towards Ireland and threatened to block Irish Home Rule if it was passed on its own because a British parliament with reduced Irish representation would make it more difficult for the Scots to attain their own objective as it was believed that this would leave them at the mercy of an increased English majority in Parliament.

The prospect of the disintegration of the United Kingdom was horrific enough to merge the Conservatives and Liberal Unionists into the Unionist Party in 1912. Defence of the Union and the Empire formed the core of the Unionist programme, and the party took time out to denounce the Workers Insurance Act for good measure. The Unionists were also able to exploit the growing divisions within the Scottish Liberal Party. Although the radicals had been instrumental in pushing Scottish Home Rule and social reform to the fore, this was not to everyone's taste. The Young Scots had used coercive methods to ensure compliance, including the threat of running their own candidates or supporting the Labour Party.[48] It was pointed out that, of forty-six Liberal candidates' manifestos in the December 1910 election, only twenty-two mentioned either Scottish or Irish

Home Rule.[49] The Unionists accused the Liberal government of being blackmailed by an 'obscure clique' who were using underhand techniques to impose their policies against the democratic wishes of the Scottish people.[50]

The threat to property and the financial burden of a Scottish parliament, not to mention the loosening of ties with the Empire, were cast up to appeal to middle-class fears.[51] The Frontbench's silence on the issue did little to dispel such notions and the fact that many of them sat for Scottish seats re-inforced Unionist suspicions. Furthermore, banging the Unionist drum appeared to be paying off as the party's by-election performances started to show signs of improvement. Radical criticism of 'London' government continued unabated and there was mounting displeasure at the tendency of the party to push 'English invaders' into safe Scottish seats at by-elections. Although the Scottish Liberal Party had always been a broad church, by the eve of World War I divisions were quite clearly hardening into a progressive social reformist, Scottish home rule wing and a more conservative, pro-leadership wing.[52] The point to be emphasised here is that the divisions in the Liberal Party were becoming apparent even before the war.

Traditionally World War I and its aftermath has been seen as a great turning point in the history of Scottish politics. After all, the Liberal Party now split and began a long process of disintegration, the Labour Party emerged from the shadows to become Scotland's largest political party and the Unionists were able to monopolise the middle class by playing on fears of Bolshevik revolution. Class became the central issue in political behaviour. It was a new age of mass politics in which the Liberals, unlike the Unionists or Labour, were unable to adapt to new demands. The post-1918 era appears to be one of profound change in Scottish politics.

The most significant change, arguably, was the rise of the Labour Party. Four key reasons are usually cited to explain why the Labour Party was able to eclipse the Liberals. They are: Liberal government failure during the war, the growth of trade unionism and working-class militancy, the Catholic reaction to the Irish War of Independence and the effect of the 1918 Reform Act. The Liberal Party and government did not have a good record during World War I. The war caused a split with the pacifist wing, the government stumbled from one crisis to another, from shell shortages to military incompetence to labour unrest on the Clyde and finally, the party split between Lloyd George and Asquith. Those Liberals loyal to Lloyd George supported the government at the price of dependency on the Conservative-dominated coalition, while the Asquith brigade faced decimation without the 'coupon' at the 1918 election.[53]

Given such circumstances, it is difficult to see how the Liberals could have recovered their position of pre-eminence in Scottish politics. The Labour Party was given a boost during the war because of increased trade union membership which fought to improve wages and conditions against a Liberal government. The pre-war radical image of the Liberal Party was shattered as it became associated with the interests of the bosses.[54] Labour activists plugged the radical vacuum and gained the party much-needed credibility as the genuine defender of working-class interests. Catholic disaffection with the wartime government's activities in Ireland was significant, but it did not entail a desertion from the Liberal Party to Labour because most did not have the vote. The extension of the franchise in 1918 is probably the most important factor in accounting for Labour's triumph in Scotland as the electorate increased from 779,000 in 1910 to 2,205,000 in 1918, with most of the new voters coming from the working class.[55] Evidence of the importance of the franchise is to be found in the difference between the election results of 1918 and 1922. In 1918 Labour was only able to win seven seats. Although there was a climate of jingoism associated with the 'hang the Kaiser' campaign which would work to the benefit of the 'Coupon' candidates, working-class militancy was still prevalent, the Irish troubles continued unabated and the Liberal Party was in disarray, all of which should have worked to Labour's advantage. The reason why Labour had to wait until 1922 for the breakthrough of twenty-nine seats was that it took time to get all their supporters registered on the electoral roll; this is reflected in the turnout figures of sixty per cent in 1918 and seventy-five per cent in 1922. Worsening economic conditions and the prospect of increased rents also helped after 1918.

The dramatic turnaround in party fortunes after the war masks some important continuities in Scottish politics. First, the techniques of mass politics such as holding large open-air meetings, making extensive use of printed propaganda, canvassing intensively and targeting winnable seats was not new, but were techniques perfected by radical Liberals before the war. The Labour Party, by using their trade union and local community networks, were able to extend such techniques to a bigger audience. Also, appealing to class interests had an established pedigree and Labour was able to capitalise on the pre-war enthusiasm for social reform, much of which had been generated by the radical Liberals. In addition, a remarkable number of radical Liberals appeared in the Labour ranks after 1918. Rev. James Barr, J.L. Kinloch, Roland Muirhead, Rosslyn Mitchell, D.N. MacKay, Walter Murray and J.M. MacDairmid were just some of those who believed that the best way forward for progressivism was through the Labour Party.

Furthermore, it should again be emphasised that the radical Liberals and the Independent Labour Party had a great deal of intellectual intercourse in the pre-war era.[56]

The greatest evidence of continuity, however, is found in the remarkable similarity between radical Liberal policy and Labour policy. Land reform, temperance, housing and education reform, free trade, church reform and Scottish Home Rule were common to both. Even nationalisation of the railways and mining had its proponents in the pre-war Liberal Party.[57] As many have pointed out, Labour conceptions of socialism were hazy and ill defined. Far more real, however, was the radical Liberal inheritance.[58]

The realities or otherwise of Red Clydeside has been one of the most productive sectors of Scottish historiography.[59] Much of the debate has centred around the extent to which the working class developed a full political and, arguably, revolutionary, consciousness. In any event, it was sufficient to win Labour two thirds of Glasgow's fifteen seats in 1922, even though voters and parliamentarians alike may not have had a keen intellectual grasp of the finer points of Marxist ideology.[60] Perhaps the most significant effect of Red Clydeside, however, was not its impact on working-class consciousness, but rather its impact on the middle class. For the Scottish bourgeoisie, the Red Clyde was no myth.[61] Indeed, in the general elections of 1918, 1922 and 1923 it was the middle class which displayed the most coherent political behaviour with local Unionist and Liberal associations forming tacit understandings in order to keep Labour candidates out.[62] Further evidence that the main driving force behind middle-class political behaviour was anti-socialism can be seen in the re-action of Scottish Coalition Liberals and Unionist MPs to the break-up of the Lloyd George Coalition government in 1922.[63] Many were against it, believing that the resultant split between the Liberal and Unionist parties would divide the middle-class vote and let in Labour candidates. Moreover, as the election of 1922 clearly showed, Labour was a much greater threat north of the border. Paradoxically, heightened class tension did much to keep Liberal Party fortunes alive in the period from 1918 to 1924. The Liberals, both Coalition and Asquithian, benefited from the anti-socialist vote largely because they had, more often than not, the best-placed candidates. In 1922 the total number of Liberal seats was twenty-eight, with thirty-nine per cent of the vote: a bigger share of the vote than either Labour or the Unionists. Liberals, of whatever faction, pushed the centre line, stressing anti-socialism and class conciliation. The collapse of the Coalition and the threat to free trade by the protectionist Unionists helped to reunite the party for the 1923 election. Although the Liberal share of the vote declined, the party was able to put in a credible performance by winning twenty-three seats. Labour increased its total to thirty-four seats, while the Unionists remained almost static with sixteen seats. The ghost of free trade had come back to haunt the Unionists with many blaming protectionism for the party's poor performance.[64] Anti-socialist calculations also worked against the Unionists to the benefit of the Liberals. Indeed, local Unionist constituency organisations showed remarkable self restraint in the general election of 1923 by allowing former Coalition Liberals a free run against Labour.[65]

Evidence that it was anti-socialism which was the key determinant of Liberal Party fortunes in the period from 1918 to 1924 can be found in the general election of that year. The Liberals had always used the threat of socialism and their ability to combat it as the key element of their propaganda. The advent of a minority Labour government in 1924 supported by the Liberal Party fatally undermined its claims to be a bulwark against socialism. Consequently, in the 1924 election the Unionists turned their flack on the Liberals to devastating effect. The Unionists won thirty-eight seats, the forward march of Labour was halted (albeit temporarily) with the party losing eight seats, bringing their total to twenty-six and the Liberals were banished to the fringes with only nine seats. Undoubtedly Labour suffered as a result of the almost hysterical anti-Bolshevik fervour in which the election was fought, although the party's period of government did establish Labour as more moderate than its opponents would have the electorate believe. Also, it confirmed the party in its reformist path towards socialism. The Unionists, likewise, improved their credibility by shaking off their 'die-hard' reputation and efforts were made to give the party a more moderate image.[66] The Liberals suffered in the squeeze for the middle ground and after 1924 the pattern was set for the future development of Scottish politics into a two-party system revolving around Labour and the Unionists.

Scottish politics after 1924 was dominated by the nation's endemic social and economic problems. For Labour this meant that growing unemployment, bad housing, threats to wages and conditions kept traditional supporters loyal. The General Strike of 1926 further exacerbated class tension with the middle class displaying a remarkable degree of support for the government.[67] The greatest impact of worsening economic conditions, however, was on political ideology with both Labour and the Unionists increasingly looking towards central British government for remedial action. The late 1920s witnessed a fundamental reorientation of Labour policy and strategy towards British state planning. Tom Johnston and John

Wheatley were instrumental in this development. Both argued that the severity of Scottish economic and social dislocation could only be overcome by utilising the resources of the British state as the Scottish economy was so rundown that it would be incapable of solving the problems on its own. This had obvious ramifications for the party's commitment to Scottish Home Rule. There would be no point having a Scottish parliament if it was unable to tackle the nation's pressing social and economic problems. This led to a fallout with the nationalist wing and the creation of the National Party of Scotland in 1928.[68] In any case, nationalism was to be increasingly identified as a bourgeois concept and of no interest to the working class.[69] Furthermore, the reform of the party organisation by Arthur Henderson in 1926 did much to increase uniformity of outlook by reducing sectarian and regional differences. Finally, Scottish Labour MPs were becoming more comfortable in their London surroundings. Their initial naked hostility to British parliamentary protocol and procedure had mellowed by the late 1920s.[70]

For the Unionists the economic problems of nation remained the bedrock of concern. The damage of increasing unemployment and the continuing presence of endemic social problems such as poor housing and health meant that the party was sensitive to the harmful effects this had on social cohesion. While notions of the market economy remained firm, the Unionists inclined more to the 'One Nation' school of Toryism with Walter Elliot, Bob Boothby and Noel Skelton emphasising class conciliation, while, at the same time, the industrialist wing of the party pursued a ruthless campaign against working-class political organisations.[71] Scottish policy began to bear an increasing Unionist stamp when Sir John Gilmour got himself promoted to full Cabinet status as the Scottish Secretary of State in 1926. Gilmour remodelled the loose administrative structure of the Scottish Office, which was situated in Dover House in London, and imposed more direct political control.[72] Although the Unionists remained remarkably cohesive in the late 1920s, while the left suffered from nationalist and communist splinters, there was an air of complacency as the party approached the 1929 general election. The worsening economic situation did not help matters and a string of by-elections in Scotland showed an improving Labour performance. Furthermore, the decision to reform local government was taken without consultation and aroused much middle-class anger.[73]

The general election of 1929 witnessed an improved Labour performance with ten seats gained, a diminished Unionist return with the loss of sixteen seats and the Liberals increasing their tally by five. The second

minority Labour government of 1929 soon found itself facing the brunt of
the impact of the Great Depression. The traumatic effects of economic dislocation mercilessly exposed the weakness of Labour's ideological commitment to socialism. Ramsay MacDonald's defence that it was the fault of the
system rather than the government illustrates the paucity of ideas about how
best to tackle the effects of mounting unemployment. While the majority
of the Cabinet remained committed to orthodox economic policy, the left,
led in Scotland by James Maxton, urged widespread nationalisation and
direct government intervention. The decision to form a 'National'
government to deal with the emergency split the party and in the general
election of 1931, Unionist-dominated 'National' candidates swept the
boards in Scotland and Labour could only hold on to seven seats.[74] The
political crisis of 1931 seriously dented the image of the Labour Party in
Scotland. First, it shook complacent notions about the inevitability of
socialism and exposed the party's weakness in the field of economic policy
generally. Second, it denied the parliamentary party the most gifted and
able Labour politicians, many of whom, such as Tom Johnston, would have
to wait several years before they could re-enter the House of Commons.
And finally, it exacerbated tensions between the left and right which
eventually culminated in the secession of the Independent Labour Party in
1932 under the leadership of James Maxton.[75]

The impact of the Great Depression dominated Scottish politics in the
1930s. Statistic after statistic showed that Scottish economy and society
were more adversely affected than those in the south.[76] The National
Government won a landslide in Scotland in the general election of 1931 as
public opinion supported a government of 'national emergency' to tackle
the baleful effects of economic dislocation. The political crisis of 1931 left
the Unionists with an undisputed hegemony in Scotland which would last
until 1945. The Labour Party, shorn of talented politicians in Westminster,
devoted much energy to organisation and rebuilding the party's electoral
bloc. Despite the severity of the depression in Scotland, Labour parliamentarians refused to promote a distinctive Scottish dimension to the nature
of economic dislocation. The emergence of a right-of-centre Scottish
National Party which had harmed Labour's electoral prospects in by-elections led to denunciations of nationalism as a product of the bourgeoisie.[77]
In spite of mounting nationalist discontent and opinion polls showing
demand for Scottish Home Rule, the nationalists found that they could
make little electoral headway in the 1930s. The SNP was riven with numerous factions. There were left-wingers and right-wingers, those who wanted
devolution and those who favoured independence and finally, a wing which

wanted to contest elections and a wing which wanted to operate through cross-party conventions. All in all, the nationalists lacked the necessary coherence to operate as an effective political party.[78]

Whereas nationalism in the 1920s was led by the left and associated with socialism and republicanism, in the 1930s it was detected in traditional middle-class quarters and complaints began to mount. The so-called 'southward drift of industry' in which Scottish businesses were packed up and moved to England caused deep resentment. Traditional Unionist allies such as the Glasgow and Edinburgh Chambers of Commerce began to express growing discontent that the government was not doing enough in Scotland. The farming community was alienated when subsidies were given for wheat but not for oats, the traditional Scottish crop. Furthermore, subsidies on sugar beet may have been good for the English farmer, but they devastated the sugar-cane refinery at Greenock. Scotland was allocated only two days for parliamentary legislation. Scottish museums and libraries received less money than those in England and Wales. These and other examples contributed to a growing perception that Scotland was not being treated fairly and, alarmingly for the Unionist party, these grievances were increasingly taking on a nationalist air.[79]

The National Government could do little to rectify the problems of the Scottish economy as that was deemed to be outwith their control. In any case, most of the heavy industrialists were members of the Unionist Party and they preferred to wait and see if the economy would pick up again rather than diversify into new industries.[80] Since there appeared to be no viable solution to the economic problem, the government faced a dilemma because it was believed that the depression was driving more and more Scots towards nationalism. According to the Secretary of State, Godfrey Collins: 'the depression has caused many minds to seek a solution of their problems by the setting up of a parliament in Edinburgh'.[81]

The threat posed by nationalism was countered in two ways. First, it was argued that any loosening of the economic ties between England and Scotland would make the situation worse. Industrialists stated that the creation of a Scottish parliament would cost the Scots both markets and government subsidies. Put bluntly, the Scots were told that if things were bad at the moment, a drift to Scottish nationalism would pull the nation into the abyss of economic catastrophe.[82] Second, the government tried to appease Scottish sentiment by acknowledging its legitimacy and attempting to divert it into symbolic or non-political channels. Administrative devolution was promoted because it would bring the government of Scotland closer to the people but it would not surrender political authority. The decision to move the Scottish Office to Edinburgh in 1937 was presented as a victory for the distinctiveness of Scottish government, offering a promise of greater Scottish autonomy.[83] The number of royal visits north of the border was increased, more money was spent on Scottish libraries, art galleries and museums and even the records taken by Edward I in the Wars of Independence in the thirteenth century were returned as a goodwill gesture to Scottish national sentiment.

The problem of economic dislocation in the 1930s softened up many Scottish politicians to the ideas of state intervention. The sense of impotence in the face of intractable social and economic problems caused much frustration in the Unionist Party and many, such as Walter Elliot, Bob Boothby and Noel Skelton, gravitated towards the centre of the political spectrum as a result of their experiences of the hardship induced by the depression.[84] Although the state apparatus was insufficient to the task, the National Government used agencies such as the Scottish Development Council, the Scottish Economic Committee, the Special Areas Reconstruction Association, the Hillington Industrial Estate and the Glasgow Empire Exhibition to promote industrial diversification and new employment opportunities. While these agencies could only dent the surface of the problem, they were important in ideologically conditioning the Unionist Party to accept the legitimacy of using state apparatus as a means of economic and social regeneration. Furthermore, although the economy started to pick up in the late 1930s as a result of rearmament, Walter Elliot at the Scottish Office was only too well aware that the only long-term security for the Union and his party lay in a fundamental restructuring of the Scottish economy which would rectify the endemic problems experienced in the 1930s.[85] The outbreak of World War II and the advent of massive state intervention provided an opportunity to breathe new life into the Scottish economy and the Union and it was grabbed with both hands by politicians from all sides.

The regime of Tom Johnston, who took over as Labour Secretary of State in 1941, has been presented as a watershed in Scottish political history.[86] Johnston set in motion numerous reforms of the government of Scotland. He instituted a large number of committees which had the remit of planning post-war reconstruction and were designed to reflect the different interests of government, industry and labour.[87] The age of corporatism had finally arrived. Johnston demanded and got substantial powers from Westminster, often by using the threat of Scottish nationalism. Planning of the post-war economy was based on the premise of massive state intervention, with the Forth Clyde Valley Plan pointing the way towards industrial diversification. Although such developments might appear radical, they were grounded in the corporatist tendencies of the 1930s. Indeed, the industrial wing of the Unionist Party was more than willing to use state support and the appointment of James Lithgow as controller of merchant shipbuilding in 1940 illustrated quite clearly that government intervention could work to the benefit of the business community.[88] A point often overlooked in the triumph of state intervention and the coming of the Welfare State is that the leaders of Scottish industry found their interests well protected and promoted by the government. Johnston's consensual approach to reconstruction was remarkably similar to the trend of the 1930s when committees and quangos were appointed to make enquiries into the state of the Scottish economy, the only difference being that the consensus was now extended to include the leaders of organised labour.

Developments in World War II were to have fundamental repercussions for Scotland's relationship with the British state. The war had witnessed an upsurge in Scottish nationalism with the SNP doing well in numerous by-elections. The Labour Party was once again veering towards Scottish Home Rule and the idea commanded a wide spectrum of cross-party support. Indeed, Labour's Scottish manifesto for the 1945 general election put the creation of a parliament in Edinburgh as the second priority after the need to defeat Japan.[89] However, the war had witnessed trends in Scotland which would be irreversible after 1945. Johnston's policy of 'the strong man in the Cabinet' had shown that the Scots could secure substantial benefits from the British state without the need for devolution. Also, the resources of the British state were greater than those that could be called upon from Scotland on its own. Furthermore, given the magnitude of Scottish social and economic problems, it was questionable whether the Scots had sufficient resources to tackle them effectively. As Johnston put it: 'What purport would there be in our getting a Scottish parliament in Edinburgh if it has to administer an emigration system, a glorified poor law and a graveyard?'[90] The coming of the Welfare State and the managed economy was welcomed in Scotland because there was much for the state to do in terms of providing better housing, health and employment opportunities. While the Scots may have harboured nationalist sentiments, their political loyalties would be determined by the prospects for social well-being and economic prosperity and, in the circumstances of the time, this meant looking to the British state to realise these aspirations. The ability of British governments to live up to such expectations would determine Scottish political behaviour for the rest of the century.

NOTES AND REFERENCES

1. I.G.C. Hutchison, *A Political History of Scotland: Parties, Election and Issues, 1832–1924* (Edinburgh, 1986), pp. 175–7, 183–5, 204–7; R. Price, *An Imperial War and the British Working Class* (1972) and M. Fry, *Patronage and Principle: A Political History of Modern Scotland* (Aberdeen, 1987), pp. 117–23.
2. Hutchison, *Political History*, pp. 218–21 and Fry, *Patronage and Principle*, p. 117.
3. Hutchison, *Political History*, pp. 211-12.
4. See G.R. Searle, *The Liberal Party: Triumph and Disintegration, 1886–1929* (1992), p. 77.
5. S.J. Brown, 'Scottish Liberalism and the South African War', *Scottish Historical Review*, lxxi (1992).
6. National Library of Scotland [NLS], Acc. 10424/63, Sir George Younger, *Confidential Memorandum: Scottish Home Rule* (1914).
7. R.J. Finlay, *A Partnership for Good?: Scottish Politics and the Union Since 1880* (Edinburgh, 1996), ch. 2.
8. Sir George Younger, *Confidential Memorandum*.
9. *Edinburgh Evening News*, 27 October 1900.
10. *The Young Scot*, 1 October 1903.
11. Finlay, *Partnership for Good?*, ch. 2.
12. *Young Scot*, 1 December 1904, p. 26.
13. John W. Gulland, *Young Scot*, November 1903, p. 16.
14. ibid., 1 December 1904, p. 26.
15. See Finlay, *Partnership for Good?*, ch. 2.
16. Based on annual programmes of speeches and meetings, 1903–14.
17. This appears frequently in articles in *The Young Scot, The Young Scot Annual Yearbook* and in the minutes of the East and North of Scotland Liberal Association MSS, University of Edinburgh Library.
18. *Young Scot*, 1 April 1905, p. 81.
19. Searle, *Liberal Party*, pp. 77–96.
20. R. Jay, *Joseph Chamberlain: A Political Study* (Oxford, 1981).
21. Lady Frances Balfour, *Lord Balfour of Burleigh* (1924), pp. 125–33.
22. *Young Scot*, 1 October 1903, p. 3 and Hutchison, *Political History*, pp. 218–21.
23. See Alan Sykes, *Tariff Reform in British Politics* (Oxford, 1979).
24. *Young Scot*, 1 October 1903, p. 7.
25. ibid.
26. ibid.
27. See Searle, *Liberal Party*, pp. 79–81.
28. *Young Scot*, 1 May 1905, p. 92.
29. ibid., p. 94.
30. NLS, Acc. 3721, box 146, 'Election Literature'.
31. Hutchison, *Political History*, p. 223.
32. Finlay, *Partnership for Good?*, ch. 2.
33. NLS, Acc. 3721, boxes 143–7, Records of the Young Scots Society.
34. Finlay, *Partnership for Good?*, ch. 2.
35. ibid.
36. *House of Commons Debates [H.C. Debs]*, vol. CLXXIX, 26 May 1908, p. 967.
37. ibid., 16 August 1911, col. 1929–30.
38. NLS, *Younger Memorandum*, 1914, p. 3.
39. For example, see press reports of the open air demonstration on 3 September and the speaking tour from 31 October to 4 November 1910.
40. Taken from press reports of the campaign, *The Glasgow Herald*, October 1910.
41. Liberal Unionist Manifesto, reprinted in *The Glasgow Herald*, 29 December 1909.
42. *Young Scots Handbook 1911*.
43. Hutchison, *Political History*, pp. 218–21.
44. NLS, Acc. 3721, box 146/2, Young Scots Society, *Report of the Annual Conference, 1911*.
45. *Young Scots Handbook 1911*, p. 2.
46. *Younger Memorandum: Scots Home Rule*, 19 May 1914.

47. See Finlay, *Partnership for Good?*, ch. 2 for further details.
48. NLS, Acc. 3721, box 146, Thomas Lockhead (General Secretary of the Young Scots Society) to R.E. Muirhead, 9 March 1912. Correspondence between R.E. Muirhead and W. Murray, September 1911.
49. *H.C. Debs*, vol. XXXIV, 28 February 1912, col. 1466–7.
50. ibid.
51. ibid., 30 May 1913, col. 503.
52. See Finlay, *Partnership for Good?*, ch. 2.
53. Hutchison, *Political History*, p. 309.
54. ibid., pp. 285–92.
55. ibid., p. 285.
56. See Finlay, *Partnership for Good?*.
57. Hutchison, *Political History*, pp. 279–80.
58. ibid.; C. MacDonald, 'The Radical Thread: Political Change in a Scottish Town, Paisley 1880–1924' (Ph.D. thesis, University of Strathclyde, 1996) and Fry, *Patronage and Principle*, pp. 119–73.
59. In particular, I. MacLean, *The Legend of Red Clydeside* (Edinburgh, 1983), I. Donnachie, C. Harvie and I.S. Wood (eds), *Forward! Labour Politics in Scotland, 1888–1988* (Edinburgh, 1989), A. McKinlay and R. Morris (eds), *The ILP on Clydeside, 1893–1932: from foundation to disintegration* (Manchester, 1991) and R. Duncan and A. McIvor (eds), *Militant Workers: Labour and Class Conflict on the Clyde* (Edinburgh, 1992).
60. MacLean, *The Legend of Red Clydeside*.
61. T. Brotherstone, 'Does Red Clydeside Matter Anymore?', in Duncan and McIvor (eds), *Militant Workers*, p. 69.
62. Hutchison, *Political History*, pp. 314–22.
63. ibid.
64. ibid., p. 322.
65. ibid.
66. ibid., p. 322–6.
67. I. MacDougall, 'Some aspects of the 1926 General Strike in Scotland' in I. MacDougall (ed.), *Essays in Scottish Labour History* (Edinburgh, 1978), pp. 170–206.
68. See R.J. Finlay, *Independent and Free: Scottish Politics and the Origins of the Scottish National Party, 1918–1945* (Edinburgh, 1994), pp. 71–126.
69. R.J. Finlay, 'Pressure Group or Political Party: the Nationalist Impact on Scottish Politics, 1928–45', *Twentieth Century British History*, 3 (1992), pp. 274–97.
70. Finlay, *Independent and Free*, p. 68.
71. A. McIvor and H. Paterson, 'Combating the Left: Victimisation and Anti-Labour Activities on Clydeside, 1900–39' in Duncan and McIvor (eds), *Militant Workers*, pp. 129–55.
72. J. Mitchell, *Conservatives and the Union: A Study of Conservative Party Attitudes to Scotland* (Edinburgh, 1990), pp. 17–26.
73. See R.J. Finlay, 'National Identity in Crisis: Politicians, Intellectuals and the "End of Scotland", 1920–1939', *History*, 79 (June 1994), pp. 241–59.
74. T. Stannage, *Baldwin Thwarts the Opposition: The General Election of 1931* (1980) and Fry, *Patronage and Principle*, pp. 175–8.
75. Fry, *Patronage and Principle*, pp. 149–74.
76. Finlay, 'National Identity in Crisis'.
77. *H.C. Debs*, vol. 272, col. 307, 22 November 1932.
78. Finlay, *Independent and Free*, ch. 4.
79. Finlay, 'National Identity in Crisis'.
80. R.H. Campbell, *The Rise and Fall of Scottish Industry* (Edinburgh, 1980), pp. 133–64.
81. *H.C. Debs*, vol. 272, col. 293, 22 November 1932.
82. Finlay, 'National Identity in Crisis'.
83. ibid.; see also the chapter by Hutchison in this volume.
84. R.J. Finlay, 'Conservatism and Unionism in Scotland Since 1918' in M. Francis, S. Reynolds and I. Zweinniger-Bargielowska (eds), *The Conservatives and British Society, 1880–1990* (Cardiff, 1996).

85. R.H. Campbell, 'The Economic Case for Nationalism, Scotland', in R. Mitchison (ed.), *The Roots of Nationalism* (Edinburgh, 1980), p. 151.

86. C. Harvie, 'Labour and Scottish Government: The Age of Tom Johnston', *Bulletin of Scottish Politics*, 2 (1981), 1–20.

87. ibid. and G. Walker, *Thomas Johnston* (Manchester, 1988).

88. Finlay, 'Scottish Conservatism and Unionism'.

89. Finlay, *Independent and Free*.

90. T. Johnston, *Memories*, p. 66.

5. SCOTLAND IN THE UNION, 1945–95: THE CHANGING NATURE OF THE UNION STATE

James Mitchell

This chapter will examine the political development of the Anglo-Scottish Union since 1945 and, in particular, it will focus on the fluctuating influences of British and Scottish nationalisms. The challenges to and new-found strengths of British nationalism during Attlee's Labour government and the post-war consensus are set against the decline of Britain as an economic and world power.

THE DYNAMIC UNION STATE

Scotland's status within the United Kingdom is the subject of much academic debate with many writers on British politics assuming that Britain is a unitary state, within which lie varying degrees of diversity. James Kellas suggested that there is a distinct Scottish 'political system', while Richard Rose maintained that Scotland was a 'sub-system' within the United Kingdom political system.[1] M. Keating and A. Midwinter, however, maintain that it is best to conceive of Scotland operating in a system of complex networks which link 'Scottish actors to one another and to non-Scottish networks' which permit some decisions to be taken entirely within the Scottish 'networks', while others are taken at the 'UK level' with 'Scotland providing a distinctive input'.[2] There is obvious confusion as to the nature of the state.

Alternatively, it can be argued that the United Kingdom has a dynamic quality and that the term 'unitary' is too crude a description of the nature of the state. Stein Rokkan and Derek Urwin have suggested a fourfold classification of state-building: the unitary state, union state, mechanical federalism and organic federalism. The key distinction in any discussion of Britain is between the unitary and union state types.

1. *The unitary state:* built up around one unambiguous political centre

which enjoys economic dominance and pursues a more or less undeviating policy of administrative standardisation. All areas of the state are treated alike, and all institutions are directly under the control of the centre.

2. *The union state:* not the result of straightforward dynastic conquest. Incorporation of at least parts of its territory has been achieved through personal dynastic union, for example by treaty, marriage or inheritance. Integration is less than perfect. While administrative standardisation prevails over most of the territory, the consequences of personal union entail the survival in some areas of pre-union rights and institutional infrastructures which preserve some degree of regional autonomy and serve as agencies of indigenous élite recruitment.[3]

It is clear that the union state ideal is closer to the nature of Britain than the unitary state. However, this typology was devised to distinguish states at their formation. For it to have value in discussions of states after their formation and as they develop over time a dynamic element must be incorporated.

In a unitary state the centre is unambiguously dominant. The changing role of the state, the international environment and the rise of social and political movements will not necessarily affect its unitary nature. Any state apparatus which reflects territorial differentiation and any responses to regionalist movements would change the essence of the unitary state as it would then incline towards a union state or even a federal state. The union state is different because it is acknowledged that integration is imperfect and though there may be administrative standardisation, the survival of distinct rights and infrastructure makes it a different kind of entity. Given that the state changes over time in response to a range of influences, it is inevitable that the territorial balance within it may change too.

It might be expected that the development of modern state activities would help unify the state and destroy sub-state communities through administrative standardisation. The decline, for example, of a religion which is predominantly found in one part of the state and which might have been significant at the inception of the state, may result in the decline of territorial differentiation. In the case of Scotland, the Church of Scotland was one of the institutions to have been given special privileges and, significantly, played a dominant role in the provision of education. Its demise and replacement with secular education could have involved centralisation and a move towards a unitary state. That this did not occur was testimony to the dynamic quality of the union state. Secularisation did not result in the abandonment of a distinct Scottish education tradition and set of institutions. The establishment of the Scotch Education Department in

1872 was an example of the state's role increasing while territorial differentiation was maintained.[4]

BRITISH VERSUS SCOTTISH NATIONALISM?

An inevitable consequence of the union state is that an official or state nationalism and sub-state nationalism (such as Scottish) co-exist. It is wrong to suggest that these nationalisms cannot exist together but equally it is necessary to be aware of the potential for conflict between them. Circumstances will determine the degree of compatibility at any given time. In order to understand this it is necessary to understand the appeal of nationalism. In his study of nationalism, Kellas distinguishes between 'psychic income' – 'those things which satisfy the mental and spiritual needs of human beings' – and material interests: 'those things which are readily quantifiable in cash terms, such as incomes and jobs' and nationalisms may offer either or both.[5]

One of the curiosities of the United Kingdom is the confused nature of state nationalism. While Scots often complain when English commentators use 'England' to mean the state as a whole, Scots are often as guilty in using Britain when the United Kingdom is accurate. Part of the confusion arises from the changes in the official nomenclature of the state. In 1961 Duncan Sandys, the Secretary of State for Commonwealth Relations, sought cabinet approval for a change in designation of the state in relations with the Commonwealth. The 'United Kingdom' or 'UK' was a 'soulless, official' designation which was 'totally lacking in popular appeal and inspires no emotions of affection or loyalty'. 'Britain' had been seen as inappropriate in the days of Empire as other countries would resent the UK arrogating to itself the term 'British' which was common to all, but new Commonwealth members never regarded themselves as British. This, it was felt, made Britain and British more appropriate in the post-colonial period. It was accepted that the full and formal designation 'United Kingdom of Great Britain and Northern Ireland' would still be necessary in treaties and legal documents and in the definition of citizenship, but 'Britain' would be used in other respects in dealings with the Commonwealth. 'Great Britain' was rejected on the grounds that it would 'inevitably be abbreviated into 'GB', which would be as unattractive as 'UK'.[6] Thus, external changes were having an impact on the name and the very essence of the state. The state never was settled. It was constantly undergoing change. Given this state of affairs it was hardly surprising that opportunities existed for the development of an alternative sense of national identity. There is no elegant adjective for the UK. As Richard Rose has commented, there are no 'UKes'.[7]

For the sake of simplicity 'British' is used and will be used here despite its obvious inaccuracy.

Over the post-war period British and Scottish nationalism have existed together, sometimes complementing each other and sometimes in conflict. Both nationalisms have had psychic and material aspects to them. The strength of British nationalism has long been the material benefits it is perceived to offer, though it would be wrong to underestimate the psychic income afforded by institutions such as the monarchy or events such as World War II or, more recently, the South Atlantic Conflict. Increasingly, however, the material benefits of the union have been found to be wanting.

There are a number of influences which had the potential to change the territorial balance within the union state. These have affected the nature of and relationship between Scottish and British nationalisms. As has already been noted the economic context has been important. The activities of social and political movements and other changes in society both threaten and offer opportunities to the union state, the changing role of the state, the international political economy, and consequences of decline or the perception of decline have all had implications for the development of Scottish and British national identities.

SCOTLAND IN BRITISH POLITICS

The key state institution manifesting the union state nature of Scotland's position in the UK has been the Scottish Office. Set up in 1885, its responsibilities and the number of civil servants it employed grew with the increasing role played by the state in the life of the nation.[8] The post-war Scottish Office resembled a mini-Whitehall in Scotland but the link with London remained powerful and the degree of autonomy was severely circumscribed. The Scottish Office was still part of the Whitehall machine and any resemblance to a form of self-government was just that – the Scottish Office had the appearance but not the substance of autonomy.[9] In financial matters the Treasury had ultimate control and no Scottish Secretary could pursue a policy which was wholly at variance with that being pursued south of the border, especially on politically sensitive matters. On the other hand, discretion was greater in areas with an established Scottish tradition, such as in the field of criminal law. The Scottish Office was (and is) a classic example of a post-unification institution of the union state: integration with the rest of Britain is less than perfect, some rights and infrastructures are preserved (or created in place of old ones) and indigenous élite recruitment preserved.

Parliament is obviously very important given the absence of a separate Scottish legislature. But even Parliament has catered for Scottish distinctiveness. A Scottish Grand Committee was set up in 1894 and in the late 1940s its functions were increased.[10] This was partly in response to home rule agitation and partly due to wider reforms of Parliament. In addition, Standing Committees set up in the 1880s to relieve legislative business have come to include two devoted to Scottish business. Again, over the post-war period there were some changes in procedure to extend their scope. More recently, the Select Committee system has been developed in Parliament. In the early 1970s a Scottish Select committee was set up and reported on matters including land ownership and land use. In the early 1980s a Scottish Select Committee was again reconstituted. As with parliamentary procedures in the late 1940s, changes in the early 1980s were partly a response to agitation for home rule and partly made in the context of wider parliamentary reforms.

PRESSURES FOR ASSIMILATION AND DIVERSITY

There were a number of pressures for greater assimilation of Scotland with the rest of Britain or, more accurately, with England in the post-war period but equally there were pressures towards greater diversity. Fifty years on from the end of the war it is not possible to say that either the pressures towards assimilation or diversification won out. The changing nature of state intervention might have been expected to have led to greater assimilation and much that was associated with the Welfare State and Keynesianism was assimilationist. The development of modern communications, in particular the electronic media, had been expected to diffuse cultural, social and political attitudes and values throughout the state if not internationally. With the same news and entertainment being beamed into homes the length and breadth of the country, the prospect of building a unified British identity appeared a possibility.

However, Britain was a union state, not a unitary state, which meant that the institutions of government and media were distinct to start with. The Welfare State which emerged was highly centralist but did have a Scottish dimension to it. The health service was organised on a Scottish basis and the education system's Scottish dimension was jealously guarded by teachers and administrators. The most notable case of assimilation at the outset was national insurance and social security. The base on which the post-war welfare system developed in these areas was Scottish but this disappeared as uniformity was imposed in the pursuit of equality. The period of relative consensus was one in which Scottish distinctiveness was accepted, although within a fairly centralised system. During this period, the Labour Party became the main promoter of centralisation.

The Unionists, as the Conservatives continued to call themselves until 1965, were the party of the unreformed union state during the period of consensus politics. They argued for greater account to be taken of the Scottish dimension but this usually amounted to little more than rhetoric and a means of embarrassing the Labour Party.[11]

The modern media and communications had a very different impact from that which had been expected by diffusionist theorists. It soon proved possible to broadcast on a Scottish or more local level. Television and radio soon reflected the situation which had always pertained in the Scottish press. The first BBC television broadcast in Scotland was in March 1952 when there were 41,000 television sets in Scotland. There are now almost 1,200,000 television sets in Scotland. Scottish television started broadcasting in 1955 and Grampian in 1961. Politically, television became the prime medium through which the electorate gained information in the late 1950s, the 1959 general election being the first election with televised coverage. In 1967–8 both Scottish television and BBC Scotland started producing political programmes. Radio Scotland only came into existence in 1974, though a service allowing for opting out of Radio 4 had existed before this. Independent radio has become comparable to the Scottish local press with a number of very successful outlets owned or controlled by a diminishing number. Relations between London and Scotland have not always been good and the tension evident in the institutions of government in the union state have been equally in evidence in the media.

Since 1945 the Scottish press has undergone dramatic change, particularly in ownership and editorial policy.[12] Over this period the decline in support for the Tories has been significant. If evidence was required to back the claim that the media affects politics, then Scotland would be a useful testing ground. The decline in Tory-supporting papers has not run in direct parallel with the decline in that party's support but does approximate with it. The most notable aspect of the print media in Scotland is its Scottishness, though this is not the same as being Scottish-controlled. The Scottish press has largely moved outside the control of Scotland.

SCOTLAND IN THE IMMEDIATE POST-WAR PERIOD

On 12 April 1945, a by-election was held in Motherwell. The war-time truce between the main parties was still in force, which gave the party which had previously held the seat a free run. On this occasion, Motherwell had been a Labour seat. The truce did not extend to the minor parties and the Scottish National Party put up Dr Robert McIntyre. The SNP had been formed in 1934 with the merger of the National Party of Scotland (formed in 1928) and the Scottish Self-Government Party (formed in 1932) and had contested a number of by-elections before the outbreak of war but had never done well. During the war it had benefited from the truce and in the dying days of the war had managed to win Motherwell. McIntyre was in Parliament for only a matter of weeks before the 1945 general election. It was a curious affair because British nationalism might have been expected to have been dominant in the circumstances. However, the politics of post-war Britain were emerging and Britishness in the union state was ambiguous. Scots had joined Scottish regiments of the British Army. Tom Johnston, the war-time Secretary of State, had instituted reforms which emphasised the Scottish dimension to British government. As Morgan has noted, the war had 'promoted fragmentation as much as it had fostered coherence'.[13] However, though it was to be another two decades before the SNP was to win its next by-election, the Scottish dimension was never far from the surface of British politics.

In the late 1940s, Scottish Convention, a home rule pressure group, organised 'Scottish National Assemblies', similar to the constitutional conventions of the late 1980s/early 1990s. The Labour government took this activity seriously. In December 1947, the Secretary of State for Scotland wrote a cabinet memorandum in which he distinguished between different groups in Scotland:

> A. – The extreme home-rulers (the Scottish Nationalist [sic] Party) who, for example, have petitioned the United Nations Organisation for their emancipation.
> This group is picturesque and articulate; but the support for it is negligible.
> B. – Scottish Convention, the less extreme wing of the Home Rule movement, demands a separate Parliament in Edinburgh for Scottish affairs, while retaining Scottish representation in the British Parliament for British affairs.
> At a 'National Assembly' held recently by the Convention detailed proposals to this end were subsequently sent to the Prime Minister with a request that he should receive a deputation. In declining to do so, the Prime Minister indicated that the Assembly's proposals might be submitted to me, and I have now been asked to meet their representatives.
> The strength of this group is difficult to estimate, as during elections its vote is not recorded because of stronger loyalty to the

main political parties. It has, however, a considerable number of
supporters in all parties.

C. – By far the largest group, and one which has strong emotional
feeling behind it in Scotland, asks that Parliament should give more
time to Scottish affairs and that, within the British constitution and
the unity of the two countries, the Scots themselves should have
further opportunities of administering in Scotland the business of
Government and of the socialised industries and other
Government-appointed organisations.[14]

Failure to make much of an impact on the government led Scottish
Convention to launch the 'Scottish Covenant', a giant petition in October
1949. The problem with the Covenant was that it carried no sanction and
the government challenged home rulers to contest elections if they felt they
had support. Nonetheless, privately it was accepted that interest in home
rule was 'always present, widespread and sincere', as Arthur Woodburn,
Scottish Secretary, informed his cabinet colleagues in December 1949.[15]

The Attlee government responded in a number of ways which resembled
those of later governments. Prevarication and reform in the Scottish Office
and parliamentary procedures were allied with stressing the value of the
union. The Attlee government had acknowledged the existence of the
'widespread desire in Scotland that the Scottish people should have
increased opportunities of dealing with affairs of purely Scottish concern'
in a white paper issued in January 1948.[16] It proposed a number of changes
in order to tackle this desire. Special parliamentary procedures dealing with
Scottish affairs were to be extended. A Scottish Economic Conference,
meeting under the chairmanship of the Secretary of State, would be established with members drawn from public and private sectors which would
be consultative. The machinery of government and administration of the
nationalised industries would be continuously kept under review with a
view to finding opportunities for developing administrative devolution. At
that stage it was not felt necessary to set up a committee of enquiry into
Scottish affairs generally.[17] Prevarication came later in the form of establishing a committee to enquire into the financial relations between Scotland
and England in June 1950 which reported in July 1952.[18] A Royal Commission on home rule was also considered and Labour was committed to
setting one up in the event of victory in 1951.

As was discussed above, the union state must respond to new challenges.
In the late 1940s these not only included the activities of nationalists and
home rulers but the Attlee government itself also instituted changes which

had considerable implications for the union state. The reform programme
of the government had a number of implications for Scotland's status. Most
significantly, the Welfare State provided Scots with reason for supporting
the constitutional status quo. The National Health Service helped cement
the union. Identification with the state was facilitated by the existence of
policies and institutions perceived to provide shelter from the cradle to the
grave, and furthermore, all of these were fundamentally British institutions.
Simultaneously, health was a responsibility of the Scottish Office and it was
possible to give a distinct Scottish dimension to the service.

Central economic planning and Keynesianism involved a high degree of
centralism. This sat uneasily alongside Labour's long-term commitment
to home rule. Within the Labour Party any enthusiasm for a Scottish
parliament was stilled by the priority attached to nationalisation and the
development of the Welfare State which it was felt required strong central
direction. The new era which Labour was entering was one in which there
was little ideological room for legislative devolution. Though it was not
until 1957 that the party in Scotland officially rejected a Scottish parliament
on 'compelling economic grounds', the Attlee government marked a shift
towards that position.

In some areas of reform, the Attlee government ran into difficulty. Its
nationalisation programme proved unpopular north of the border where
the Tories argued that it would 'denationalise' industry by taking responsibility for these industries out of Scotland and placing them in the hands
of bureaucrats in London. In 1949, the Scottish Unionist Party produced a
policy paper, 'Scottish Control of Scottish affairs'. Its name implied that the
party was sensitive to the desire for Scots to have a greater say in Scottish
policy, but this was only to take advantage of national sentiment and the
paper merely proposed to extend administrative devolution. In a memorandum to the cabinet in 1950, Scottish Secretary Hector McNeil acknowledged that there was a 'strong' feeling in Scotland that nationalisation was
seen as a form of centralisation and that Labour was vulnerable on this
matter.[19] In this context, the Conservatives seemed more likely to accept
legislative devolution and certainly played the Scottish card to the full to
Labour's embarrassment in the 1940s and early 1950s.[20]

Nonetheless, the Attlee government instituted reforms which were to
have far-reaching implications for Scots. Opportunities existed for Scots
who previously would have had no hope of gaining a higher education.
Nationalisation helped to sweep away many of the discriminatory employment policies which helped maintain sectarianism. The rise of local and
regional planning with the building of new towns and peripheral schemes

meant that old communities were disrupted. In these urban communities overcrowding was common and opportunities few. The new towns did for a period look like offering new hope though the peripheral schemes around Glasgow, Dundee and Edinburgh never did offer the same opportunities as those elsewhere. Part of the strength of the new towns lay in changes in the international political economy. Multinationals seeking bases in Britain or Europe found support and encouragement there at a time when they were expanding their international networks.[21]

THIRTEEN YEARS OF CONSERVATIVE RULE:
A VERY BRITISH AFFAIR

Despite the Conservatives' rhetoric while in opposition in the late 1940s, the thirteen years of Conservative rule from 1951 saw little in the way of territorial innovation. A Royal Commission on Scottish Affairs under Lord Balfour was set up which reported in 1954, by which time nationalist agitation had all but disappeared. Balfour recommended a number of extensions of administrative devolution – electricity, food, animal health, roads and bridges – to the Scottish Office, which were accepted by the Conservatives. These added to the piecemeal growth of Scottish Office responsibilities and taken together with other functions gave it a broad range of responsibilities which allowed it to develop an important planning function from 1962 when the Scottish Office was reorganised and the Scottish Development Department was established.

Though nationalist and home rule agitation was at its lowest post-war ebb in the 1950s, there was much that happened which was later to be of significance in changing attitudes which affected the nature of Scotland's position in the union. The British Empire was coming to an end. Indian independence had been proclaimed in 1947 and a decade later Ghana became the first of a succession of African states to gain independence from Britain. European integration was slowly taking place. The Treaty of Rome was signed in March 1957. In May 1959, Scottish unemployment doubled with the ending of national service and the deflationary effects of government policies. By February 1960, Scottish unemployment topped the 100,000 mark. All was not well. Britain's great appeal to the Scots existed so long as it delivered. Britain was beginning to have problems in providing both 'psychic' and material income to the Scots. It was becoming increasingly difficult to sustain the myth of British 'Greatness', especially in Europe where the process of integration would in time fundamentally alter attitudes regarding the nation state. The British state was failing to realise the post-war aspirations of the Scots.

BRITAIN'S DECLINE: THE 1960s

Not only did Britain appear to have failed to keep its side of the bargain, but there was some evidence that Scotland was being abused in the process. The desire to maintain a semblance of British greatness resulted in the development of the nuclear-powered submarine Polaris. In November 1960, Prime Minister Harold Macmillan announced that it would be based in the Holy Loch in Scotland. Polaris, however, like its successor Trident, was to prove little more than a costly symbol.

Harold Wilson's Labour government made little difference. High hopes were built up around promises to modernise the economy but in the 1960s the Labour government staggered from one crisis to the next. Bombastic British nationalism was still evident. In December 1964, Wilson announced that the Polaris base at the Holy Loch would be retained. Industrial relations difficulties and exchange-rate crises afflicted the government and the symbolically significant devaluation of the £ sterling took place in November 1967. Much of this reflected Britain's weak status as a trading nation. Wilson's 'New Jerusalem' crumbled: the Department of Economic Affairs was disbanded in October 1969 and the Ministry of Technology disappeared a year later. National Planning soon turned into crisis management. But most significantly, Britain failed to provide the material income Scots had come to expect.[22]

While Labour attempted to modernise the country, Edward Heath tried to modernise the Scottish Tories. The party had reached its high point in 1955 when it won 50.1 per cent of the Scottish vote, but had been in decline since then. By the mid-1960s it was being suggested that the weakness of the party north of the border might cause it to lose office at Westminster in the future. A number of initiatives were begun, but there was a contradiction in the approaches adopted. On the one hand it was decided to abandon the name, Scottish Unionist Party, which had given the party a distinctly Scottish identity. The new name – Scottish Conservative and Unionist Party – assumed that assimilation was the norm and that territorial differentiation was backward looking. On the other hand, in May 1968 Heath made his 'Declaration of Perth' at the Scottish Tory conference. It was a response to the rise of the SNP and this grandly-titled speech committed the party to establishing a Scottish legislature. This assumed that Scottish distinctiveness was important. Heath had told Richard Crossman that he believed that Scottish nationalism was the most powerful new force in British politics.[23]

The impression that all was not well was the important backdrop against which the SNP picked up support in the 1960s. In local and by-elections

the SNP made gains and finally made its breakthrough when Winnie
Ewing won Hamilton from Labour in a sensational by-election in November 1967. Academic and journalistic interest in the distinctive nature of
politics north of the border increased. In 1966, Ian Budge and Derek
Urwin published *Scottish Political Behaviour*, the first major study of Scottish
politics which challenged the then orthodox diffusion model of politics by
suggesting that despite centuries of close political association in a single state
Scottish identity had not disappeared. In 1967–8, both the BBC and STV
started transmitting political programmes.[24]

Labour retained a centralist outlook, although the Scottish Office under
Willie Ross attained a degree of autonomy from Westminster never known
before. Ross jealously protected his Scottish territory and its interests. It was
not a particularly democratic form of politics and sat uneasily alongside
1960s' counter-culture and participatory ideals, but it was a distinctly Scottish and quite conservative form of politics. Labour failed to deliver in terms
of 'material income' and the perception of decline made British nationalism appear somewhat outdated. In 1969, as in similar situations in the past,
a Royal Commission was set up – to 'spend years taking minutes' in Harold
Wilson's memorable phrase – giving the appearance of action but really
only buying time for the government.

BRITAIN UNDER THREAT: LIFE IN THE 1970s

The 1970 general election saw the SNP win its first seat at a general election
when the Western Isles, the last constituency to be declared, was won by
Donald Stewart. Otherwise it was seen as a poor election for the Nationalists. Not for the last time, SNP pre-election hype had far outstripped the
party's performance and allowed its opponents to suggest that it was a
spent force. In reality, the party's 11.4 per cent of the Scottish vote was
a creditable performance and provided it with a base which allowed it to
break through at the elections in 1974. Events conspired to help the SNP
in 1974. The discovery of North Sea oil allowed the party to argue that
Scottish nationalism offered both material and 'psychic' income. 'It's Scotland's Oil' proved the most potent slogan in the SNP's history. In October
1973, the Royal Commission on the Constitution reported and instead of
achieving what Harold Wilson had intended, its publication fuelled the
forces for constitutional change. Its timing could not have been more
propitious for the SNP. A week later, voters in the Glasgow Govan by-
election returned Margo MacDonald of the SNP.

The winter of 1973–4 was a time of crisis in British government. External events exacerbated difficulties at home. War in the Middle East and

the ensuing energy crisis combined with industrial relations problems to create an image of Britain as a country in deep trouble. North Sea oil seemed to offer Scotland a way out of its difficulties. In February 1974, the SNP won seven seats with 21.9 per cent of the Scottish vote and in October it won eleven MPs and 30.4 per cent of the vote. In an article in the *New Statesman* in September 1974, John Mackintosh argued that Scottish nationalism had a new appeal. He noted the 'decline in self-esteem and self-confidence of the British' with which 'we are all familiar'. He maintained that the SNP had forced the other parties to fight on their ground. Whatever the others offered – assemblies or a share in oil revenues – would be inadequate 'so long as there is no proper pride in being British'.

Labour was forced to change its anti-devolution policy. Ironically, support for devolution was forced on the Labour Party in Scotland by its London bosses. With little conviction, the Labour government staggered along and passed an unworkable scheme of devolution. Whatever its merits it would have required major revisions to make it work. Devolution dominated parliamentary time in the late 1970s and the Scotland Act, 1978 was passed only by conceding a referendum with a clause stipulating that 40 per cent of the eligible electorate plus a majority of voters had to vote for the measure. The referendum was held on 1 March 1979 after the 'Winter of Discontent'. Labour was unpopular and the country was in difficulty. Scots voted only narrowly for the measure on offer – 51.6 per cent voted Yes and 48.4 per cent voted No – revealing that the Scots were fairly evenly divided on the issue. Having indicated overwhelming support for a Scottish parliament over many years, the measure itself was seen as inadequate and its association with a failing government did not help. It was the supreme irony. A measure designed principally to appease Scottish nationalist sentiment had become associated with the poor economic performance of a British government. Just when confidence in Britain was at one of its lowest points in post-war history, Scottish home rule was thwarted because it was not seen as an alternative to British decline but was associated with it.

THE THATCHER YEARS: MANAGING BRITAIN'S DECLINE

In the first volume of her memoirs, Margaret Thatcher's exasperation with the Scots is made clear during her time in office. She admits that there was 'no Tartan Thatcherite revolution' and that the balance sheet of Thatcherism in Scotland was lopsided: 'economically positive but politically negative'.[25] Thatcherism has been the subject of much debate. In one respect it was a continuation of what had gone before. It was an attempt to articulate decline both in the sense of devising policies to manage decline and also to

offer an ideological justification and legitimacy for these policies. Both
aspects had territorial implications. Mrs Thatcher had little time for, nor
understanding of, the ways in which traditional unionism catered to
Scottish sensibilities. Bluntly put, no prime minister since 1945 failed to
appreciate or failed to accept the need for a distinct Scottish dimension.
Britain was a unitary state as far as Mrs Thatcher was concerned. Again, her
memoirs provide evidence of this. Previous Conservative leaders had fully
endorsed the existence of separate Scottish institutions and the party in the
past had celebrated the fact that it had established and played the most
significant part in the development of the Scottish Office. Administrative
devolution was very much part of the Tory tradition. Mrs Thatcher's comments on the Scottish Office show a very different attitude:

> The pride of the Scottish Office – whose very structure added a
> layer of bureaucracy, standing in the way of the reforms which were
> paying such dividends in England – was that public expenditure per
> head in Scotland was far higher than in England.[26]

She maintained that the Conservative Party was not an English Party but a
Unionist party, but: 'If it sometimes seems English to some Scots that is
because the Union is inevitably dominated by England by reason of its
greater population.'[27] Though factually accurate, these are typically insen-
sitive words. Previous prime ministers would instead have stressed the
importance of catering for Scottish distinctiveness.

But it was not simply because Mrs Thatcher was a 'little Englander' that
she was unpopular in Scotland. Her attitude to Scotland was based on her
belief that Scottishness got in the way of her project to reverse decline and
put the 'Great' back into Britain. She failed to appreciate the widespread
support in Scotland for the steel industry or why a Tory candidate in the
north east of Scotland should be amongst those most vociferously arguing
for the retention of Ravenscraig steel mill south of Glasgow. The de-indus-
trialisation of Scotland had been well in progress before Mrs Thatcher
entered Downing Street but her style and insensitivity were all too evident.
It might have worked to her party's advantage had the alternative British
nationalism borne fruit. With the brief exception of the South Atlantic
Conflict, the Conservatives failed to capture the Scots' imagination with a
British appeal and even then the Scots were less enthusiastic than the English in wrapping themselves in the Union Jack. Rising unemployment and
the growing gulfs in society did not help make the case for Britain.

In the 1980s external events once more intruded and had an impact
on domestic territorial politics. Mrs Thatcher's success in re-negotiating

Britain's budgetary contribution at Fontainebleau in 1984 paved the way for the next phase of European integration. The Single European Act and Single Market were to be part of her downfall. The flip side of Mrs Thatcher's opposition to diversity as represented by a union state interpretation of Britain was opposition to loss of sovereignty, as she saw it, to Brussels. British nationalism was becoming parochial and centralist. Perhaps in reaction to this, the Scots became increasingly pro-European. Having been one of the most reluctant European parts of Britain in the 1970s, Scotland became one of the most pro-European in the 1980s. The SNP reflected this change. During the 1980s it gradually abandoned its anti-European Community stance and in 1988 formally launched its 'independence in Europe' policy. The Scottish nationalists were adopting a more pragmatic line on Europe than their British counterparts. The SNP were beginning to sound relevant, modern and international.

In addition, the Conservatives' pursuit of social and economic policies which were socially divisive and damaging to the Welfare State, at least as perceived in Scotland, gave the Scottish nationalists an opportunity. The poll tax was the culmination of this. Because it was introduced in Scotland a year ahead of England, it was easy to portray the government as treating Scotland as a guinea-pig. The perception that the Welfare State was under threat was also significant. Those institutions created by the Attlee government which had provided the material incomes which helped bind Scots into the union now looked under threat from a government which stressed its Britishness. Opinion polls and elections showed support for the SNP rising and the desire for independence higher than ever before with the constitutional status quo and the Conservatives in decline. The Scots were showing consistency in their support for the state but it was the Welfare State that they supported. The difference was that increasingly a belief was developing that the territorial state which would best protect that state was a Scottish state within the European Community rather than a British state which was becoming increasingly isolated.

The 1992 general election saw a slight rise in Tory support and there was no Mrs Thatcher and no poll tax to blame for the party's poor electoral performance. John Major was remarkably popular in Scotland. Taking these factors into account, the 1992 election was not very good news for the SNP. The SNP hype once more far outweighed its potential support and what was a good result in terms of increased votes proved a disappointment when the party failed to win any additional seats and lost the Govan constituency it had won at a by-election in November 1988. But politics in Scotland had not become polarised between the SNP and the Tories. Most Scots saw themselves as both Scottish and British, wanted a reform of the constitution, not its complete overthrow. Labour and the Liberal Democrats had worked together in the Constitutional Convention from 1989 to draw up plans for a Scottish parliament. In part this was a response to Nationalist pressure and served to draw support away from the SNP but it did signify the growing importance of the Scottish dimension and dissatisfaction with the existing arrangements in the union state.

CONCLUSION

Shortly before becoming Labour MP for Berwick and East Lothian in 1974 John Mackintosh identified the key problem for both his party and the Conservatives:

> Only one thing will halt or reverse the onward march of the SNP and that is a period of government so that it ends with a satisfied electorate eager to vote positively for a party that has once again restored the feeling that Britain is a successful, worthwhile country to belong to for those who do have other places where they can go and other traditions and titles to which they can turn.[28]

The Scots have an alternative partly because of the nature of the state they currently live in. Had Britain become a truly unitary state the alternative might not have existed (or at least be seen to exist). That Britain remains a union state, despite the Thatcher years, and that the Scottish dimension has in some respects become more important, means that the exit option remains. Scottish and British nationalisms have not always sat together easily over the post-war period. The 'psychic' and 'material' incomes offered by each has changed, reflecting the dynamic nature of the state itself. Labour's challenge in the 1980s was to find a new balance in the union state. In 1945, the Attlee government offered material income to the Scots in the form of the Welfare State and support for employment and other outputs of Keynesian economics. Britain's decline has changed matters. Each new government requires to convince its people that they should show loyalty to them, or at least to the state.

The failure of the Conservatives in Scotland looks unlikely to be reversed. The Conservatives have become a party with a territorial base of support beyond Scotland. It may yet revert to accepting Britain as a union state but it may take time before the Scots trust the Tories in anything like the numbers they once did. In the post-Thatcher era it could be that the Conservatives will once again wish to become a 'one nation' party – in every sense of that term. If not, the challenge will be Labour's. It is a challenge to reconstitute the state within the union state tradition but in a manner in keeping with the modern world, which will include taking account of European integration. Constitutional change might go some way to appeasing the Scots but the new politics of Scotland is more complex. Psychic and material demands may be provided by being both Scottish and European. Materially and psychologically, Britain's appeal has declined since the war. Democratic nationalism is contingent and requires to be constantly renewed and loyalties to be won again.

NOTES AND REFERENCES

1. J. Kellas, *The Scottish Political System* (Cambridge, 1989).
2. M. Keating and A. Midwinter, *The Government of Scotland* (Edinburgh, 1983).
3. S. Rokkan and D. Urwin, 'Introduction: Centres and Peripheries in Western Europe' in S. Rokkan and D. Urwin (eds), *The Politics of Territorial Identity: Studies in European Regionalism* (London, 1982), pp. 3–4.
4. See Iain Hutchison's chapter in this volume.
5. J.G. Kellas, *The Politics of Nationalism and Ethnicity* (London, 1991), pp. 66–7.
6. Cabinet Papers, C (61) 46, *Britain or UK: Memorandum by the Secretary of State for Commonwealth Relations*, 24 March 1961.
7. R. Rose, *Understanding the United Kingdom* (London, 1982), p. 11.
8. See the chapter by Hutchison in this volume.
9. For an alternative view see L. Paterson, *The Autonomy of Modern Scotland* (Edinburgh, 1994).
10. See J. Mitchell, *Strategies for Self-Government* (Edinburgh, 1996).
11. See J. Mitchell, *Conservatives and the Union: A Study of Conservative Party Attitudes to Scotland* (Edinburgh, 1990), pp. 17–38.
12. J. McInnes, 'The Press in Scotland', *Scottish Affairs*, 1 (London, 1992), pp. 137–50.
13. K.O. Morgan, *The People's Peace; British History 1945–90* (Oxford, 1992), p. 23.
14. Cabinet Papers, (47) 323, 6 December 1947.
15. ibid., *Scottish Affairs*, 12 December 1949.
16. Cmnd. 7308, *White Paper on Scottish Affairs* (HMSO, 1948).
17. ibid.
18. Catto (Chairman), *Report on Scottish Financial and Trade Statistics*, Cmnd. 8609 (HMSO, 1952).
19. Cabinet Papers, (50) 101, 11 May 1950.
20. See Mitchell, *Conservatives and the Union*, pp. 48–50.
21. See the chapter by Peter Payne in this volume.
22. See Morgan, *The People's Peace*, pp. 277–317.
23. R. Crossman, *Diaries of a Cabinet Minister*, vol. II (London, 1977), pp. 550–1.
24. I. Budge and D. Urwin, *Scottish Political Behaviour: a case study in British homogeneity* (London, 1966).
25. Margaret Thatcher, *The Downing Street Years* (London, 1993), p. 618.
26. ibid., p. 619.
27. ibid., p. 624.
28. J.P. Mackintosh, 'The new appeal of nationalism', *New Statesman*, 27 (September 1974).

6. WE'RE A' JOCK TAMSON'S BAIRNS: SOCIAL CLASS IN TWENTIETH-CENTURY SCOTLAND
David McCrone

If the nineteenth century was a century of status, then the twentieth century has been a century of class. Just as social relations last century were characterised by personalised, hierarchical interactions between unequal status groups, so we might characterise our own century as dominated by impersonal, economic transactions between those who have unequal amounts of power in the market place. A glance at the key milestones of twentieth-century Scottish history seems to reinforce the point. The century opened with the formation of the Labour Party which made its mark with the phenomenon of 'Red Clydeside' and reinforced the view that politics were almost exclusively about class. Such a view became the orthodoxy with the events of the General Strike in 1926, and the Labour landslide of 1945 is usually represented as the culmination of the quest by the working class for political as well as social power with the coming of the Welfare State. Finally, the period since 1979 has been dominated by the counter-ideology of Thatcherism which, while coming from a diametrically opposed political standpoint, seems to reinforce the view that class is the chief motor of both Britain and Scotland. After all, if Scotland proved to be stony ground for the New Right, was it not because the Scots were much more resolute in their structure and culture of class?

There is, however, a counterpoint to this refrain, played in the minor key. A view has been growing since the 1950s that class has been losing its political and explanatory power. Political scientists have written at length about the 'de-alignment' of class, and sociologists have pointed to non–class cleavages such as gender and ethnicity as important predictors of life chances. We might need, then, to refine the opening sentence. Perhaps the first half of the century was stamped by the mark of social class, whereas in the second competing dimensions of inequality have challenged its explanatory authority. Certainly the key political debates of the second half of the century have not gravitated around class. The 1950s and 1960s were the decades of 'affluence' and the advent of the 'classless society'. It took a major sociological study of so-called affluent car-workers in Luton (J.H. Goldthorpe et al., *The Affluent Worker in the Class Structure*) to contradict the view that social class no longer mattered, but it did little to silence the politics of affluence. By the 1970s Scottish nationalism appeared to reinforce the view that class was dying as a political force, even in Scotland, one of its heartlands. The rise of the SNP added a new dimension to Scottish politics hitherto dominated by the 'class politics' of Labour versus Tory. In the 1980s, Thatcherism emerged triumphant south of the border, and Essex man and woman were created to give the lie to the view that class mattered in English politics.

It is clear from this brief overview of the significance of class that much of the evidence concerns its predictive quality for political behaviour or, more generally, for social and political action. If we are to reach a conclusion about its significance, we will first have to work out more precisely what we mean by 'class'. The view that class matters less and less usually takes as its starting point the belief that it has lost its explanatory power to predict social and political behaviour on its own and that other factors have to be taken into consideration. It is necessary to be precise about what we mean by class, and what it is we are trying to explain. Class will be treated here in a fairly orthodox Weberian way:

> We may speak of a 'class' when (1) a number of people have in
> common a specific casual component of their life chances, insofar as
> (2) this component is represented exclusively by economic interests
> in the possession of goods and opportunities for income, and (3) is
> represented under the conditions of the commodity or labour
> markets.[1]

Of the two classical theories of social class, Marxian and Weberian, the former is in a pretty poor state. Lockwood argues convincingly that in Marxist analysis there is much conflict over the concept of class, and not much in the way of a theory of class conflict. Class struggle is expected, but when it does not happen, then it is explained away either by appeal to dominant ideology in a thoroughly utilitarian way, or by reference to an unproblematic schema of class structure in which the mechanisms between structure and action are presumed rather than proved.[2]

If we wish to connect structure and action, then we have to be much more explicit about the mechanisms between them, the connecting chain, as it were. Simply put, we ought to think of at least three links in this chain: class structure – how class is 'objectively' constructed and reproduced; consciousness – the level of culture and meaning which surrounds class and other systems of inequality; and action, usually, but not exclusively, political. The usual, and somewhat misleading, connection is to imply that action derives from consciousness which in turn is read off structural features. If certain actions do not occur – such as 'class' politics – that is because there are breaks higher up the chain, at the level of culture and ideology, and further back to structure itself. This is a model which has currency far beyond its Marxian origins. Hence, many of those who proclaim a political process of class de-alignment argue that it reflects a changing class structure. Put simply, non-Labour voting reflects in part a major reorganisation of the social structure. To point out that the links in the chain are complex and frequently less than predicatable is to re-situate Scotland in a meaningful way. The debate about the politics and sociology of twentieth-century Scotland has frequently taken liberties with its history as well as the conceptual treatment of social class. Class has not been absent from social and political debate, merely somewhat distorted. Let us review some of the ways in which this has happened.

There are two opposing views about Scotland's class structure. Either it is simply a mirror of the British one, or it is qualitatively different. Neither position is tenable, however, largely because the terms used are not adequately clear. On the one hand, the unitary character of the British state, and its early reorganisation as the world's first industrial power, have been used to imply the homogeneity of its class structure, Scotland included. In this view there is no such thing as a separate sociology of Scotland because the social, economic and political forces are essentially the same as those in Britain. On the other hand, nationalists have taken one of two opposing views. The right-of-centre one is that 'class' is an alien – frequently English – imposition into the community of Scotland. Hence the comment from the late historiographer royal, Gordon Donaldson: 'It is true to this day that Scotland is a more egalitarian country than England, but as a result of class consciousness horizontal divisions into classes have become ... more important than vertical divisions into nations'.[3] Here we find a central idea about class in Scotland, which owes more to culture than to structure. In other words, Donaldson touches on the powerful 'lad o' pairts' myth which argues that social mobility – the ability to 'get on' in Scotland – is significantly more open than in England. We will examine this myth, not to disprove it – myths cannot be 'proved' or 'disproved' – but to make a central point about class, namely, that structural similarities between countries do not in any way preclude their alternative interpretation. In other words, far too little attention has been given to the middle link in the chain – consciousness, or more precisely culture.

The view that class was an alien imposition from England has been supplanted in recent years in nationalist quarters by a more radical view that Scotland is itself a 'class', or rather an 'ethno-class colony' of England. This view gained considerable currency in the 1970s as it chimed with a burgeoning sociology and politics of development in the Third World and owed much to writers on colonialism such as Immanuel Wallerstein and Michael Hechter. Both attributed colonial status to Scotland, and were involved in debates with Scottish historians and sociologists about the trajectory of Scottish economic and social development. The view that Scotland was itself a (subordinate) class was taken up by writers like Dickson and Payne who flirted with the colonialist thesis.[4] Although this thesis may have been replaced with the view that Scotland was not a colony of England but a successful junior partner in the wider process of British imperial colonialism, the political value to be had from such a piece of rhetoric is still resonant in the 1990s.

Nothing has given sociology in Britain its distinctive character more than the study of class. From the 1950s the study of social class has been at the centre of the discipline in these islands and its chronology is marked by major studies of social mobility.[5] Reviews of the concept and the literature continue to be published and debates still occur in the sociological journals with titles like 'How many classes are there in contemporary British society?', 'Is Britain a class-divided society?', 'The promising future of class analysis: a response to recent critiques', and 'Does class analysis without class theory have a promising future?'.[6] Such a debate suggests not simply that British sociologists are still fascinated by social class (some critiques argue that this is a fatal fascination), but that it is still a highly contentious subject.[7] Few, however, would disagree with the comment that 'classes must be seen, not as veritable geological formations, once they have acquired their original shape, but as phenomena in a constant process of formation, reproduction, re-formulation and de-formation.'[8] Let this be our starting point for our discussion of social class in Scotland.

To underscore the thesis, it will be argued that in terms of the first link in the chain – class structure – there is very little to distinguish Scotland from the rest of the UK (or, indeed, most other advanced industrial societies). However, at the other end of the chain – social and political action – there are important differences of behaviour and meaning, most notably in how Scots behave and think politically. The clue lies in the middle link in our chain, consciousness and culture. It will be argued that there are systems of meaning in Scotland which act as prisms through which structures are refracted to provide alternative explanations for similar structural changes. The point is that we do not experience 'structure' directly, although we are aware of those which change around us. For example, people are confronted by and have to cope with unemployment and redundancy which result from the changing occupational structure. They do not 'know' the structure directly, merely the impact it has on their lives.

There is nothing especially novel about this approach to class. After all, we would not expect workers in France to see the world in the same way as English workers because there are different systems of political and cultural meaning available to each. We only find it surprising that Scots do so because we assume a homogeneous class structure carries with it a corresponding, almost determined, class culture, and that membership of the same state reinforces homogeneity. Insofar as history matters, or more precisely, politics and institutions matter, then we have to disentangle structure from culture, lest we conclude that action always follows structure in a predetermined way. It is also one of the benefits of Weberian analysis that history as well as contingency matter in this model of class. Class action is highly contingent and undetermined, and not the outcome of deeper 'historical' forces.

In his paper 'How many classes are there in contemporary British society?', George Runciman estimated that in 1910, the working classes of Britain accounted for seventy-five per cent of the population, with the upper and middle classes around fifteen per cent (the rest he labelled the 'underclass').[9] He estimated that by the 1990s, the 'working class' stood at half of the population, the middle classes at forty-five per cent, and the underclass five per cent. While we might argue about the exact figures for Scotland, we would be wise to accept that in broad terms the structure was similar. We will never know for sure because the Registrar-General only began to collect and publish data on 'socio-economic groups' in 1961. Nevertheless, a review of the industrial structures of Scotland – that is, the industries people worked in – as well as for those in the rest of the UK shows quite clearly that Scotland was not a deviant case.[10] While we cannot automatically assume that people were employed in the same way in these industries north and south of the border (it would be possible for, say, ships and marine engineering to employ disproportionately more, or less, unskilled manual workers in Scotland than in England), industrial orders (IOs) do give us a considerable clue about class structure too. On the evidence of the IOs, there are no grounds for saying that Scotland in the nineteenth century had an industrial structure which was particularly 'deviant' from the British norm. Scotland was especially well-adapted to take advantage of Britain's highly advantageous structural position in the world economy which was at that time shaped around Britain's own commercial interests.

At this stage it might be appropriate to defend the assumption that 'class' is about occupations, what people do for a living. That is a phrase which is much nearer to the sociological truth than it first appears. For most people their life chances are determined by what they do for a living, what they work at, because that is the source of their income. It characterises their life security, gives them access to housing, education and so on. Runciman, for example, argues that three key criteria matter: 'control' – an ability or otherwise to control or organise the work process; 'ownership' – the legal title to some productive property; and 'marketability' – the institutionally recognised possession of an attribute, skill or asset with income-generating powers.[11]

Hence, we can follow Edgell's characterisation that while we can argue about the relative distributions in a population, there are in modern market societies three main classes: a dominant class based on the ownership of capital; an intermediate class whose power derives from the acquisition of educational or organisational skills; and a subordinate class based on the possession of physical labour.[12] In modern times, the conventional rankings are those of the Registrar-General whose socio-economic groups are 'differentiated by life-style', and a more sociologically derived schema by Hope-Goldthorpe which brings together 'market' and 'work' situations (Runciman's marketability and control aspects respectively).[13] These are described as:

> Occupational categories whose members would appear, in the light
> of the available evidence, to be typically comparable, on the one
> hand, in terms of their sources and levels of income and other
> conditions of employment, in their degree of economic security
> and in their chances of economic advancement; on the other hand,
> in their location within the system of authority and control
> governing the processes of production in which they are
> organised.[14]

To return to our industrial/class history of Scotland, we can see that the middle decades of this century, 1931–71, saw the continuation of the similarity of Scotland to the rest of the UK, although the proportion of skilled manual workers was slightly higher. The industrial structure was

TABLE 1
Sectors as % of total employment in Scotland

Year	Agriculture, forestry, fishing	Mining and quarrying	Manufacturing	Intermediate	Services
1911	12	8	36	19	19
1931	10	6	30	25	24
1951	7	5	35	22	24
1961	6	4	33	24	26
1971*	3	2	33	21	33
1981	2	2	25	20	43

* Major categorical revision.
Source: D. McCrone, *Understanding Scotland: The Sociology of a Stateless Nation* (1992), p. 76.

marginally more differentiated from that of Britain as a whole than had been the case in the previous century. In 1931 and 1951 Scotland remained the economic region with the industrial structure closest to the British mean, and in 1961 and 1971 was only overtaken by north-west England. The general process of convergence which has taken place between the economic regions of the UK has not been mirrored within Scotland, that is, in terms of the internal regions of Scotland.[15] Perhaps the rather widespread assumption that Scotland did have a fairly specialised economy, based on heavy industry, textiles and engineering, reflects the propensity of economic historians to write the history of Scotland as a whole in terms of that of west-central Scotland. Scotland was not a specialised region of the UK but one which had a very similar profile to Britain as a whole. This will have clear implications for its class structure, as we shall see shortly.

The intermediate step between outlining industrial orders and the social class structure is to describe sectoral change in Scotland. Taking 1991 as our base line (there was a major recategorisation in that census making comparison with previous censuses problematic), we can see that Scotland like Britain had been transformed in the second half of the century (Table 1).

It is from 1951 that what sociologists call the 'occupational transition', the shift from manufacturing employment to services, has occurred, in line with other advanced industrial societies. The growing share of services, from nineteen per cent in 1911 to forty-three per cent by 1981 has been the major motor of economic and social change (we must recall in passing that this category has changed considerably, from domestic service employment to occupations concerned with state service functions like education and social services). The changing occupational structure and concomitant patterns of social mobility, coupled with new opportunities for women, have ushered in major political and social change.

TABLE 2

Socio-economic groups as % of total employment in Scotland

		1961	1971	1981 (adjusted)
1, 2.	Employers, managers and administrators	7	8	9
3, 4.	Professionals	2	3	5
5.	Intermediate non-manual	6	8	11
6.	Junior non-manual	21	21	22
7.	Personal service	4	6	6
8.	Foremen and supervisors (manual)	2	3	3
9.	Skilled manual	28	23	20
10.	Semi-skilled manual	13	13	11
11.	Unskilled manual	8	9	7
12.	Own account workers	2	2	2

Source: McCrone, *Understanding Scotland*, p. 79.

We are now in a position to describe the main socio-economic changes in Scotland since these data were collected and analysed in 1961 (Table 2).

The trends, which Scotland shares with the rest of the UK, have been for the expansion of white-collar work, notably professional employees, and intermediate non-manual workers (teachers and non-managerial workers). Manual workers have declined as a percentage of those in employment, from just over half (fifty-two per cent) in 1961, to just over forty per cent in 1981. In comparison with the rest of the UK, while Scotland has a higher share of manual workers in employment, the general decline is in line with the decline across the rest of the country. In comparison, Scotland has a lower share of non-manual workers, especially in the private sector, and of own-account workers.

In similar vein, the trend for women to participate increasingly in the labour force has been a feature north and south of the border. In Scotland, however, as far as married women are concerned the trend has been one of convergence. Until well after 1945, the economic activity rate for married women in Scotland was only two-thirds that of the rest of Britain, and it was not until the late 1970s that Scotland caught up. By 1981, fifty-seven per cent of married women in Scotland under the age of sixty were economically active. The expansion of new occupations for women runs alongside the feminisation of certain occupations such as clerical work, in which the percentage of clerks who were female rose from about half in 1961 to three-quarters by 1981. The thesis that Scotland has in some way become deskilled in comparison with England and Wales is not sustainable. The similarities on both sides of the border are greater than the differences, and the patterns of women's employment mirror those of England and Wales more than those of men. If we treat women as quintessentially 'deskilled' workers, then it is not possible to make a case that Scotland has become proletarianised.

We are now in a position to bring these data up to date by looking at the 1991 census, and to draw some conclusions about Scotland's class structure in comparison with England and Wales. It is important, however, to counsel caution about straightforward comparisons with historical data, given categorical revisions in the last decade. Nevertheless, the shape of social class structure in Scotland is now quite different. The fall in the proportions of manual workers continues to fall (at just over forty per cent), and while skilled manual workers are still the largest category at nineteen per cent, employers and managers (Socio Economic Groups (SEG) 1 and 2) are now seventeen per cent. If we group SEGs 1 and 2 (employers and managers), 3 and 4 (professionals), own account workers (12), and farmers (13 and 14), thirty-one per cent of economically active heads of households are now 'middle class'. SEGs 8, 9, 10, 11 and 15 (manual workers plus agricultural workers) represent forty-one per cent with twenty-four per cent in the intermediate categories. The comparison with Great Britain is interesting. (Table 3).

The shortfall in 'middle class' workers in Scotland is largely accounted for by the difference in 'own account' workers (six per cent compared with nine per cent), whereas the larger 'manual working class' in Scotland is due in part to proportionately more skilled manual workers (nineteen per cent compared with eighteen per cent).

If we adopt the Registrar-General's sixfold classification of social class (again, for persons who are economically active heads of households) we find the comparison in Table 4.

The different patterns of employment between men and women alluded to earlier are reflected in the social class profiles for each gender (Table 5).

The complexities of class definition are reflected in these distributions. We cannot conclude, for example, that women are more 'middle class' than men simply because they do non-manual jobs. Over three times as many women as men are in IIIN (non-manual skilled occupations) yet three times as many men as women are in category I (professional etc occupations). Similarly, around half of men (fifty-one per cent) are in manual jobs compared with less than one-third of women (thirty-one per cent). Again, it is the similarity with the British pattern which is noteworthy rather than the differences.

Looking at structure is valuable but limiting. The census gives us a snapshot of the social structure at decennial intervals, but says nothing about

TABLE 3
SEGs of economically active heads of households (% by column)

	Scotland	GB
'Middle class' (1, 2, 3, 4, 12, 13, 14)	31	37
'Intermediate' (5, 6, 7)	24	23
'Manual working class' (8, 9, 10, 11, 15)	41	36

Source: 1991 Census, general volume part 2: table 8.6, pp. 172–3.

TABLE 4
Social Class of Households (% by column)

		Scotland	GB
I	Professionals, etc.	7	7
II	Managerial and technical	28	30
IIIN	Skilled non-manual	12	12
IIIM	Skilled manual	29	28
VI	Partly skilled manual	15	14
V	Unskilled	6	5
	Others	3	3

Source: 1991 Census local base statistics: table 90 (Scotland); table L90 (GB).

TABLE 5
Social Class and Economic Position (% by column)

	Men		Women	
	Scotland	GB	Scotland	GB
I	6	7	2	2
II	23	26	26	27
IIIN	10	10	36	38
IIIM	31	31	7	7
IV	16	15	15	16
V	6	5	9	7

Source: 1991 Census, table 91 (Sc); table L91 (GB).

social mobility in the intervening periods. For that, we need to turn to social mobility data. Here we are reliant on major British and Scottish surveys of inter-generational mobility taken in the mid-1970s. The limitations of these studies derives less from their age (nearly twenty years old) than from the sexist character of the assumptions that women's class can largely be read off that of their male partners. In the climate of part-time working and gender parity in the labour market twenty years later this would now be untenable. Nevertheless, what these studies show clearly are the mobility implications of the expansion of non-manual work in the post-war period.[16]

The results for Scotland, and England and Wales are, almost without exception, similar. A substantial proportion of the 'service class' is drawn up from manual working-class backgrounds.[17] Fully one-third of respondents in class I had fathers who were in manual occupations, and for class II ('subaltern or cadet levels of the service class') the figure was forty-three per cent. In other words, there is (or was, in the 1970s) substantial social heterogeneity in the upper echelons north and south of the border. On the other hand, the manual working class is much more homogeneous and self-recruiting, and more working-class in its origins in both England and Scotland. While there is considerable upward mobility into classes I and II, there is very little downward mobility into IV and V. This lack of reciprocity is due to the fact that while the size of the manual working class has fallen, that of the service class has grown. This allows the offspring of the service class to be retained in the top classes, while there is (or has been in a period of economic growth in the long post-war boom) room for upward movement into top jobs from below. We should bear in mind, however, that social opportunity is by no means equally distributed. The opportunities for class I sons to 'self-recruit' was over four times greater than we would expect from perfect mobility, while the inflow into class I from IV and V was only about half of what might be expected. Access to 'top jobs' is clearly class-skewed.

The patterns of social mobility between Scotland, and England and Wales are quite similar, with the exception of the 'petty bourgeoisie' which in Scotland shows a greater capacity for self-recruitment and reduced social mobility, possibly due to the number of small farmers and smallholders in this category north of the border. We should not be surprised at these similarities. Scotland, England and Wales have common occupational characteristics by virtue of early industrialisation and the demise of the peasantry. Not even crofting in Scotland makes much of a dent in the patterns, with the exception of the class IV patterns alluded to. It would, then, be perverse to conclude from these data that Scotland has taken a different mobility route from the rest of the UK. Scotland has a slightly smaller middle class and a slightly larger manual working class, but the processes of social mobility which have created these structures are similar on both sides of the Tweed. This may seem an obvious point to make, but it is an important one, as we shall see in our discussions of the next two links in our chain of class – culture, and action. If Scotland is 'different' in its politics, it is not simply because its class structure is different.

Of the three links in the class chain – structure, consciousness and action – the middle one is the least understood. To most sociologists of class, for example, and perhaps historians too, consciousness is translated into individual awareness of one's class position. It is, in Marx's phraseology, the difference between *Klasse an sich* and *Klasse für sich*. We need to recognise that whether or not people become class conscious and the extent to which they do is dependent on broader social and cultural forces impacting on individual consciousness. At its most basic, it allows sociologists to ask a battery of survey questions about images of class, in addition to ascertaining occupations.

If we were doing a comparative study of class in different societies, say France and Germany, we would assume that between structure and action there operated a culture, a meaning system generated in part by different political cultures, which translated structural aspects into possibilities for action. We would not assume that a particular structural configuration of class automatically led to identical social or political action. We are aware that these cultures, for want of a better word, are historically constructed and refracted through, among other things, political agenda. This may seem a trite point, but when it comes to Britain in general and Scotland in particular, we seem to forget about it. Put simply, 'class' in Scotland will not be interpreted and explained in the same way as in England, simply because key institutions such as law, education and religion, will mediate structures and experiences to produce different political and social outcomes. Associated with these institutions are cultures and meaning systems, which frame structure and action.

We do not have to look far in Scotland for such distinctive cultures of class. What has been called 'the Scottish myth', the belief that Scotland is a more egalitarian society than England, and that social mobility is somewhat easier, has a long cultural history. It was probably in the mind of Gordon Donaldson when he commented that 'class' seemed to be an alien import into Scotland, a 'more egalitarian country than England'. It is also true that the egalitarian myth is fairly impervious to falsification. No amount of counter-evidence to show that there are abiding socio-economic differentials on a whole host of social phenomenon – educational attainment, morbidity, quality of housing, and so on – seems to be enough to banish the myth. That is because myths are not meant to be proved or disproved. In Andrew McPherson's words: 'The demythologiser is as likely to de-historicise, to discount the significance of the interplay over time of changing forms and ideas, as is the prisoner of myths who interprets present institutions as the unchanged expression of a timeless ideal'.[18] Lest we think Scots are particularly prone to this sort of thing, we should remind ourselves of the power of the American Dream. The notion that hard work coupled with ability will lead to achievement unless you are particularly unlucky is a powerful value in the USA. It is a story, a narrative, of considerable power which helps to define Americans to themselves and, they hope, other people. It is an identity-myth, saying who they are and who they are not. In like manner, the Scottish myth – with interesting parallels with the American one – is a truth held to be self-evident, that all men [sic] are created equal.

This myth has been explored at length elsewhere and it is not appropriate to do so at length here.[19] Suffice it to say that the myth – in an anthropological sense, a perspective, a guide to help interpret social reality – does not describe or explain features of the social structure. Myth draws selectively from the past, but its key purpose is to provide a contemporary reservoir of legitimation for belief and action. The Scottish myth lends itself to two main interpretations, an activist one which seeks the resolution of the apparent contradiction between real social inequality and an egalitarian ideology in favour of the latter. However, there is also a second, more conservative interpretation of the myth, that if man is primordially equal, then social structural inequalities do not matter, and nothing needs to be done. It is sufficient that 'we're a' Jock Tamson's bairns'.[20]

The Scottish myth had its educational manifestation in the 'lad o' pairts', a talented youth (almost always male) who had the talent but not the financial means to 'get on'. This myth was embedded not simply in the whimsical stories of late nineteenth-century fiction, but had its educational counterpart in what Andrew McPherson has called the 'Kirriemuir career', the route taken by many senior educators in Scotland to power and influence. The 'Kirriemuir career' was a 'symbolic world bounded by Angus, standing for East and North and with Kirriemuir at its heart, by Dumfries in the South and in the West by a Glasgow academy, perhaps The Academy'.[21] The image of small-town, conservative Scotland which the lad o' pairts exemplified belonged historically to the late nineteenth and early twentieth centuries. The social opportunity which was being celebrated did not belong to collective achievement but to individual endeavour. It drew on a 'meritocratic' ideal not an egalitarian one. As Allan MacLaren commented:

> the egalitarianism so often portrayed is not that emerging from an economic, social or political equality; it is equality of opportunity which is exemplified. All men are not equal. What is implied is that all men are given the opportunity to be equal. Whatever the values attached to such a belief, if expressed today, it would be termed elitist not egalitarian.[22]

The lass o' pairts had no iconographic equivalent in Scottish education, and critics have pointed out that the egalitarian tradition in Scotland has hidden the gender inequalities in education.[23]

It would be misleading, however, to suggest that the myth depended on 'facts' for its meaning. To be sure, there had to be some validation (or at least not overmuch counter-evidence) for the myth to ring true. Robert Anderson has shown that in the late nineteenth and early twentieth centuries, a substantial number of students at Scottish universities, especially Glasgow and Aberdeen, came from 'disadvantaged' backgrounds (manual working-class, and peasant origins respectively).[24] By 1910, twenty-four per cent of students at Glasgow came from the manual working class, and twenty per cent at Aberdeen from peasant stock. Even as late as 1947, as Keith Hope has shown, 'the native tradition of meritelection [educational opportunity] in which educational selection of the 'lad o' pairts' was a recognised mode of social ascent of the poor [sic]' was supported by survey evidence to the extent that 'Scotland, as we would expect, is more merit-elective than the United States'.[25] Again, cross-national surveys suggest that the skilled manual working class in Scotland after 1945 had similar educational opportunities to mainland Europe, whereas this class was noticeably at a disadvantage in England.[26]

The Scottish myth is kept alive not simply because people believe it to be founded on fact (or more precisely because it is not totally at odds with reality), but because there are institutional mechanisms such as the education system which are its carriers. In other words, we are dealing here not with some disembodied set of beliefs and values, but with coherent meaning systems which are given institutional expression in Scotland. Ideas about class and social opportunity are firmly embedded in Scottish civil society. That is the clue to understanding the culture of class. How people act will not be the result of automatic responses to structural dictates, but will result from the meanings, values and ideas which structural aspects have in the society. People do not experience 'structure' *per se*, but are aware of the ways in which it changes, bringing opportunity, or the lack of it. More broadly, class *tout court* in Scotland has to be interpreted in the frame of meaning, social, cultural and political. This means that class will carry its meanings within it, embedded in its culture. Structure alone will not be enough to carry it into action. And vitally, historical memory will play a strong part in the story. The narrative of class in Scotland is one in which issues of national identity play across issues of class. Scotland's relationship with England has taken on 'class' connotations to the extent that class and nationality are often insinuated. We need only to look at the position of the anglicised lairds to appreciate the point. Throughout this century, the shift-ing relationships of class – between lairds and bourgeoisie, national and local bourgeois, bourgeois and worker – have often been refracted in this way.

There can be no class without politics, and no politics without the state. Hence, as the Scottish semi-state – the Scottish Office – has taken on more direct powers of governance, so class relations are played out through the medium of state power. One of the key processes of the twentieth century has been the expansion of the Scottish state apparatus, and with it a Scot-tish agenda.[27] This has been a complicated process which is not necessarily a linear one. The semi-state which had been repatriated to Edinburgh in 1885 became the mechanism for restructuring the Scottish economy. It became a powerful administrative apparatus, or 'negotiated order'.[28] We do not need to claim that Scotland had a separate political system to accept that a set of policy communities operate in which the values and culture of decision-making élites help to sustain a distinctive set of institutions and relationships through which class operates. We are now in a position to understand the final link in our chain of class, social and political action.

In recent years, one of the key themes of political science and political sociology in Scotland has been the divergence in electoral behaviour north and south of the Tweed. That there is something to be explained is obvious enough. Since the 1960s, electoral patterns in Scotland, and especially the fortunes of the Conservative Party, have diverged. Much of the debate has been about how much of this divergence can be explained by 'structural' factors, and how much of the variation remains unexplained. In other words, can we simply account for the divergence between Scotland and England (and even those categories cannot be treated without some caution) in terms of differences in social structure because Scotland has more people in the manual working class, more employed in the state sector and more council tenants than England? The answer is – not entirely. This is not the place to lay out the fine details of the argument and the com-plexities of the data and their statistical transformation. It is enough to say that the predicted Conservative vote in Scotland on the basis of the social structure is systematically lower than we would expect. Whether we call this residual which we cannot explain by structural factors 'the national effect' or the cultural component, it is clear that there is real difference.[29]

To some historians, of course, this may seem obvious enough and some-what tedious. Politics in Scotland has always been about more than naked social class. The land questions, being Orange or Green, rural or urban, east or west, have each coloured Scottish politics, as well as class relations. It is not necessary to overstress the difference. The division between rough and respectable within the working class has currency north and south of the border, but the ways in which it has expressed itself – in social relations, where people lived, who they interacted with, which football team they supported, and so on – have taken on Scottish characteristics. That is not to say, of course, that this is a distinction unique to Scotland, simply that it has taken on Scottish colouring. Class relations in Scotland, just like any other society, take on the substance of social relations generally. They are not expressed in 'pure' form, whatever that may look like. They are always 'naturalised'. The interaction between religion and social class is one of the most interesting and contentious. There is little doubt of its historic importance, and there is a new line of argument suggesting that it has not died as many have claimed. Some argue that support for the Conservative Party from Protestants has not eroded significantly, merely that fewer people consider themselves Protestant these days, and that ethnic and religious factors are still powerful determinants of social identity.

Just as religion has been losing its force as a key determinant of identity and political behaviour as the century has progressed, so nationalism has grown in importance. The emerging Scottish frame of reference from the late 1960s fixed a new dimension in politics. The arrival of North Sea oil fuelled the perception of Scotland as a separate unit of political and economic management and opened up the political possibility of an alternative Scottish future. The SNP in the 1970s was in the right place at the right time, making explicit the 'national' dimension of the post-war consensus, and providing a political alternative when the British settlement began to fail. At the height of its electoral success in 1974, the SNP did well across all social classes, but especially among skilled manual and routine non-manual workers. The October 1974 election study showed the undoubted 'classless' appeal of the SNP, a feature of both strength and weakness. Although the party did well among all social classes in Scotland, its particular attraction was for those who were socially and geographically mobile in the 1970s. The lack of a class connotation for the SNP was perhaps a key factor for the upwardly socially mobile. Such people were susceptible to a kind of political perspective which was different from the one with which they had grown up. In other words, there was a shift to a more 'privatised' lifestyle, in which television provided an appropriate frame of political and social reference.

To be sure, this process of what Raymond Williams called 'mobile privatism' was not unique to Scotland, because these social changes were happening in the rest of the UK and beyond.[30] The rise of the SNP, however, gave these processes a particularly Scottish resonance in the 1970s.

The party captured the generation entering the electorate in these years who, in England, gravitated to the Conservatives or the Liberals. Again, the point is worth underlining. Class and politics – or more precisely, structure and action – do not produce identical outcomes north and south of the border. The national dimension matters, and operates as a prism through which structural forces are refracted. It remains, then, to underscore this point by a glance at the 1992 evidence, collected by Jack Brand and James Mitchell in the Scottish Election Survey. Taking the Registrar-General's classification in line with the one we used earlier, we can see the difference between Scotland and England and Wales with regard to class voting (Table 6).

The Tories do less well in every social class in Scotland, and among class I, professionals, only thirty-eight per cent vote Tory compared with fifty-six per cent in England and Wales. Labour does proportionately better in Scotland among intermediate groups (II and IIIN), and least well among class V, where the SNP makes considerable inroads. Labour and the SNP are the main competitors for the unskilled working-class vote in Scotland. In general, the SNP does better the lower the social class. In a reversal of its position in 1974, the SNP does better in lower social classes (Table 7).

A similar pattern is shown using Goldthorpe-Heath social class categories, with the Conservatives doing especially badly in Scotland among the 'salariat' (thirty-two per cent compared with fifty-one per cent in England and Wales) and the 'routine non-manual' group (twenty-six per cent versus forty-eight per cent). Labour does proportionately better among these groups in Scotland (twenty-three per cent versus seventeen per cent; and thirty-three per cent versus twenty-five per cent), with the Liberal Democrats doing worse in Scotland in every social class. In other words, only about one-third of the Scottish salariat votes Tory compared with over fifty per cent in England and Wales. Similarly, only one-quarter of the routine non-manual class in Scotland votes Conservative compared with just under fifty per cent south of the border.

It is not necessary to labour the point about the different relationship in Scotland between social class and voting. The weak appeal of the Conservatives north of the border is spread throughout all social classes; Labour does better in Scotland among all classes, with the exception of unskilled manual workers where the SNP success among that group is a reflection of the policy change in the 1980s to attack Labour as the biggest party north of the border. In other words, class matters, but it is refracted through the somewhat different political party system here.

An understanding of social class in Scotland requires not simply an

TABLE 6

Social Class and Vote: Scotland (England and Wales) (% by row)

		Conservative	Labour	LibDem	SNP
I	Professional	38 (56)	14 (16)	24 (18)	14 (n/a)
II	Managerial	32 (50)	25 (18)	15 (24)	19 (n/a)
IIIN	Skilled non-manual	30 (51)	28 (22)	10 (15)	20 (n/a)
IIIM	Skilled manual	15 (35)	38 (28)	9 (12)	21 (n/a)
IV	Partly skilled	13 (30)	45 (45)	4 (13)	22 (n/a)
V	Unskilled	13 (22)	34 (51)	9 (8)	27 (n/a)

Source: Scottish Election Study, 1992.

TABLE 7

Social classes voting SNP (% by row)

1974

Employers and managers	27
Professional	30
Intermediate	40
Junior non-manual	26
Foremen and supervisors	18
Skilled manual	35
Semi-skilled manual	23
Unskilled manual	23

Source: Scottish Election Survey, October 1974.

1992

Professional	14
Managerial	19
Skilled non-manual	20
Skilled manual	21
Partly skilled manual	22
Unskilled	27

Source: Scottish Election Survey, 1992.

appreciation of how the social structure has altered in the course of this century, but also the culture of class and its relationship to social and political action. Just as there is no straightforward relationship between structure and action – the former does not automatically translate itself into the latter – so the sets of meanings and values surrounding social class, the culture of class, is a vital ingredient in a comprehensive understanding. Too often inferences are made from a simplistic reading of voting patterns about the declining importance of class as the motor of the distributive system. We should take little reminding that it has never been easy to read class from politics, structure from action. Scottish history shows many examples of the difficulty of doing this, and yet it is all too easy to assume that once upon a time there was a straightforward relationship. Class relations are frequently encoded and difficult to read, but we cannot deny the importance of social class as the key motor of life-chances at the end of the century, just as it was at the beginning. It is only the form, not the substance, which has changed. If class still matters, then so, vitally, does history.

NOTES AND REFERENCES

1. H. Gerth and C.W. Mills, *From Max Weber* (1948), p. 181.
2. D. Lockwood, 'The Problem of Class Action' in D. Lockwood (ed.), *Solidarity and Schism: 'The Problem of Disorder' in Durkheimian and Marxist Sociology* (Oxford, 1992).
3. G. Donaldson, *Scotland: Shaping the Nation* (London, 1974), p. 117.
4. A. Dickson, 'Scotland is Different, OK?' in D. McCrone, S. Kendrick and P. Straw (eds), *The Making of Scotland: Nation, Culture and Social Change* (Edinburgh, 1989) and G. Payne, 'Occupational transition in advanced industrial societies', Sociological Review, 25 (1977).
5. D. Glass, *Social Mobility in Britain* (1954); J. Goldthorpe, *Social Mobility and Class Structure in Modern Britain* (Oxford, 1987); G. Payne, Employment and Opportunity (1987); J. Goldthorpe, D. Lockwood, F. Bechhofer and J. Platt, *The Affluent Worker and the Class Structure* (Cambridge, 1969); H. Newby, C. Bell, D. Rose and P. Saunders, *Property, Paternalism and Power: class and control in rural England* (Madison, 1978); F. Bechhofer and B. Elliot, *The Petite Bourgeoisie: comparative studies of the uneasy stratum* (1981) and G. Marshal, D. Rose, H. Newby and C. Vogler, *Social Class in Modern Britain* (1988).
6. R. Crompton, *Class and Stratification: an introduction to current debates* (Cambridge, 1993); S. Edgell, Class (1993); G. Runciman, 'How many classes are there in contemporary British society?', *Sociology*, 24 (1990); G. Evans, 'Is Britain a class-divided society? Re-analysis and extension of Marshall et al's study of class consciousness', *Sociology*, 26 (1992); J. Goldthorpe and G. Marshall, 'The promising future of class analysis: a response to recent critiques', *Sociology*, 26 (1992) and R.E. Pahl, 'Does class analysis without class theory have a promising future?', *Sociology*, 27 (1993).
7. P. Saunders, *Social Class and Stratification* (1990).
8. G. Therborn, 'Why some classes are more successful than others', *New Left Review*, 138 (1983).
9. Runciman, 'How many classes are there in contemporary British society?'.
10. D. McCrone, *Understanding Scotland: The Sociology of a Stateless Nation* (1992), ch. 3
11. Runciman, 'How many classes are there in contemporary British society?'.
12. Edgell, *Class*.
13. C. Marsh, 'Social class and Occupation', in R. Burgess (ed.), *Key Variables in Sociological Investigation* (1986).
14. Goldthorpe, *Social Mobility and Class Structure*, p. 40.
15. McCrone, *Understanding Scotland*.
16. McCrone, ibid., pp. 109–11.
17. Goldthorpe, *Social Mobility and Class Structure*.
18. A. MacPherson, 'An Angle on the geist: persistence and change in Scottish educational tradition', in W.M. Humes and H. Paterson (eds), *Scottish Culture and Education, 1800–1980* (Edinburgh, 1983).
19. McCrone, *Understanding Scotland*.
20. ibid.
21. MacPherson, 'Angle on the Geist'.
22. A.A. MacLaren (ed.), *Social Class in Scotland* (Edinburgh, 1976). p. 2.
23. J. Fewell and F. Paterson (eds), *Girls in their Prime: Scottish Education Revisited* (Edinburgh, 1990).
24. R. Anderson, *Education and Opportunity in Victorian Scotland* (Oxford, 1983).
25. K. Hope, *As Others See Us: Schooling and Social Mobility in Scotland and the United States* (Cambridge, 1984), p. 30.

26. W. Mueller and W. Karle, 'Social selection in education systems in Europe', International Sociological Association, 12th World Congress of Sociology, Madrid.
27. McCrone, *Understanding Scotland*.
28. C. Moore and S. Booth, *Managing Competition: Meso-corporatism, pluralism and the negotiated order in Scotland* (Oxford, 1989).
29. McCrone, *Understanding Scotland*, p. 170.
30. R. Williams, *Television: Technology and Cultural Forms* (1974).

7. URBANISATION IN TWENTIETH-CENTURY SCOTLAND
Richard Rodger

It is a commonplace to associate profound urban change with industrial-isation. Yet such transformations as those witnessed in the nineteenth century pale when placed against the experience of the twentieth century. Despite a decelerating rate of urbanisation, towns and cities have been fun-damentally reorganised, spatially and economically, by new energy sources, transport systems, and changed political priorities. The skyline, built-up area, and the colours, materials and designs of buildings have been altered radically in the twentieth century; cultural events and festivals have amplified the function of the urban; and retailing and distributional activi-ties are undertaken increasingly from the margins of an orbital road system. Aided by private road transport and changed residential patterns, the centri-fugal force of the twentieth-century city has replaced its earlier centripetal role. To commuters, shoppers, and a diverse group of recreational interest groups, the benefits of community-based activities have been overwhelmed by an emphasis on individual personal interests. Accordingly, concepts of public service and citizenship have weakened.

Even though in 1900 their own livelihood was always vulnerable, to the Govan riveter, Coatbridge foundryman, Dundee jute-worker, Peterhead fisherman, or Kilsyth miner the disappearance of his entire industry would have been unimaginable. The effects of such terminal economic decline on individual places have been profound in demographic terms and the quality of the twentieth-century urban environment, as have changes in the transport network, housing amenities and leisure activities. Socially and culturally, these and other influences have very considerably affected the character of Scottish towns and cities. The shrinkage of distance, principally by air and road transport and by the media, has had a homogenising impact on the geographical margins of the United Kingdom.

Physically, the Scottish townscape at the end of the twentieth century is in certain fundamentals radically different from that at the beginning of the century. Cobblestones have been replaced by tarmac, electric lighting has replaced gas lights and mantles indoors and on the pavements, traffic lights and street signs abound where none existed, advertising hoardings have been replaced by neon signs and corporate logos, and brick, glass and plastic have overwhelmed traditional materials of stone and slate. As the icons of Scottish industrialisation have passed away, the locomotive shops at Springburn and Cowlairs, Templeton's carpet factory, the Fairfields yard, Tennants' St Rollox chemical factory, the North British Rubber Company, as well as breweries, distilleries and creameries in towns too many to list – so the distinctive industrial landscape of mills, furnaces and warehouses has been demolished and replaced by pre-fabricated 'tin-sheds' and industrial units capable of adaptation as firms come and go.

The brutalism associated with urban development has been a recurrent and international experience. As with the nineteenth century, when un-controlled urban development brought environmental damage and public health risks on an unprecedented scale, so in the twentieth century urban change has in some cases been drastic. The intrusion of urban motorways, shuttered city-centre shops, shattered inner-city tenements, proliferating TV aerials and satellite dishes, and the ubiquitous concrete structures of the post-1945 era have been as thoughtless as Victorian development which cared little initially for the adverse effects of urbanisation on the Georgian city. Reformist strands have offset some of the worst excesses through conservation strategies, such as those advanced by the Saltire Society since the 1930s and more recently taken up in Glasgow's merchant city and the renovation of Glasgow's East End; pedestrianising and 'traffic-calming' strategies have moderated some of the effects of the automobile revolution, and a realisation that the social consequences of high-rise tower blocks are unacceptable has produced a greater emphasis on smaller-scale, informal housing developments.

These changes in the texture of urban Scotland are the product of two groups of influences. The first, beyond the scope of this chapter but of central importance, is associated with national and international scientific and technological changes which have altered the nature of industry in the twentieth century. To some extent, therefore, common denominators exist between the Scottish urban experience and that of other parts of western Europe and North America. The second group of changes has been dis-tinctively local and reflects the way in which individual burghs have them-selves instigated changes in the urban environment. Often the coincidence of macro-level changes and local circumstances has resulted in a distinctive outcome, and it is to these that most attention will be paid.

The chapter establishes a new index of urbanisation between 1891 and 1981, both individually and for groups of towns and cities, considers housing and planning changes as one means of exploring physical and spatial alterations to the Scottish townscape in the twentieth century, and concludes by arguing that changes in town and city environment have accelerated the decline in community-based activities, undermined social interaction, and diminished public service and the concept of citizenship. The changing nature of Scottish towns and cities in the twentieth century has thus forged a new urban consciousness, different in fundamental ways to that which generated municipal socialism and class-based conflicts before 1920.

INDICATORS OF URBANISATION

Size, density and function are the three indicators which are most closely associated with urbanisation. For practical purposes, attention is generally devoted to the size of urban places and their relationships over time, and this approach is followed here.

During the nineteenth century, the Scottish population became increasingly urbanised. Indeed, after England, Scotland was the most urbanised country in the world in 1911: 60 per cent of Scots lived in settlements of more than 5,000 population and 50 per cent in burghs of 20,000 or more inhabitants. The proportions had doubled in the eighty years 1831–1911. Though some places were rocketed to prominence at the beginning of the century by new processes, technological breakthroughs and locational advantages, such as Clydebank and Motherwell, Scotland remained a country in which the four largest cities – Glasgow, Edinburgh, Dundee and Aberdeen – retained their dominance. In 1851, 22 per cent of Scots lived in these four cities; by 1911, the proportion had risen to 30 per cent (or to 35 per cent by anticipating the absorption of Govan, Partick and Leith). The rate of growth in the four cities reached a peak of 37.6 per cent in 1951, tailing off to 30 per cent and then to 28 per cent in the 1981 and 1991 Censuses.

This system of regional centres rather than a single dominant metropolitan city differentiated the Scottish urban system from that of most of Europe. This can be seen in the rank size order graph (Figure 1) in which absolute population size is plotted against the ranked position of a town or city. If the relationship is one of proportionality, that is, if the second largest burgh is half the size of the largest, and the third largest is a third, the fourth

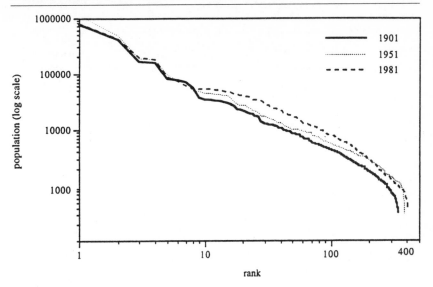

Figure 1

Rank Size Distribution of Scottish Burghs 1901, 1951 and 1981*

* Information on sources for this graph and tables in this chapter may be obtained by writing to the author, Dr Richard Rodger at the Department of Economic History, University of Leicester, University Road, Leicester LE1 7RH.

a quarter and so on, then the log scale graph would show a straight line. This is to a considerable degree what occurred in the Scottish urban system throughout the twentieth century. No abrupt discontinuity exists, as with the predominance of London, Paris, Mexico City, or major cities of the Pacific rim, where the second and subsequent tiers are significantly smaller than the principal metropolitan centre. Indeed, this approximation of a straight line is typical of British imperial urban systems generally, such as those in Ireland, India and Canada, where no dominant city or power base was permitted to develop.

In view of the rapid urbanisation during the nineteenth century, it was arithmetically inevitable that the process would slow in the twentieth century. A doubling of the urban proportion to 60 per cent between 1831 and 1911 simply could not be sustained. Throughout the twentieth century, however, the proportion of Scots living in towns and cities has continued to rise. Direct comparisons between the nineteenth and twentieth centuries are impossible – there have been four important changes to the way the census enumerators defined burghs and urban places – but a quantitative assessment of the continuing magnetic pull of Scottish burghs can be seen from Table 1.

TABLE 1

An Index of Urbanisation in Twentieth-Century Scotland (1931=100)

	Overall Scottish index	205 larger towns and burghs	306 smaller urban places
1891	71.6	71.5	n/a
1901	84.5	86.6	65.8
1911	93.0	93.6	89.2
1921	98.2	98.5	96.4
1931	100.0	100.0	100.0
1951	106.7	105.9	112.7
1961	107.9	105.6	n/a
1971	112.2	109.1	131.1
1981	112.5	106.7	147.5

Note: too few smaller urban places on which to form a reliable index value.

Over the ninety years 1891–1981, and using 1931=100, the index of Scottish urbanisation, based on 511 locations, increased from 71.6 to 112.5. The Scottish urban population continued to increase appreciably, therefore, with 57 per cent more inhabitants in towns and cities in 1981 compared to 1891. For the larger urban locations, most of the increase was concentrated in the years before 1931.

Regional variations in the patterns of twentieth-century Scottish urbanisation are presented in Table 2. For the towns in what might be described as a crescent of semi-rural Scotland the pace of expansion 1861–91 had slowed and the relative stagnation of the years 1891–1911 is evident. Only some urban expansion in the towns north and west of the Great Glen ran counter to the more gentle pace in towns throughout the rest of Scotland. Almost everywhere, the indices of urbanisation declined in the years straddling World War I, in the 1920s, and into the 1930s. Only a measure of economic recovery in the 1930s and a variety of factors in the 1940s meant that towns expanded by 1951, though this was barely perceptible in the border burghs and those in Banff, Moray and Nairn. In many Perthshire towns, across the entire south of Scotland, and north of the Great Glen including the northern isles, the pace of urban expansion was moderated a little in the 1950s, though the upward trajectory was resumed almost universally with considerable vigour from the 1960s (see also Table 1).

In the towns and cities of the central belt and the north-eastern counties the pre-1914 urban expansion was maintained only in Lanarkshire and the Lothians during the 1911–21 decade. War-time demands for coal, shipbuilding and repair meant that Fife burghs like those of Clydeside were less affected than other places, but the unmistakable message was of a slackening in the rate of urban expansion in the industrial heartlands of Scotland.

TABLE 2

Comparative Levels of Scottish Urbanisation: Percentage of Inhabitants in Settlements of 1000+, by counties, 1861–1971

County	1861	1891	1901	1921	1931	1951	1961	1971
Lanark	86.3	90.4	92.3	92.4	94.9	96.6	97.3	97.4
Renfrew	82.0	91.1	89.1	91.7	93.3	95.2	95.2	95.9
Midlothian	81.3	87.7	90.4	91.7	93.5	95.0	96.1	96.1
Angus	74.8	83.4	84.9	84.7	85.5	86.2	87.3	88.9
Clackmannan	65.3	70.9	79.8	83.0	85.5	88.8	92.9	91.0
Dunbarton	63.1	76.1	81.3	86.7	86.7	90.0	94.2	95.1
Selkirk	62.2	86.9	81.8	82.8	83.0	84.5	85.5	87.7
Aye	61.6	70.2	73.4	73.4	76.2	80.8	87.4	90.1
Scotland	57.7	70.6	74.3	77.3	80.1	82.9	85.5	87.0
Stirling	55.9	68.2	67.2	76.5	83.6	84.7	88.1	89.0
Fife	55.2	65.2	69.7	79.0	81.1	84.8	85.9	86.7
West Lothian	53.5	56.7	63.2	60.9	72.4	73.4	81.9	87.1
Bute	51.0	58.6	65.0	62.4	66.9	68.4	61.2	58.9
Moray	45.6	51.9	50.9	54.8	57.2	55.1	67.4	71.9
Kinross	44.6	50.4	47.9	48.2	49.3	49.5	52.1	54.8
Roxburgh	44.4	52.5	54.6	54.4	56.8	59.4	65.1	70.0
Aberdeen	43.9	57.2	61.3	66.1	67.3	70.5	73.2	76.8
Perth	39.5	46.1	49.1	49.8	51.7	56.6	58.7	62.2
Wigtown	35.0	31.5	33.1	33.5	33.1	41.3	42.7	47.0
Banff	34.7	49.7	53.4	55.6	57.1	59.4	57.9	60.4
Nairn	34.2	40.1	48.3	50.9	50.7	53.9	58.2	72.7
East Lothian	33.0	45.6	42.3	51.8	56.7	61.5	69.5	73.3
Dumfries	31.7	38.2	41.3	43.8	54.3	58.5	64.7	69.2
Kirkcudbright	27.8	37.9	39.8	37.7	27.5	29.6	30.3	33.5
Peebles	27.8	57.6	57.1	59.0	61.7	55.0	55.4	59.2
Caithness	26.6	33.5	34.3	39.4	40.9	45.6	56.7	60.9
Berwick	19.8	22.9	23.1	23.6	23.8	27.1	29.6	34.4
Argyll	18.8	33.4	38.2	41.8	33.1	46.0	45.2	43.5
Orkney	16.5	18.5	21.5	22.2	23.1	27.5	30.9	36.7
Kincardine	16.3	38.2	47.3	49.0	51.8	57.8	63.6	67.4
Inverness	15.5	26.6	27.9	29.2	31.9	42.5	49.5	56.6
Ross & Cromarty	13.1	17.5	20.0	16.3	16.1	18.9	23.4	32.0
Zetland	9.8	13.7	15.2	25.2	24.8	28.6	33.2	35.4

Notes: (i) The population described as urban is, for 1861 and 1891, that of the towns and villages with a population of 1000+; for 1921 and 1931, it is that of burghs and Special Districts (Lighting and Scavenging) with populations of 1000 and over. The remainder of the population is rural.
(ii) Separate figures are not given for Sutherland before 1961. The urban population accounted for 17.9 per cent of the total in 1961, and 21.5 per cent in 1971.
Source: Census of Scotland 1931 Table 11, p. 15; Census of Scotland 1951, Table 4, pp. 20–5; General Register Office, *Index of Scottish Place Names* (HMSO, Edinburgh 1974), pp. 171–2.

The decade of World War I did prove something of a watershed for the pattern of Scottish urban expansion, though this probably had more to do with the structure of Scottish industry, foreign competition and economic depression than with the war itself. Though absolute urban decline affected Lanarkshire burghs from 1945, Fife burghs from the 1960s, and the Lothians from the 1970s, it was only in the Renfrew and Dunbartonshire,

TABLE 3
An Index of Urban Growth for the Principal Scottish Burghs 1891–1981 (1931=100)

	Glasgow	Edinburgh	Dundee	Aberdeen	Paisley	Greenock	Kilmarnock	Perth
1891	61.0*	75.2	87.3	65.9	76.7	80.3	74.7	86.0
1901	82.0	89.8	91.8	91.8	91.8	86.3	89.7	94.4
1911	86.4	91.3	94.0	98.0	97.7	95.2	91.2	103.0
1921	95.0	95.7	95.9	95.0	98.1	102.8	93.8	95.4
1931	100.0	100.0	100.0	100.0	100.0	100.0	100.0	100.0
1951	100.1	106.3	101.0	109.3	108.4	96.6	110.6	116.3
1961	96.9	106.7	104.2	110.8	110.8	94.4	124.7	118.4
1971	80.5	102.5	105.0	119.5	113.2	84.9	140.3	120.7
1981	70.3	95.7	99.3	113.9	98.3	74.8	136.7	123.6

Note: * includes Govan, Partick and other areas included within Glasgow burgh extensions in 1891 and 1912.

and Stirling and Clackmannan towns that urban expansion broke loose from the relative decline which had affected urban Scotland from the second decade of the twentieth century.

Within this broad regional pattern there were significant local differences. The experience of the four major cities and the other principal burghs which had been so significant in nineteenth-century Scotland is presented in Table 3. This reveals the underlying urban experience of twentieth-century Scotland: the sustained accretions of the nineteenth century at a rate in excess of the overall Scottish index of urbanisation slowed in the inter-war years, and was in general decline after 1951. Only with specific advantages, such as the oil industry expansion in Aberdeen, or the development of light industry and distribution in Perth and Kilmarnock, was it possible for urban expansions in these areas to continue beyond 1961. In the specific case of Glasgow, the post-1945 overspill policy and New Town development strategies which decanted population far and wide – to Arbroath, Erskine, Irvine, Cumbernauld, North Berwick, Corpach, and Hamilton, for example – made serious inroads into the population base of the city.

Amongst the larger towns and cities there was considerable variation in the trajectory of urban expansion. Though the index for the larger burghs shows an increase from 71 in 1891 to 100 in 1931 and 107 in 1981, there were 28 places where by 1981 the index was over 200, and a further 38 where the index was more than 150 by 1981. Penicuik (index = 640; 1931 = 100), Whitburn (517), Ellon (486), Fort William (438), Denny and Dunipace (420), and South Queensferry (418) exceeded all others amongst the established burghs by 1981, but places such as Stranraer, Stonehaven and Stornoway experienced growth after World War I at rates formerly associated with burghs in the Forth-Clyde valley. For many such townships, the pace of urban growth, accelerating particularly after 1950, was a largely unfamiliar experience, with administration, schooling and leisure services often inadequate.

A typology of twentieth-century urban Scotland is shown in Table 4. This is statistically based on hierarchical cluster analysis, that is, on comparing the population profiles of 188 locations for each census between 1891 and 1981, and grouping the coefficients generated as measures of similarity. Clusters of six major types have been produced. Table 4 should be read as a continuum, beginning with Brechin, moving downwards vertically, and then on to the second column, beginning with Cove and Kilcreggan. Where breaks occur, these represent clusters which differ in some way from the major characteristics of the column. Thus while Anstruther and Cullen are in the same general group of burghs in long-run decline, they differ from Abernethy and those places above the break since they did not participate in the slight recovery which Brechin, Maybole and others experienced between 1931 and 1951.

For the first cluster, the column beginning with Brechin, the unifying characteristic is that population levels were generally in decline until 1931. For some places (Abernethy, Alva, Alyth, Ballater, Brechin, Burghead, Campbeltown, Coldstream, Coupar Angus, Crail, Duns, Forfar, Huntly, Laurencekirk, Maybole, Moffat, Portsoy, Whithorn and Wigtown) there was a temporary respite in the 1930s and 1940s in this long-run population loss as a result of protracted economic depression and the diminished appeal of emigration, either within urban Scotland or beyond. However, in the 1950s these small towns, mostly on the geographical periphery of Scotland, continued their downward trajectory, thereby resuming the shared experience with Aberchirder, Anstruther, Cullen, Galashiels, Langholm, Pittenweem, Rothes and Tobermory whose downward spiral was uninterrupted until the 1960s. For almost all of this cluster of towns in long-run decline – exceptions were Wigtown, Whithorn, Pittenweem, Laurencekirk, Newmilns and a trio of important border towns, Galashiels, Hawick and Selkirk – the decline was reversed to varying degrees in the 1960s and 1970s, with more widespread car ownership and some economic and industrial reorientation enabling a measure of expansion. This reversal was enough in Duns, Forfar, Abernethy, Aberfeldy, Ballater, Dufftown, Coupar Angus, Galston and Lauder to edge population levels in 1981 above those of 1891 for the first time.

In one sub-group of burghs (Hawick, Selkirk, Innerleithen, Tayport and Keith) the long-run decline was so very gentle that it might be more

TABLE 4

Typology of Scottish towns and cities based on cluster analysis

Long-run decline (44)	Early twentieth-century expansion (43)	Pronounced post–1945 expansion (19)	Stagnation or decline and modest recovery (27)	Steady expansion (39)	Dramatic recent expansion (8)
Brechin	Cove and	Linlithgow	Newton Stewart	Kintore	Penicuik
Burghead	Kilcreggan	Tain	Blairgowrie	Forres	Fort William
Campbeltown	Dunoon	Stewarton	Kirkwall	Carnoustie	Denny and
Whithorn	Elie and	Lochgilphead	Bridge of Allan	Stonehaven	Dunipace
Maybole	Earlsferry	Banchory	Dollar	Lerwick	S. Queensferry
Aberchirder	Rothesay	Invergordon	Inverbervie	Lossiemouth	Johnstone
Langholm	Millport	Irvine	Montrose	Inverness	Prestonpans
Tobermory	———	———	Dalbeattie	Stranraer	Bonnyrigg
Coldstream	Buckie	Dunblane	Macduff	Dingwall	Thurso
Duns	Greenock	Kirkintilloch	Auchterarder	Lanark	
Alva	Portknockie	Cumnock	Kirkcudbright	Barrhead	
Forfar	Aberlour	Milngavie	Kelso	Leslie	
Alyth	Findochty	———	Lockerbie	Haddington	
Arbroath	———	Helensburgh	East Linton	Airdrie	
Abernethy	Cowdenbeath	Nairn	Kirriemuir	Stirling	
———	Lochgelly	Alloa	Fortrose	Loanhead	
Anstruther	Glasgow	Armadale	Biggar	Ardrossan	
Cullen	Clydebank	Elgin	Peterhead	———	
Galashiels	Buckhaven and	Annan	Callander	Inverkeithing	
Wigtown	Methil	Stornoway	Eyemouth	Tranent	
Banff	Musselburgh	Tillicoultry	Jedburgh	Grangemouth	
Wick	Falkirk	———	Falkland	Largs	
Portsoy	Auchtermuchty		Lochmaben	Prestwick	
Pittenweem	Gourock		Turriff	———	
Rothes	———		Dalkeith	Bathgate	
Keith	Kingussie		Cupar	Renfrew	
Hawick	Darvel		Dunbar	Dumfries	
Aberfeldy	Fraserburgh			Troon	
Selkirk	Melrose			Inverurie	
Innerleithen	Kinross			Oban	
Tayport	Bo'ness			St Andrews	
Ballater	Edinburgh			Dornoch	
Newmilns	Newburgh			Kilmarnock	
Ladybank	Paisley			Ayr	
Dufftown	Dundee			Hamilton	
Coupar Angus	Crieff			Kilsyth	
Laurencekirk	Burntisland			North Berwick	
Huntly	Peebles			Girvan	
Crail	Kirkcaldy			Dunfermline	
Moffat	Markinch			Cockenzie and	
Lauder	Sanquhar			Port Seton	
Doune	Leven			Saltcoats	
Galston	Perth				
Stromness	Castle Douglas				
———	Port Glasgow				
Cromarty	Dumbarton				
	Coatbridge				
	Aberdeen				
	Newport				

appropriately termed stagnation, with the indices condensed into a range of about ten points. For another sub-group (Ladybank, Coupar Angus, Dufftown, Huntly, Ballater, Newmilns, Laurencekirk, Moffat, Crail and Lauder) the trend was similar to the overall pattern for the cluster, but for an increase in the 1890s and more exaggerated decennial changes. Individual aberrations such as the expansion of Stromness in the 1890s, Cromarty in the 1900s, and more modestly in Lauder and Moffat in the 1911–21 decade, though exceptional, were still broadly consistent with the profile of long-run decline which characterised this group of 44 places, a selection of which appear in Figures 2–4 (charts 28, 31, 42). The geographical locations and economic activities of these towns which were mostly concerned with woollens, fishing, and with market-town, secondary administrative and distributional functions provides some explanation for the long-term decline. Superseded by the proliferation of alternative fabrics, heavier capitalisation in the fishing industry in a restricted number of ports, and a greater concentration of retailing activity in the larger urban centres, they were increasingly by-passed by growth in neighbouring towns and cities.

The second cluster share a late nineteenth- and early twentieth-century expansionary phase, followed by a slight decline in the 1920s. Four variant clusters within this group can be differentiated within the second column of Table 4.

First, there was a sub-group (the Clyde resorts – Cove and Kilcreggan, Dunoon, Millport and Rothesay – and Elie) which enjoyed a short-run expansion concentrated around World War I which was sufficient to double or even treble numbers. The abrupt increase was matched by an equally abrupt decline, and with the exception of Cove, the resorts then went into a steady decline. Second, there was a group of Banffshire burghs (Aberlour, Buckie, Findochty and Portnockie) which peaked in 1911 and thereafter went into an uninterrupted decline, exaggerated in recent decades by the pull of oil-related economic development in Aberdeen and the Moray Firth. Buckie excepted, population levels in 1981 were below those of 1891. While the relative remoteness and insulation of the Banffshire burghs may have favoured urban expansion in the period before 1920, this proved a handicap thereafter. The rhythm was replicated in Greenock, though for different reasons. The third cluster within this group experienced a more exaggerated version of this 'Banffshire' profile. A pronounced Victorian and Edwardian expansion was curtailed in the 1920s, but where decline followed, as in Lochgelly, Cowdenbeath, Falkirk and Glasgow, it was not so severe that it wiped out earlier population growth, and in some cases

(Musselburgh, Buckhaven and Methil, Clydebank and Gourock) there was even a modest resumption of the upward trend. The final sub-group of twenty-four towns and cities in this cluster includes the three cities of Edinburgh, Aberdeen and Dundee, major urban centres such as Kirkcaldy, Perth and Paisley, some heavy industrial and engineering centres (Coatbridge, Burntisland, Leven, Port Glasgow and Dumbarton) and county and market towns (Melrose, Kinross, Crieff, Peebles and Castle Douglas). The common denominator for this cluster is the modest pre-1914 pattern of expansion, followed by a rather similar trajectory after 1921 until the 1950s and 1960s when the long-run steady expansion came to a halt in a downturn which varied slightly in timing but was for the most part apparent in the 1960s. Adaptation to technical change and an ability to develop complementarity in the economic base enabled these towns and cities to avoid reliance on single products and markets in periods of depression and thus to continue their gently expansionary course.

The defining characteristic of the third cluster in Table 4 is the pronounced post-1945 expansion such that population levels in 1981 were two to three times above those of 1931. The initial experience varied somewhat. For the first sub-group (Linlithgow, Lochgilphead, Tain and Stewarton) stagnation and even decline before 1931 was evident; in the next category (Dunblane, Kirkintilloch, Cumnoch and Milngavie) there was a general upward trend to 1931; except for Tillicoultry and Nairn, this rising trajectory was more decisive in the final sub-group. A cluster with considerable homogeneity in statistical terms, the geographical diversity suggests a range of explanatory influences: in central Scotland (Linlithgow, Tillicoultry, Alloa, Kirkintilloch, Milngavie, and Helensburgh, for example) more efficient and independent access to work in larger urban centres heightened the strategic importance of these locations and extended the geographical range of suburbanisation, a feature which also applied to Banchory; in Annan, Elgin and Nairn, the concentration of distribution networks and services such as hospitals and schools assisted the expansion; and in Stornoway, Invergordon, Armadale and Irvine, economic development policies stabilised and then expanded urban concentrations.

The single cluster which forms the fourth column of Table 4, beginning with Newton Stewart, generally lost population before 1931 and regained it subsequently with a net addition in most cases. For the most part this rhythm of urban contraction and expansion was confined to the smaller county and market towns outside the central belt. There are no urban locations in west-central Scotland represented in this category. This cluster of towns, which includes Kirkcudbright, Eyemouth, Jedburgh, Falkland,

Montrose, Dollar, Blairgowrie, Fortrose and Kirkwall, differs from the preceding group, headed by Linlithgow, in that there was more of a contraction before 1931 and less of an expansion afterwards. It differs from the first cluster, headed by Brechin, in that the spiral of urban contraction was both arrested and reversed. But in geographical terms, the borders, Perthshire and northern and north-eastern burghs are represented in all three columns (clusters 1, 3 and 4). Subtle, and often highly individual explanations are therefore required as to why a place falls within one cluster and not another. To take one geographically restricted grouping, the pronounced expansion of Kirriemuir in Strathmore during the 1890s was at odds with the considerable contraction of neighbouring Blairgowrie. The power of macro or national level influences was mediated by local economic and geographic factors. The rhythm of stagnation or decline followed by recovery is shown in charts 36 and 41.

The fifth cluster in Table 4, headed by Kintore in Aberdeenshire, enjoyed a measure of steady expansion which unified this grouping, and distinguished it from the other clusters. Only in fifteen per cent of observations was there a decline in the population indices of these thirty-nine towns, equivalent to less than one occasion per burgh between 1891 and 1981. Where there was a decline, it was almost always recorded in the 1920s. By 1981, the urban expansion of this grouping overall was sufficient generally to have doubled the populations recorded in 1891. The subgroups within this cluster differ in their pace of expansion: the quintet of Inverkeithing, Tranent, Grangemouth, Largs and Prestwick has an almost identical profile to the pattern described above, but started from a lower base with all the indices below 60 in 1891. Accordingly, the pre-1920 expansion was more pronounced than elsewhere in the cluster. In the lower reaches of the third sub-group, for example, in Dumfries, Kilmarnock, Ayr, Hamilton and Dunfermline, their higher initial levels of urbanisation meant that the pace of post-war expansion was more modest than for the cluster as a whole, the population indices for 1971 and 1981 being more in the 130s and 140s than the 180s which was the case for smaller places such as Carnoustie and Dingwall. One interesting regional and arguably typological variant was the abrupt decline of the Ayrshire seaside towns in the 1920s – Girvan, Saltcoats, Troon, Largs, and more modestly, Ardrossan, Ayr and Prestwick. This pattern, which also applied to St Andrews, Cockenzie and Port Seton, North Berwick, Carnoustie, and as noted earlier in the second cluster in relation to the Clyde resorts and Elie, indicates an abrupt interruption to the Scottish-based holiday industry. For some, recovery was never forthcoming, and for others, it was commuting, retirement, and an array of commercial activities in conjunction with their former resort functions which enabled them to resume their earlier expansionary course.

The distinctive feature of the final cluster of nine towns is dramatic expansion in the 1950s and 1960s, moderated only slightly in the 1970s. Though there was some small expansion before 1950 in what often were established burghs, the pace of change since has not been approached by other towns or cities in Scotland. In large measure this can be explained either by the commuting possibilities, for example, offered from Queensferry, Denny, Penicuik and Johnstone along the Edinburgh–Glasgow axis, extreme examples of a phenomenon observed elsewhere, and by deliberate economic development strategies designed to attract new industry and distribution activities. Where these coincided, as in Penicuik or Whitburn, then the pace of expansion was meteoric. Elsewhere where regional economic policy fostered growth around a particular node, as in Thurso and Fort William, this too offered spectacular urban growth, on a scale previously unknown, and which in the case of Fort William also coincided with leisure and tourism developments.

Locations with small populations are normally excluded from indices of urbanisation. By tracking expansion and contraction in a given set of places no allowance is made in most studies of urbanisation for those places which either through persistent expansion punctuate the upper echelons of the urban hierarchy, or because of their remoteness may still function as important urban nodes despite their modest size – a place with 500 population in Argyllshire may be equally significant as places of 50,000 in Lanarkshire. Overall, such locations initially might be considered 'minor', though some grew continuously and sufficiently to merit a place in the league table of major Scottish burghs.

The dynamism of this group of smaller places (see Table 1) provided a boost to the overall index of Scottish urbanisation in the twentieth century, even though the proportion of Scots living in such places remained relatively small. Predictably, the drama of the transformation was most pronounced in the New Towns. Cumbernauld and East Kilbride were in 1981 respectively forty and thirty times their 1931 size. Both Newton Mearns and Alness (Ross-shire), places with greater longevity, expanded tenfold during this fifty-year span, and Polmont, only twenty-third in its rate of expansion amongst the smaller burghs, still managed almost a fivefold increase on its 1931 levels of population. Altogether at least 144 smaller centres of Scottish population increased at rates of growth in excess of the average for the major towns and cities.[1] Just as the slowdown developed amongst the larger established towns and cities, so, inversely, the expansion in the minor urban centres can be dated to the inter-war years and more emphatically after World War II.[2] To a large extent this is the corollary to the pattern identified in the second cluster in Table 4, where the four cities and many of the major industrial concentrations experienced early twentieth-century expansion followed by a decline in absolute size.

Those smaller urban centres which did not enjoy a period of expansion between 1930 and 1980 were relatively few. Approximately 25 per cent of urban concentrations down to those around the 500 population mark declined. Newcastleton, Milnathort, and Port William were amongst those for whom population levels changed very little over the half century, but for New Deer, Ecclefechan, New Pitsligo, Kelty, Harthill, West Calder, Dalmellington, Strathmiglo and Kirkonnel there were 15–20 per cent fewer inhabitants in 1981 than in 1931. For Thornton, Carstairs, Coalburn, Tighnabruaich, Corssgates, Muirkirk, Portgordon and Walkerburn the decline was 25–33 per cent. While South Queensferry enjoyed a period of considerable growth (index = 418), across the Forth Road Bridge North Queensferry was in serious decline, plunging to an index of 68 in 1981.

Pronounced post-1945 expansion in smaller urban communities is a reflection of declining economic opportunities in older industrial centres, of relatively lower house prices which were not offset by the costs of commuting, and the broader employment opportunities for men and women in certain strategically chosen locations.

THE REDESIGNED TOWNSCAPE

The urbanising process in the twentieth century has produced fundamental shifts in the character and composition of Scottish urban life. Of these, spatial changes have been the most visible. Between 1919 and 1939 the style, form and amenities of Scottish housing changed almost beyond recognition. Working-class housing estates created throughout urban Scotland on the fringes of the built-up area were constructed using layouts, designs, and materials which were at variance with Scottish traditions of urban form. Predominantly compact, irregular and informal before 1914, working-class living arrangements were replaced by diffuse, low density housing in which common facilities were exceptional. The reference points of a Scottish system of social relations were thus dislocated. Domestic and family rhythms were redefined in a manner more abrupt than on English housing estates where the absence of conventional working-class support mechanisms – pawnbroker, pub, bookmaker, and meeting hall – were also felt acutely, but where at least the physical characteristics of housing represented less of a cultural jolt. Indeed, some of the first council housing in

Liverpool and Leicester was barely distinguishable from earlier private-enterprise terraced housing, and was designed deliberately to minimise opposition to municipal provision.[3]

The replacement of four- and five-storey tenement block life by two- and three-storey semi-detached housing represented a decisive shift in cultural norms for Scots. Even the bricks and tiles, some as in the Abercorn/Northfield estate in Edinburgh with their red and orange colours, introduced a housing style familiar to very few Scots, most of whom were more accustomed to stone and slate materials, mostly in dour, smoke-stained shades of grey, or a darkened reddish sandstone barely discernible beneath the soot of the industrial west of Scotland. For Scots, brick was 'merely a post-script' and not a traditional building material.[4]

The instrument for this transformation was the Treasury in London. Scottish Board of Health housing proposals after 1919 required the approval of London civil servants before financial subsidies were forthcoming. Since seventy per cent of all Scottish housebuilding between 1919 and 1941 was public housing, that is, initiated by municipalities (compared to only twenty-eight per cent in England and Wales),[5] the homogeneity of design, density, form, and colour produced a particularly monotonous visual effect in Scottish towns and cities. Indeed, symptomatic of the concern for the dreary, uniform physical appearance of Scottish housing was the fact that in 1934 a high-level delegation visited Berlin to see if greater variation might be introduced into the built environment. This is not to say that housing production in England and Wales was noted for its architectural diversity, but at least the ubiquitous semi-detached suburban house was produced by a number of private-enterprise builders, whereas each Scottish municipality was tied to just a handful of designs that met with Treasury approval. Notwithstanding recent reassessments[6] of the responsiveness of Scottish municipal building departments in the innovative use of new materials and methods, for example, steel- and wooden-framed structures, clinker and concrete materials, steel window frames, technological developments such as cement and plaster guns, and systematised shutter methods of construction using unskilled building labour, the design and layout of individual houses and overall projects owed much to a conception of housing largely determined by English values, experience and aesthetics.

The dominant housing ideology was based upon garden-city principles and influenced by English middle-class suburban values. Curved perspectives and cul-de-sacs, open spaces and low building densities, broken building lines, rustic aspects, and individual garden plots were the crucial characteristics of garden-suburb design.[7] Scottish experience of these before

indices
(1931=100)

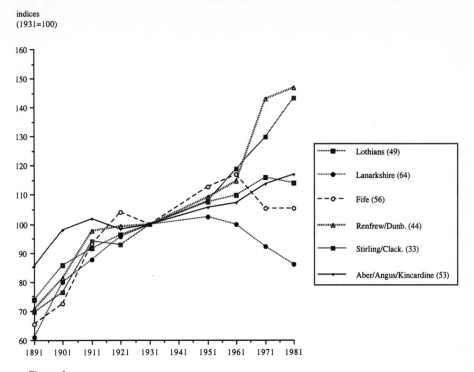

▪·······	Lothians (49)
•·······	Lanarkshire (64)
–○–	Fife (56)
▲·······	Renfrew/Dunb. (44)
▪——	Stirling/Clack. (33)
◆——	Aber/Angus/Kincardine (53)

Figure 2a

Urbanisation in Scotland 1891-1981: the Lothians, Fife, Central and West of Scotland

indices .
(1931=100)

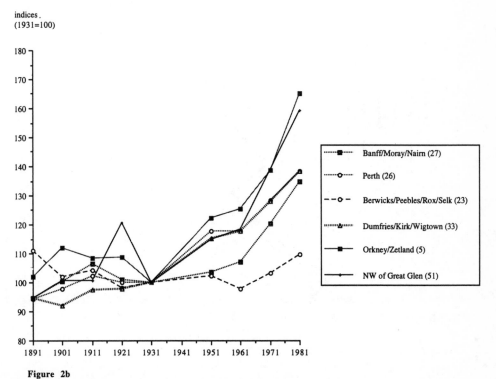

▪·······	Banff/Moray/Nairn (27)
○·······	Perth (26)
–○–	Berwicks/Peebles/Rox/Selk (23)
▲·······	Dumfries/Kirk/Wigtown (33)
▪——	Orkney/Zetland (5)
◆——	NW of Great Glen (51)

Figure 2b

Urbanisation in Scotland 1891-1981: Northern, Southern and North-Western Counties

indices
(1931=100)

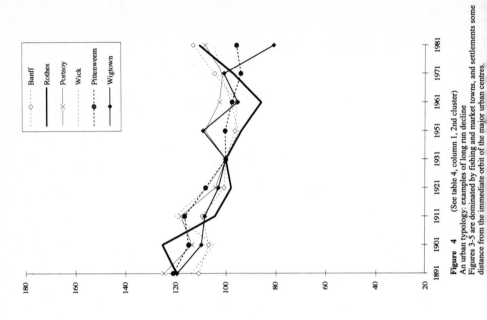

Figure 4 (See table 4, column 1, 2nd cluster)
An urban typology: examples of long run decline
Figures 3-5 are dominated by fishing and market towns, and settlements some
distance from the immediate orbit of the major urban centres.

indices
(1931=100)

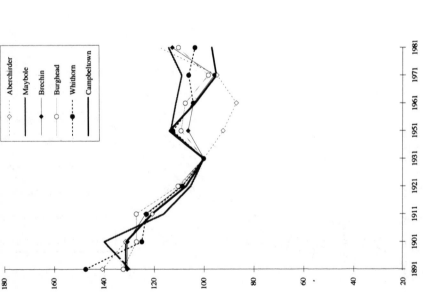

Figure 3 (See table 4, column 1, 1st cluster)
An urban typology: examples of pronounced long run decline
Figures 3-5 illustrate differing degrees of severity in long run decline.

indices
(1931=100)

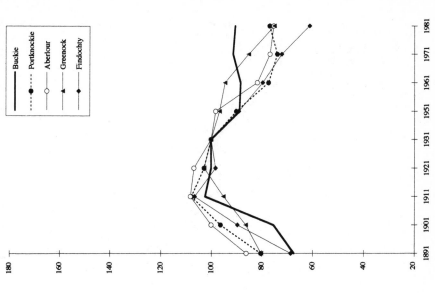

Figure 6 (See table 4, column 2, 2nd cluster)
An urban typology: early twentieth century expansion and continuous post-
1920s decline

indices
(1931=100)

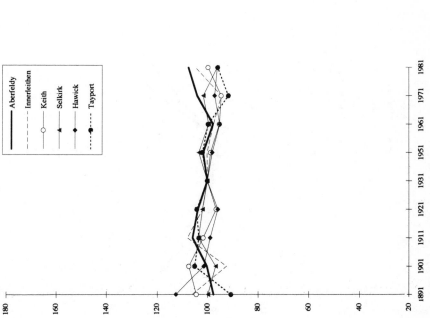

Figure 5 (See table 4, column 1, 2nd cluster)
An urban typology: examples of stagnation and moderated long run decline
Figures 3–5 are dominated by fishing and market towns, and settlements some
distance from the immediate orbit of the major urban centres.

indices
(1931=100)

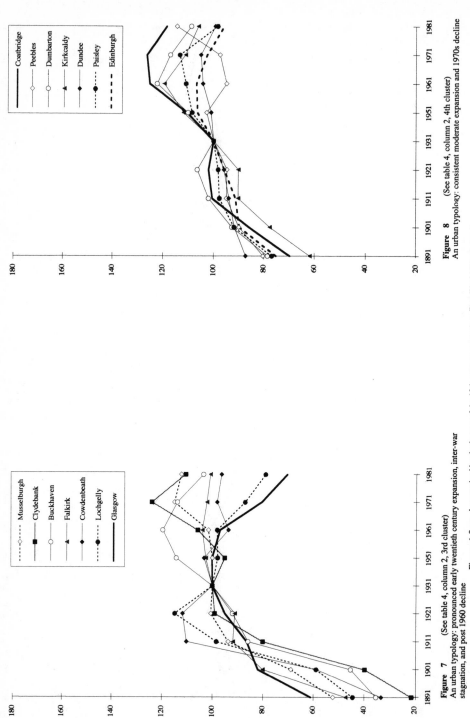

Figure 7 (See table 4, column 2, 3rd cluster)
An urban typology: pronounced early twentieth century expansion, inter-war stagnation, and post 1960 decline

Figure 8 (See table 4, column 2, 4th cluster)
An urban typology: consistent moderate expansion and 1970s decline

Figures 6-8 are characterised by the legacy of the 19th century expansion. Post World War I experiences differed appreciably, with some burghs in long term population decline, others offsetting the Victorian legacy.

indices
(1931=100)

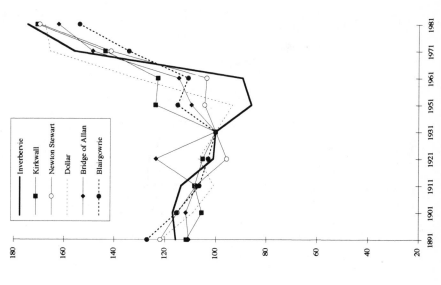

Figure 10 (See table 4, column 4, 1st cluster)
An urban typology: pre 1945 decline and pronounced post 1945 expansion
Figures 10 and 11 illustrate similarities with figures 3–5 in their long-run pre-
1939 stagnation and decline, but an ability to offset this after World War II.

indices
(1931=100)

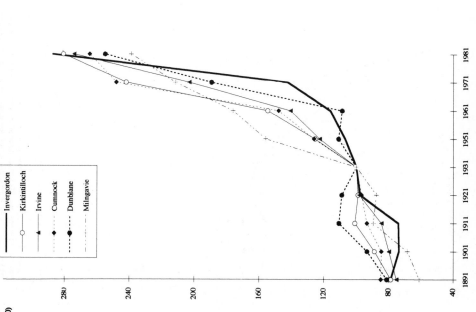

Figure 9 (See table 4, column 3, 1st and 2nd clusters)
An urban typology: pronounced post 1945 expansion
Long run expansion interrupted during the inter-war years and resumed
emphatically after World War II.

indices
(1931=100)

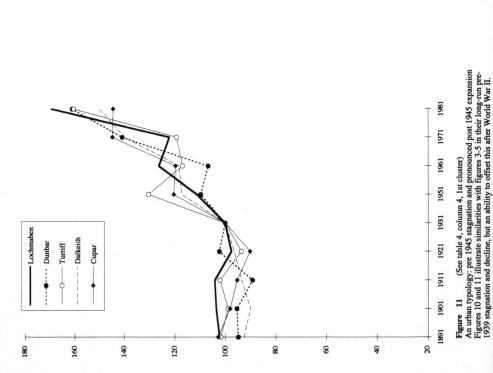

Figure 11 (See table 4, column 4, 1st cluster)
An urban typology: pre 1945 stagnation and pronounced post 1945 expansion
Figures 10 and 11 illustrate similarities with figures 3-5 in their long-run pre-
1939 stagnation and decline, but an ability to offset this after World War II.

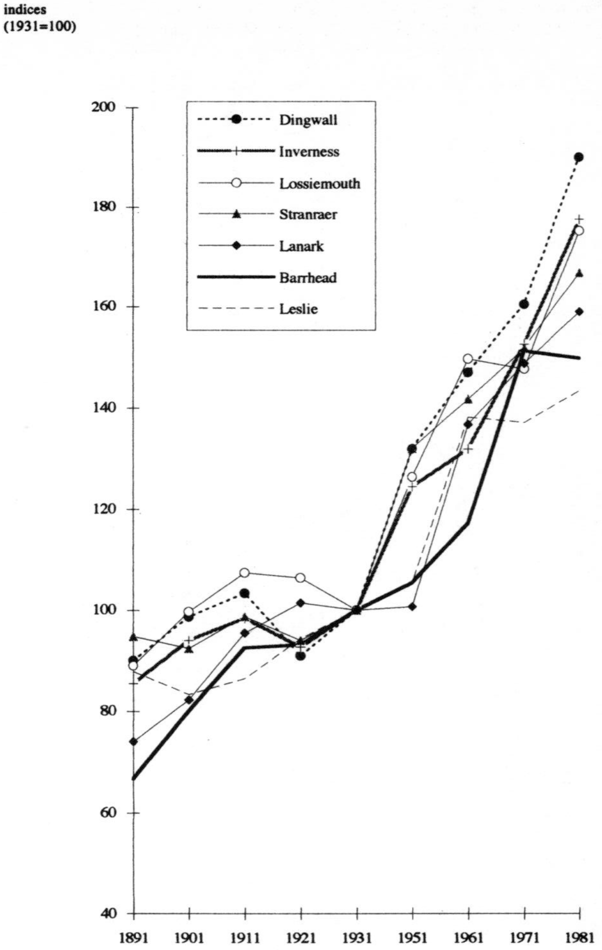

indices
(1931=100)

Figure 12 (See table 4, column 5, 1st cluster)
An urban typology: twentieth century expansion
Figures 12 and 13 show fairly consistent and pronounced gains during the
20th century, moderated only slightly in the inter-war years.

indices
(1931=100)

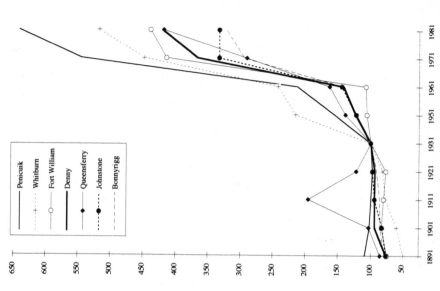

Figure 14 (See table 4, column 6, 1st cluster)
An urban typology: dramatic post 1960s expansion
Modest urban growth followed by dramatic post 1950s expansion based on commuting, suburbanisation and an element of tourist led growth.

indices
(1931=100)

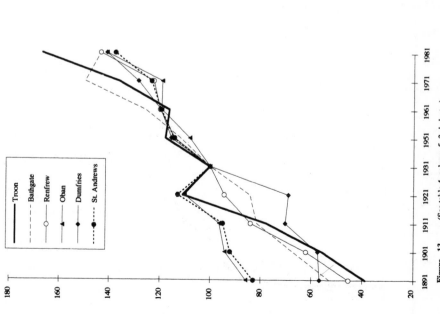

Figure 13 (See table 4, column 5, 3rd cluster)
An urban typology: successive twentieth century expansion
Figures 12 and 13 show fairly consistent and pronounced gains during the 20th century, moderated only slightly in the inter-war years.

indices
(1931=100)

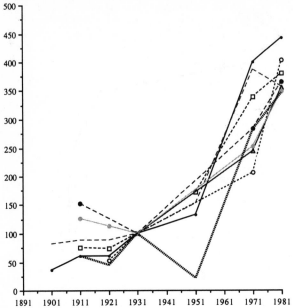

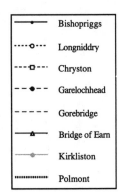

—•—	Bishopriggs
----o----	Longniddry
----□----	Chryston
--●--	Garelochhead
----	Gorebridge
—△—	Bridge of Earn
—•—	Kirkliston
••••••••	Polmont

Figure 15a

The Expansion of Smaller Urban Centres 1901-81

indices
(1931=100)

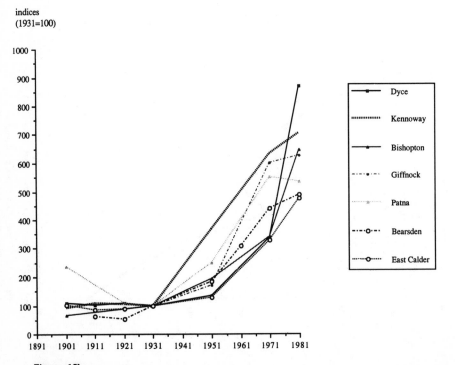

—■—	Dyce
••••••••	Kennoway
—■—	Bishopton
—•—•—	Giffnock
•••••••	Patna
---o---	Bearsden
••••o•••	East Calder

Figure 15b

Meteoric Expansion of Smaller Urban Centres 1901-1981

World War I had been limited to two projects: forty houses built by the Glasgow Garden Suburb Tenants Ltd at Canniesburn and fifty-eight houses built by the Scottish Garden Suburb Tenants Ltd at Gourock and Greenock. Like the project to house torpedo workers at Greenock, two government-inspired wartime schemes at Gretna and Rosyth were developed to lure key munitions and naval shipbuilding workers to strategic plants.[8] However limited, these projects were overseen by the Local Government Board for Scotland, which in accepting garden suburb principles, defined the basic assumptions concerning how people should be housed after the war.[9] Yet Hull had its Garden Suburb, Liverpool had Wavertree and Thingwall, and London had Hampstead and Ruislip. These, together with garden-suburb and public-utility schemes in fifty-eight towns and cities south of the border, familiarised large numbers of English and Welsh residents with garden-city principles before 1914.[10] Independently of ideological pressures, private builders in England had themselves turned to garden-village styles in an effort after 1904 to counteract the cyclical downswing in house-building by adding interest and stimulating demand for their schemes.[11] By 1918, 'the garden suburb reigned supreme' and the housing debate had momentarily resolved itself; the way was set for the creation of 'one of the standard visual symbols of twentieth-century Britain – the low-density council-housing estate.[12] This visual reference point was an entirely foreign one to Scottish residents. It was a form of English cultural imperialism.

Between the wars, the colonisation of Scottish burghs by a cottage and villa-flat style of housing provision was common. Prior to 1914, such cottages and self-contained villa flats, though not unknown, were sufficiently unusual to deserve special mention when they were built.[13] Under the terms of the earliest subsidies (the legislation of 1919 and 1923), almost half of Glasgow's new housing stock was of cottages, and together with flatted villas, 85 per cent of housing under the 1919 act and 75 per cent under the 1923 act was either in cottages or in flatted villas.[14] Glasgow's housing scheme Mosspark, clearly influenced by garden-city principles, was developed on a contoured site, but even under greater financial stringency later projects, such as those at Hamiltonhill and Possilpark, also attempted to retain the elements of garden-suburb layouts. While the flatted tradition was well known to Scots, the design and physical form in which it was provided represented a radical departure. Though the 1924 act reversed the balance between cottages (24 per cent) and villa flats (59 per cent), a substantial volume of new Scottish housebuilding was in a physical form which represented a significant departure from the pre-1914 townscape. Moreover, the location of such housing estates on the fringes of the city disturbed the essentially compact character of the Scottish Victorian city, another feature which distinguished the Scottish urban experience from that of English boroughs.

Throughout Scotland, plans put before the Board of Health between 1919 and the late 1920s relied heavily on a combination of cottages and two-storey flatted villas. Visually, and in relation to their lay-out, these were unlike the four-storey tenement blocks which had dominated late nineteenth-century Scottish housing. In respect of the use of traditional materials, in the earliest Edinburgh housing planned under the subsidy arrangements, only 21 per cent used traditional stone, and Glasgow Corporation was so imaginative in the encouragement of cement, concrete, clinker and other non-traditional materials, that over 20 per cent of the 16,000 houses built under the 1919, 1923, and 1924 acts used these materials.[15]

The physical and visual effect of the financial subsidies provided through the Treasury in London was to produce a cross-border convergence in the style of public-sector housing. This was not surprising. The garden-suburb principles upon which the influential Tudor Walters Report was founded were embraced by the Scottish representative on the committee, J. Walker Smith, who was the Chief Engineer at the Scottish Local Government Board, and Controller of Housing and Town Planning. Indeed, between 1910 and 1917, the Scottish Local Government Board had 'a most creditable track record, having built or otherwise commissioned over 3,000 houses in Scotland, nearly all of them "cottages" (as distinct from tenements) and all at "garden city" densities'.[16] Wilson produced detached cottage and semi-detached, double-flatted designs which owed a great deal to utopian experiments in England; and, as has been noted, the interiors bore a 'striking resemblance' to cottages built for Rowntree's workers at Earswick (York).[17] Where Scottish women had an input into official enquiries into housing and town planning, the terms of reference were again pre-determined by official thinking, and women's deliberations were often marginalised to a consideration of the details of cupboards, cooking arrangements and bath sizes, rather than a more fundamental consideration of issues associated with financial constraints and overall design features.[18]

This centralisation of decision-making was therefore a critical factor in harmonising the type of housing provision after World War I. As the Glasgow City Engineer noted in 1919, the new financial subsidy 'gives the Local Government Board (in London) absolute autocratic powers', and he decried the absence of 'freedom of action given to a local authority'.[19] It was the Scottish Office, itself 'an arm of Westminster-based government',[20] the (English) Local Government Board, and the Treasury particularly which controlled the purse strings and sanctioned the design and layout of housing proposals. The extent and nature of local municipal intervention in housebuilding before 1914 had generated intense political debate, but there had been no doubt that the agenda for that debate was locally determined. Arguably, after 1919 it was central government which prevented the local authority from undertaking its housing task, and of fulfilling electoral promises and voters' aspirations. Though Daunton concludes that 'regional diversity was not apparent in the council houses built between the wars',[21] the form it took owed more to English than to Scottish traditions of housing.

As floor plans indicate, internal space became more specifically delineated. Amenities became exclusive, rather than shared. Sleeping, bathing and eating areas were clearly defined, and amenities internalised – private rather than public. For many residents in these 'general needs' cottages and flatted villas of the 1920s, their own front door and small individual garden plots were novel departures. Internally, though the flatted villas possessed something of the Victorian tenement flat layout, being on a single level and with rooms accessed from the hall, again the interiors offered sinks, bathroom and toilet combined, kitchen, a coal bunker, and hot-water supplies. These advances in 1920s municipal housing provision were undeniable, as was the fact that for numerous families the patterns of daily life were redefined in a manner more akin to that to which the English working classes had been accustomed for at least fifty years.

The significance of the early council-housing projects was not that they immediately redefined daily living styles for large sections of the working class. Initially, they were occupied, in fact, mainly by non-manual classes – 80 per cent of the first 700 post-war Edinburgh council-house tenants were in this occupational category.[22] As in English boroughs where much the same social composition existed in early council housing, management problems, for example concerning rent arrears, noise and maintenance, were minimal. The significance of the inter-war housing developments was that the cottage and flatted villa insinuated itself into the acceptable fabric of post-war Scottish society. A discontinuity had been introduced into the tenemental tradition.[23]

Despite the transition in the external appearance of Scottish housing between 1920 and 1940, the tradition of overcrowding continued.[24] This was because of 'the deplorable results of persistence in the policy of building undersized houses', and because new houses were already on the margin of overcrowding when first let.[25] In Scotland, 64 per cent of all

TABLE 5
English–Scottish Contrasts in the Size of New Housebuilding 1919–39

Local Authority	Dwellings of 4 rooms and more (%)	Dwellings of 5 rooms and more (%)	Parlour type dwellings (% with 2 living-rooms)
Scottish burghs			
Aberdeen	27	2	–
Dundee	15	2	–
Edinburgh	13	2	–
Glasgow	28	4	1
English boroughs			
Birmingham	94	23	23
Manchester	83	21	21
Leeds	66	20	11
Liverpool	89	35	33

Source: Scottish Housing Advisory Committee, *Planning Our New Homes* (HMSO, Edinburgh, 1944), p. 18.

inter-war council housing was of three or less rooms, and 26 per cent accordingly, of four or more rooms; in England the ratios were almost the reverse, with 20 per cent of all council housing of three or less rooms, and 80 per cent of four or more rooms (see Table 5).

The Census of 1931 showed that overcrowding in Scotland was six times more acute than overcrowding in England and Wales, and another official report observed that

> overcrowding in houses built by local authorities in Scotland was found in 1935 to be higher than overcrowding throughout the country as a whole and over four and a half times as great proportionately as overcrowding in houses built by local authorities in England and Wales.[26]

Notwithstanding the adoption of English garden suburb styles and densities and the transformation of the Scottish townscape which resulted from Ministry-approved designs, Scottish housing interiors remained cramped. There was a degree of continuity in this regard, even though new amenities introduced electricity and hot and cold running water, and exteriors were re-designed to incorporate garden suburb principles.

During the 1920s, therefore, at a critical phase in defining a new urban form in Scottish towns and cities, the path chosen relied heavily upon an English housing tradition. There is no evidence to show that serious consideration was given to the reproduction of an up-dated and modernised form of the tenement with which the Scottish working, lower middle and

middle classes were familiar. Yet the continental European housing tradition with which Scotland had much in common continued to emphasise
high-rise block structures after 1920.

'BUNGALOW BELTS': A FOREIGN INVASION?

While English cultural values were invading the provision of public housing after World War I, a second front opened up in the private sector.
The Saltire Society, which had assumed the cultural mantle of a Scottish
nationalist revival, lamented the proliferation of bungalows, which were
viewed as an insidious form of English invasion. Even south of the border
powerful attacks were mounted from the mid-1920s on this type of housing from professional architectural and planning associations through the
national press, supported by prominent landowners and, in the 1930s, from
the Council for the Protection of Rural England. They objected vociferously to the proliferation of retirement, seaside and weekend bungalow
homes, as well as to the extension of bungalows to English cities. The use
in Britain of the pejorative term 'bungaloid' dates from 1927.[27]

English bungalow development was vigorous immediately after the war[28]
but it took almost ten years to reach Scottish burghs in substantial numbers.[29] From 1929, building-society advances to owner occupiers in Edinburgh for the purchase of tenement flats, which had been buoyant in the
1920s, declined appreciably and though this was initially in part due to
the enveloping economic depression, it was also due to the emergence of
the large number of suburban bungalows for sale, which punctured lower
middle-class demand for tenement flats built before 1914.[30]

Though the economic and social background to private building development was often common to English and Scottish towns and cities – suburbanisation, demographic trends, extended bus and tram routes, a search
for alternative housing forms and materials in the light of post-war shortages – the physical and visual impact was distinctively different. Semi-
detached villas, often with pseudo-Tudor beams, were the common form
of private housing in England and Wales. This housing type was virtually
absent in Scottish burghs during the period 1919–39. Instead, swathes of
private bungalow development dominated the inter-war Scottish suburban
expansion, and although finely graduated internally and externally in terms
of social class, the initial impression was of a homogeneous housing form.

Bungalows were concentrated in areas throughout Edinburgh – Col-
liesdene, Marionville, Blackhall, Craigleith, Craiglockhart, Greenhill,
Carrickknowe, Kingsknowe, Corstorphine; these areas were colonised by
single-storey, three- and four-bedroom houses on individual plots. Other

Scottish burghs, the larger cities of Glasgow, Aberdeen and Dundee and the smaller towns too, were also subject to a rash of bungalow building, on a scale and density never previously (or subsequently) experienced, and in concentrations rarely found in English boroughs.[31]

Allegedly, bungalows possessed three principal advantages over conventional housing forms: no specialised plant; a single buyer; and complete control over the plot.[32] Yet foundations and roofing costs, covering a greater area as they did, were higher proportionately than in a semi-detached or terraced house,[33] and in Scotland land costs were historically appreciably higher than in England, as the rent-control policy introduced in 1915 acknowledged explicitly. If at all, the economics of bungalow-building pointed to English rather than Scottish locations. Nor were Scottish rural traditions of cottage-style dwellings noticeably more entrenched than in Northumberland, or indeed other English counties. Again, geographical preferences seem to indicate no decisive reasons for such Scottish concentrations of bungalows. With their crescents, squares, and varied vistas, 'bungalow belts' assumed some of the garden suburb characteristics which had been widespread in English boroughs before 1914.

But the rapidity with which this novel form of housing was adopted in Scotland could not have been anticipated. Arguably, the bungalow offered a familiar domestic form – rooms accessed from a central hall-way – and did so in a horizontal rather than vertical setting. In this respect, though a radical departure from earlier organisational features of Scottish tenement housing, there were certain features which were more akin to tenement flats of the middle classes than the terraced housing of the English. In Edinburgh and Glasgow, where owner occupier levels were lower in 1914 than in English boroughs, builders may have recognised a latent middle-class demand for property ownership which had been thwarted for much longer than in some parts of the kingdom where the building industry had been more buoyant than in Scotland in the decade before 1914.[34]

The proliferation of the bungalow in Scottish towns and cities also co-incided with a degree of disenchantment with the tenement flat amongst tenants. In 1943, a survey noted that 25 per cent of housewives preferred to continue living in a tenement flat, but of those who did express an interest in moving, 39 per cent identified bungalows as their preferred housing type.[35] Amongst housewives unwilling to move, the highest proportion (66 per cent) was already housed in bungalows, and only 21 per cent in tenement flats. The Wartime Report noted that 'The preference for the single storey self-contained house (bungalow) is related to the housewives' experience of the tenement of [sic] flatted house and life in a congested neighbourhood'.[36] The consumer preference for private ownership of bungalows was thus formed in the inter-war years, and did much to make the fortunes of Scottish builders such as Ford and Torrie, and Mactaggart and Mickel, and improved the Scottish prospects of national firms such as Barratts and Wimpey after World War II.

Thus in the years between the wars, the bungalow, which had been a rarity in Scottish burghs before 1914, assumed a dominance in the domestic psyche of Scots. Though there were North American and Asian origins, and English precedents, by the early 1920s bungalows had insinuated themselves into a Scottish townscape which had formerly been largely unfamiliar with the style. Equally significant, bungalow developments accelerated the spatial segregation of Scottish towns and cities, a process which the nineteenth-century tenemental tradition had to some extent contained. More than ever before, the Scottish middle classes were able to distance themselves from the city, spatially and emotionally, as the indices of urbanisation in the major towns and cities show. Council housing, too, was clearly differentiated in class terms, with the early schemes associated with a higher social class, and subsequent clearance and de-crowding programmes focused more towards the unskilled and socially disadvantaged. Thus housing developments allied with changing 'bus transport and car ownership in the inter-war years formalised social fissures within Scottish society.

THE RECONSTRUCTION OF THE SCOTTISH URBAN LANDSCAPE POST-1945

After World War II, as elsewhere in the United Kingdom, Scottish municipalities were obliged to draw up urban redevelopment plans: comprehensive reviews of land use and projected developments. These provided useful summaries of the status quo, and indications of how an increasingly powerful town planning profession conceived future urban development. The underlying assumption of these municipal planning blueprints was their own autonomy.

Wartime bombing in west-central Scotland together with the absence of housing repair and maintenance, and the continued decline of private rented accommodation due both to the problems associated with factoring and continuing rent-control policies, prompted a search for urgent housing solutions after 1945. Labour and materials shortages inclined planners to centrally co-ordinated housing designs, often using non-traditional and prefabricated materials. This approach was reinforced by restrictive building licensing policies and financial subsidies deployed by the Under-Secretary of State, George Buchanan.

More importantly, perhaps, the autonomy of Glasgow Corporation and its elected officials' responsibility to ensure the decent housing of its citizens was challenged directly. The assault on the fiscal base and thus on the political leverage of Glasgow by reducing the power and autonomy of the Housing Department was launched through the Clyde Valley Regional Plan, published in 1946. Limitations to the power and size of Glasgow were achieved by reducing the population of the city centre, but instead of distributing this around the peripheral suburban land identified earlier for the purpose by the Glasgow City Engineer and later by the Housing Director, a green belt constricted the urban expansion of Glasgow. The Clyde Valley Plan explicitly identified re-housing as feasible only out-side the city boundaries. Seven miles from the city centre, the East Kilbride Development Corporation (founded 1947) meant large-scale housing provision was possible on open-field sites.[37] The displaced population was thus redistributed throughout the region, and beyond. Strategic planning decisions at a regional level were used to neuter the civic planning func-tions historically discharged by the municipality. Private housebuilding 'failures' between 1919 and 1939 were used to justify ceding significant future housebuilding responsibilities to New Town Development Corpor-ations (Cumbernauld was commissioned in 1956) and the Scottish Office blocked land allocations, for example at Castlemilk, to limit housing development options within Glasgow itself.[38] Though the Scottish Office relented somewhat over green-belt sites, the shortage of land for housing not surprisingly inclined the Corporation to a high-density housing strategy, abandoning cottages and flats and the principles enshrined in the regional plan for three- and four-storey tenements (Pollok/Priesthill, 9,000 dwellings; Castlemilk, 8,500; Drumchapel, 7,500; and the Easterhouse area, 10,000) in something approaching a repeat of the nineteenth-century expansion on the margins of the city.

Conflicting approaches to inner-city redevelopment were significant not just for Glasgow and the Strathclyde area, but for Scotland as a whole. The diametrically opposed planning philosophies – municipal autonomy con-trasted with regional planning – had implications for the development of nearby communities, and the victory in the 1940s and 1950s of regional planning and overspill policies meant that many small towns and even villages were quite quickly submerged by an influx of 'newcomers' whose accents and customs were different. Schools, health and other services were often insufficient to adjust in the short term to such influxes.

To state that the course of post-war urban development in Scotland was determined by the outcome of the contest between municipal autonomy versus centralisation would be an oversimplification, but it did produce an underlying dynamic to subsequent policy phases in Glasgow and beyond. Thus, as a reaction to the ascendant regional planning approach, Glasgow Housing Department built high-density low-rise dwellings in the 1950s, and then recaptured the initiative after 1957 by switching to high-density multi-storey tower blocks in the 1960s, built haphazardly on any available site. Municipal power was reasserted. The construction of twenty-storey flats at Royston in eight months during 1960 convinced the Housing Committee that they could retain control over housing provision for Glaswegians by means of an intensive programme of high-rise housebuilding within the city boundaries. Thereafter, a concentrated burst of 1960s multi-storey housebuilding, unrivalled in any other British city, meant that 75 per cent of all local-authority completions were in such high-rise flats. Red Road, Balornock (1962), Springburn (1963) and Pollokshaws (1965) passed into local and sometimes national folk-lore as the high-rise council housing phase held sway in Glasgow. Significantly for municipalities elsewhere, technical issues were resolved, and the Glasgow example was copied in other Scottish cities.[39] The quick technological fix which high-rise flats presented, however, was undertaken without much attention to the social context of the buildings constructed.[40]

The rhythm of council housebuilding was replicated in many other urban centres, large and small, throughout Scotland. These trends were reinforced by the Scottish Special Housing Association (SSHA), a quango active in some sixty different locations and the second largest landlord in Scotland, with almost 100,000 dwellings at its zenith.[41] The SSHA was involved in a variety of housing strategies – to supplement general housebuilding programmes, to support economic development, to complement overspill housing, to accommodate the special needs of the elderly and infirm, and in the 1980s, to repair and refurbish inner-city properties.[42] Varied responsibilities, therefore, enabled the SSHA to develop an important role in Scottish housing after 1945.

The durability of the SSHA can be attributed to astute perceptions of changing housing needs and the identification of successive housing initiatives, to innovative technical developments and the expansion of professional services connected with housing, and to access to policy formulation and implementation at the level of the Scottish Office. To a certain extent this last factor also made the SSHA an agent of the Scottish Office in the attempt to implement the housing policy of a central government often at political odds with Labour councils in Scottish burghs. Nor has the SSHA been neutral in the ongoing tension between the Scottish Office in Edinburgh and Glasgow Corporation. For long anxious about the political autonomy of Glasgow, the Scottish Office has used various strategies to restrain the Glasgow power base in Scotland, ranging from the reorganisation of local government and the countervailing power of Strathclyde region, to overspill policies, and to the impact on council revenues of rental levels and housing standards influenced by SSHA activities. To some extent, therefore, the role of the SSHA as a political agent and in its own evolving role has meant that the character of urban development in Scotland has been affected.

The dominance of the public sector throughout urban Scotland is well known. In some of the specific areas mentioned above, as much as 98 per cent of the housing stock was owned by Glasgow Housing Department. In 50 local authorities throughout Scotland, council housing in 1981 represented at least 70 per cent of the total housing stock. In Coatbridge, Bellshill, Livingston, Irvine, Clydebank, Motherwell and Wishaw more than 80 per cent of households lived in properties rented from the local authority. The private landlord, responsible in 1900 for about 90 per cent of all dwellings, owned no more than 6 per cent in 1990, and so the customary experience of housing management has for Scottish tenants changed from the private factor to a bureaucratic and centralised administrative structure in local council offices. This decline of landlordism was to a considerable extent a direct, though not a linear, consequence of the expansion of the public sector, and since 1945 – not from 1979–80 with the Conservative government's encouragement to tenants to buy their own council homes and favourable mortgage finance arrangements – reflects the steady growth of owner occupancy which had taken a firm root in the inter-war years.

Criticisms of Scottish housing have proved remarkably consistent throughout the twentieth century: the destruction of neighbourhoods and resultant social havoc in communities; the inhumanity of council housing as represented by its scale, height and monotony of design and colour; the insensitivity of housing management; the social dereliction caused by the absence of amenities and leisure facilities; the destabilisation of local economies. Overcrowding has remained a consistent source of criticism. In addition, the complexity of bureaucracy had an intimidating effect upon tenants; the tension between central government objectives in Whitehall, those in the Scottish Office in Edinburgh, and the concerns of local councils created confusion, delay, frustration, and diffused the political will.[43]

The ethos of housing policy was for long governed by the notion that quantitative provision was itself sufficient; little importance was attached to participation by prospective tenants. Even when tenants were vociferous it served only to amend the particular form in which policy was imposed from above, and gave no great scope for participation in the initial decision-making process. It was in part as a reaction to such criticisms that recent grassroots involvement, tenants' associations, smaller council housing management units, diverse tenure, and scope and responsibility for local initiatives were moulded together to form a more intimate, responsive approach to housing provision. Such initiatives were derived from the experience and appraisal of long-term housing strategies; they were not an overnight ideological shift.

CONCLUSION

Civic consciousness has for long been highly developed in Scottish burghs. From early modern times 'Nichtbourheid Buiks' recorded the rights and responsibilities of property owners and acknowledged mutual interests, later enforced through the Dean of Guild Courts.[44] The Common Good fund in Aberdeen and Edinburgh, as elsewhere, was used to develop poli-cies which had a collective benefit – the purchase of land for parks, or the acquisition of feus to enable streets to be formed or access improved.[45] In the nineteenth century, the City Improvement Trust in Glasgow, and similar bodies set up in Edinburgh, Dundee, Leith, Greenock and else-where in the 1860s and early 1870s, anticipated similar projects in English boroughs, and recognised that the imbalance between public benefit and private costs required the intervention of the municipal authority.[46] Crucially, the concept of civic responsibility was also different in Scottish law where cross-subsidisation between municipal activities, for example between the gasworks and tramway operations, was not permitted, unlike English law where operational profits could be used to reduce local tax burdens on property owners.[47] Though the label of municipal socialism was in no small measure associated with the West of Scotland before 1914, a similar philosophical approach underpinned most civic thinking through-out urbanising Scotland. The precepts of Scottish urban administration, therefore, explicitly acknowledged mutuality.

Scottish towns and cities were the catalysts for an emerging nineteenth-century concept of citizenship in which prominent individuals in Scottish burghs – men as different as Thomas Chalmers, Patrick Geddes, and also Medical Officers such as J.B. Russell and A.K. Chalmers in Glasgow, and Henry Littlejohn in Edinburgh – acknowledged the inter-connections between social problems and the physical condition and circumstances of the population. They recognised the degenerative possibilities of Darwinian evolution. In England in the late nineteenth and early twentieth centuries, T.H. Green and L.T. Hobhouse argued that concern for the common good was a measure of citizenship; Scottish burgh officials, however, had already moved in this direction. Building on a concept of the common good, volunteers, philanthropists and the city fathers in Scotland shared a vision of a social integration as a pre-condition for a civilised society. It was this vision which guided civic social policy before 1920, with slum-clearance programmes, for example, reinforced necessarily by moral rearmament. The Rent Strike of 1915 'was based upon the moral economy of the late nineteenth century',[48] where mutuality and the effects of the actions of one interest group upon another were explicitly recognised. Unfairness, unreasonableness, were resisted. It was a matter of practical and philosophical engagement.

The scale and persistence of urban poverty and deprivation during the inter-war years combined with an increasing reliance upon the state to transform the expectations of citizens themselves.[49] Not infrequently, as with 'Homes for Heroes' and other propagandist utterances, the state was itself directly responsible for raising expectations, possibly to legitimise its own interventionist role. Volunteers and philanthropists were ousted by public authorities. This was specifically the case in housing and planning, where local authorities worked increasingly through planning offices, and after 1945 as part of a national network, were increasingly isolated from residents. The former insistence of Victorians that social and spatial considerations – the local context – should be taken together in the reconstruction of the urban environment was submerged in narrow technical solutions to urban problems: 'the more power the planners got from a constant stream of legislation, the more their work was divorced from direct two-way contact with ordinary citizens'.[50] Rationalism, functionalism and an unshakeable belief in macro-level policy making enhanced after 1945 by Keynesian economic management and Labour Party commitment to equal entitlements for citizens; this meant that local and individual solutions were relegated to obscurity. Civic autonomy was increasingly contested because of public expenditure considerations, standardised and financed as this was from London. Council-housing developments between the wars were a case in point, and since 1945, regional planning has by definition and by intent removed key strategic decisions from the municipalities. To contain the power and political influence of Glasgow Corporation, and to advance the leverage of the Scottish Office, the creation of regional authorities throughout Scotland has also set tensions between Grampian and Aberdeen, Lothian and Edinburgh, the Borders Region and the border burghs.

The insinuation of a further tier of administration has distanced residents from elected representatives. What distinguished nineteenth-century civic development was the close identification of benefactors and volunteers with a particular place. Endowments, often of a tangible nature – statues, fountains, park benches, clocks, memorials, and contributions to the up-keep of institutions – were concerned frequently with the beautification of the environment as an antidote to the corrosive moral effects of urbanisation. Though the quality of the moral environment was an issue which the municipality itself embraced in the nineteenth century as libraries, museums and galleries were built, the pace and character with which the cultural agenda was developed depended largely upon the vision and political will of local individuals. This flexible, organic development of nineteenth-century Scottish towns and cities, sensitive as it was to local priorities and resources, preserved the relationship between citizens as both residents and as instruments of urban change. In the twentieth century, this has been replaced by a pace and scale of urban change amounting to wholesale redevelopment that is beyond the comprehension of willing local residents who have thus been denied an input. Appeals and enquiries have provided a platform for local inhabitants, though often only in high-profile planning developments. Indeed, twentieth-century urban change has been neither partial nor incremental, and thus local individuals, with their communities and neighbourhoods destroyed or substantially altered by grandiose developments, have had no stake in the outcome, in stark contrast to the nineteenth century, and accordingly have lost interest in shaping a new urban environment.

This century, detaching residents from the planning processes and by distancing them from decisions affecting property and communities, the importance of public service has been downgraded. In ceding the responsibility for providing local amenities and services to centralised authorities where audits, quality control and administrative efficiency are important considerations, the danger is that policy and local inhabitants' interest lose touch with one another, and the outcome is unacceptable. In no small measure, as indicated above, this was the case with council housing between the wars, and with high-density and multi-storey projects in the west of Scotland after 1960. As has been observed,

> urban equilibrium was achieved in the past through a long process
> of trial and error … where a composite urban environment is

emerging in a continuous historic process, the chances of inflicting aesthetic mischief and unhuman rigidity are much smaller.[51]

Local inhabitants have not been entirely blameless in their increasing disinterest in playing a civic role. Property ownership, new leisure facilities, motoring and a host of other factors have unknotted local ties, provided independent recreational possibilities, and detached individuals and families from former community structures. The city itself has accelerated this process, unhinging individuals from decision-making processes which govern the quality of their lives. Urbanisation in twentieth-century Scotland, thus, has witnessed a transition not only in the physical and spatial relations within towns and cities, but also in a fundamental realignment of the relationship of individuals to the urban milieu, and to perceptions of their own citizenship.

NOTES AND REFERENCES

1. Almost certainly more than 144 smaller places exceeded the growth rate achieved in the major centres, but data is not directly comparable, and thus the exact number cannot be obtained.
2. This contrasts with the view developed by I.H. Adams, *The Making of Urban Scotland* (London, 1978), pp. 245–58, in which he traces the recovery of small towns, specifically border towns, to the 1960s.
3. S. Marriner, 'Cash and concrete. Liquidity problems in the mass production of "homes for heroes"', *Business History*, 18 (1976), p. 155.
4. G.Y. Craig, 'Topogrphy and building materials', in J. Gifford, C. McWilliam and D. Walker, (eds), *The Buildings of Scotland: Edinburgh* (London, 1984), p. 25.
5. Scottish Housing Advisory Committee, *Report on the Distribution of New Houses in Scotland*, Cmnd. 6552, 1943–4, para. 23.
6. N.J. Morgan, '"£8 cottages for Glasgow citizens": innovations in municipal house-building in Glasgow in the inter-war years', in R. Rodger (ed.), *Scottish Housing in the Twentieth Century* (Leicester, 1988), p. 145.
7. M. Miller, *Raymond Unwin: Garden Cities and Town Planning* (Leicester, 1992) gives a detailed account of the principles. See also S.V. Ward, 'The Garden City introduced', in S.V. Ward (ed.), *The Garden City: Past, Present and Future* (London, 1992), pp. 1–9.
8. D. Whitham, 'State housing and the Great War', and J. Minett, 'Government sponsorship of New Towns: Gretna 1915–17 and its implications', in R. Rodger (ed.), *Scottish Housing*, pp. 89–103, and 104–24; S.M. Gleave, 'The influence of the Garden City movement in Fife, 1914–23, with particular reference to Rosyth', unpublished M.Phil. thesis, University of St Andrew's, 1988. I.H. Adams, op. cit., p. 205, argues that the garden suburb idea was forced on Scotland prior to World War I.
9. G. Darnley, 'Pattern book to design guide – dictation or suggestion?', *Built Environment*, 5 (1980), pp. 12–21.
10. H.R. Aldridge, *The Case for Town Planning* (London, 1915), p. 419. I am grateful to A. Sutcliffe for reminding me of this listing, based on E.G. Culpin, *The Garden City Movement Up-to-Date* (London, 1913).
11. A.A. Jackson, *Semi-Detached London* (London, 1973), pp. 61–2.
12. S.M. Gaskell, *Model Housing: From the Great Exhibition to the Festival of Britain* (London, 1986), p. 151, quoting W. Ashworth, *The Genesis of Modern British Town Planning* (London, 1959), p. 196.
13. C. McWilliam, *Scottish Townscape* (London, 1975), pp. 152–6.

14. Corporation of Glasgow Housing Department, *Review of Operations, 1919–47* (Glasgow, 1947). I am grateful to Annette O'Carroll for reminding me of this source, and for supplying data drawn from it.
15. N.J. Morgan, '£8 cottages', op. cit., p. 140; Letter from the Edinburgh City Architect, 18/3/1919, Edinburgh City Record Office, Housing and Town Planning Committee, Box 4 1(1). Reference supplied by Annette O'Carroll.
16. D. Whitham, 'National politics and local tensions', op. cit., pp. 102–3.
17. J.K. Young, 'From laissez-faire to "Homes fit for Heroes": housing in Dundee 1868–1919', unpublished Ph.D. thesis, St Andrew's University, 1991, pp. 641–2 (brackets added).
18. ibid., pp. 629–31; L. Christie, 'Gender, design and ideology in council housing: urban Scotland 1917–1944', *Planning History*, 15 (1993), pp. 6–13.
19. Quoted in Morgan, op. cit., p. 128.
20. J.K. Young, op. cit., p. 637.
21. M.J. Daunton, 'Introduction', in M.J. Daunton (ed.), *Councillors and Tenants: Local Authority Housing in English Cities 1919–1939* (Leicester, 1984), p. 27, also makes the point about the harmonisation of design and housing form in the English regions.
22. A. O'Carroll, thesis, p. 250.
23. S. Damer, *From Moorepark to 'Wine Alley': The Rise and Fall of a Glasgow Housing Scheme* (Edinburgh, 1989), pp. 74–6, shows the three-tier hierarchy of council housing in Glasgow.
24. A.D. Gibb, 'Policy and politics in Scottish housing since 1945', in R. Rodger (ed.), *Scottish Housing*, pp. 156–8.
25. Scottish Housing Advisory Committee, *Planning Our New Homes*, (HMSO, Edinburgh, 1944), p. 19.
26. ibid. The Committee acknowledged that room sizes were generally somewhat larger in Scotland.
27. A.A. Jackson, *Semi-Detached London*, p. 99; A.D. King, *The Bungalow: the Production of a Global Culture* (London, 1984), pp. 245–6. See also pp. 156–92. Remarkably, there are no index references to Scotland in this account, nor textual ones in the chapter entitled 'Britain 1918–80'.
28. A.D. King, op. cit., p. 159.
29. Amongst the first in Edinburgh were those sold by James Millar in 1927 at Blackhall, according to C. McKean, *Edinburgh Portrait of a City* (London, 1991), p. 212.
30. A. O'Carroll, 'The development of owner occupation in Edinburgh 1918–1939', unpublished Ph.D. thesis, Heriot-Watt University, 1994, pp. 234 et seq.
31. A.A. Jackson, *Semi-Detached London*, p. 135, notes that in Staines and Uxbridge in Middlesex, and on cheap suburban land in Essex, there were considerable clusters of English bungalows 'en masse'; A.D. King, *The Bungalow*, p. 164, notes that bungalows were 'thick on the ground' in Hayes, Upminster, Rainham and Hornchurch, and (pp. 170–1), refers to clusters of bungalows by the sea in four main geographical concentrations each within 50–70 miles of major population concentrations – the Sussex and Hampshire coast; North Wales (between Llandudno and Prestatyn); and the coastal strips of Lancashire and Yorkshire. These are explained by shorter working hours, paid holidays, better road and rail connections, and a forty per cent increase in motor vehicles between 1931 and 1935.
32. A.D. King, op. cit., pp. 164–5.
33. Scottish Housing Advisory Committee, *Planning Our New Homes*, p. 12.
34. R. Rodger, 'The Victorian building industry and the housing of the Scottish working class' in M. Doughty (ed.), *Building the Industrial City* (Leicester, 1986), pp. 151–206.
35. D. Chapman, *The Location of Dwellings in Scottish Towns*, Department of Health for Scotland, Wartime Social Survey, New Series 34 (Edinburgh, 1943), p. 29. The burghs sampled include Edinburgh, Glasgow, Aberdeen, Dundee, Paisley, Falkirk, Kilmarnock, Hamilton, Inverness, Hawick, Buckhaven and Methil.
36. ibid.
37. R. Smith, 'The origins of Scottish New Towns policy and the founding of East Kilbride', *Public Administration*, 52 (1974), pp. 143–59; A.D. Gibb, op. cit., pp. 159–67. Scottish New Towns began with East Kilbride (1947), and then Glenrothes (1948), Cumbernauld (1956), Livingston (1964) and Irvine (1968) followed. Stonehouse was planned in 1975 but cancelled in 1976.
38. R. Smith, 'The politics of an overspill policy: Glasgow, Cumbernauld and the Housing and Town Development (Scotland) Act', *Public Administration*, 55 (1979), pp. 79–94.

39. M.G. Horsey, '"Give the people homes!" Britain's multi-storey housing drive', unpublished Ph.D. thesis, University of Edinburgh, 1991.
40. For an examination of this issue see P. Dunleavy, *The Politics of Mass Housing in Britain 1945–1975: A Study of Corporate Power and Professional Influence in the Welfare State* (Oxford, 1981), pp. 99–103.
41. T. Begg, *50 Special Years: A Study in Scottish Housing* (London, 1987).
42. For an extended discussion of these points see R. Rodger and H. Al-Qaddo, 'The Scottish Special Housing Association and the implementation of housing policy 1937–87', in R. Rodger (ed.), *Scottish Housing*, pp. 184–213.
43. T. Hart, 'The comprehensive development area', Occasional Paper No. 9, University of Glasgow Social and Economic Studies (1968).
44. R. Rodger, 'The origins of Scottish town planning', in G. Gordon and B. Dicks (eds), *Scottish Urban History* (Aberdeen, 1983), pp. 75–80, and 'Conscience civique et representations des interets: l'interventionnisme municipal en Ecosse 1860–1914', *Geneses*, 10 (1993), pp. 6–30.
45. See for example, T. Hunter and R. Paton, *Report on the Common Good of the City of Edinburgh* (Edinburgh, 1905).
46. C.M. Allan, 'The genesis of British urban development with special reference to Glasgow', *Economic History Review*, 17 (1965), pp. 598–613; P.J. Smith, 'The housing-relocation issue in an early slum clearance scheme: Edinburgh 1865–1885', *Urban Studies*, 26 (1989), pp. 100–14, and 'Slum clearance as an instrument of sanitary reform: the flawed vision of Edinburgh's first slum clearance scheme', *Planning Perspectives*, 9 (1994), pp. 1–27. For a useful contemporary account of Scottish Improvement Schemes, see Royal Commission on the Housing of the Working Classes, PP 1884–85 XXX. Evidence of Walker Q.18290–1; Gentle Q.20594–208703; Crawford Q.18701–66; Turnbull Q.20084–157; Collins Q.19316–19896; Laing Q.20270–300; Simpson Q.19945–20000; D. Crawford Q.188479.
47. W.H. Fraser, 'Municipal socialism, in R.J. Morris and R. Rodger (eds), *The Victorian City: A Reader in British Urban History 1820–1914* (London, 1993), pp. 258–80.
48. R.J. Morris, 'The ILP 1893–1932: introduction', in A. McKinlay and R.J. Morris (eds), *The ILP on Clydeside, 1893–1932: From Foundation to Disintegration* (Manchester, 1991), p. 11.
49. I should like to acknowledge the help I have received in discussions with Helen Meller concerning some of the ideas contained in this section. For a fuller account see H. Meller, 'Urban renewal and citizenship: the quality of life in British cities, 1890–1990', *Urban History*, 22 (1995), pp. 63–84.
50. Meller, op. cit., p. 65.
51. A Glikson, *The Ecological Basis of Planning* (The Hague, 1971), p. 111, quoted in Meller, op. cit.

I would like to acknowledge the help I have had from Bryn Hamer in inputting census data, and from Jim Clark and Vicky Gibbons in calculating the indices of urbanisation on which much of this paper is based. Advice and support from Sylvia West concerning the cluster analysis on which many of the statistical findings are based is also gratefully acknowledged.

8. THE SCOTTISH HIGHLANDS: FROM CONGESTED DISTRICT TO OBJECTIVE ONE

Ewen A. Cameron

It is not the intention of this chapter to provide a detailed account of the chronology of twentieth-century Highland history. Rather, the approach is thematic and it will attempt to evaluate the elements of continuity and change which have shaped the modern Highlands. In significant areas it will be shown that recent changes which have been hailed as radical have, in fact, deep historical roots. The most important factor in determining the course of twentieth-century Highland history has been the government's growing involvement since 1886. There have been two important themes in the development of government policy. In the years prior to 1930, the primary concern was with land, although the rise of a more comprehensive approach has seen it relegated to a lower place on the agenda. Secondly, there has been the use of the historical legacy to justify special treatment for the Highlands. The definition of the Highlands has long been a controversial area. However, for the twentieth century we have some guidelines to follow in the form of the definitions provided by the government in the establishment of institutions with Highland responsibilities. The first and most enduring was provided in 1886 with the creation of the seven Crofting Counties. It established the area to be covered by a new code of legislation which has endured with minimal changes. This has not only affected the lives of crofters but has created a basis for the government to argue that this area was deserving of treatment by special criteria. So, although it is the case that crofting is a minority pursuit within the crofting counties, it has been the basis of the government's definition and treatment of the Highlands for over 100 years.[1] Furthermore, it should be noted that the geographic Highlands are not coterminous with the officially-defined Crofting Counties.

For historians and policymakers alike, the success or failure of Highland policies since the late nineteenth century has been judged in terms of their demographic impact.[2] Although at times the idea of concentrating economic and demographic growth has been flirted with, the explicit concomitant, writing off other areas which had declined so far as to be beyond recovery, was never fully grasped.[3] The demographic pattern of the Highlands has been one of depopulation through out-migration since the mid-nineteenth century. Emigration was a key feature of Highland society in the twentieth century, although the rate of emigration dropped in the depressed condition of the world market in the 1930s and again in the 1960s as the former Dominions, the traditional destination for Highlanders, began to impose restrictions on entry.[4] This continuous loss of population has been the primary concern of government in the twentieth century. While temporary migration had been a key feature of Highland society since the late eighteenth century as crofters ventured further afield to boost their incomes, in the twentieth century this migration has become increasingly permanent because of poor economic and social opportunities.[5] Highland depopulation, however, has not been a straightforward process as there have been important variations over time and place. Indeed, there are a number of paradoxical elements to this process.

First, in spite of the predominantly rural nature of the Highlands, it has been the urban areas rather than the rural areas which have experienced population growth and they have often grown at the expense of the rural community. This was a criticism of post-1945 economic policy which concentrated growth in the eastern Highlands. Second, influxes of small numbers of people, attracted by a single factor such as a new industrial plant or other employment opportunity, have had a major impact on the demographic structure, although they often prove to be short-lived. The nuclear power station at Dounreay in the 1950s, the industrial developments in Easter Ross and Locharber since the 1960s and the Shetland oil industry in the 1970s have all produced isolated points of growth (see Tables 1 and 2). The third paradox has been the demographic role reversal with the central belt which has seen its population contract since the 1980s while that of the Highlands has increased. Whereas Highland depopulation was caused by out-migration, the recent increase has been caused by in-migration which has far exceeded natural growth.[6] The 'White Settlers' have attracted criticism from some on account of their insensitivity towards traditional lifestyles, although, on the positive side, the influx of energetic individuals who are sensitive to their new environment can inject much-needed life into moribund communities.[7] This has been heralded as a major watershed by some, but given the history of short-term demographic fluctuations, it

TABLE 1
Percentage Population Change by Decades in the Crofting Counties

	1900s	1910s	1920s	1930s	1940s	1950s	1960s	1970s
Shetland	−1.1	−8.6	−16.1	−7.0	−3.0	−7.8	−2.8	57.8
Orkney	−9.8	−6.9	−8.3	−2.3	−1.4	−12.2	−8.6	11.7
Caithness	−2.7	−11.6	−9.2	0	−11.7	20.7	1.5	−1.5
Sutherland	−6.5	−11.8	−9.6	−5.0	−10.5	−1.4	−3.0	8.4
Ross	2.6	−8.5	−11.0	−1.3	−2.4	−4.8	1.2	18.5
Inverness	−3.2	−5.5	−0.5	−1.2	4.8	−0.7	7.3	24.1
Argyll	−3.8	8.4	−18.1	−1.9	−2.6	−6.3	1.0	2.7

TABLE 2
Population Change in Highland Local Authority Areas 1981–91

	Total Change	Natural Change	Migration
Highland Region	6.2	1.0	5
Districts			
Badenoch & Strathspey	13.5	−1.7	15.2
Caithness	−3.5	1.3	−4.8
Inverness	11.5	2.6	8.9
Lochabar	−1.1	1.0	−2.1
Ross & Cromarty	7.1	2.5	4.6
Skye & Lochalsh	14.9	−2.8	17.7
Sutherland	−0.8	−4.4	3.6
Argyll & Bute	−1.1	−2.5	1.3
Islands			
Western Isles	−5.7	−3.9	−1.8
Orkney	4.0	−0.5	4.5
Shetland	−3.8	3.2	−7.0

is too early to confirm this. Yet, it would appear to be a more comprehensive and multifaceted growth than the isolated and monocausal rises experienced earlier in the century.

Land was the key issue in Highland policy down to 1930. The 1886 Crofters' Holdings Act had established tenurial security but extant problems included a shortage of land and, more importantly, a lack of economic security. The Congested Districts Board (CDB) argued in 1897 that 'an agricultural holding should be of such an extent that its occupier could depend entirely on it, or mainly, for a comfortable living'.[8] There was an important Conservative ideological thrust to the policy behind the CDB which sought to make crofters the owners of their land.[9] While the land issue was the major focus of the Board's work, taking up the majority of its budget (52.6 per cent), significant portions of its resources were devoted to infrastructural improvement (24.5 per cent) and the development of agriculture and fisheries (16.1 per cent).[10] The implicit objective of the Board was to move the Highland economy away from reliance on very small holdings supplemented by incomes from other activities, but due to its lack of compulsory powers and insufficient funds, the CDB was unable to make much progress.

The CDB was abolished in 1912 and its role assumed by the Board of Agriculture for Scotland. The Crofters' Commission which had been established to oversee the implementation of the 1886 Act was also abolished and its role was taken on by the Scottish Land Court. The primary reason for this was a different Liberal approach to the land question which stressed secure tenancy rather than extended ownership. From 1906 the Liberal government strove to pass a Land Settlement Bill which was delayed until 1911 due to opposition from the Conservative-dominated House of Lords. The Land Settlement (Scotland) Act was nationwide in its application but most activity was in the crofting counties. This heralded a new era which lasted until the mid-1920s as concerted efforts were made to create new holdings in an attempt to relieve congestion. However, due to political pressure from the crofting counties, inadequate legislation and initial proprietorial opposition, the effect was the opposite to that intended and congestion was perpetuated.[11]

It has been said of the cumulative effect of the land settlement legislation of 1911 and 1919 that 'the agrarian and social injustices perpetrated by the creators of the land system that had taken shape during the clearances had been permanently removed – from the crofting community's Hebridean heartland at any rate'.[12] To some extent this view can be *quantitively* substantiated. From 1912 to 1925, 1,571 new holdings were created and a further 894 holdings were enlarged. This represents 26.1 per cent of the serious applications for land. If the focus is narrowed and the extent of land settlement in the Hebrides is considered, 932 new holdings were created and 676 holdings were enlarged representing 39.5 per cent of the serious demand for land.[13] When the *qualitative* aspects of the exercise are considered, however, the notion of reversing the clearances has to be modified. Due to the extent of the demand for land and its vociferous expression, the political imperative was to settle as much of it as possible. Government surveys of the size of holdings in the 1930s exemplify the perpetuation of small crofts produced by this situation. In the crofting counties as a whole two thirds of all holdings were under 15 acres and in specific areas such as Sutherland, Harris and Lewis around half of all holdings were under 5 acres. In the Hebrides 83 per cent of all holdings were under 15 acres.[14]

There was very little land settlement after the mid-1920s as the bulk of the available land had been used. Renewed emigration had been a marked feature of Scotland in the 1920s wiping out the entire natural growth of the population. Within this there was substantial emigration from the Highlands and Lewis in particular.[15] In the 1930s economic conditions worsened dramatically and depopulation slowed down as employment opportunities contracted. Unemployment doubled between 1930 and 1936.[16] This brought to a head some of the disadvantages of the uniform system of small crofts as opportunities for auxiliary employment contracted and the resources which could be provided by the holding became more important. The government was firmly of the opinion that any further land settlement had to enlarge crofts rather than to create more.[17] A campaign by the Highland Development League helped to put pressure on the government by demanding a new and more comprehensive approach to the problems of the Highlands. Its rhetoric scarcely touched on the results of the land settlement operation, however, and its slogan, 'A New Deal for the Highlands', drew inspiration from contemporary events in America and the Tennessee Valley Authority in particular.[18]

Land settlement was reviewed towards the end of World War II and the conclusion was reached that holdings were too small and the overall policy had 'failed to establish within the Highlands an agricultural economy which either procures the maximum utilisation of land or provides an encouragement to the young generation to follow an agricultural career'.[19] After 1945 land policy in the Highlands was shifted in an attempt to cope with the rigidity of the tenurial structure which was imposed by legislation between 1886 and 1919. Security of tenure in its initial form had a number of inbuilt conditions to prevent it leading to decay. The most important of these conditions were the residence and cultivation qualifications. The former was removed inadvertently by a Court of Session decision in 1917 and the latter was impossible to enforce in the absence of a statutory definition of good or bad cultivation.[20] These provisions, added to the structure of smallholdings, drove down the standard of cultivation, reduced the incentive to reside on the croft and created absentee tenants and derelict holdings. The post-war Labour government responded to this situation by establishing the Commission of Enquiry into Crofting Conditions chaired by Thomas Taylor, the Principal of the University of Aberdeen. Taylor's brief was to re-establish the link between security of tenure and vitality in the crofting community. The Commission was well aware of the need to amalgamate holdings and deal with absentee tenants, as well as the difficulties of dealing with a system which provided rating concessions for crofters and access to the system of agricultural supports which had been established during the war. As crofting agriculture declined, the croft became important as a domestic base for an often aged population which could not simply be moved aside.

There was vigorous debate within the Commission. The Skye Crofting activist, Mrs Margaret MacPherson, felt herself to be isolated as other members declined her proposals for land nationalisation.[21] Rejecting state ownership, the Commission proposed the establishment of an administrative authority which would have powers to deal with absentee tenants and to reorganise crofting townships.[22] The two most important results to emerge from the Taylor Commission were the establishment of the Crofters Commission in 1955 and the creation of the Crofting Counties Agricultural Grants scheme. By 1991 this scheme had poured over thirty million pounds into the seven crofting counties.[23] Prior to 1955 crofters had access to the agricultural subsidies which had been established during the war. These were designed for larger-scale agriculture and, as such, did not have much impact on the crofting communities.[24] The 1955 schemes indicated an explicit return to the notion that crofters should receive special treatment. Furthermore, the structure of subsidy has helped to reduce crofting agriculture to an ovine monoculture which has had damaging environmental consequences. Whilst the environment is often superficially perceived as 'unspoilt' or characterised as a wilderness, there has been considerable criticism of land-use, the influence of commercialised sport and the structure of land holding. All of which draws attention to the fact that the Highland environment is in a far from 'unspoilt' condition. The human impact on the Highland landscape has been profound.

The Treasury required reassurance that this type of subsidy would not encourage agricultural pressure groups all over the country to demand similar provisions.[25] The Scottish Office resorted to the age-old tactic of pleading that the Highlands were a special case. This had begun in the 1920s with scare tactics over land raids in an attempt to fund land settlement and continued until the 1960s with official terminology designed to create a 'mystique' which would impress (or confuse) the Treasury.[26] In a European context, the problems of the Highlands were not unique. The Irish government also experienced problems caused by late nineteenth-century land legislation as land purchase produced an even more rigid system; a fact pointed out by the Taylor Commission. The contrast can be made with the crofting system which can be regulated, even if in a limited manner, by government agencies.[27]

The regime to administer crofting established in the aftermath of Taylor has remained largely intact. There were marginal reforms in 1961 after Commission proposals to pursue large-scale consolidation of small crofts were headed off. In the late 1960s the Commission proposed wholesale conversion of crofting tenancy to ownership, but this was deeply unpopular. In any case, the Bill proposing the changes fell with Edward Heath's Conservative government in 1974. The only result of the long period of thought was the 1976 Crofting Reform (Scotland) Act which provided favourable opportunities for individual crofters to buy their land from their landlords, although few have done so. Resistance to all these reforms is grounded in the special advantages which the original crofting legislation conferred on crofters. This argument was used in Kilmuir in 1904 to counter CDB blandishments about ownership and it has remained the main obstacle to all reform of the basics of crofting. A recent attempt to pass the estates in Skye and Raasay, which had been acquired by the government in the 1920s, into Community Ownership encountered similar objections and nothing came of the proposal. It is this catalogue of resistance to tenurial change which makes the recent purchase of the Assynt estate by its crofters so groundbreaking. However, the reliance on public campaigning and fund-raising predicated on the assumption that this was a special case suggests that this will not be a model for other crofting communities to follow.

One of the most important developments of the latter half of the twentieth century has been the impact of the European community (EC). Unlike rural communities in Ireland, the European Economic Community was viewed pessimistically in the crofting communities and a substantial 'no' vote was registered in the Highlands in the 1975 referendum.[28] This view has softened as the crofting communities have taken increasing advantage of European Community funding initiatives. The series of development programmes in the 1980s provided a model for growing involvement by the Highlands and Islands Development Board (HIDB) in crofting.[29] European support culminated in the attainment of Objective One status under EC regional policy which has relevance for the Highlands as a whole and not just the crofting areas.[30] Despite the government's concentration on crofting matters there are other aspects of the land issue which have remained beyond the remit of government. The unchecked land speculation which has gone on in post-war Scotland is almost unique in a European context.[31] This aspect of the land issue has proved intractable, due not only to a lack of political will, but also to the insurmountable difficulty of collecting information on the subject.[32]

The achievement of Objective One status is confirmation of the development of a more comprehensive approach to the Highlands. The attempt to develop wider aspects of the Highland economy has been driven by the fact that existing crofts are very small and there has been a need to at least consider the opportunities for wage earning outside basic agriculture. Concerted attempts to develop the economy expanded after 1945 and although the CDB had a remit in this area, it was not really pursued, due to the overwhelming concentration on the land issue. The search for a more comprehensive approach reached its peak in the 1960s with the establishment of the HIDB which was one of the first institutions with Highland responsibilities not to have as its primary concern crofting and the land use. The antecedents of a more comprehensive approach to the development of the Highland economy emerged in the 1930s when it was believed that policies formed in London did not take sufficient account of Scottish circumstances. This extended to business circles and was expressed most obviously by the Scottish Development Council and its associated body the Scottish Economic Committee.[33] It has already been noted how the Highland issue was regarded as unique even in a Scottish context. Despite the vast land settlement operation since 1919 the Highlands were still regarded as a problem area in Scotland.

The Scottish Economic Committee turned their attention to the Highlands in 1936 with the creation of a sub-committee under the direction of Edward Hilleary, a Skye landowner. The report, which emerged in 1938, led to few tangible results due to the outbreak of war in September 1939. However, it established a number of themes which would form the basis of a more comprehensive approach to the Highlands in the post-war period. It proposed the appointment of a Highland Development Commissioner who would have overall control of the design and implementation of Highland policy.[34] It was careful, as was the government, to point to the difference with the Special Areas. The latter had been defined by legislation of 1934 and 1937 as areas with high rates of unemployment which required special assistance. The problems of the Special Areas were related to specific industries while the problems of the Highlands were rooted in fundamental aspects of the Highland landscape and social structure.[35]

Because of the smallness of holdings and the large extent of marginal land the Hilleary Committee concluded that 'A large percentage of crofts and holdings are incapable of providing a livelihood, and the necessity for the establishment of local industries supplying auxiliary employment therefore becomes evident.'[36] This theme was pursued in the post-war era with a more comprehensive approach to Highland economic policy and similar thinking was evident in the Report of the Taylor Commission in 1953 and in the early work of the Highlands and Islands Development Board.[37] Although the war signalled the end of debate between the Treasury and the

Scottish Office over the Hilleary Report, the years from 1939 to 1945 did see some significant developments for the Highlands. At a fairly prosaic level the Rural Water Supplies and Sewerage Act of 1944 was a basic contribution to the infrastructure of the Highlands which should not be underestimated. A larger development was signalled by the Hydro-Electric Development (Scotland) Act of 1943 which Tom Johnston argued was 'an instrument for the rehabilitation of the Highlands'.[38] Indeed, Johnston's period at the Scottish Office was important in creating a climate where interventionist policies were viewed more positively and his advisory council of ex-secretaries spent much of its time considering post-war reconstruction, with the Highlands high on the agenda.[39]

In the immediate post-war period, Highland policy was considered in a more integrated manner.[40] The Advisory Panel on the Highlands and Islands was established in 1946 and although it had no real power, it could raise awareness and until 1965 it took a very wide view of the issues facing the Highlands.[41] The most significant legislative development was the Distribution of Industry Act of 1945 which was important in its own right but also in the development of Highland policy up to the 1960s. The Act established Development Areas which were defined on the criteria of unemployment. The government, through the Board of Trade and Scottish Industrial Estates Ltd, had powers to stimulate industrial development in these areas. The Highlands were brought into this structure in 1948 when the area around the Cromarty and Beauly firths was scheduled as a Development Area.[42] This began a debate about the best way forward in the industrial development of the Highlands. The theoretical basis of a growth point was the potential stimulation it would give to the surrounding areas. However, many were worried that it could 'accentuate the drift from the remoter areas'.[43] Easter Ross has been the area most often mentioned as a Highland growth point. Whilst it has good harbour facilities and an ideal geographical layout for large-scale industrial and residential construction it also has some of the best land in the Highlands.[44] The paradox of obliterating the latter when it is in such short supply has been commented on.[45] Concentration of growth has been a constant criticism of the Highlands and Islands Development Board, especially following the disastrous period in the early 1980s when the Highland economy was struck by the closure of the Invergordon Aluminium Smelter and the Fort William Pulp Mill.[46]

Labour policy was outlined in 1950 in *A Programme for Highland Development*, which advocated the development of basic industries, such as agriculture and fishing, the creation of permanent employment and improvement of infrastructure. There was little that was controversial or

novel and when the Conservatives produced a progress report on the rather
limited implementation of these policies in 1959, they did not change the
direction of the policy.[47] The most important development of the 1950s
was the ongoing work of the North of Scotland Hydro Electric Board
(NSHEB). Its precise role was the subject of some controversy as debate
focused on two issues. First, whether the Board should concentrate on the
expensive job of providing a comprehensive domestic supply or provide
cheap power in an attempt to attract energy-intensive industries to the
Highlands. The Cooper Committee which investigated the issue in 1943
concluded that a comprehensive rural supply would be ruinously expensive
and that the Board should concentrate on attempting to attract industry.[48]
However, the stewardship of Tom Johnston gave the domestic consumer
priority and he steadfastly refused to offer cheap power deals to industrial
consumers at their expense. The programme of rural electrification
proceeded to virtual completion by the early 1960s.[49]

The second controversial area concerned the so-called 'social clause'
of the NSHEB. This stated that the Board should collaborate with any
relevant authority to improve social and economic conditions in the Highlands. Although expenditure under this clause was minimal, it provided the
core of the identity of the NSHEB: so much so, that any threat to tamper
with its independence caused a political storm in the Highlands. This
happened twice, at the time of nationalisation of the electricity industry in
1947 and when a proposal for a single Scottish Board was considered in the
1960s.[50] The NSHEB, regardless of its failure to achieve the wider objectives of Highland development, which were probably unrealistic anyway, is
regarded with a loyalty matched only by that for the Crofters' legislation
in the Highlands. This is primarily based on its provision of a domestic
electricity supply, which can be regarded as one of the outstanding achievements of any public-service body in post-war Britain and was certainly the
most fundamental contribution from any agency in twentieth-century
Highland history.

An important theme to re-emerge in the 1950s was the need for an overarching Highland development authority. The Scottish Trade Union Congress was the main proponent of this, but had little impact on an indifferent
Conservative government. As the 1964 election approached, however, the
Conservative administration became worried about the political impact of
its years of inaction which contrasted badly with the Labour Party's enthu-
siastic espousal of a Highland Development agency. There was also the usual
anxiety – which cropped up whenever special action for the Highlands was
being considered – that it could be regarded as a precedent in other areas

of the country.[51] The 1953 Balfour Commission on Scottish Affairs argued against such a body on the grounds that it would duplicate the facilities of existing authorities.[52] This was the stock argument against any new authority and it was essentially the same argument that was used in the late 1930s against the Hilleary Committee's proposals.

The formation of the HIDB in 1965 is usually seen by historians as part of the wider planning objectives of Harold Wilson's Labour government, although the idea had a long pedigree in the Highlands.[53] Indeed in its first report, the HIDB looked back to the Tennessee Valley Authority which had been one of the inspirations for the Highland Development League in the 1930s. The sources are not yet available for anything other than an interim judgement on the work of the HIDB, but it is possible and important to place the HIDB in a historical context. Previous attempts have been confined to superficial comparisons with the CDB. There are several important areas of continuity even though the HIDB was the apogee of the move to a more comprehensive approach to the Highland problem. Like most other policies in the twentieth century the approach of the HIDB was measured in terms of the likely impact on population. The initial strategy of the HIDB also drew on a refinement of the growth-point strategy of the Distribution of Industry Act. The major growth point was to be the Moray Firth area but this was to be supplemented by Caithness, Fort William and by smaller growth points in the west of the region. However, the HIDB's policy was complemented by the growth of the oil industry in the early 1970s and the extent to which these developments were located in Easter Ross and the Northern Isles.[54] This was an approach which was being considered contemporaneously by the Irish government and was attempted prior to the abandonment of the policy in the 1980s. The third element of the HIDB's approach which was consistent in historical terms was the tactic of attempting to develop crofting through bolstering the prospects for employment in the crofting areas.[55]

The HIDB has been criticised for not concentrating sufficiently on the land issue and for not paying enough attention to social criteria. The rejection of proposals to develop the Strath of Kildonan and Mull, two areas which had long been recognised as representative of the worst problems facing the Highlands came at a time, in the early 1970s, when the HIDB was more interested in industry. The HIDB was not equipped for tackling the land issue. Its powers of compulsory purchase were not suitable for the acquisition of large areas of land in the manner of the Congested Districts Board or the Board of Agriculture for Scotland.[56] However, in the mid-1970s there were signs of a shift of attention towards the land issue. The

Board argued in 1976 that 'A sound approach to land use can contribute more to economic health of every part of the Highlands and Islands than any other single policy.'[57] Perhaps the most sensible assessment of the HIDB was that it carried insufficient weight to have a great deal of impact on the Highlands. Other institutions had been around for longer, such as the Department of Agriculture, the Crofters' Commission and the NSHEB and, more importantly, some events were simply beyond the control of the Board, most notably the rise and fall of the oil industry. The major failures of the Board have to be examined in the light of this basic fact. This point is illustrated by the failure to deal with the land issue and, most notably, the closure of the Invergordon Aluminium Smelter which had its origins in the simultaneous rise in energy prices and collapse in demand for aluminium; neither of which could be blamed on the HIDB. Nevertheless, the HIDB found itself unable to affect the course of events as the Scottish Office and the Energy Department haggled over the power contract for the smelter. There was also a strong element of continuity in the NSHEB's refusal to contemplate providing cheap power for an industrial facility.[58]

Throughout the post-war period two important industries were constantly discussed as possible panaceas for the development of the Highland economy and the reversal of depopulation: tourism and forestry. The concentration on these industries related to the apparent under-utilisation of trees and scenery in the Highlands. For as long as governments have been interested in the Highlands the fishing industry was presented in much the same light and for much the same reason. World War II had seen maximum utilisation of the Highland woods for the war effort with large areas, particularly in central Inverness, being denuded of trees.[59] In a British context, the war-time projection was for the devotion of five million acres of land to afforestation. However, this was to be done on a purely economic basis with efficiency rather than repopulation being the motivation, although it was recognised that forestry could help to revitalise rural areas.[60] There was constant criticism that the Forestry Commission did not have an outlook similar to the NSHEB and stuck very closely to the strict economic planting criteria.[61] The second panacea was tourism which had a history going back to the nineteenth century, most of it associated with élite sporting pursuits.[62]

The problems of tourism in the Highlands in the post-war period were twofold. First, the facilities for a mass form of tourism had to be created in a climate of enterprise among conservative hoteliers who had to be persuaded to lengthen the season to accommodate larger numbers.[63] The apogee of this approach was the creation of a comprehensive tourist facility at Aviemore.[64] The second issue related to the impact of tourism on the Highland economy because it was not enough simply to bring tourists to the Highlands. For real stimulation of the economy, tourists had to be able to take advantage of a range of goods and services produced in the Highlands. As one Scottish office clerk summed up the situation in 1958: 'It would be possible for hundreds of parties to travel thousands of miles in the Highlands, carrying their own tents and tinned food, buying only a few cairngorm brooches made in Birmingham and providing employment only for county roadmen and garbage collectors.'[65] The impact of the NSHEB was central here. The provision of a domestic electricity supply to the Highlands created a new institution, the Bed and Breakfast establishment. This provided a new source of income which evaded the clutches of the taxman and provided an important prop for remote crofting communities.

As tourism has moved into the realm of offering a 'heritage experience' for visitors, the Highlands have becomes a key icon in the marketing of Scotland. Presentations of the history and the landscape of the Highlands have been sanitised in the interests of this process. Scenery, preferably without people, has been marketed as the key attraction of the Highlands, while their cultural vitality and linguistic distinctiveness have been played down. The appropriation of the Highlands for this purpose has a long historical pedigree beginning in the eighteenth century, but arguably it has reached a peak in the late twentieth century.

There are strong elements of continuity in the history of the Highlands in the twentieth century. Perhaps the strongest is the consideration of the region as distinctive in policy terms. One could argue that the replacement of the HIDB by Highlands and Islands Enterprise (HIE) represents a breach of continuity in this regard. However, this can be countered by noting that Highland policy has long been subject to the dictates of political ideology. Also, there is a paradox at the heart of continued special treatment for the Highlands. The implication is that despite prior special treatment more is needed. Whether this is due to the failure of earlier policy or the prospect of a political backlash should it be discontinued is unclear. The paradox was neatly summed up by an HIE official commenting on the announcement of Objective One status: 'One minute we're telling everybody how well our economy is doing, the next minute we're getting special EC aid as one of the poorest areas in Europe.'[66]

The enlarged EC has been forced to take more account of underdeveloped rural areas than the original Europe of six nations. In a national context, governments have been forced to develop policies for problem regions when they pose political problems. This was true of the Highlands in the 1880s and in a modern context the theme is exemplified by the example of southern Italy.[67] While the slump from Objective Five b to Objective One status could be regarded as the ultimate European recognition of the longstanding problems of the Scottish Highlands, it can also be placed in the historical context of exceptional treatment of the Highlands. The vociferous political lobbying which preceded the announcement of Objective One status was crucial. The Highland GDP, at seventy-nine per cent of the EC average, was in strict terms four per cent too high to qualify.[68] Nevertheless, Objective One has helped to focus attention on longstanding problems such as transport infrastructure. It has also raised possibilities which have been submerged for many years, most notably, the prospect of a university in the Highlands.[69] The failure of a campaign for a university in the 1960s was regarded by those involved as a major setback for the area. This is an interesting exception to the special-case scenario as the campaigners were warned by the Scottish Office to play down Highland particularism in favour of mainstream educational arguments.[70]

There are signs of renewed confidence in the Highlands in the period since the mid-1980s. There have been signs of activism on linguistic issues and on crofting. Confidence has proceeded so far as to facilitate, if not sustain, arguments that crofting is an environmentally-friendly model of land tenure which could be usefully exported.[71] However, this confidence is in direct contrast to enduring economic and social problems, as the EC has recently recognised.

NOTES AND REFERENCES

1. H.A. Moisley, 'The Highlands and Islands – A Crofting Region?', *Transactions of the Institute of British Geographers*, 31 (1962), pp. 83–4.
2. T.C. Smout, 'Scotland 1850–1950' in F.M.L. Thompson (ed.), *The Cambridge Social History of Britain, 1750–1950, Volume I, Regions and Communities* (Cambridge, 1990), p. 259; Scottish Record Office [SRO], Scottish Economic Planning Department Files, [SEP] 12/7/2, A Sketch of the Economic Resources of the Highlands and Islands and of the Measures necessary to secure full development, 1 June 1948; SEP 12/219, Recent Population Changes in the Highlands and Islands, June 1959; SEP 12/166, Scottish Development Group: Study of the Highlands and Islands (Population), January 1964.
3. SRO, SEP 12/117, Scottish Development Group, Minutes of 1st Meeting, 30 January 1964; SEP 12/198, Advisory Panel on [the] Highlands and Islands [APH], Sub-Committee of Development and Transport Groups, Minutes of Meeting 11 December 1964.
4. M. Anderson, 'Population and Family Life' in A. Dickson and J.H. Treble (eds). *People and Society in Scotland, 1914–1990*, vol. III (Edinburgh, 1992), pp. 12–16.
5. T.M. Devine, 'Temporary Migration and the Scottish Highlands in the 19th Century', *Economic History Review*, 32 (1979), pp. 344–59; SRO, AF 81/24, Commission of Enquiry into Crofting Conditions: note by Mr Robert MacLeod.
6. P. Boyle, 'Modelling population movement into the Scottish Highlands and Islands from the remainder of Britain, 1990–91', *Scottish Geographical Magazine* [SGA], 111 (1995), pp. 5–12.
7. E.A. Cameron, '"White Settlers" in the Highlands', *Highland Fund Annual Report, 1994*,

pp. 21–4; M.C. Jedrej and M. Nuttall, 'Incomers and Locals: Metaphors and Reality in the Repopulation of Rural Scotland', *Scottish Affairs*, 10 (Winter 1995), pp. 112–26.

8. Congested Districts Board, *Annual Report, 1897*, p. ix.

9. For a detailed review of the work of the CDB see E.A. Cameron, *Land for the People: The British Government and the Scottish Highlands, 1880–1930* (Edinburgh, 1995), chapters 4, 5.

10. A.S. Mather, 'The Congested Districts Board for Scotland', in W. Ritchie, J.C. Stone, A.S. Mather (eds), *Essays for R.E.H. Mellor* (Aberdeen, 1986), p. 200.

11. For the political and ideological background and detail on land settlement see E.A. Cameron, 'Politics, Ideology and the Highland Land Issue, 1886 to the 1920s', *SHR*, 72 (1993), pp. 60–79.

12. J. Hunter, *The Making of the Crofting Community* (Edinburgh, 1976), p. 206.

13. E.A. Cameron, 'Public Policy in the Scottish Highlands: Governments, Politics and the Land Issue, 1886 to the 1920s' (unpublished Ph.D. thesis, University of Glasgow, 1992), pp. 237–8.

14. SRO, Highland Development Files, DD 15/54/1/1–13, Acreages of Holdings in the Crofting Counties, 1935.

15. M. Harper, 'Crofter Colonists in Canada: An Experiment in Empire Settlement in the 1920s', *Northern Scotland*, 14 (1994), pp. 69–108; M.E. Vance, 'British Columbia's Twentieth Century Crofter Emigration Schemes: A Note on New Sources', *Scottish Tradition*, 18 (1993), pp. 1–27.

16. Scottish Economic Committee [SEC], *The Highlands and Islands of Scotland: A Review of the Economic Conditions with Recommendations for Improvement* (1938), p. 179.

17. SRO, DD 15/7, Department of Agriculture Memorandum on the Report of the Scottish Economic Committee on the Highlands and Islands of Scotland, 16.

18. Video Interview, F.J. MacDonald and Rev T.M. Murchison, Glasgow University Audio Visual Services; see also representations from various branches of the HDL in SRO, DD 15/4.

19. PP 1944–5 V, *Land Settlement in Scotland: Report by the Scottish Land Settlement Committee*, 44.

20. Court of Session Cases, 1917, 453–63, *Rogerson* vs *Chilston*; J. Scott, *The Law of Smallholdings in Scotland* (Edinburgh, 1933), p. 71; SRO, SEP 12/7/4, APH: Future of Crofting Communities, Small Landholders Act: Note by the Secretary (Matthew Campbell), 1950.

21. SRO, AF 81/25, Commission of Enquiry into Crofting Conditions, Note by Mrs MacPherson; interview with Mrs Margaret MacPherson, July 1994.

22. PP 1953–4, VIII, *Report of the Commission of Enquiry into Crofting Conditions*.

23. Crofters' Commission, *Annual Report*, 1991, p. 22.

24. SRO, SEP 12/7/1, APH, General Memorandum, 7 November 1947.

25. SRO, Agricultural Credit Files, AF 71/106/4a, C.H.M. Wilcox (Ministry of Agriculture Fisheries and Food) to G.M. Wilson (Treasury), 8 March 1956; AF 71/106/6a, Wilson to M. Campbell (Department of Agriculture for Scotland), 15 May 1956.

26. Cameron, 'Public Policy', p. 240; SRO, SEP 12/171, J. Russell to E. Gauld, 3 December 1963; DD 15/74, Note on the Definition of the Highlands, 13 December 1960.

27. P. Commins, 'Land Policies and Agricultural Development', in P.J. Drudy (ed.), *Ireland: Land Politics and People* (Cambridge, 1982), p. 235; SRO, AF 81/8, Summary of evidence given to Commission of Enquiry into Crofting Conditions by Dr Frank Fraser Darling, 20 March 1952.

28. D.A. Gillmor, 'Agricultural Development', in R.W.G. Carter and A.J. Parker (eds), *Ireland: A Contemporary Geographical Perspective* (London, 1989), p. 174.

29. Hunter, *Claim of Crofting*, p. 167; SRO, Crofters' Commission Files, CRO 3/2/20, Agricultural Support in Less Favoured Areas: Memo by the Crofters' Commission to the House of Commons Agriculture Committee, 13 November 1981.

30. M. Blacksell and A.M. Williams, 'The Development of the European Community: Its Spatial Dimension', in M. Blacksell and A.M. Williams (ed.), *The European Challenge: Geography and Development in the European Community* (Oxford, 1994), pp. 97–9.

31. Other European countries have legislative checks on this type of activity; see P. Commins, 'Land Policies', in Drudy (ed.), *Land Politics and People*, p. 221; Naomi Mitchison pointed to the relevant Danish legislation in 1953, SRO, SEP 12/9/1, APH, Note on Danish Agriculture by Mrs Mitchison, June 1953.

32. The attempts to do so have merely exemplified the difficulties; see R. Millman, 'The Marches of Highland Estates', *SGM*, 85 (1969), pp. 172–81; R. Millman, 'The Landed Properties of Northern Scotland', *SGM*, 86 (1970), pp. 186–203; J. MacEwan, *Who Owns Scotland?* (Edinburgh, 1981).

33. R. Saville, 'The Industrial Background to the Post War Scottish Economy', in R. Saville (ed.), *The Economic Development of Modern Scotland, 1950–1980* (Edinburgh, 1985), pp. 12–16.

34. SEC, *Highlands and Islands*, pp. 29–30; for an alternative view of this idea see Sir A. MacEwan, 'A Dictator for the Highlands? The Strengths and Weaknesses of the SEC's Report', *Scots Magazine*, 30 (1938–9), pp. 293–8.

35. R.H. Campbell, 'The Scottish Office and the Special Areas in the 1930s', *Historical Journal*, 22 (1979), pp. 167–83; SRO, DD 15/12, Memo Concerning Development Commissioner, June 1939.

36. SEC, *Highlands and Islands*, p. 144.

37. *Report of the Commission of Enquiry into Crofting Conditions*, PP 1953–54, VIII, pp. 71–80; HIDB, *1st Annual Report, 1965–66*, p. 4.

38. SRO, SEP, 12/94, Memo on Developments in the Highlands and Islands, 1944; for the North of Scotland Hydro Electric Board see P.L. Payne, *The Hydro* (Aberdeen, 1988), pp. 44–5.

39. C. Harvie, 'Labour and Scottish Government: The Age of Tom Johnston', *Bulletin of Scottish Politics*, 2 (1981), pp. 12–14; C. Harvie, 'Labour in Scotland During the Second World War', *Historical Journal*, 26 (1983), pp. 929–31; R.H. Campbell, 'The Committee of Ex-Secretaries of State for Scotland and Industrial Policy, 1941–45', *Scottish Industrial History*, 2 (1979), pp. 1–10.

40. SRO, SEP 12/94, Report of the Inter Departmental Committee on Highland Development, 1945, p. 40.

41. Hunter, *Claim of Crofting*, p. 75; W.W. Knox (ed.), *Scottish Labour Leaders 1918–1939: A Biographical Dictionary* (Edinburgh, 1984), p. 194; for an idiosyncratic but revealing insider's view of the work of the Panel see N. Mitchison, *Saltire Self Portraits, No. 2* (Edinburgh, 1986), pp. 10–32.

42. *Highland Opportunities* (HMSO, 1959); *Statement on the Distribution of Industry in Relation to Development Areas*, PP 1948 II 463, pp. 31–2.

43. SRO, SEP 12/118, Scottish Economic Conference: A Sketch of the Economic Resources of the Highlands and Islands and of the Measures necessary to secure full development, 1948; SRO, SEP 12/2, APH, Minutes of the 11th Meeting, 11 June 1948, Comments by Sheriff Cameron.

44. SRO, SEP 12/7/1, Potential Development of the Cromarty Firth Area by H.A. Rendel Govan. The author was the Planning Consultant to Ross and Cromarty District Council and thus not entirely disinterested.

45. J. Bryden and G. Houston, *Agrarian Development*, 65; J.S. Smith, 'Land Transfers from Farming in Grampian and Highland, 1969–1980', SGM, 97 (1981), pp. 169–70, 173–4.

46. J.S. Smith, 'The Invergordon Aluminium Smelter – Growth Policy Gone Wrong? A Note', *SGM*, 98 (1982), pp. 115–18; J.T. Hughes, 'HIDB Development Policy: A Response', SGM, 99 (1983), pp. 121–4.

47. *A Programme of Highland Development*, PP 1950 XIX; *A Review of Highland Policy*, PP 1958–59 XXV; 'Highland Development', *Economist*, 15 July 1950.

48. *Report of the Committee on Hydro-Electric Development in Scotland*, PP 1942–43 IV.

49. Payne, *Hydro*, pp. 56–9, 193; SRO, AF 81/3, Evidence of the North of Scotland Hydro Electric Board to the Commission of Enquiry on Crofting Conditions.

50. Payne, *Hydro*, pp. 114–15, 200–23; *Electricity in Scotland: Report of the Committee on the Generation and Distribution of Electricity in Scotland*, PP 1962–63, XVII.

51. SRO, SEP 12/1, Minutes of the Meeting of the Highlands Committee, St Andrews House, 2 October 1962; SEP 12/117 APH, Minutes of the 9th Meeting, 29 October 1964.

52. *Royal Commission on Scottish Affairs*, 1952–54, PP 1953–54 XIX, p. 83; see also SRO, SEP 12/9/1.

53. C. Harvie, *No Gods and Precious Few Heroes: Scotland since 1914* (Edinburgh, 1993) p. 143; M. Lynch, *Scotland: A New History* (London, 1992), p. 442.

54. HIDB, *2nd Annual Report, 1967*, pp. 17–18; *6th Annual Report, 1971*, pp. 6–7; *8th Annual Report, 1973*, p. 20; *9th Annual Report, 1974*, p. 12.

55. HIDB, *1st Annual Report, 1965–66*, pp. 2–5; J.A. Walsh, 'Regional Development Strategies' in R.W.G. Carter and A.J. Parker (eds), *Ireland*, p. 445.

56. HIDB, *9th Annual Report, 1974*, p. 7.

57. HIDB, *11th Annual Report, 1976*, p. 5; Hunter, *Claim of Crofting*, pp. 157–67; J. Grassie, *Highland Experiment* (Aberdeen, 1983), pp. 69–98.

58. For contrasting views of this episode see Grassie, *Highland Experiment*, pp. 102–29; M. Shucksmith and T. Lloyd, 'The HIDB, regional policy and the Invergordon closure', *National Westminster Quarterly Review* (May 1982), pp. 14–25.

59. W.C. Wonders, 'The "sawdust fusiliers": the impact of the Canadian Forestry Corps in the Scottish Highlands in World War II', *Northern Scotland*, 8 (1988), pp. 51–68.

60. *Post War Forestry Policy, Report by H.M. Forestry Commissioners*, PP 1942–43 IV; SRO, SEP 12/98, Proposed Scottish Programme for Upland Areas: Memo by the Scottish Office, 11 March 1958; SEP 12/260, Cabinet Working Party on Forestry Policy, Minutes of Meeting, 25 April 1958; for an alternative view of forestry as an engine of repopulation see J. Hunter, 'Against the Grain', in K. Cargill (ed.), *Scotland 2000: Eight Views on the State of the Nation* (Glasgow, 1987), p. 68.

61. SRO, SEP 12/2, APH, Minutes of 37th Meeting, 22 February 1952; APH Minutes of 55th Meeting, Meeting with Forestry Commissioners.

62. W. Orr, *Deer Forests, Landlords and Crofters: The Western Highlands in Victorian and Edwardian Times* (Edinburgh, 1982), pp. 29, 37–44; R.W. Butler, 'The tourist industry in the Highlands and Islands' (unpublished Ph.D. thesis, University of Glasgow, 1973), pp. 63, 66, 72, 78–9.

63. SEP, 12/56, The Promotion of the Tourist Industry in the Counties of Inverness, Ross and Cromarty, Caithness and Sutherland.

64. D. Getz, 'Tourism and Rural Settlement Policy', SGM, 97 (1981), pp. 158–68; G. Pottinger, *The Secretaries of State for Scotland, 1926–1976* (Edinburgh, 1979), pp. 151–2.

65. SRO, SEP, 12/56, Minute by R.E.C. Johnston, 18 August 1958; APH Meeting with the Secretary of the Scottish Tourist Board, 2 April 1958.

66. *The Financial Times*, 3 July 1993.

67. D. Sassoon, *Contemporary Italy: Politics, Economy & Society since 1945* (London, 1986), pp. 35–6, 57, 229; P. Ginsborg, *A History of Contemporary Italy: Society & Politics, 1943–1988* (Harmondsworth, 1990), pp. 138–9, 162, 229, 331; M. Clark, *Modern Italy, 1871–1982* (London, 1984), pp. 357–61.

68. *The Independent*, 25 February 1993; *The Glasgow Herald*, 25 February 1993.

69. *The Glasgow Herald*, 25 February 1993.

70. SRO, SEP 12/117, Scottish Development Group, Minutes of 2nd Meeting 1964, 27 February 1964; Interview with Mrs Margaret MacPherson, July 1994.

71. D.J. MacLeod, 'Gaelic: the dynamics of a renaissance', in W. Gillies (ed.), *Gaelic and Scotland: Alba agus a'Ghaidlig* (Edinburgh, 1989), pp. 222–9; R.G. Rogerson and A. Gloyer, 'Gaelic Cultural Revival or Language Decline?', *SGM*, 111 (1995), pp. 46–53; J.M. Bryden, 'Crofting in the European Context', *SGM*, 103 (1987), pp. 100–4.

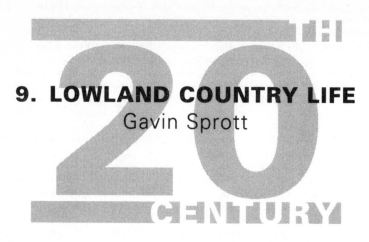

9. LOWLAND COUNTRY LIFE
Gavin Sprott

Modern farming is one of the pillars of industrial society, the supply of food being as important as fuel and raw materials. Moreover, farming is an industrial activity. Yet it has not always been so in the sense of being a commercial and market enterprise. Over the last two centuries the history of the lowland countryside is of the industrialisation of farming, and it is not commonly understood that this process only matured in the mid-twentieth century. Two things have dominated the countryside for much of this century – wars and the maturation of the Agricultural Revolution.

In the 1840s and 1850s lowland country life developed a pattern that would last, with some modification, for a century. The start of that period was the one of 'high farming'. The capital from Empire and urban industry flowed into intense investment: sub-soil ploughing and draining, the breaking in of hitherto unworkable carselands, and yet another generation of steadings which reflected a capital investment which only the laird, and not the tenant, could afford. The threshold was crossed from regional to national markets. This was possible through the combination of a new farming press which could carry advertisements,[1] the penny post and a developed banking system, and of course railways, enabling the transport not only of produce but of machinery. Railways and steam shipping opened up markets for livestock and animal products which had hitherto been inaccessible. The national character of high farming is caught in the first edition of Henry Stephens's *Book of the Farm* (1844). Although Stephens's family had farmed at Balgavies near Forfar, the work had a universality that made it relevant to readers all over the United Kingdom, and generated a demand for the five up-dated editions that followed until 1908.

Stephens's first edition was written just before the factors mentioned above had their full effect. Substantial progress had been made in levelling the rigs as a result of effective sub-soil drainage. By 1876 the picture would include not just reaping machines, mowers and the first potato diggers, but also the first binders – reaping machines that also threw the crop off as ready-bound sheaves, and achieved a very significant cut in harvest labour.

If prosperity developed high farming, depression fossilised it, and the binder was just one element in that depression. European farming was severely affected by the expansion of American agriculture and by the mid-1870s France and Germany had opted for protection. The British remained committed to free trade because of empire produce from Canada and Australasia, and, more importantly, the domestic political agenda dictated a cheap food policy – not *panem et circenses* but bread and slums. This was known among the farmers as 'the Great Betrayal', and would inform their politics and dictate the expectations which were realised in 1947 with the establishment of the annual price review.

The same storm which blew down the Tay Bridge on the last Sunday of 1879 also ushered in a series of very bad seasons. Between this time and the end of the century ten per cent of the best land went out of production, and grain production dropped by fifteen per cent. England was even harder hit, with twenty per cent of arable land out into grass.[2] Lowland Scotland survived the depression better as a result of several factors. These were principally the high levels of investment during the preceding years, professional competence, and a growing regional specialisation that supplied developing markets. In general, the long rotations – up to six years – with up to half the ground in rotation grass made for a more flexible regime.[3]

Other crude statistics tell their tale. In the forty years between 1871 and 1911, the numbers of skilled ploughmen and shepherds fell by a third. By 1910 the annual spring exodus of emigrants through the Clyde had reached a staggering sixty thousand, many of these people from the land, and from the north east and the south east. At the beginning of the twentieth century, that left just under two hundred thousand people on the farms of Scotland.[4] Paradoxically, this period was no worse for farm servants than other times. Their wages kept their value while the cost of provisions fell. Only in those parts of Scotland quite remote from the competing labour markets of urban industry were rural wages significantly lower than in the towns.[5]

At the turn of the century the structural differences between the various lowland regions were quite marked. South-east and east-central Scotland remained the main cropping area. There was a perceptible shift from wheat to oats in the face of foreign imports, which served better as stock-feed anyway. The north east was riding high on the remarkable success of the Aberdeen-Angus breed in the previous quarter century,[6] and imported

Argentinian beef could not match it for quality. Dairying in the west and south west catered for the now substantial central-belt conurbation. The extraordinary maze of rural branch lines provided dependable transport for fresh milk. The central and western borders faced harder times, as the competition of Australasian wool and mutton remained severe.

The regional differences were reflected in the occupational balance in the labour force. In the cropping areas of the south east in particular the work was very labour intensive, and married farm servants were the rule, because the regime was dependent on female outworkers. The strongly arable emphasis, including root crops such as potatoes and turnips, required a lot of hand-work – planting, singling, weeding, the associated harvests, then the shawing and *waeling* or dressing. It was difficult for a man to get a *single fee* – a job which did not involve a man's wife and daughters or a hired woman as part of the bargain.[7] On the smaller family farms of the south west, the women were as vital, and more on a par with the men, as they usually took charge of the milk-processing side of the job. The massive physical task of the twice-daily milking would have been impossible without female labour.[8]

Further north we move into the world of the bothy and chaumer. In Angus, the heartland of the bothy area, single farm workers tended to be young. (There is an interesting and almost direct parallel in the composition of the crews of sailing ships.[9] Both occupations offered a freedom and mobility that appealed to the young.) When they gave up the bothy, it was often to leave the land for the town or for farming abroad, often in Saskatchewan, Alberta or the South Island of New Zealand.

The real and continuing grouse that farm servants had until after World War II was housing and social conditions.[10] The evidence suggests that over the years conditions improved, but so slowly that they made little difference to inhabitants. The nineteenth century had its associations for improving the domestic lot of farm servants to which the great subscribed, and the Highland and Agricultural Society regularly and dutifully promoted this cause; but even so, little was done.[11] Until the period after World War II, the common arrangement was two rooms and a closet. One room was the kitchen, the other commonly a bedroom, and the closet a small room in between which might serve as a scullery, but was more commonly a store with bedding crammed in if required. However, it was not the smallness of the accommodation that bothered people,[12] but lack of easy access to water, inadequate sanitary arrangements, and above all, damp. The houses were built with no damp-proof courses, and often with little thought to the natural run-off. The inside walls were usually plastered, and were often so damp that wallpaper soon curled at the edges, and the bottom foot supported a rich fungal growth. If the unimproved floors were not clay, they were made from flags or bricks set in sand. If the surrounding drainage was poor, these would also be damp.

The one legal sanction against poor housing was if it posed a sanitary threat. The Public Health (Scotland) Act of 1897 required that everyone had 'reasonable access' to wholesome water. However, a trek of one hundred and fifty yards to the nearest well was not uncommon.[13] A nearby outside stand-pipe was considered pretty reasonable. One privy might be shared between several cottages, to the point that people would collect old doors which they flitted with them to construct their own privies instead.[14] These privies would consist of a plank with a hole and a bucket underneath.[15] In the 1930s one in three lowland country dwellings had no sanitary conveniences at all.[16] The flushing water closet we now take for granted was virtually unknown in farm servant housing at the beginning of this century. By 1936 about a quarter of the houses had one.[17] The approach of the law – and of public-health officials – was one dominated by the mentality of poor-law administration. They often considered that 'the open life of the country' made the provision of sanitary conveniences somewhat superfluous. That might be so on a small family farm with a convenient byre or a choice of parks at the back of the house, but in the closely populated rows of a big East Lothian *toun* it was very inadequate, and the evidence suggests that people found the situation degrading. It was only in the 1930s that public health authorities became aware of the farms as a source of infection through milk, and their potential as a source of typhoid.

Various reasons have been advanced for this state of affairs, some of them purely practical, such as the lack of a water supply and sewage infrastructure in many parts of the countryside (septic tanks were only just coming in). From 1925 government grants were available to improve sanitation, but they were rarely taken up, because farming was in such a state that there was often no money to make up the owner's contribution. Reports made by public-health officials varied so widely for similar areas that not only were the statistics meaningless, but the inspections a pretence. There was probably an attitude among officialdom that it was all a waste of time. The size of the inspectorate was totally inadequate to the task. Also, they were reluctant to use the ultimate sanction, a closing order, as that would make the housing situation worse. The Secretary of State's Housing Advisory Committee of 1937 was severely critical of all this, stating that the owner's financial embarrassment was no excuse for not complying with the law.[18]

With the prospect of moving to another house at the end of the term, workers would endure bad conditions and hope for better. Where the farm was part of an estate, as was the norm before 1914 and still common enough after World War I, the maintenance and repair of farm servants' housing often fell between the two stools of laird and farmer. The farm servant's limited twelve-month fee made complaints easy enough to parry with promises. The farmer's obligation was to keep the housing in the state that he found it at the beginning of the tack, which would be nominally fit for habitation. If it was wretched, then it would stay wretched. If the farmer had to press the laird for improvements, workers' housing would be at the bottom of his list. This is perhaps borne out by the marked difference in the quality of farm-servants' housing and of those working directly for the estate, such as keepers and gardeners, who would nearly all have some form of sanitary convenience, were twice as likely to have a water supply and a WC inside the house, and had less than half the normal incidence of damp.[19]

A farmer's sense of social responsibility could for instance include kindness to a loyal and long-established farm servant who had fallen into ill-health, but would not include a general commitment to changing the lot of the working population. Although in the 1920s most farmers and farm servants still spoke very much the same language, there was a considerable social gulf. The servants were *wark-fowk* who had made their bargain at feeing time. Improvements were a matter of condescension, although we should bear in mind that condescension was a quite acceptable basis for a relationship in this era, and is indeed inherent in the term *farm servant*, deriving as it does from the notion of master and servant.

After World War I, when many farmers bought their own farms (see below), it appears that some did not include the cost of housing maintenance previously borne by the estate in their calculations, and this was compounded by the post-war depression.[20] Often it was the farm-servants' wives who would give the farmers the rough edge of their tongues, whereas for the men that could be deemed a breach of contract meriting dismissal.[21]

Women were often the agents of domestic change, because it was primarily on them that the burdens of poor housing mainly fell. Despite the increase of the travelling cadgers and vanmen in the country districts before World War I, and the greater convenience in purchasing household necessities, there was a hunger of a different sort. In 1917 the Board of Agriculture for Scotland sponsored the foundation of the Scottish Women's Rural Institutes. From the inauguration of the first one at Macmerry in East Lothian, they were an immediate success. Within 5 years there were 242 branches with a membership of 14,000. The idea spread to the rest of Britain. Perverse evidence of their worth is that initially the 'rurals' met with considerable male opposition. The yearning for a more interesting social life was also reflected in a steady drain of population to the towns. And however hard it might turn out to be, the prospect of emigration was an attractive one, and many lowland farm servants followed that trail up to the outbreak of World War I, lured on by the travelling salesmen of the Canadian Pacific Railway with the promise of their *quarter* of land, and more if they made a go of it.

Although poor housing was often blamed at the time for rural depopulation, there was no obvious link between the exodus and the areas of worst housing. Nor was unemployment a problem in the pre-war lowland countryside. The farming press was always regretting the loss of skilled labour. It was also one of the pressures that kept up the development of labour-saving equipment and the further stretching of the already long rotations.

In political terms the rural population did not matter. That may seem strange considering the developments afoot in the pre-war years, but the tide seemed to have set in a different direction. The main expansion of New World farming had all but run its course. Many projects that had once been only pipe dreams were coming to fruition. In 1899 the West of Scotland College of Agriculture was founded, and in 1901 and 1904 similar colleges were founded in Edinburgh and Aberdeen, all with government recognition.[22] In 1912 came Joe Duncan's Scottish Farm Servants' Union, and in the same year the Board of Agriculture for Scotland and the Scottish Land Court. The same controversy raged over the Board as does today over a Scottish parliament, stemming from the fear that Scottish interests would be marginalised. The record in that sector, however, indicates the opposite. In 1913 the Chamber of Agriculture sponsored the formation of the National Farmers' Union.

It appeared that the state of lowland as well as Highland rural society was after a fashion becoming a political issue. The landowning interest raged at the prospect of introducing crofting into lowland agriculture. Liberal politicians wrote elegant pamphlets about the state of the land, echoing the Tolstoyan *Narodniki* of mainland Europe and looking with envious admiration at the farmers of Denmark and the Netherlands where small farmers were in the majority, secure in their holdings and prospering within a strong co-operative framework. In other contexts, in Germany, Poland and Hungary, following World War I these notions would march into another era of peasants' parties, eventually to be exploited with the Fascist catch-phrases of *Blut und Boden*. But never in Scotland. The Crofter MPs were absorbed into the mainstream of British Liberal and latterly Labour politics. The fact is, by the turn of the century the United Kingdom was so urban and Empire-orientated that rural social issues did not matter. There is a history of extraordinary differentials between town and country. Urban workers had the vote in 1867 while country people had to wait until 1884. There was unemployment insurance for every worker from 1920 – except for farm workers, who got a cut-down version in the Agricultural Wages (Regulation) (Scotland) Act of 1937.[23]

The do–it–yourself pre-industrial ethos of anti-government independence displayed in the *Turra Coo* incident may also explain something. Following Lloyd George's National Insurance legislation of 1911, local farm servants backed Robert Paterson in Lendrum, by Turriff, in not paying the levy. Their argument was that supposedly healthier country people would not fall ill so readily as factory-bred *tounsers*, so why should they subsidise them? When one of Paterson's beasts was poinded towards paying for his contribution, there was a comical public disturbance that passed into popular legend in the north east. There was a real *roch* and boisterous streak in the old rural population, their instinct being to settle scores directly, whether with a mean farmer by leaving him a *clean toun* and a bad name at the term, to bait a sharp-tongued farmer's wife by raiding her eggs or indeed the hens, or to exert group pressure in very local terms, as in horsemen's societies. However, the effect of such behaviour was always limited, and once the economic depression had set in after World War I, it was not such a threat.

The alternative, Joe Duncan's organised union, faced various obstacles besides the ethos of the *Turra Coo*. Although the pattern of movement from one fee to another was usually within a well-defined district, it was enough to make keeping track of a membership so time-consuming as to be impossible. Nor were farm servants a homogenous group. As engine drivers in the city were quaintly described by their well-heeled admirers as 'the aristocrats of the working class', the same might have been said of the shepherd in a rural context, and the differential in status between a shepherd and a woman outworker was considerable. Such demarcation within what were already isolated groups was fatal. It would take two wars and the levelling effects of powered mechanisation to change this.

Then there was that other substantial segment of the rural population, the tradesmen such as blacksmiths, joiners, masons, slaters and millwrights, on whom the farms were totally dependent. Equally important were the various semi-skilled trades – the dykers and ditchers, the mole-catchers and rabbit-catchers, and then the considerable gamut of estate workers – gamekeepers, foresters and the whole range of staff it took to run a 'Big Hoose' and its policies.[24] Here we have a complex society that is totally foreign to the simplistic food factory that modern planners and politicians imagine the countryside to be and to have been. Right up to the post-war years it was a hybrid society, half peasant, half industrialised.

In the *Scottish Farmer Year Book* of 1903 an anonymous correspondent asked 'what would by the state of this country if the lines of communication from the wheat plains of the outside world were interrupted?'. Later the same author referred to 'the trial of strength which was sure to come one day'. He had a point. Britain produced only a quarter of the food it consumed, and parliamentary committees did consider this alarming scenario, concluding that the Royal Navy would keep the supply lines open. That turned out to be correct, but only just.

On the outbreak of World War I, recruitment affected the countryside as much as the towns, and in the case of the Crofting Counties, more so. The nineteenth-century volunteer movement had a strong rural following,[25] and that carried over into the reforms that created the Territorial Army and Royal Naval Reserve in 1906.[26] In the end, over two-fifths of Scotland's countrymen went to war, and from that it would be fair to infer one half of the male population in the prime of life.[27] At the outset there was the expectation that the war would be a few short rounds of rapid cut-and-thrust. It was the German attempt to break the ensuing deadlock by submarine warfare, and the prospect that Britain would starve and actually lose the war that stimulated a plan to manage agricultural output on a grand scale. In addition, 1916 was a rotten harvest with half the grain yields of 1914, and staples such as potatoes produced little more than four tons to the acre.

Lloyd George's administration grasped that military victory depended primarily on what was christened the 'Home Front'. The hitherto leisurely Agricultural Executive Committees were galvanised into action and a massive sowing programme put in hand for the spring of 1917. Contrary to the popular myth, conscription did not aim to provide cannon-fodder, but a structured war industry, and agriculture was part of that. Thus farming became a reserved occupation. The Women's Land Army was created, the retired and the young were mobilised, the latter by suspending the school leaving age of fourteen. Above all the Corn Production Act of 1917 guaranteed both prices and wages. The whole combination was remarkably effective.

In 1921 the Corn Production Act was repealed, and with that the whole framework of wage agreements. In one respect the people who lost out most were women, because during the war their wages had been brought close to those of men, to prevent them going off to the better-paid munitions factories in the towns. The countryside was plunged back into depression. With depression came a collapse in land prices, and over the next few years a drastic turnover in land ownership in Scotland. Just under two-fifths of the land changed hands; if that were to be calculated by productive capacity, this proportion would be even larger. With all this came a fundamental shift in the social character of the countryside. Long-established estates vanished, the years of depression having left many of them burdened with debt. On top of that there could be a series of death duties incurred by war casualties. Of course, many estates survived, sometimes much cut-down, but they no longer dominated the social organisation of the countryside as they had before.

The principal buyers were the sitting tenants. Those farmers who had been careful with the proceeds of war-time production were often in a position to buy, and usually at a pretty low valuation. This lurch towards owner-occupation started something that has continued to the present day. In the late 1880s the number of registered holdings was about 80,000, with a quarter of these under five acres. Overall, owner occupation was just under a tenth. By 1930 owner occupation had trebled to two-fifths, by 1960 it was over a third. The trend accelerated. By 1991 the number of holdings had shrunk from 61,000 in 1960 to just under 31,000, interest-ingly, a third of these still under 50 acres. Overall, two-thirds of farms were owner-occupied. The remaining third included farms owned and managed for trusts and companies, or estate farms with managers. The number of farms which are tenancies within estates with the old-fashioned tenant and laird relationship is comparatively small.[28]

The tenancies which did develop after World War I were the govern-ment holdings, rather like veterans' farms for retired Roman soldiers. They are an interesting phenomenon, but for the lowlands not numerically or economically significant.[29] The idea was that they would not just satisfy a popular demand, but provide a stepping stone towards more substantial tenancies (which they did not). For many the attraction would not have been the land but the house.

Nevertheless, the hours of work were changing. Before the war a ploughman would be up at five to groom and feed his *pair o' horse*, and be back at the stable door for *yokin time* at six, whence he would finally return twelve hours later, with the horses still to attend to. He would have two hours off from, say, eleven to one, his *mid-yokin*, although any old horse-man will aver that this break was geared to the working capacity of the horses, not the men. After the war, this was reduced to ten hours a day from the stable door. The biggest prize was the dawn of the Saturday half-day. Until World War I the only holidays were Sundays, New Year's Day, and the feeing days. There could also be other informal concessions, such as time off before moving to a new fee to put the garden in, or attendance at a ploughing match or agricultural show. These latter underline the fact that even leisure activities were dominated by work. The bothy songs were about work, as were the domestic interests of the 'Rural'. The *kirns* or *meal 'n ale* celebrations that marked the end of the *hairst* celebrated work.[30] Until 1937 the week-long holiday away from work that many townsfolk had was rare. The labour organisation might be industrial, but the ethos was not.

The inter-war period saw underlying structural changes that would prove to be of long-term rather than immediate significance. In 1919 the Forestry Commission was founded with the intention of making good the devastation of timber that had occurred during the war, one of the prime movers being Sir John Stirling Maxwell.[31] The government acted directly in supporting the foundation of significant research bodies such as the Rowett, Morden and Macaulay institutes. Although these might have appeared as frivolous luxuries in the middle of a grim depression, practical heavyweight scientific research was desperately needed. The potato crop in particular (the potato was as much a staple as grain) was riddled with disease, and the scientific basis of animal and crop husbandry had advanced little since the turn of the century.[32] The work of John Boyd Orr alone at the Rowett Institute on animal and human nutrition was of world significance.

Encouraged by the Scottish Agricultural Organising Society, fledgling co-operative marketing organisations such as egg producers in the north east and Orkney, which had been stopped in their tracks by the war, showed renewed signs of life. Sheer desperation engendered by periodic glut and a chaotic fragmentation of the market drove potato and milk producers towards the formation of the respective marketing boards. However, that did not happen without a struggle and resort to the compulsion of legislation, in the Agricultural Marketing Act of 1931.

A turning point was the appointment of Walter Elliot as Minister of Agriculture in 1932. The preceding two years marked the absolute nadir of farming this century, when crop prices hardly returned the cost of sowing them. Instead of offering the timid do-nothing excuses of his predecessors, Elliot – a skilled border farmer himself – immediately moved to restrict imports and stave off a total collapse of cattle and sheep prices. Other measures followed, the most interesting of which were schemes to retrieve the badly run-down state of the land. Much ground had hardly seen lime or drainage work since the late 1870s.

It was a sea-change which was to develop its own momentum. When the balloon went up again in 1939, there was at the outset the assumption that after the war farming would not be left to slide back into depression. This was institutionalised in the annual price reviews from 1947, and with that the framework of confidence that produced the investment in powered mechanisation. The organisation of agriculture during World War II built on the lessons of previous experience. This time plans had been well laid before hostilities broke out. An interesting contrast is that at the outset, if the Nazis fielded a much more professional army, the British had a more professional war economy, and farming was part of that. During World War II, rationing was much more refined and based on scientific rationale. The principal beneficiaries were the slum-dwellers of the towns, many of whom now had the first decent diet in their lives. The difference for country people lay in the Restrictions on Engagements order of 1940, which restricted farm workers from moving out of the industry, and the ponderously entitled Essential Work (Agriculture) (Scotland) Act of 1941, aptly shortened in common speech to the 'Stand Still' Act. This stopped farm servants moving from one fee to another without good reason, and effectively broke the habit of flitting from one place to another. With this came the spread of the weekly wage, setting a pattern that would continue after the war. At this time there was also an almost revolutionary improvement in housing. Unless estates or farmers provided decent accommodation, they could not get workers. In the event, as post-war farming moved into prosperity, the money was there to achieve this. In all, the farming population was to become more settled than it had been for two centuries.

As we know, the invention of the tractor and combine were a major part in decisive change. The genius of Harry Ferguson had a lot to do with the development of the tractor. His parents farmed at Growell in Co. Down. Ferguson was a sixth-generation Ulster Scot. He escaped the farm early to join his elder brother's garage business in Belfast, where he developed a wide mechanical knowledge, which included cars and aircraft. By 1933 he had developed his prototype tractor, and in 1936 this went into production as the Ferguson-Brown, in partnership with the Huddersfield firm. The essential and novel element was the three-point linkage at the rear of the machine, which was controlled by two hydraulically-operated arms. On these three points were mounted implements designed for the system. The implements thus became part of the tractor, and for the first time the tractor's full power could be taken advantage of. The implements could be raised, lowered and changed by one man at the touch of a lever. Because of the hydraulically-controlled semi-rigid mounting, the drag of a plough bound down the tractor wheels, giving a smaller machine greater grip on the ground, the so-called weight-transfer.

One might imagine that this would have been an immediate success, but it was not. There was not only the expense of the machine, but the system implements to go with it.[33] Even although the depression was beginning to lift a little at that point, money was still very scarce, and not many were sold. In all, about 1,250 Ferguson-Brown machines were made. But the basic idea was there.

The combine was more a process of evolution. It started in the US in the nineteenth century, principally with the firm of Holt (which became Caterpillar). The first combines were essentially travelling threshing mills with a cutter bar and conveyor belt added, and before the first tractors they were pulled by monster teams of mules or horses. In 1926 some were exported to Europe, but their success was very limited, because they were designed to thresh the short and light-strawed prairie crops, not the longer and coarse-strawed varieties of northern Europe. In England in 1928 Clayton and Shuttleworth produced a much-improved design, and it was one of these that came to Lord Balfour's farms of Whittinghame and Cairndinnis in East Lothian in 1932. It was to be one of the very few work-ing in Scotland for many years. The same machine is now preserved in the Scottish Agricultural Museum, perhaps the oldest combine in working order in the world. Farming during World War II still used horses.[34] Mech-anisation showed in the Government Tractor Service, where powered machinery was used as a flying squad where cultivation was falling behind. By 1942 machinery was pouring in from the US as part of Lend-Lease. This included a few Ford Ferguson tractors. Ferguson had fallen out with David Brown and taken up with the aging Henry Ford. Ford's engineers, in particular Sorensen, had weeded out the weak points in Ferguson's design and got production on a sound footing.

In the event, Ferguson was to fall out with Henry Ford's successors, and after the war the same basic design was transferred to the Standard works at Coventry. Here was TE 20, 'the Wee Grey Fergie' of popular memory, or 'the Ferguson menace' to the trade rivals. Half a million were produced. Meanwhile combine design advanced rapidly, the first self-propelled models coming out in the late 1940s, and the first recognisable modern combines in the mid-1950s with the Massey Harris then Massey Ferguson 700 series (made in Kilmarnock).

It is with the combine rather than the Ferguson-system tractor that we can make a dramatic comparison between the old ways and the new. With horse working, first the *road* had to be cleared along the edge of the field with a scythe to let the binder in without damaging the crop. The binder, often with a special three-horse yoke, threw off the sheaves already bound. These then had to be stooked. A hard blow, and they would have to be stooked again, perhaps several times, until they had sufficiently *won*. Then they would be thrown down so that the *erse o' the shaef* could dry, and then they were *led*, or loaded on to a cart and taken into the cornyard, where they were built into a *ruck* or stack. This was a skilled job, and the stack had to be thatched and roped. The crop would win further in the stacks, which then had to be pulled apart and threshed, either one by one as required in the fixed barn mill, or those that remained in the spring by the travelling high-speed mill. The grain from the barn mills often had to be *dichtit* or winnowed separately. By contrast, a combine does all this in one operation.[35]

The change-over to the new regime came with great rapidity. By 1952 horses were dwindling rapidly. By the end of the decade they were becoming unusual. By the end of the 1960s they were a rarity. With the horses went the whole labour-intensive system – the ploughmen and their families, the tradesmen, and in many cases the old steadings themselves which had been designed round horse-working. The depopulation and all the attendant factors are not hard to imagine. This is best illustrated by one remarkable fact. In the lowland countryside today, those connected with farming, either directly as farmers or workers, or indirectly as agricultural engineers, vets, dealers etc., are now a minority within the rural population.[36]

When the original Six (Germany, France, Italy, Netherlands, Belgium, Luxembourg) signed the Treaty of Paris in 1951, creating the European Coal and Steel Community, the UK was taken up with the Festival of Britain, and did not take any notice. The Suez fiasco that would signal the end of Britain's great power status still lay five years ahead, as did English nationalist dreams of a 'new Elizabethan age'. But, as we know, that community evolved into the European Economic Community in 1957, by which time the German Economic Miracle was in full swing. In 1962 the common coal and steel policy was reinforced by a common agricultural policy. This had the two related objectives of keeping people on the land, and raising their standard of living to that of townsfolk. Now Britain tried to scramble aboard the Community, but in 1963 and again in 1967 General de Gaulle said *non!* Following his death in 1969 the CAP received a fresh impetus, as did the British efforts to gain entry. This was finally agreed in 1972.

In the euphoria that surrounded Britain's entry, land prices rose sharply, because the CAP held out the prospect of a longer term agricultural policy than the old annual price review. Support was effected by setting a floor for prices by 'intervention' buying by the Community, and storing the surplus. Hence came the accumulation of the fabled beef, butter and grain mountains and wine lakes. In Scotland this produced a significant structural change, as the support followed the long-established mainland European ethos of putting 'bread' or grain first. On many farms, particularly on the eastern side of the country, the tradition of mixed livestock and arable farming was abandoned. Such a move tends to be a one-way ticket, as the livestock production cycle is much longer, thus the return on investment is much slower. Furthermore, the skills of stockmanship are not so easily drummed up from the pages of a book. Pure arable also had other inducements – no longer the constant tie of beasts to be looked after.

Other consequences followed, such as the growth of contracting for many basic operations from ploughing to harvest. Farming through contractors was once laughed at as the lazy farmer's road to ruin, but now with the efficient utilisation of machinery, there were many tasks that could be done at less cost than the individual farmer could achieve. An alternative which had its origin in Germany and spread to lowland Scotland in the 1980s was the machinery ring, which meant a group of farmers sharing the most modern and efficient tools. This took on first in the Borders, then Aberdeenshire and Angus and the Mearns. This application of mechanical rationale which had started with the Ferguson system and the combine harvester reinforced the trend to depopulation. The agricultural workforce is still contracting at the rate of 2 per cent a year.

Productivity has been maintained not just through machinery but scientific development. There is a popular urban myth that this is a monster that must be caged and chastised rather than encouraged and responsibly directed. It is through intelligent plant breeding that strains can be developed that are naturally disease resistant rather than dependent on various sprays to protect them. In economic terms, new strains of cereals are vital to Scotland. The now ubiquitous winter barley as well as wheat which will thrive in Scotland's northern climate enables farmers to compete on even terms with their counterparts in, say, the clement climates of the Loire and the Po valleys. In this broader European perspective the climate can grant Scotland some advantages. The cooler climate and relative isolation of specialist enterprises makes for a high health status, enabling the surer production for instance of good seed potatoes.

Another and new area of specialisation that astonished country people half a century ago is the total change of pig and poultry production.[37] Again Scotland profits from high health status, because unlike for instance in the Netherlands or Denmark, the intensive breeding and production units are isolated from one another. The desirability of such regimes is now often questioned. If however the urban public wish low-intensity free-range pig and poultry products, they will have to pay for them. All these issues high-light a new dimension of animal welfare and environmental questions where urban lobbies are making new demands of the countryside.

This has extended to the financial support for farming. 'Set-aside' or paying farmers to take land out of production is one alternative to inter-vention buying and thus reducing production 'mountains'; quotas as imposed on the dairy industry are another. Yet other factors have worked to the British farmers' advantage, in particular the consistently poor value of British currency, because EC financial support is calculated in Ecus (originally the 'green pound' system) yielding a favourable rate of payment.

However, this picture of fewer and richer farmers has not been without some pretty rough patches. The severe inflation of the late 1970s caught many farmers who had run up big debts through investment on the hop, and well into the following decade there were bankruptcies, particularly in the north east, and not a few tragic suicides among people who were good farmers but poor accountants. This brought to the surface much specu-lation within the farming community as to the changed nature of the life, as if people had only just woken up to the change in personal terms. Instead of the farmer presiding over a *toun* that was often a small village of the *pleuchies* and their families, the *herd* and the *cattilie*, not to mention the *byre wumman* and the *kitchie lass*, as often as not he and his family are there on their own with their machines and bulk-handling systems. It can be an iso-lated and lonely existence. Where the farm will support it, there is a trend for some farming families to send their children to private boarding schools so, like Jane Austen's Bennet family, they are 'rising into property and gen-tility' and becoming integrated into a social circuit that has its roots in income rather than location. In the West – from Dumbarton south to Galloway – where livestock still predominates, there is a country population concentrated in small farms (by British standards) sufficient to maintain something of the older ethos and language. In other areas, that ethos is increasingly maintained in the small country towns. For instance, in the eastern Borders, there has been an overall increase in population, but it is concentrated in centres such as Galashiels and Kelso, while landward areas such as upper Lauderdale or Longformacus are still declining in population.

There are important aspects and trends that statistics do not yet reveal which could be important for the future. One is the drift towards part-time farming, the creeping 'crofterisation' of the lowland countryside that the landed interest so dreaded at the beginning of the century. Some committed traditional farmers may dismiss this as 'hobby-farming', but increasingly they are being forced into developing other activities themselves, centring more general business enterprises in the countryside. The use of modern communication technology has reinforced this trend.

One countervailing restriction lies in the planning laws. These arise from the urban bureaucrat's conception that the countryside is either a food factory or a weekend playground that must not be 'spoilt'. Many other parts of Europe are having to come to terms with the same industrialisation of farming. The view from the summit of Menez Hom in Brittany reveals an astonishingly different picture of a populated landscape, because when people leave the farm, they can still have their homes on the land, continuing to build in a modern Breton vernacular.

As the opening of the corn-lands of America and Australia so affected European farming into the beginning of this century, so will the collapse of state socialism in Central and Eastern Europe affect the whole continent in the coming century. Once areas such as Hungary, the Ukraine and Romania – which contain vast tracts of very fertile ground – recover from up to three-quarters of a century of mismanagement, corruption and plain abuse, then the balance for the rest of Europe's farmers will change yet again.

NOTES AND REFERENCES

1. The history of Scottish agricultural journalism is well accounted for in Angus MacDonald, *The Scottish Farmer – One Hundred Years* (East Kilbride, 1993).
2. D.T. Jones, J.F. Duncan, H.M. Conacher, W.R. Scott and J.P. Day, *Scotland during the War* (Oxford, 1926), p. 132.
3. Within its reduced compass, it was also more productive, as the crop that followed on the longer *lye* was higher-yielding. The same phenomenon is occurring with set-aside today, where a heavier yield (up to twenty per cent) follows on ground that has lain fallow. The tendency in England was to put more ground in permanent grass and reduce the arable to a smaller four-shift core. This was a retrograde step, and may account for the success of Scots farmers who settled in southern and eastern England when the unfortunate natives went bust during the inter-war depression.
4. Jones et al., *Scotland during the War*, p. 198.
5. See T.M. Devine, 'Scottish Farm Labour in the Era of Agricultural Depression, 1875–1900' in T.M. Devine (ed.), *Farm Servants and Labour in Lowland Scotland 1770–1914* (Edinburgh, 1984).
6. Although Hugh Watson, in Keillor, Strathmore, founded the breed, it was the McCombies in Tillyfour and Grant of Ballindalloch who had made the breed commercially formidable. South American and Texas breeders are still regular attenders at the Perth sales, aiming to improve their stock. The Shorthorn, which in the middle of the last century bid fair to relegate the native breeds to the sidelines, itself developed a distinct Scottish strain which is still important in the north-east.

7. The late Allan Hamilton, of a family of East Lothian farm servants, recollected many such examples. The break-up of the strict bondager system towards the end of the nineteenth century in fact threw more emphasis on the husband and son/wife/daughter team, which commonly involved three and sometimes up to six members of the same family in what was generally known as *double hinding*. Many farms had a *wumman gaffer*, a man in charge of the woman outworkers. Multiple fees involving several family members also occurred on the big low-ground farms of Easter Ross.

8. The milking machine developed very much by fits and starts, first in south west Scotland from late last century. Although workable machinery – which included a pulsator to replicate the natural sucking action of a calf – was available by 1905, as with the tractor, it took a long time before this invention became widespread. The availability of family female labour on the small farms of west and central districts inhibited its spread until later. Only in the 1950s with the electrification of the countryside did hand-milking become a rarity.

9. See G. Sprott, 'Who were the Sailormen?' in *Review of Scottish Culture* No. 2 (1986).

10. When the government was in discussion with agricultural labour in 1917 with a view to fixing equitable wages, Joe Duncan of the Scottish Farm Servants' Union protested that this did not take into account that housing – which was among other things in effect part of the wage – was so much worse in Scotland.

11. Some individuals do stand out. For instance the Roseberry estates rebuilt a lot of accommodation to provide what were then the best standards. There may be some connection between this and the Earl's enthusiasm for the poetry of Robert Burns.

12. For instance, Allan Hamilton recalled that when his father was promoted to be manager of the Co-operative Society's farm at Long Newton by Gifford c.1926, they found themselves in a house with an upstairs and two more bedrooms. So few were their possessions (they all went into two box-carts) and so unused were they to the space, that the extra rooms lay empty.

13. *Royal Commission on the housing of the Industrial Population of Scotland, Rural and Urban*, 1917, p. 168. Chapter XV is devoted to rural housing, and reveals a miserable picture.

14. ibid., p. 167.

15. On one farm in south Angus known to the author, a visitor from the town complained about the want of a lock on the privy door. The farmer was puzzled – 'faa 'ad want tae steal a bucket o' s★★★?'

16. Scottish Housing Advisory Committee, *Report on Rural Housing in Scotland 1937*, p. 85.

17. *Report on Rural Housing 1936*, p. 23.

18. *Report on Rural Housing 1937*, p. 15.

19. *Report on Rural Housing 1936*, p. 85.

20. Jones et al., *Rural Scotland during the War*, p. 178.

21. The late Harry Davidson, Bankfoot, Perthshire, recalled this as common enough to be a standard ritual. But the farmer still had the last word, or in this case, non-word. *Speaking time* was the period near the end of a term when a farm servant would be asked if he wished to *bide*. If the farmer said nothing, that was a sign that the contract would not be renewed.

22. As distinct from the School of Agriculture in Edinburgh University, which had been founded in 1790; although they would also develop a formidable research record, the new colleges concentrated on practical skills for practical farmers.

23. There is an interesting discussion of these issues by B. Robertson, 'The Scottish Farm Servant and his Union: from Encapsulation to Integration' in I. MacDougall (ed.), *Essays in Scottish Labour History* (Edinburgh, 1978).

24. See G. Sprott, 'The Country Tradesmen' in Devine, *Farm Servants and Labour in Lowland Scotland*.

25. There are curious relics of the Volunteer movement still to be seen, such as the wall-mounted trophies and mementoes in the public halls at Melrose. There are still numerous 'Drill Halls' throughout rural Scotland that attest to this phenomenon.

26. This in particular provided a magnet for recruits from the crofting counties, for the annual bounty helped to pay the rent.

27. Jones et al., *Scotland during the War*.

28. Ministry of Agriculture and Food & Department of Agriculture for Scotland, *A Century of Agricultural Statistics 1866–1966* (HMSO, 1968).

29. See L. Leneman, *Fit for Heroes? Land settlement in Scotland after World War I* (Aberdeen, 1989).

30. The reach of rip-roaring *course* humour would still come back to work, for example at a clipping, with an imaginative comparison between individual *yowes* and the women of the district.

31. Some of his experimental planting can still be seen as mature timber on Corrour Estate in Inverness-shire.

32. This despite the efforts of Sir Patrick Wright, the first principal of the West of Scotland Agricultural College, who did much to translate and introduce German scientific knowledge in the chemistry of agriculture to Britain, and initiated programmes of systematic crop trials.

33. The tractor cost £224 (compared with £135 for the Fordson on steel wheels and £180 on rubbers), the initial range of mounted implements – including a two-furrow plough, a spring-tine cultivator, rigid-tine cultivator, and a ridge plough – cost £26 each.

34. Only in Buchan did the tractor make much headway between the wars, due to the endemic horse-sickness in that district. This gave Aberdeenshire the distinction of being the most highly mechanised area of Britain at the time.

35. The author recalls some years ago looking at a small fifteen-acre field near Kirriemuir, remarking how a combine would clear it in a morning. His companion recalled how in 1922 in the same field a wind-laid crop had been cleared in the same time – but with over forty people working, some with scythes, others binding and stooking.

36. *Scottish Rural Profile* (HMSO , 1991).

37. The author recalls an incident at Ballintuim in Strathardle in 1959. A man was buying eggs in the local shop, and demanded 'nane o thae damned battery hens' eggs but richt waalkin-about hens' eggs'.

10. GENDER APARTHEID?: WOMEN IN SCOTTISH SOCIETY
Arthur McIvor

Class divisions fractured Scottish society in the early years of the twentieth century, but so too did discrepancies based on gender; these, however, have been investigated far less systematically, and this chapter aims to look at the degree of 'gender apartheid' experienced this century.

Despite a flurry of recent research, there remain massive gaps in our knowledge of the changing patterns and continuities in Scottish women's lives.[1] Research has focused predominantly upon the industrial west of Scotland and on Dundee. Basic quantification of social and economic indicators relevant to Scottish women as citizens, consumers and workers remains quite thin, whilst the vast potential of oral evidence (to explore in particular the 'inner world' of women's lives) remains largely unexploited.[2] Scottish women's history lacks the maturity of the discipline in England, whilst it has suffered somewhat from being subsumed within the British experience as a whole, when there may be a distinctively Scottish story to tell.[3] A largely unbridged chasm remains between the work of social scientists working on women in contemporary Scottish society and historians whose focus has been the pre–World War II period.

Scotland had an intensely patriarchal society in 1900. Women were widely regarded as second-class citizens, whose labour was valued at less than half the rate of that earned by men and whose property-holding and voting rights were severely prescribed. Charles Robinson, Motherwell Trades Council delegate to the Scottish Trade Union Congress, personified such attitudes. Speaking in 1918 against a resolution proposing a union campaign to break down occupational segregation, Robinson argued that the involvement of women in industry during World War I was demoralising, had 'a depressing effect upon public morality' and that a woman's 'natural sphere is the home'.[4]

FAMILY, HOUSEWORK AND MARRIAGE

The experience of women in the twentieth century is intimately bound up with their lives within the family and the household and this 'private sphere', in turn, has had a critical role in women's involvement in the 'public sphere' of paid work and politics. The cult of domesticity which gathered momentum through the Victorian period dictated that by 1900 the inalienable cultural norm in Scotland was that the primary role of women in life was the servicing of a male 'breadwinner' within the home and family. According to the 1911 Census of Scotland, only one in twenty employed women was married. Reality was more complex: a minority of single, independent women had a different experience; women within the poorest families had to engage in paid work because their husbands (as unskilled labourers) failed to earn a 'family' wage; and there were different aspects to domesticity for working-class and middle-class women.[5] More-over, the decennial census seriously under-recorded female economic activity, underestimating part-time, casual and seasonal employment.[6] Nevertheless, for most married women in Scotland before 1914 life pivoted around the tasks of reproduction, child rearing, housework and servicing family needs. Women were socialised into acceptance of a domestic role and the subordinate socio-political status this entailed. This acculturation process led most women not only to acquiesce, but to actively support and endorse traditional notions of the family and the sexual division of labour.[7] Domesticity was limiting, but also secure and widely regarded as 'respectable' within the prevailing world view of the Edwardian period.

During the course of the twentieth century significant changes have taken place within the private sphere of the home and the family in Scot-land.[8] Undoubtedly, the critical change was the control women achieved over their fertility (see Table 1). From the 1870s to the turn of the century there was already a modest fall in Scottish fertility rates, notably amongst the middle classes, bringing the average family size down to six.[9] The trend continued downwards until World War II, with a rise thereafter linked to a fall in the mean age of marriage (see Table 2). From the 1960s, fertility rates fell back drastically again, though the downward trend slowed markedly in the 1980s. This movement is linked intimately to the wide-spread availability of oral contraceptives from the late 1960s and to delayed marriages from the late 1970s. Nevertheless, the decline in family size is clearly a long-term phenomenon which pre-dates the 'pill'.

One comparison is worth noting: the fall in fertility initially occurred more rapidly in England than Scotland. Thus, Scottish families remained substantially larger than English families in the first half of the twentieth

TABLE 1

General Fertility Rate (per 1,000 women aged 15–44)

	Scotland	England and Wales
1900–2	120.6	114.7
1910–12	107.4	98.6
1920–2	105.9	91.1
1930–2	78.8	64.4
1940–2	73.7	61.3
1950–2	81.4	72.1
1960–2	97.8	88.9
1970–2	83.3	81.4
1980–2	62.2	61.8
1990–2	59.3	63.8

Source: Central Statistical Office, Annual Abstract of Statistics, No. 130 (1994).

TABLE 2

Mean Age at Marriage in Scotland: Females

1901–10	26.2	1961–70	24.1
1911–20	26.7	1971–80	24.7
1921–30	26.5	1981–90	26.6
1931–40	26.4	1991	28.5
1941–50	26.0	1992	29.1
1951–60	25.1		

Source: Central Statistical Office, Scottish Abstract of Statistics, No. 22 (1994).

century.[10] Class structure is of primary importance in explaining such differentials: Scotland had a smaller middle class than England.[11] Religion may also have played some part, because Scotland had a larger proportion of Catholics than England in the first half of the twentieth century.[12] Moreover, the birth-control campaign appears to have experienced more opposition in Scotland than in England. Elspeth King has exposed the severe problems birth-control campaigners faced in inter-war Glasgow.[13] A range of views existed, but on the whole the Scottish labour movement between the wars had a regressive attitude towards birth control. Prominent members of the Independent Labour Party, including John Wheatley, Stephen Campbell and James Maxton, were amongst those who voted and campaigned against the extension of public information and medical advice on contraception.[14] In respect of both family size and formal economic activity, however, Scotland was little different to England by the 1980s, and regional variations within Scotland had by this time narrowed,[15] revealing that, as in so many other areas of social and cultural life, there has been a trend towards convergence between Scotland and the rest of Britain over the course of the twentieth century.[16]

Smaller families combined with the incremental improvement in life expectancy had a significant impact upon women's lives across all social classes. In 1900, Scottish working-class women would have spent around a third of their lives (i.e. fifteen to seventeen years) producing, nursing and nurturing children up to the age of ten. Indeed, given average life expectancy of forty-seven in the 1900s, few women would have experienced life without dependent children within the home. By the early 1990s, with the average number of children per family at two and life expectancy up to seventy-seven years, this maternal care period had contracted to constitute around fifteen per cent of a woman's life span.

The last quarter of the twentieth century has also seen some erosion of married family life in Scotland. Between 1971 and 1991 the marriage rate (including remarriages) fell by 16 per cent – a larger proportion of marriages have broken up and there has been a sharp rise in births outside marriage.[17] Typically, in the early twentieth century marriages were dissolved on the death of one partner: only 142 individuals sued for divorce in Scotland in 1900.[18] Divorce and co-habitation rates have risen sharply since the 1960s. In 1960 there were less than 2,000 divorces in Scotland. In 1991 there were 12,400 and 75 per cent of these cases were initiated by women.[19] Double standards in divorce law were removed in the 1920s, making it possible for women to divorce men on the same grounds. The Divorce (Scotland) Act of 1938 introduced a wider range of grounds for divorce, including (for the first time) cruelty. The provision of legal aid to women in divorce cases in 1949, 'no-fault' divorce law reforms in the late 1960s and 1970s, and the passage of the Family Law (Scotland) Act in 1985 appear to have had particularly beneficial results – the latter providing for a fairer distribution of family resources and property upon marital breakdown.[20] Marital and partnership breakdowns have led to a rapid growth in single-parent families, which now constitute around one in five Scottish families.[21] Not least because of the continuing undervaluation of female labour, this situation has exacerbated the problem of poverty amongst single-parent families (90 per cent of which are headed by women).[22]

The decline in live-in relatives, fewer children, artificial contraception, labour-saving devices, rising housing standards and improved health and longevity combined to have positive effects upon Scottish women's lives through the course of the twentieth century. Such substantive changes went some way to emancipate women from the stultifying drudgery that characterised housework and family responsibilities at the end of the nineteenth century, and provided women with more freedom and autonomy, not least in sexual behaviour.[23] M. Anderson emphasises such positive amelioration in his evaluation of changing family life in twentieth-century Scotland.[24]

But is this too sanguine an interpretation? Did relationships, the distribution of resources within families and the sexual division of labour within the Scottish home undergo any radical transformation through the course of the twentieth century?

A distinctive and traditional sexual division of labour existed within the early twentieth-century Scottish home. Indeed, according to the Census, significantly fewer Scottish married women before World War I were engaged in paid work outside the home compared with their English counterparts, though there were wide regional variations here, with Dundee standing out as the obvious exception, being similar to many textile towns in north-west England in having a less sex-segregated division of labour within the home.[25] With specific reference to working-class families, Lynn Jamieson has noted how 'all family members took it for granted that a whole range of household tasks were women's work'.[26] Daughters were expected to contribute help with household chores and child-minding from an early age, whilst evidence suggests that sons and fathers were exempt from all but a few specialised tasks – cleaning and mending shoes, decorating, chopping sticks and sometimes bringing in coal and water and running messages.[27] Even when young women entered full-time employment they typically continued to be responsible for many domestic tasks and lacked the customary privileges conferred on young men on their entry to full-time work.[28] All this was bound up with entrenched notions of masculinity and femininity.

Helen Corr has demonstrated how formal education in the early twentieth century helped to perpetuate such gender divisions, favouring domestic skills for girls, technical skills for boys.[29] Girls were prepared carefully for a life of servicing, one way or another, the male earner. In response to the question 'did your father help your mother with any jobs in the house?' one Stirlingshire woman commented: 'No. No. No, my father was very well looked after in the house, even to the fact that his tea was poured out for him, and everything was just there for him to sit down. He was the worker o' the house.'[30] Long habituation and socialisation meant that such sex stereotyping of roles within the working-class family was invariably accepted without question, as simply part of the fabric of everyday life. An Edinburgh woman recalled life for her mother in the 1930s thus: 'She was always working, she never got out anywhere. That was her life.' She continued: 'I had six brothers and four sisters. As we got older we did more work. My brothers were treated like gentlemen. That was general. I was second youngest but the ones before me got a lot to do. We didn't mind; that was our life.'[31]

The labour demands of family responsibilities and household work around 1900 needs to be stressed. This was a multi-faceted and highly responsible job, seven days a week; nursing, caring, feeding and minding children; washing and ironing laundry; frequently shopping (often twice daily), preparing and cooking food; washing up, scrubbing, sweeping, washing, polishing and blackleading equipment (such as the iron kitchen range). Laundry in itself was a massive task, which for larger families absorbed a full day and a half a week: soaking, boiling, bleaching, scrubbing, rinsing, 'blueing the whites', starching, hanging up and ironing. Clothes were often made and repaired within the home, whilst women also invariably shouldered the burden of responsibility for financial budgeting and general household management. Moreover, all this activity was performed with the minimum of mechanical aids – the domestic revolution was an incremental process, but few working–class families even had access to electricity before the 1930s. Thus the domestic labour process was physically debilitating – doubly so where poor women engaged in paid work to supplement family income. There appear to have been, however, significant regional and class differences in the ideology and practice of domesticity.

The internal life of the Scottish family remains relatively mysterious and badly in need of more systematic research. We know very little about how relationships, resource distribution and the sex-based division of labour within Scottish families changed over the course of the twentieth century. Ann Oakley's detailed, pioneering and context-sensitive studies of unpaid housework in London in the early 1970s have not yet been replicated north of the border.[32] In the area of domestic violence, J. Young and S. McIntyre have argued that wife-beating was endemic within Scottish working-class homes in the late nineteenth century and this was evidently still a prevalent practice in Glasgow in the 1970s.[33] On the basis of research in Glasgow police records, R.E. Dobash and R. Dobash argue that the state legitimised domestic violence by refusing consistently to prosecute offenders.[34] Domestic violence remains a feature of marital life at the end of the century, but to what extent this insidious practice has changed over time is unclear.

Three final points on this subject are worth making. All are important caveats to the 'quiet revolution' thesis which hypothesises that a cluster of reforms and changes through the twentieth century conferred full rights of citizenship upon women.[35] First, it has been persuasively argued that despite the so-called 'revolution' in domestic technology there has been little, if any, fall in the number of working hours spent by full-time housewives on housework and childrearing.[36] This apparent paradox has been explained by the fact that as the technology improved standards in all areas of the domestic labour process – childcare, cleaning- cooking, laundry etc. – have increased commensurately. Nevertheless, labour-saving domestic technology has been emancipatory in its impact in the sense of providing more choice over the allocation of time within the general context of household and childcare work. What appears to have happened is that childcare and socialisation have become more important within the family.[37]

Second, the data suggest the emergence in recent years of a more equitable system of unpaid domestic work distribution within the home. Change in this respect, however, is limited and appears to have gone furthest in professional, middle-class families. Segregated roles and sex-typing in domestic labour clearly remains the norm, even, apparently, where both partners are working full-time.[38] According to one quite comprehensive time–budget study, British women averaged 26 hours more than men per week on housework in 1961, whereas by 1983–4 women averaged 16 hours more than men on such unpaid labour within the home.[39] Howard Kahn's recent study of the domestic labour of 100 wives in Edinburgh appears to confirm the findings of A. Oakley and J. Gershuny – high levels of monotony, fatigue and stress and marginal involvement of men in the running of the home and family.[40] Change in this respect appears to have been a long time coming and has still not fundamentally altered the division of labour within the home at the end of the twentieth century.

Third, evidence suggests that unequal distribution of resources within the home continued through the twentieth century. Oral and other evidence indicates that married men before World War II typically kept a portion of their income as personal pocket money (for booze, tobacco, newspapers etc.), thus enhancing their access to regenerative and diversionary recreational activities.[41] Unfortunately, there appears to have been no recent work on such matters specifically relating to Scotland. However, Vogler's study of 1,200 British households in the 1980s shows that only around one in five used more egalitarian financial/income pooling systems, such as joint bank accounts.[42] In the majority of households men continued to have access to larger quantities of personal spending money than women. Moreover, economic dependence on the husband's higher wage increased women's vulnerability to future poverty in cases of marital breakdown. This was part of a vicious circle. The undervaluation of female labour in the formal economy could be used to rationalise an unequal sexual division of labour within the home (with women designated the lion's share of housework) on the strategic grounds of maximising family income. Then the time spent on such unpaid work in the home in turn disadvantaged women (in the sense of loss of accrued employment experience) in the formal labour market. This situation demonstrates the continued strength of patriarchal values, which remain deeply embedded within the Scottish family.

It remains difficult to come to any firm conclusions on the changing role of women within the family in Scotland because of the dearth of detailed research. Clearly, however, much of the context in which women were operating within the family has altered since c.1900 and the pace of change has accelerated since 1945.[43] As discussed, smaller families, household mechanisation, longer lives, control over fertility, improving standards of health and housing have done much radically to alter the physical environment in which women have operated and this had had something of an emancipating impact. Women have also chosen different patterns: delaying marriage until almost thirty; leaving the family home earlier to co-habit with a partner; divorcing rather than tolerating unsatisfactory partners; more frequently combining economic with domestic work.

However, change in the private sphere of the home and family has lagged behind ameliorative changes in the public sphere of women's lives since 1900. Despite some tangible movement towards the more symmetrical household, particularly amongst middle-class, professional groups, the 'new man' remains a distant ideal. Female subordination and economic dependency within the home, the persistence of a marked sexual division of labour, the maldistribution of resources within the family and the survival of chauvinist attitudes and patriarchal values continue to characterise the Scottish family. Thus the notion of a radical transformation, or 'quiet revolution', in women's position and role within the family in Scotland during the course of the twentieth century lacks credibility. At the very least such an hypothesis has to be used very cautiously, and hedged with an array of caveats and qualifications.

WOMEN AND EMPLOYMENT

During the twentieth century labour markets have been transformed and significant changes have occurred in women's experience of waged work in Scotland. Amongst the most important developments have been the movement of married women from the home into paid employment, an erosion in occupational segregation by gender, rising real wages and declining gender wage differentials, growing female trade union membership and the legal banning of gender-specific discriminatory employment practices. However, at the same time, regional and class differences in experience have remained quite significant and gender inequalities have continued, albeit in

a somewhat diluted form. In other words, progress towards equal opportunity in the Scottish workplace has been made but the process is by no
means complete as we near the end of the twentieth century. What is most
evident and should be stressed is the dogged persistence throughout the
twentieth century of structural inequalities and discrimination against
women at the point of production.

Taking the basic measurement of economic activity rates (that is the proportion of the population participating in paid employment according to
the Census), the period 1900–1930s witnessed relatively little change. From
the 1930s, however, female economic activity rates rose sharply. Over the
period 1901–31 around thirty-five per cent of women between school
leaving age and retirement were officially classified as economically active.
By 1991 the figure was sixty-seven per cent. Before World War II marriage
was a key watershed, drawing women back into the domestic sphere and
into a different mode of economic activity invariably involving a combination of irregular wage earning and unpaid services and manufacturing (of
food, clothing etc.) for family consumption. What had changed by the end
of the twentieth century was that female economic activity invariably took
place outside as well as inside the home.

Before World War II strong social and institutional pressures existed to
ensure that married women were kept out of the formal economy. The
heightened participation of women in the workplace during World War I
had little long-term effect, with few holding down war-time jobs thereafter
due to trade union opposition and the Restoration of Pre-War Practices
Act. Discrimination against married and older women in the labour market abounded in the inter-war period. The marriage bar remained firmly
in place in teaching, and many other occupations exercised an informal bar
and, indeed, preference for younger, unmarried workers.[44] Moreover, a
stigma was clearly attached to those married women who continued to
work in the formal economy. One Edinburgh shop assistant recalled:

> If you were allowed back to work after marriage they would have
> said 'what a shame she's got to go and work'. So even if you were
> hard up, the last thing was to go back to work. It was not the done
> thing – Oh no! In those days the man was supposed to be the
> provider.'[45]

Oral testimony suggests that this was an accepted and rarely-challenged
norm. One woman (born 1919) from Springburn in Glasgow noted: 'My
mother didn't work at all. No way. Women just didn't work in those days.
It took ye to keep a house'.[46] However, there were marked regional vari-

TABLE 3

Female Employment in Scotland, by Marital Status, 1911–91
(expressed as a percentage of total females employed)

	Married	Single	Widowed/Divorced
1911	5.3	87.3	7.4
1921	6.3	86.7	7.0
1931	8.5	85.9	5.6
1951	23.4	69.0	7.3
1961	38.7	61.3	61.3
1971	57.8	42.2	42.2
1981	62.0	38.0	38.0
1991	60.4	39.6	39.6

Source: Census of Scotland, 1911–91.

ations in experience. Many of the Lanarkshire towns dominated by heavy industry had significantly lower proportions of married women in employment (e.g. Glasgow: 5.5 per cent; Motherwell: 2.0 per cent), whilst Dundee stands out with almost a quarter (23.4 per cent) of married women officially classified as in paid work in 1911. This was largely the product of demand for cheap female labour in the jute manufacturing industry. Dundee thus developed a distinctive factory culture not dissimilar to many of the cotton-weaving towns of north-west England.[47]

Things evidently began to change in the 1930s, and at an accelerated pace after World War II. Full employment after 1945 provided more job opportunities whilst the pool of single women in the labour market shrank because of the rising school-leaving age and longer periods spent in full-time education. Enhanced participation in the labour market by married women has been facilitated by smaller family size, rising real wages and growing expectations fuelled by the revived feminist movement of the 1960s and 1970s. However, a crucial causal factor has been the expansion of part-time job opportunities outside the home. Between 1951 and 1981 the proportion of total female jobs in Scotland that were part-time (i.e. defined as a working week of under thirty hours) rose from less than five per cent to forty-one per cent. Significantly, at the latter point, only around seven per cent of all male Scottish employees worked part-time. Hence, whilst job experience ranged widely, the 'bi-modal' or M-shaped profile of female employment became more prevalent in Scotland during the course of the twentieth century. Typically this meant an initial eight- to ten-year period of work outside the home until reaching early- to mid-twenties, followed by a period of several years of unpaid work within the home, rearing children, and capped off by a return to work in the formal economy on a full or part-time basis until retirement.[48]

Where did women work? The decennial Scottish Census illustrates the broad parameters of change in labour markets and the type of work performed by women in Scotland since the turn of the century.[49] Several points are worth highlighting.

The overall pattern is very similar to developments within the British economy as a whole. At the very broadest level, there has been a marked shift from manual, industrial, primary employment towards tertiary, clerical, service and distributive work. Agriculture in Scotland, for example, employed over 40,000 women in 1901 and only 4,300 in 1991. However, this transition towards services took place rather more slowly in Scotland than England, reflecting, in part, the poorer, more proletarianised nature of the Scottish economy. The major employment growth area for Scottish women has been the non-manual, services sector – insurance, banking, business services, public administration, local government, teaching, nursing and shopwork. Indeed, 75 per cent of all Scottish women employed in the formal economy were clustered in these occupations by 1971, compared to less than 20 per cent in 1901. The twentieth century has witnessed a revolutionary transformation in the gender composition of clerical labour in Scotland. Secretarial, typing, sales and routine clerical work have become dominated by female labour, with female employment in banking, insurance and public administration increasing almost fourfold since World War II. A further component of the expansion of opportunities for women has been increased employment in the professional and scientific sector with the post-war expansion of state health services and education. Between 1951 and 1981 the numbers of female nurses and teachers in Scotland doubled.

The manufacturing sector has also seen considerable change since 1900. The traditional sectors of textiles and clothing, where over a third of all women in the Scottish labour market (over 200,000) found employment before World War I, suffered catastrophic contraction as foreign competition eroded markets, forcing closures and rationalisation. In 1991, less than 25,000 women were employed in textiles and clothing, around 1 per cent of the total Scottish female labour force. On the other hand, the process of technological change, new mass-production assembly-line techniques, deskilling and more sophisticated division of labour led to a substantial increase in the proportion of females employed in light engineering, food and drink processing and transport and communications. However, much of this expansion has stagnated since the late 1960s. Thus female employment in engineering rose from around 3,000 in 1901 to over 60,000 in 1971, thereafter dropping back to 32,000 by 1991.

Perhaps the most significant change in the occupational profile of women workers in Scotland in the twentieth century has been the virtual extinction of the indoor domestic servant, the largest single occupation for women before World War II, accounting for some 20 per cent of the total female labour force. However, counterbalancing this has been rising job opportunities for women in the low-paid personal services sector with the expansion of private and state sector employment, including institutional cleaners and caterers. Working in shops also became more common, with women employed in distribution rising from 54,000 in 1901 to peak at 157,000 in 1971. However, job opportunities in this sector stagnated in the 1970s and 1980s, partly as a consequence of the growth of giant stores and the expansion of labour-saving micro-chip technology.

The evidence from the Census therefore supports the notion of significant erosion over the course of the twentieth century in horizontal occupational segregation. A much wider range of job opportunities was open to women by the 1990s compared to the 1900s. Nevertheless, a distinct sex-based division of labour continued to characterise the employment market. In 1991 around 70 per cent of women workers were clustered in just four (personal services, clerical, professions, distribution) out of 16 broad occupational orders.[50] Moreover, it was predominantly women who performed the lesser paid, lower status part-time jobs. Indeed, around 90 per cent of all part-time workers (around 500,000) in the early 1990s were women. The position of part-time female workers perhaps best reflects the continuing undervaluation, degradation and discrimination exercised against women in the post-war labour market in Scotland. Part-time workers remained amongst the least organised and most exploited sections of the post-war Scottish labour force – low paid, with low status, often working unsocial hours and with few of the employment rights enjoyed by full-timers.

Gender segregation in employment had undoubtedly become more blurred towards the end of the century, but it remained pervasive nonetheless. Many areas of manual employment continued to be monopolised by male workers, women patently failing, for example, to penetrate in any significant numbers the traditional bastions of heavy-metal working, mining and shipbuilding. Within 'newer' occupations, moreover, women tended to be gathered in the lowest status, poorest paid, menial jobs, whilst the most skilled, responsible and best-paid jobs went to men. Breaking the employment profile down in a rather different way by socio-economic status reveals the persistence of vertical occupational segregation and gender apartheid in job opportunities.[51]

Upward social mobility into the top status jobs is evident over 1961–91 from Table 4 for both male and female workers. However, in relative terms the position has changed little over these years. What remains persistent is the over-representation of women in the subordinate grade jobs and obdurate under-representation in the employing, managerial and professional categories (see the summary Table 5). At the bottom of the pile, the proportion of women in the lowest status jobs has hardly changed, while a larger proportion of male workers has experienced upward mobility. Significantly, the unskilled manual group has become considerably more feminised. Such data tend to support those who have argued that women have a separate class status to men and should not be subsumed within the class position of the male breadwinner.[52] These figures also support the notion that upward social mobility for women in Scotland has been slower than that of men over the past three decades or so. One important reason for this has been the characteristic degradation in job status achieved by women on re-entering the labour market after an absence rearing children. Not only has this pattern led to 'deskilling', but it has been exacerbated by the fact that married women were more geographically immobile. One survey has estimated that around thirty per cent of women returning to work after having children experience a fall in previous job status.[53]

Part of the 'quiet revolution' argument is based upon the notion of growing economic independence through the twentieth century for women as real earnings and the real value of state welfare benefits rose. However, as has been shown, the undervaluation of female labour has remained an enduring feature of Scottish society. The differential between male and female earnings changed little over the period 1900–39 and eroded only slowly over the period 1939–70. In the 1900s, women in Scotland earned around forty-five per cent of average male earnings. Work performed by women was invariably labelled as unskilled, irrespective of objective elements such as task range, discretionary content and training period. Moreover, the patriarchal notion of 'lesser worth' was firmly enshrined and institutionalised within state welfare policy.[54] The prevailing notion of the 'family wage' for the male earner and the 'supplementary' wage (pin-money) for the female worker had serious implications for women in general and independent unmarried working women in particular. As late as 1970 Scottish women averaged only fifty-four per cent of male earnings. Thereafter, as a consequence of equal-rights legislation, the gap narrowed sharply, though gender wage differentials remain a marked feature of the Scottish economy in the 1990s, as Table 6 indicates.[55]

TABLE 4

Scottish Workers by Socio-Economic Group, 1961 and 1991
(as percentage of total workforce by gender)

	1961		1991	
Group	**Male**	**Female**	**Male**	**Female**
1. Employers	3.1	1.5	3.7	1.7
2. Managers and administrators	4.7	2.1	12.1	7.0
3. Self-employed professionals	1.0	0.1	1.2	0.3
4. Professional employees	2.3	0.6	5.7	1.7
5. Intermediate non-manual	3.5	10.7	10.0	20.1
6. Junior non-manual	12.3	38.7	9.2	35.6
7. Personal service	0.9	11.7	1.8	8.3
8. Foremen/women and supervisors (manual)	3.4	0.4	3.6	0.8
9. Skilled manual	36.2	9.4	23.5	2.8
10. Semi-skilled manual	12.8	14.6	12.7	8.4
11. Unskilled manual	8.8	7.3	4.9	9.7
12. Own account workers	2.0	1.2	5.7	1.9
13. Farmers (employers and managers)	1.9	0.3	0.8	0.1
14. Farmers – own account	1.1	0.2	1.1	0.3
15. Agricultural workers	4.0	0.9	1.6	0.4
16. Armed forces	1.4	0.1	1.4	0.1
Total (thousands)	1504	712	1143	930

Source: 1961: S. Kendrick, 'Occupational Change in Modern Scotland', *Scottish Government Yearbook* (1986), pp. 246–7; 1991: Census of Scotland.

TABLE 5

Job Distribution in Scotland by Gender (expressed as a percentage
of total workforce by sex), 1961 and 1991)

	1961		1991	
Group	**Male**	**Female**	**Male**	**Female**
Proportion of workers in top jobs*	13.0	4.6	23.5	10.8
Proportion of workers in lowest jobs†	22.0	57.7	15.9	53.6

* Represents the grouping of categories 1–4 and 13 in Table 4.
† Represents the grouping of categories 6, 7 and 11 in Table 4.

TABLE 6

Gender Wage Differentials: Scotland and England Compared, 1906 and 1992

	Adult male earnings (£ weekly)	**Adult female earnings (£ weekly)**	**% col. II to col. I**
Scotland 1906	1.43	0.65	45.2
England 1906	1.51	0.69	45.3
Scotland 1992	324.60	221.90	68.4
England 1992	343.60	244.20	71.1

Sources: 1906: Board of Trade Earnings and Hours Inquiry (Sept. 1906); 1992: Dept of Employment, New Earnings Survey (1992), Part E, Tables E110.1, E113.1.[56]

Ingrained attitudes about men as the primary earner, combined with the proliferation of part-time employment from 1945, limited the erosion of gender wage differentials and helped to keep women at the lower end of the employment hierarchy. Evidence suggests that at least in the post-1945 period the gap between male and female earnings was wider in Scotland than in England. If, as R.H. Campbell and E.H. Hunt have asserted, the west of Scotland heavy industries had become relatively high wage payers by UK standards by the 1900s, the evidence suggests that the opposite was the case by the 1990s as far as the main industries employing women were concerned.[57]

A major cause of this persistent gender wage differential has been (and continues to be) the economic penalty women pay for withdrawal from the labour market to have and rear children. Joshi has calculated that women taking eight years out of employment potentially reduce their lifetime earnings by forty-six per cent in comparison with a woman who remains childless. Moreover, equal pay has been difficult to achieve because of the persistence of sexual discrimination working at a number of levels, including skills acquisition, normal hours worked and access to overtime. Child-care facilities remain inadequate. Moreover, the post-1945 state-initiated formal incomes policies restrained wage rises which penalised service sector workers (where overtime and bonus payments were rare) compared to blue collar workers. Employers have proven to be persistently reluctant to promote women or to train women for skilled and responsible positions. One such example is higher education, where very few women achieve entry into senior lectureships, readerships or chairs. Many trade unions recognised during the equal pay debates in the 1970s that this was the crucial issue: 'Without equal opportunities, equal pay is only a partial success', commented the Scottish Schoolmasters' Association. Another service sector union reported: 'Frankly, what concerns the Association of Broadcasting Staff much more is the apparent discrimination against women in the filling of posts, particularly higher graded posts.'[58]

Gender differentials in educational attainment were also a pivotal cause of undervaluation in the labour market. Sex-typing in education eroded painfully slowly, thus contributing to sustaining inequalities and constraining women's chances of upward social mobility. For much of the twentieth century there existed double standards in educational provision for girls and boys, including a markedly greater chance of young men gaining qualifications through higher education than women. There continues to be marked gender differentials in the type of degree courses undertaken, though by the 1990s the gender balance in access to degree level courses in

TABLE 7

Proportion of Females to Total Population Educated to Degree Level in Scotland:
by age cohort, 1991

	% female
Aged 18–29	49.7
Aged 30–44	40.6
Aged 45–59	27.1

Source: Census of Scotland, 1991

Scotland was roughly equal. In the latter respect progress in Scotland had been markedly slower than in England.[59]

Trade unions, it might be argued, have played a vital role in protecting workers' interests against rapacious employers and the vagaries of volatile labour markets, and there is a positive correlation between high-wage industries and levels of trade union density. It follows, therefore, that participation in such collective organisations by women could enhance their living standards, contribute to economic independence as well as having spin-offs in terms of better contractual conditions and a more conducive work environment. However, whilst collective protest and industrial action by women were not unknown before World War I, in common with other areas of public life women were largely excluded from the male-dominated world of the Scottish trade unions.[60] Such organisations predominantly consisted of skilled craftsmen, and, as few crafts allowed female apprentices, women were effectively prevented from gaining access to skilled work or union protection. For much of the twentieth century Scottish trade unions were clearly part of the problem in that they absorbed and reflected the dominant sexist values of the day, rather than championing the cause of gender equality.[61] Female union membership levels were lower (proportionately) than in England and whilst there were a number of actively involved women prior to World War II, representation in decision-making positions within the union hierarchy was marginal.[62]

From the 1930s female trade union membership accelerated (see Table 8). Women were drawn more systematically into the institutions of the Scottish labour movement and, as members, reaped some of the benefits of collective organisation for mutual protection. By the end of the twentieth century, Scottish women were amongst the best-unionised in Britain.[63]

Male chauvinism within the Scottish trade unions has undoubtedly declined through the twentieth century. Change, however, came very slowly, though from the 1970s trade unions in Scotland became more sensitive to the needs and aspirations of the female segment of their membership. This was partly in response to the revived civil rights and feminist

TABLE 8
Female Trade Union Membership in Scotland

	Female membership	Percentage of total female labour force	Percentage of total STUC members
1923–4	78,470	12.3	24.2
1931	48,125	7.2	19.7
1939	57,047	8.5	14.9
1945	136,879	20.5	22.3
1951	140,189	21.0	18.8
1961	155,000	21.8	20.0
1971–2	277,648	34.0	30.4
1979*	353,000	40.3	35.2
1992–3	n/a	38.0	36.0

Note: * The 1979 figures are taken from E. Breitenbach, 'A Comparative Study of the Women's Trade Union Conference and the Scottish Women's Trade Union Conference', Feminist Review, Spring 1981, No. 7, pp. 69–70.[64]

Source: STUC, Annual Reports; Census of Scotland; Department of Employment, Interim Report of the Standing Commission on the Scottish Economy (Feb. 1988).

movements and to growing female membership of unions and the crisis many trade unions in Scotland suffered as a result of the erosion of their traditional base as coal-mining and other heavy industries contracted. Many unions thus initiated positive action programmes to facilitate change: they attempted to improve female representation and created Women's Committees while special conferences and changes have been evident in recruitment policy, for example, with reduced subscription rates for part-time workers and those on maternity leave. Moreover, issues particularly pertinent to women workers have been increasingly embraced, such as child-care, sexual harassment, employment rights of part-time workers, health issues, access to education, parental leave and equal pay.

While women remained seriously under-represented within the largest Scottish unions recruiting women, as Table 9 demonstrates, there have been significant improvements in the access of women to decision-making positions within the STUC, the result, partly at least, of policies of positive discrimination. In 1980 there was only one female member of the 21-strong STUC General Council and of 580 delegates to the STUC Congress only 39 (7.1 per cent) were women. In 1994 there were 12 women on an expanded General Council of 37 and of 503 delegates to the STUC Congress, 118 (23 per cent) were women.[65] Patriarchal values within the labour movement proved extremely difficult to eradicate and must be held at least partially responsible for the persistence of gender apartheid within Scottish society. There are, however, tangible signs towards the end of the

TABLE 9

Representation of Women within a Sample of Unions in Scotland, 1991

Union	Total members	Female members	Percentage of women	Total FTO•	Female FTO*
TGWU	104,021	24,025	23	48	3 (11)
GMB	107,530	44,264	41	30	3 (12)
NALGO	78,414	48,863	62	18	8 (11)
NUPE	59,816	39,778	67	16	2 (11)
USDAW	41,909	27,940	67	18	1 (12)
EIS	46,489	30,781	66	12	2 (9)
COHSE	27,161	22,627	83	6	1 (5)
BIFU	24,000	13,440	56	4	0 (2)
Total	489,340	251,718	52	152	20 (73) = 13.2%

Note: ★ FTO denotes full-time officers. The numbers in brackets indicate the amount of female FTO posts which should exist in proportion to the number of women members.

Source: J. Anzani (ed.), Report on a Survey of Women in Trade Unions, STUC Women's Conference, Perth, Nov. 1992. Note: Total membership is based on 1991 questionnaire returns, not affiliated membership.

twentieth century that the overbearing male chauvinism of the Scottish trade union movement is being dismantled and that gender equality in the workplace is at last being prioritised on the trade unions's policy agenda. This, at least, is no longer regarded as solely a man's world.

CONCLUSION

Despite the slowness of change, women in Scotland at the end of the twentieth century have a higher status and more respect as citizens, and enjoy more autonomy, more choices and a less prescribed existence than their Edwardian counterparts. In this respect political and legal reforms have been important, as well as widening job opportunities and access to the protection offered by trade unions. Control over fertility, however, has been the most critical development. Despite improvements in conditions for women, however, the ability to vote and open access to the institutions of power (e.g. local and national government) have not been translated into anything like near equal representation of women. In the mid-1990s, only 9 per cent of British MPs were women (7 per cent of Scottish). In the early 1980s, only 13.7 per cent of Scotland's 1,639 local councillors was female.[66] Indeed, occupational segregation, the undervaluation of female labour and a distinctive sexual division of labour within the home and family have remained persistent features of Scottish women's lives through this century.

Finally, fragmentary evidence suggests that Scottish society was more patriarchal than English society at the beginning of the twentieth century and that despite some convergence it remains so at the end of the century. Occupational segregation appears to have been more marked; gender wage differentials were somewhat wider; Scottish families were larger and a significantly smaller proportion of married women worked in Scotland before World War II than in England. Moreover, until recently, gender differentials in educational attainment were wider in Scotland than England and before 1939 there were also proportionately fewer women in trade unions in Scotland than in England. Scottish women were also under-represented (compared to English women) in Parliament and local government. However, a great deal more research is required before such conclusions can be anything other than tentative, and before a much clearer picture can be outlined.

NOTES AND REFERENCES

1. See in particular the two collections of essays: E. Breitenbach and E. Gordon (eds), *The World is Ill-Divided* (Edinburgh, 1990); E. Breitenbach and E. Gordon (eds), *Out of Bounds* (Edinburgh, 1992).
2. See, however, L. Jamieson, 'Limited Resources and Limiting Conventions: Working Class Mothers and Daughters in Urban Scotland, c1890–1925', in J. Lewis (ed.), *Labour and Love: Women's Experience of Home and Family, 1850–1940* (London, 1986); C.G. Brown and J.D. Stephenson, 'The View from the Workplace' in Breitenbach and Gordon, *The World*; C.G. Brown and J.D. Stephenson, '"Sprouting Wings"? Women and Religion in Scotland, c1890–1950' in Breitenbach and Gordon, *Out of Bounds*. See also J. Faley, *Up Oor Close: Memories of Domestic Life in Glasgow Tenements, 1910–1945* (Glasgow, 1990).
3. Scottish women's history lacks the benefit of broad surveys such as those of J. Lewis, *Women in England, 1870–1950* (London, 1984) and *Women in Britain since 1945* (London, 1992).
4. Scottish Trade Union Congress, Annual Report (hereafter cited as STUC, AR), 1919, pp. 83–6. For similar attitudes expressed within the STUC see STUC, AR, 1916, pp. 76–7; 1918, pp. 50–1.
5. Gordon, 'Women's Spheres' in Fraser and Morris (eds), *People and Society, Vol.II, 1830–1914* (1990), p. 218.
6. These were activities usually hidden from view within the home, such as childminding, washing, mending, sewing, knitting and the taking in of lodgers.
7. Oral evidence strongly supports this argument. See, for example, the transcripts from the Stirling Women's Oral History project (1988).
8. For a detailed introduction into this debate see Lewis, *Labour and Love*.
9. Gordon, 'Women's Spheres', pp. 216–17. The average size of professionals' completed families was around four persons in 1900.
10. M.W. Flinn (ed.), *Scottish Population History* (London, 1977), pp. 346–7.
11. See J. Foster, 'A Proletarian Nation? Occupation and Class Since 1914' in A. Dickson and J.H. Treble (eds), *People and Society* (1992).
12. I am grateful to Callum Brown for confirmation of this suggestion. However, Catholics constituted only around fifteen per cent of total Scottish population.
13. E. King, *The Hidden History of Glasgow's Women* (1993), p. 144.
14. J.D. Young, *Women and Popular Struggles: A History of Scottish and English Working Women, 1500–1984* (1985), pp. 137–9.
15. Flinn, *Scottish Population History*, pp. 326–7: In the early years of the twentieth century thirty-one per cent of women never married in the north of Scotland, compared to just twelve per cent in the west lowlands.

16. Edwin Muir commented on the converging tendency in Scottish and English culture as early as the 1930s. See his *Scottish Journey* (London, 1935). For a general discussion of cultural convergence see T.C. Smout, 'Patterns of Culture' in Dickson and Treble (eds), *People and Society*.

17. *Regional Trends*, 11 (1975), p. 48; J. Haskey and K. Kiernan, 'Co-habitation in GB', *Population Trends*, 58 (Winter 1989), pp. 23–5; *Regional Trends*, 28 (1993), p. 47; M. Anderson, 'Population and Family Life' in Dickson and Treble (eds), *People and Society*, p. 30. Births outside marriage in Scotland constituted around six to eight per cent of total live births in 1900 and twenty-nine per cent in 1991. There was undoubtedly a greater tendency at the beginning of this century, however, to marry if a courtship ended with a pregnancy. Flinn has argued that pre-marital sex was not an uncommon feature of working-class courtship patterns before 1914 (though this would have been very unusual within middle-class courtship), with around a third of working-class marriages producing a child within six months of marrying. See Flinn, *Scottish Population History*, pp. 359–60.

18. R. Marshall, *Virgins and Viragos: A History of Women in Scotland from 1080 to 1980* (1983), p. 301.

19. Equal Opportunities Commission (EOC), *Equality Issues in Scotland*, p. 76. This reverses the position at the beginning of the century when a majority of divorce cases were filed by men (fifty-three per cent UK).

20. EOC, *Equality Issues*, pp. 77, 89. See also E. Breitenbach, 'The Impact of Thatcherism on Women in Scotland', *Scottish Government Yearbook* (Edinburgh, 1989), p. 179.

21. *General Household Survey* (1990). In Scotland the number of one-parent families approached 100,000 in 1981. Earlier in the twentieth century the premature death of husbands produced significant numbers of lone mothers, so this is not altogether a new phenomenon.

22. C. Glendinning and J. Millar (eds), *Women and Poverty in Britain: the 1990s* (London, 1992), pp. 3–10, 42–4. In 1961 around seventeen per cent of lone parents in the UK claimed supplementary benefit compared to over seventy-five per cent in 1991. It is important to stress, though, that poverty in these terms is defined as relative, rather than the type of absolute poverty found by Booth and Rowntree at the turn of the nineteenth century.

23. Most of the legal sanctions against homosexual/lesbian activity have been removed and popular attitudes to all types of sexual activity are now more liberal than in c.1900.

24. Anderson, 'Population and Family Life'.

25. Census, Scotland and England and Wales, 1911: four per cent of married women in Scotland were occupied in paid work in 1911, compared to ten per cent in England.

26. Jamieson, 'Limited Resources', p. 66.

27. Faley, *Up Oor Close*, pp. 58–60.

28. ibid., pp. 66–7; Stirling Women's Oral History Project, Transcripts D2, P2.1, G1, B4, X3.1, L.1, V2.1.

29. H. Corr, 'The Schoolgirl's Curriculum and the Ideology of the Home, 1870–1914' in Glasgow Women's Studies Group, *Uncharted Lives* (1983).

30. Stirling Women's Oral History Project (WOHP), Transcript G1.

31. Pentland and Calton Reminiscence Group, *Friday Night was Brasso Night* (Edinburgh, 1987), p. 10.

32. A. Oakley, *The Sociology of Housework* (London, 1974); *Housewife* (London, 1974). Oakley stresses the persistence of sharply segregated gender roles in the family, low participation rates of men and the alienating, monotonous, isolated nature and low status of this work.

33. See J. Young, *Women and Popular Struggles*, p. 141 (where it is argued that domestic violence was considerably more prevalent in the Fife coalfield than in South Wales); see also S. McIntyre, *Little Moscows* (London, 1980). For the 1970s see R.E. Dobash and R. Dobash, *Violence Against Wives* (London, 1979).

34. See Dobash and Dobash, *Violence*. Only around one in ten offences of domestic violence resulted in arrest in the 1970s, whereas over three in four cases of public offences resulted in arrest.

35. The best example of this argument in the Scottish context is R. Marshall, *Virgins and Viragos*.

36. See, for example, C. Hardyment, *From Mangle to Microwave: The Mechanisation of Housework* (London, 1988); C. Davidson, *A Woman's Work is never Done* (London, 1982); R.S. Cowan, *More Work for Mother* (London, 1989).

37. L. Davidoff, 'Rationalisation' in D.L. Barker and S. Allen (eds), *Dependence and Exploitation in Work and Marriage* (London, 1976), p. 147. What is also important is that there has been a marked fall in the overall number of full-time housewives since 1945, partly the result of greater mechanisation in the home.

38. J. Gershuny, et al., 'Time Budgets', *Quarterly Journal of Social Affairs*, vol. 2 (1986), pp. 13–39. Gershuny found that where both partners were in full-time employment, the female partner spent around double the time spent by the male partner on unpaid domestic work.

39. ibid. Over the same period there was a greater proportionate growth in total time devoted to leisure by full-time employed women compared to men. See also H. Joshi (ed.), *The Changing Population of Britain* (London, 1989), pp. 160–1. I have not been able to find any more recent figures than 1983–4, nor any time-budget material specifically relating to Scotland (Gershuny does not break his sample cohort down by region).

40. H. Kahn, *Scotland on Sunday*, 27 November 1994.

41. L. Jamieson, 'Limited Resources', pp. 66–7.

42. C. Vogler, 'Labour Market Change and Patterns of Financial Allocation within Households', Working Paper 2, ESRC Social Change and Economic Life Project (1989). See also Glendinning and Millar, *Women and Poverty*.

43. For an overview of post-1945 developments from a British perspective see Lewis, *Women in Britain*. See also H. Harman, *The Century Gap* (London, 1993), which argues that there have been fundamental changes in the way women view themselves in the twentieth century, and a commensurate lag in society's attitudes and government social policy to address such change.

44. STUC, AR, 1931, pp. 69–71; 1934, p. 73.

45. Pentland, *Friday Night*, pp. 19–20.

46. M. Burniston, cited in Faley, *Up Oor Close*, p. 53.

47. E. Gordon, 'Women, work and collective action: Dundee Jute workers, 1870–1906', *Journal of Social History*, 21 (1987); B. Kay, 'They fairly Mak Ye Work', in B. Kay (ed.), *Odyssey* (Edinburgh, 1980), pp. 36–45; W. Walker, *Juteopolis* (Edinburgh, 1979). In 1981 Dundee continued to have one of the highest female activity rates in Scotland at sixty-seven per cent compared to the Highlands and Islands at forty-eight per cent. See R. Mitchison, 'The hidden labour force: women in the Scottish economy since 1945' in R. Saville (ed.), *The Economic Development of Modern Scotland, 1950–1980* (Edinburgh, 1985), pp. 190–3.

48. G. Joseph, *Women at Work: The British Experience* (London, 1983), pp. 163–4. This pattern is becoming modified as an increasing number of women choose to return to work between childbirths.

49. For an attempt to quantify changing employment patterns and evaluate the changing nature of work for Scottish women see A.J. McIvor, 'Women and Work in Twentieth Century Scotland' in Dickson and Treble (eds), *People and Society*, Tables 1 and 2, pp. 139–40.

50. For Britain as a whole, Joshi has shown that in 1981 64 per cent of all female part-time workers are located in only 7 of the 549 disaggregated job categories. See Joshi, *The Changing Population*, p. 159.

51. C. Hakim, 'A Century of Change in Occupational Segregation, 1891–1991', *Journal of Historical Sociology*, 7, No. 4 (December 1994).

52. G. Marshall, H. Newby, D. Rose and C. Vogler, *Social Class in Modern Britain* (London, 1988), pp. 63–84. Here a persuasive argument is put against John Goldthorpe's use of the family unit as a determinant of class status, rather than the individuals (including dependent women) within a family.

53. Joshi, *The Changing Population*, pp. 169–70.

54. For example, in gender differentials in unemployment pay and statutory minimum wages set in the Trades Boards.

55. The differential is even greater if earnings over a lifetime are considered, because until recently women retired five years earlier than men. Moreover, there has been a greater tendency for women in their fifties to reduce their involvement in paid work, whereas men are much more likely to continue full-time employment to the official retirement age.

56. The 1906 figures represent averages derived from twenty-two industries where information is consistently provided on both male and female full-time earnings in the Board of Trade Labour

Department wages survey of that year. The 1992 figures are average gross weekly earnings of full-time workers on adult wage rates.

57. E.H. Hunt, *Regional Wage Variations in Britain, 1850–1914* (London, 1973); R.H. Campbell, *The Rise and Fall of Scottish Industry, 1707–1939* (Edinburgh, 1980).

58. STUC, Women's Advisory Committee Agenda and Report (18 November 1972).

59. See *Regional Trends*, 28 (1993), Table 5.11.

60. See Gordon, *Women and the Labour Movement*; Glasgow Labour History Workshop, *The Singer Strike, Clydebank, 1911* (Glasgow, 1989); Reynolds, *Britannica's Typesetters*; W.W. Knox, *Hanging By a Thread: The Scottish Cotton Industry, c1850–1914* (London, 1995), pp. 164–72.

61. For a more detailed discussion see Breitenbach, *Women Workers*, and McIvor, 'Women and Work', pp. 153–6, 159–61, 165–7.

62. For results of a 1938 STUC Women's Advisory Committee survey see McIvor, 'Women and Work', p. 155.

63. In 1992 38.4 per cent of Scottish women were members of trade unions, compared to 30.9 per cent in England. See the Employment Gazette (January 1993), p. 686; *Regional Trends*, No. 28 (1993), p. 98.

64. Breitenbach calculated that the STUC statistics of 300,000 under-represented female membership in Scotland by around 53,000 in 1979, or around 17 per cent. Because of the problems in distinguishing specifically Scottish membership within British-based unions these figures must be regarded as a rough guide to trends, rather than definitive statistics.

65. I am grateful to Audrey Canning for providing these figures from the STUC archives.

66. N. Abercrombie, Warde, et al., *Contemporary British Society* (1990), p. 239. Scotland had particularly low levels of female representation at the local level. The UK average was 18.1 per cent in 1982.

I would like to acknowledge a debt to the following, who provided help with information and references: Audrey Canning, Ronnie MacDonald, Helen Corr, Pat Thane, Callum Brown, Neil Rafeek, Eleanor Gordon, Jan Gershuny and the late Jane Stephenson for access to the transcripts of the Stirling Women's Oral History Project.

11. POPULAR CULTURE AND THE CONTINUING STRUGGLE FOR RATIONAL RECREATION

Callum G. Brown

I

Many historians have argued that popular culture in the twentieth century has been replaced by 'mass culture', something which is little more than mere leisure activities. Peter Burke suggests that 'almost everyone shares the common culture of television' in which passive viewers 'live in a "phantom world" of pseudo-events' where public culture has been privatised.[1] James Walvin regards cinema, radio and war as collectively 'the catalyst for the great social change of the twentieth century', democratising and levelling popular culture in a context of shortening working hours and lengthening holidays.[2] T.C. Smout has described Scotland's popular culture this century in terms of a long struggle, shared by all European countries, to maintain a distinctive identity in the face of the homogenising forces of a common Western culture.[3] The question arises whether, since 1900, the Scots, as others, have experienced a popular culture, as defined by Richard Johnson: 'the common sense or way of life of a particular class, group or social category, the complex of ideologies that are actually *adopted* as moral preferences or principles of life.'[4]

In Victorian and Edwardian Scotland, public culture was an object for struggle, often class struggle, in which the élites engaged to convert plebeians from the pernicious hedonism of drink and urban 'low life', and create new loyalties – to God, employer, municipality and nation.[5] The Bible, teetotalism and 'rational recreation' were deployed to polarise culture by offering in mechanics institutes, prayer meetings, temperance parades and concerts of sacred song a use of recreation for social as well as individual redemption. The notion implicit in the 'mass culture' interpretation of the twentieth century is that this design started to fail after 1900 because it was becoming redundant: as rising standards of living helped to erode class divisions, so culture was being socially levelled. 'Certainly by the second half of the twentieth century,' writes T.C. Smout of Scotland, 'it becomes less appropriate to speak of a working-class culture separate from a middle-class culture.'[6]

Recent research in England, however, has shown that not only did 'rough' culture survive (and modernise) well into this century, but so too did the struggle to regulate and eliminate it.[7] This chapter explores aspects of popular culture in Scotland since 1900 using this theme of rational recreation's robust survival and evolution. The study of this topic in Scotland is in its infancy, and massive gaps exist in our understanding of the social impact of new cultural forms (like the cinema and broadcasting) and of the Scottish dimension to developing perspectives in the field (such as gender and culture, and informal street culture). The chapter looks briefly at the principal trends in the commercialisation of leisure, assesses the nature of voluntary organisations, and examines the activation of state agencies in the attempted suppression of working-class 'rough' culture between c.1905 and the end of the economic slump in 1933. Finally, it reviews the strategy adopted by the state after 1935 aimed at the continued promotion of rational recreation.

II

The nature of what was identified by Scottish social élites as 'rough culture' had changed little between the nineteenth and twentieth centuries. Drink, gambling, sexual promiscuity, street and domestic violence have been constant themes. Working-class culture had its roots in the harsh work and domestic environments of congested Scottish towns and cities; the public house, the football ground and the street remained key venues in which popular culture was located. Yet there were important changes. The nature of leisure constantly evolved throughout the twentieth century, in part through developments in taste and in part through advances in technology. Commercialisation of leisure, and especially of new forms of pastime, occurred with accelerating rapidity after 1900, and with this came increasing state regulation and intervention. But in addition, the campaign of puritans, especially in the Presbyterian churches, to control or suppress 'rough culture' achieved some new and distinctive successes in Scotland.

From the itinerant fair to the public house, the commercial sector had long been considered immoral by religious and civic authorities.[8] Music halls, the successors of the mid-Victorian 'free-and-easies', were being challenged by the 1890s by more reputable variety theatres: Glasgow's Empire of 1897, the Pavilion of 1904, the Coliseum of 1905 and the Alhambra of 1910

– the latter reputed to be 'the best equipped theatre North of London'. The variety theatre seems to have attracted more of the élites than did the music halls; certainly the opening night at the Pavilion in 1904 witnessed 'quite a preponderance of ladies and gentlemen of quality in evening dress', including magistrates, merchants, shipowners and lawyers.[9] But this was probably not typical. The élites tended to frequent the serious drama theatres where they liked to promenade in the boisterous 'pit'; as one Glasgow commentator wrote in 1900: 'I have seen more diamonds in the Theatre Royal pit than ever I witnessed in the stalls or the balcony'.[10] Yet, variety by c.1920 was better regulated – in part through inspection and licensing, and partly through improvements by professional impresarios such as Edinburgh's H.E. Moss. Moss Empires established British-wide acceptance for variety, it has been argued, by greater manipulation of audience behaviour (ending encores and censoring stage material). But the music hall still lingered into the 1930s, as in Glasgow's Britannia (later Panoptican), maintaining a 'rough' edge to the working-class night out. As one customer there recalled: 'Many of the patrons who were under the influence of the "water of life" spent the best part of the evening either admiring themselves in these [distorting corridor] mirrors or making up their minds as to whether they should sign the pledge or not.'[11]

Despite a move to the Scottish provinces, into cine-variety, and to the summer seasons at seaside resorts like Dunoon and Rothesay, variety theatre started to decline in the 1920s and 1930s. In 1897, Alfred Hubner was making regular screenings of short cinefilms in Glasgow's Skating Palace, and by 1900 the Glasgow firm of Lizars was touring Scotland with its cinema projector, showing silent, scratchy films of Boer War locations at meetings of the Rechabites. The first purpose-built cinema, the Electric Theatre, was opened in Sauchiehall Street in May 1910, and by 1914 there were at least twenty, though by one estimate perhaps sixty-six, in that city alone. At its peak in 1938, there were one hundred and four cinemas in Glasgow, forty-one by 1965 and by 1992 eleven (though with a total of forty-two screens).[12] In 1937, a survey of eight thousand West Lothian school children found that thirty-six per cent attended cinema once a week, twenty-five per cent more than once per week, and only six per cent never attended (the remainder being occasional attenders).[13] A survey of 1946 showed that forty-three per cent of Scottish children went to the cinema once a week, thirty-seven per cent twice or more times a week, with only twenty per cent never attending. Scotland was a strong cinema-going region in Britain, though a 1943 survey showed that people in the north of England and London went more often than Scots.[14]

Cinema-going peaked in 1946 (with 1.635 billion admissions in Britain). It represented the apex of public leisure, a lineage which ran from music hall to 1990s' multiplex cinema. Mass audiences for music hall, variety theatre and for sport (notably, but not exclusively football) were seen as an unstoppable social development, but one that portended social problems. The gathering of large numbers of people in theatres and the new football stadia was physically dangerous, as witnessed in disasters such as the collapse of terracing at Ibrox in 1902.[15] Fear of the disorderly crowd, exacerbated by drink, was ever-present. Municipal licensing of entertainment venues was repeatedly tightened-up in the larger towns between the 1880s and 1920s, including in 1901 in Glasgow the banning of standing (and thus disorderly) audiences in theatres, the banning of barmaids, and imposition of early closing in public houses – a permissive power of licensing courts used as late as 1938 in Clydebank, where pubs closed at 9pm.[16]

More illustrative of élite concerns with the commercial sector were the very vigorous and widespread incursions into mass entertainment by voluntary organisations and by municipal authorities. The Corporation of Glasgow was the leader in this field, starting Penny Concerts in the late 1880s, which by the 1899 season attracted a total of 216,161 people to five venues. The Penny Concerts were more restrained and less flamboyant than commercial music halls, attracting 'the fair sex in large numbers … for the reason that they can go unprotected'.[17] Voluntary organisations were responding to the music hall as well. The Rechabites, Good Templars and the Glasgow Abstainers Union provided until the 1930s social evenings at venues throughout Scotland. Most took the form of small-scale dances or variety events, but the Abstainers Union attracted audiences of up to 3,500 people every Saturday night in the Glasgow City Hall until 1914 for evenings of a 'high moral tone'.

The cinema, through its sheer popularity, cheapness, accessibility and continuous showing, posed a much greater challenge to rational recreation than did the music hall. Teachers condemned it in the 1930s for its effect upon school work: 'it is the "Do-Nothingism" of the cinema which is proving in so many cases a handicap to the schools', wrote one headmaster.[18] The Government's Scottish Young Offenders Committee of 1925 had mixed feelings, seeing the cinema as better than the pub, but in need of 'real' censorship. Some town councils, like that in Kirkintilloch in the 1910s and 1920s, put on highly successful cine-variety shows in the town hall, charging up to one-third less than commercial competitors, with large profits being used to run children's galas, public lectures, opera evenings with Beecham artists, and a subsidised public clothing scheme – with sufficient left over in one year, 1920, to bank £1,043 in the Common Good Fund.[19]

Joining the cinema as the great night out in the first half of this century was the dance hall. Dancing in the Victorian period was a significant element of the 'rough' end of popular culture, and moral panic continued to be aroused by dance halls (as with Alexander McArthur and H. Kingsley Long's 1935 novel *No Mean City*). But ballroom dancing also became a refined art form of the common people. 'Dancin' daft' Glasgow had 159 registered dance halls in 1934, declining thereafter to 96 in 1952, though the total capacity stayed roughly constant (33,000 people nightly in 1934, a low of 26,000 in 1943, but rising to 30,000 in 1952).[20] A study of 537 Glasgow males aged 20–22 in 1953–5 listed their top six leisure activities as playing or watching football (50 per cent), the cinema (48 per cent), and dancing (41 per cent).[21] The *Glasgow Herald* estimated that 30,000 people went dancing in Glasgow weekly, a third of them on a Saturday night.[22] It was only in the later 1950s and the 1960s that their popularity waned, though dancing was to be revived in the 1970s by the rise of discos and night clubs, and the 'rough' character of the pastime has for the most part survived.

Twentieth-century pastimes differed from earlier recreations not just in technology and commercialisation, but also in scale. The attendance of 149,547 people at the Scotland *v* England soccer match at Hampden Park in 1937 seemed remote from the Yuletide 'ba" games still played throughout the century in places like Kirkwall – games in which any of the hundreds of players 'can do just as he likes with [the ball] provided the opposition do not stop him'.[23] Yet, modern-rules football resonated with the collective culture of the city street as much as its precursor did in the village: a culture of community teams, pub banter, 'hard men' and the street bookie. But in places like Glasgow, described by R.J. Holt as 'the most avid of footballing cities', wider identities have been constructed. Sporting events emerged as occasions for affirming loyalties to religion, nation, social class and to gender, as well as to neighbourhood. Football has been the game of machismo skills, in which the 'star' players were avidly watched for signs of 'effeminate' weaknesses.[24] Rugby extolled until 1995 the amateur ethos of the Scottish middle classes, with comparatively low weekly audiences paying homage to the 'old school'. Football attracted incomparable crowds – overwhelmingly proletarian – of over 130,000 (especially in the late 1930s) to watch the great club matches. And at both rugby and soccer internationals, especially those against England, audiences rose to even greater heights.

But soccer has represented both shared and conflicting traditions within the industrial working classes of Scotland. Sectarian loyalties between Catholic and Protestant became articulated in club support for, respectively, Glasgow's Celtic and Rangers, Edinburgh's Hibs and Hearts and, early on, for Dundee's Hibs (from 1923 United) and Dundee F.C. As other forms of sectarian division lessened in Scottish society (in housing and occupation, though not in education), especially after 1950, so the 'Old firm' was reaffirmed, not just in Glasgow's but also in Scotland's schismatic popular culture. The divide between Orange and Green has been increasingly transformed into a divide between Blue and Green, giving rise to an ever-present threat of violence, the last major incident being the Scottish Cup final riot of 1980.[25] Yet football also became a focus for a Scottish national identity, an ostensible unity of the Scots observable especially at the annual match with England, which in the late 1930s attracted 60,000 Scots on trips to Wembley.[26] However, the fervency of national support did not obliterate the sectarian division, and in the case of the inter-war period may well have been enhanced by it. Even in the 1990s, support for the Scottish national team is still weak amongst the predominantly Catholic fans of Celtic (who strongly identify with Ireland), and is instead drawn disproportionately from Protestant Rangers' supporters[27] – who, as Holt points out, saw themselves from early in the century as 'bastions of true Scottishness'.[28] The Scottish football crowd, with both its fixed and periodic loyalties, was a public-order problem throughout the century, capable at its most passionate moments (as in the economic recessions of the 1930s and the early 1980s) of producing unsurpassed social breakdown.

Taken together, the cinema, dance hall, music hall and football stadium represented the institutionalisation of a 'rough' culture. Despite licensing and increasing control, they embodied a culture about which the state was very suspicious.[29] It was also a culture which the promoters of rational recreation in the voluntary sector targeted explicitly, especially as it related to the male 'juvenile delinquent'.

III

The mainstay of rational recreation in the Victorian period, the voluntary organisation, faced extinction after 1900. In 1901 Ian Maclaren (Rev. John Watson), author of *Beside The Bonnie Brier Bush* (1894) and other Kailyard novels, expounded on the recent transformation of the church into a leisure centre, 'more concert room than church', where men and women came 'for petty pleasures' rather than to worship God. The 'up-to-date religious institution', as he called it, was composed of endless 'socials', the entertainment evening, the Chicken-pie dinner, and, as he elaborated, 'the candy-pull':

> This [Christian] agency, if that be the right word, is a party of
> young men and women who meet for the purpose of pulling candy,
> and, in the case of the co-operation of the sexes, is said to be a very
> engaging employment. It may be that candy-pulling on the part of
> the Y.M.C.A. is confined to one sex, and is therefore shorn of half
> its attraction, but one clings to the idea that in these days of
> 'pleasant' religious evenings the young men would not be left to
> their own company.[30]

The choice for rational and religious recreation after 1900 was stark – stick to providing devotional and 'elevating' functions only, and risk decline or demise, or provide more exciting entertainment to stay in the rapidly evolving marketplace.[31] The devotional-based Sunday school, the largest youth organisation in Scottish (and indeed British) history, reached its all-time peak membership of 497,433 in the three main presbyterian churches in 1894, and then started its long twentieth-century decline: from a high of 53 per cent of Scots children aged 5–15 years in 1891 to 38 per cent in 1931 and to 11 per cent in 1981.[32] Non-devotional youth organisations which went the way of the 'candy-pull' fared better in the short term. The teetotal movement still offered into the 1920s an alternative culture environment, including teetotal hotels, pubs and refreshment rooms, a massive teetotal literature, and wide-ranging leisure activities including the Band of Hope's magic lantern shows and the Good Templars' teetotal dances. The teetotal message was the most enduring of the values in *fin-de-siècle* rational recreation, with enjoyment increasingly the key, but the message remained very confrontational. Local-veto plebiscites offering the prohibition option started in June 1920 leading, over a period of three decades, to significant contests between the religious community and the licensed trade,[33] whilst the British Women's Temperance Association was very active in mining and fishing villages, bringing into their White Ribboners parades young girls dressed in white to stand as the victims of drunken fathers. One woman from Stirlingshire recalled how, as a young girl in the 1920s, she was placed at the head of a parade, watched by her father who had not known of her White Ribboner enrolment; he 'was standing at the corner when he saw us coming down with the white banners, and somebody said: "My, Archie, see who's leading it?" He says, "Aye, an' I'm going to the pub tonight." '[34]

The 'moral preferences' of cultural choice had still to be made, but the temperance movement had essentially lost its battle in Scotland by World War II. Organisations based on devotional activities and a didactic puritanism did not survive well in the new social climate dominated by cinema and radio. Organisations fared better when the *form* of rational recreation may have meant more to young people than did the message. The Boys' Brigade, founded in Glasgow in 1883, exploded in popularity after 1893 when it introduced a Saturday football league (together with cricket and swimming).[35] It had 12,796 members in Scotland in 1900 and 26,575 10 years later, reaching 35,922 in 1934, and 55,000 in 1988. A Scottish Office survey in 1988 found a total of 215,000 members in the Boys' Brigade, Girls' Brigade, Boy Scouts and Girl Guides, 53 per cent of them female; there were a further 192,500 members of youth clubs, more than half of them in Catholic Youth Clubs.[36] The nature of these organisations has changed less during the century than might be thought. Boys' Brigade focus, for instance, has remained both religion and discipline, the official policy being to emphasise the spiritual above the militaristic.[37] The early success of sport as an attraction to recruitment has remained; for the BBs in 1914, sport was 'a training ground for those higher mental and moral qualities which the Brigade seeks to cultivate'.[38] From the 1960s, increasing professionalisation of youth leadership led, by 1988, to 65 per cent of sports played in Scottish voluntary organisations being supervised by specialist coaches or trained youth leaders.[39]

In the 1930s independent sports clubs started to be co-ordinated by national federations, and from 1947 by a single umbrella group, sponsored by the Scottish Office, called the Scottish Joint Consultative Committee on Physical Education. It successor, the Scottish Council for Physical Recreation, had 115 member sports and sports-related organisations by 1959, and through it much Scottish Office funding to the voluntary sector was channelled.[40] The dominance of football and rugby was increasingly challenged by grant-aided minor sports which after the 1960s achieved great levels of popularity – including those like snooker which early in the century were the subject of state disapproval.

In absolute terms the voluntary sector has continued to grow during the twentieth century, and especially since the late 1930s. But that growth coincides with an even larger expansion by the commercial sector, and gradually had a diminishing claim to be 'voluntary'. The level of support since the key legislation in the mid-1930s was variable and sometimes inconsistent; the total level of Scottish Office grants to voluntary organisations actually fell between 1948 and 1958. But the provision of facilities (playing fields, sports halls, swimming pools and camps for annual retreats) enjoyed a more steady development, and by the early 1960s youth and sports organisations were heavily dependent on a widening mixture of Scottish Office and local authority grants and subsidies (for salaries, administration, premises, equipment, national camps and staff training). At the same time, 'state' youth clubs were started by virtually all local authorities after 1945 with Scottish Office sanction; by 1958–9 they had 50,050 members and 152 paid youth leaders in Scotland.[41] To a significant extent, the voluntary sector had by then become subsumed within a state policy on rational recreation.

IV

There was little in 1900 which could be described as a Scottish Office 'policy' on leisure and popular culture. Drinking laws and occasional responses to police or church concerns aside, it was only from about 1905 that a growing number of files were started on various aspects of recreation. Three persistent themes emerged: first, fear that rural society was going to collapse because of weak social life; second, fear that popular recreations caused juvenile delinquency and wider social disorder; and third, fear that the voluntary sector was in danger of collapse, taking with it the moral fibre of the country. The next two sections focus on the second and third of these anxieties.

The single most important piece of legislation for the control of popular culture in Scotland in the twentieth century was the Burgh Police (Scotland) Act of 1892, as amended in 1903 and 1911, which remained in force until the reform of local government in 1975.[42] In over 400 sections, it allowed local authorities – by adopting clauses in the Act – to prohibit or control practically every major and minor leisure activity imaginable: from the two bulwarks of cultural enforcement, the offences of breach of the peace and being drunk and incapable, to controls on places of entertainment, refreshment and bathing, and illegal activities like betting. Against children, the Act allowed local authorities a battery of specific powers, ranging from banning the flying of kites to the prosecution of anyone who 'makes or uses any slide upon ice or snow'. The amended Acts of 1903 and 1911 added another 80 clauses to the list, including a specific crime of betting in common stairs, the licensing of billiard and bagatelle rooms (from which children were banned), and the sanitary inspection and registration of ice-cream and aerated-water shops and all refreshment places.

It is interesting that whilst the four largest Scottish cities had private Acts covering many of these matters, the adoption of the 1892 Act by smaller burghs came in a flurry, starting with Clydebank in 1905. The primary concern was to control the proliferating billiard and bagatelle rooms, and specifically to exclude both alcohol and children from these venues. A licence-holder was required not to 'knowingly permit or suffer persons of notoriously bad fame, or girls and boys' on the premises. As the town clerk of Clydebank put it, 'adjournments from public houses to billiard rooms at [ten o'clock] with a supply of liquor is so common that the Council desire to do all in their power to prevent it … in the interest of good order in billiard rooms'.[43] In 1910–14, and again in the mid-1920s, dozens of Scottish burghs queued up to emulate Clydebank and obtain Scottish Office approval for regulation of these rooms.[44] In a West Lothian survey of 1937, it was found that between twenty-one per cent and sixty per cent of school children visited billiard rooms more than three times a week, the worst places for this being Livingston and Bathgate.[45] Playground bylaws in the 1920s offered further restrictions on children's behaviour, adding to existing bylaws in many burghs which banned street sports.[46]

As children grew older, the state's concern increased over their cultural influences. Ice-cream and aerated-water shops sprang up in the 1890s, spreading during the 1910s to virtually every burgh in Scotland. The trade was dominated by Italian immigrants, and the shops and parlours quickly won a vast popularity amongst young people, and became notorious for unchaperoned liaisons between boys and girls, for drunken disturbances as men came out of pubs, for breaching the Sabbath, and for gambling. And in one place at least, they also became associated with socialism.

In Stirling in December 1906 Alexander Chalmers was found dead in a close off Broad Street, adjacent to Beneditto Giannandrea's ice-cream shop. In two consecutive court cases, the publican of the Red Lion Inn was found not proven on a charge of having sold Chalmers a half gill of whisky whilst Chalmers was intoxicated, but Giannandrea pled guilty to having allowed him to consume the whisky in his ice-cream shop, and was fined fifteen shillings or ten days in gaol.[47] One night two years later, the same area of Stirling was rocked by a major disturbance when the police arrested an intoxicated Martin Heally – who had a long history of convictions for being 'drunk and incapable' – in the same ice-cream shop. Those described by the Chief Constable as the 'usual crowd of roughs' tried to liberate him on the way to the police station. The Chief Constable reported:

> These hooligans congregated after the public houses were shut in these dens of iniquity, the ice-cream shops, and after being put out of these places at twelve o'clock, they gathered on the street and committed these offences … These roughs were parading the streets

all night, and it was a question whether they or the police were to be the masters.[48]

Heally got 60 days in gaol. All over Scotland, the ice-cream shops caused moral outrage. In Lerwick they became the target for a religious campaign by Protestant clergy between 1905 and 1913. The local members of the British Socialist Party met in one, and when the ministers wanted it and the others closed on the Sabbath, the socialists sided with Sunday opening. A mass demonstration in 1905 outside the socialists' meeting place, Harry Corothie's ice-cream shop on the North Esplanade, attracted 1,500 people, who took part in a religious service, complete with harmonium, which was conducted from the back of a lorry. After much public agitation, two plebiscites and a sheriff's inquiry, the outcome at municipal elections in 1913 was the routing of the two socialist candidates from the council by four 'Sunday Closing' candidates of the anti-ice-cream party.[49] Sunday opening of ice-cream shops was still causing controversy in the 1920s, even in small burghs like Doune in Perthshire.[50]

Coinciding with, and originally connected with the moral panic over ice-cream shops, was the panic over gambling. The Victorians made it an illegal and unrespectable activity, largely through the 1853 Betting Act (which came into force in Scotland in 1874). Four forms of betting caused the greatest concern: street betting, slot machines of chance (which evolved into fruit machines), the football pools, and the totalisator (the tote). It was discovered in 1916 that what were called 'Clown' and 'Clown Pickwick' automatic machines were being 'dumped' in Scotland after having been declared illegal by English courts, and installed in ice-cream shops. On the insertion of a penny, these machines randomly disbursed prizes of coupons for twopence or fourpence entitling the recipient to purchases in the shop. The Scottish Office rushed through a special Act of 1917 banning games machines of all kinds in Scotland, including those which were not games of chance, resulting in bizarre court cases – as when Glasgow Corporation was fined £20 for allowing automatic machines, which were legal else-where in Britain, to be used in the Kelvinhall New Year Carnival of 1925.[51] Despite vigorous protest by the Showman's Guild in Scotland, the Scottish Office found itself in a hole: having inadvertently banned all forms of auto-matic machine, the powerful anti-gambling lobby (led by the churches) would not countenance a retreat.[52] With the arrival in Scotland in 1929 of the fruit machine, chief constables supported allegations, starting in Dundee, that 'a ring of foreigners, Italians' was running their installation in ice-cream and grocers' shops. Though the police were confronted with a new defence of using machines 'for amusement only', undercover detectives did surprisingly well in catching the insertion of money: in Glasgow in 1935 there were 106 convictions for using money-operated fruit machines.[53]

The moral crusade had widened to cover the use of children in gambling, which rose in popularity in the early 1920s. In January 1924, the Education Authority of Glasgow issued a letter to all teachers and parents asking them to get their children to sign a pledge which said: 'I promise to abstain from Betting and Gambling and I shall discourage the habit among my companions.'[54] With support from Education Authorities and the United Free Church, the government quickly agreed to The Betting (Juvenile Messenger) (Scotland) Act 1928, which made it illegal to procure a child under sixteen years to carry a betting slip or verbal bet. The first prosecution was of an unfortunate Glasgow father who sent his son with a bet to a street-corner bookie; the son, accused of truanting, told his school teacher who then informed the police.

Scottish gambling law before 1874 had been laxer than that of the rest of Britain, but during the 1910s and 1920s it was becoming markedly tougher. The Scottish Office's concern did not stop with children. Football pools in Scotland, like fruit machines, were suspected of being controlled by Italians. Pools betting was initially built on top of ordinary horse-race betting and, according to police intelligence, became, during World War I, a highly organised and capitalised business aimed at the middle-class punter. The Chief Constable of Glasgow alerted the Scottish Office in December 1916 to around 16 main offices and 19 letter-drop offices in central Glasgow being used for the receipt of postal betting, chiefly on football as horse-racing was mostly suspended because of the war. Increasingly during the 1910s and 1920s, betting was by telephone with some bookies having 6 or more phones in their offices.[55] The pools merely added a new dimension to the burgeoning fixed-odds betting handled by street bookies. In Edinburgh, the numbers of convictions rose from 141 in 1922 to 303 in the first 9 months of 1932, the vast majority under the Street Betting Act. These figures were negligible compared to those from Glasgow. In 1930, whilst Edinburgh dealt with 266 betting offences, Glasgow dealt with 2,759, exactly two-thirds of the Scottish total. Secret evidence by the Scottish Office to the 1932 Commission on Gambling proposed a legislative onslaught on the 'social evil', including Post Office interception of postal bets, and – incredibly – a prohibition of all news of foreign lotteries (including the impounding of Irish newspapers giving winning numbers) because of their potential to corrupt.[56]

Another new concern over gambling was greyhound racing, which first started in Manchester in 1926; by December 1932 there were 22 tracks in Scotland (four in Glasgow, and the others mostly in small industrial towns) with another six about to open. The worry here was the tote, especially as its popularity at greyhound tracks had given rise to private 'Tote Clubs' in the major cities. Tote clubs first emerged in 1932 when 37 were formed in Scotland during the year. A club in Paisley became the model for the Royal Commission to condemn; a police report was quoted in full in which the Paisley Tote Club tried to pass itself off as a social club 'to encourage social intercourse and rational recreation', but the police report noted the absence of furnishings, newspapers or games (except one pair of boxing gloves and one dominoes set), and counted 284 persons on the premises when the police raided.[57]

The level and variety of gambling – whether conducted in the street, the pub or place of work – was, by the early 1930s, out of control in Scotland as it was in Britain as a whole; with a national turnover of as much as £400 million and possibly 15 million gamblers, suppression was by then imposs- ible.[58] John Prendergast's memoirs as a Glasgow bookmaker describe the years 1932–4 as a period of intense struggle between bookies for their 'pitch', and of extensive police activity. Nonetheless, he recalled being introduced in 1933 to the 'unspoken code of conduct':

> the police would not arrest a watcher after he had given the 'Edge Up' warning cry; nor would they interfere with the bookie when he was paying out at night ... most of the time, with any luck, they'll turn a blind eye to your bookmaking activities and only arrest you when your 'turn' comes round.[59]

This situation emerged in evidence to the 1932 Royal Commission that Scottish police forces and the courts were conniving with bookies, fining each exactly £100 once a year, but otherwise allowing them to operate unhindered. A secret Scottish Office survey of chief constables in 1933 showed very divided opinions – some wanting greater enforcement of existing laws on gambling, and others favouring local authority licensing of bookies. P.J. Sillitoe, Chief Constable of Glasgow, wrote: 'The bettors [sic] of the middle class would, I think, welcome the recommendation [to legalise postal betting], removing as it does the illegality and consequent furtiveness of their transactions.'[60] This sort of view prevailed against the critics; though the Interim Report of the Royal Commission recom- mended the closing down of all betting at greyhound tracks, all tote clubs and the football pools, the Betting and Lotteries Act 1934 legalised the tote on licensed racecourse and greyhound tracks, but banned it elsewhere.

Scottish Office files indicate that the moral panic over gambling, drink and 'rough culture' as a whole reached a peak during the slump years of 1932–33. The impact of the volte face over gambling in 1934 was great. By the early 1950s, before the full legalisation of off-course ready-money betting in 1961, bookies were operating openly in shop premises with grills, television sets and properly printed betting slips – to the point where they even allowed newspapers to print photographs of them.[61]

More profoundly, the change of the mid-1930s signalled the state's concession of defeat to working-class 'rough' culture as a whole. The Scottish Office and the police were relieved, in part because the courts (both lesser courts and the High Court of Justiciary) had been choked with prosecutions and well-financed appeals from wealthy bookies. In part also, there was unease in the 1920s and early 1930s for the anti-Catholic character of Church of Scotland campaigns for moral reform, especially in view of the rise of sectarianism in municipal politics, and the increase in dance halls and gang violence.[62] The moral crusaders in the presbyterian churches found their cause receding on a broad front in the mid-1930s. The local-veto plebiscites under the Temperance (Scotland) Act of 1913 started in June 1920, but only 40 out of 586 wards voted for local prohibition, and nearly all of these voted 'wet' in re-polls in the later 1920s and 1930s. The abolition in 1929 of both parish councils and directly-elected education authorities further reduced presbyterian influence in social policy and schooling. Clearly another factor was increasing division over 'rough' culture within the middle classes, many of whom were cinema-goers and dance-hall enthusiasts, and some of whom were making legal credit bets (only cash betting was illegal) and drinking at licensed restaurants (which remained legal under local prohibition). The social hypocrisies compounded the impracticalities, and with the state's abandonment of the puritan crusade on behalf of a post-Victorian 'godly commonwealth', there was in the 1930s an implicit acceptance of working-class 'rough' culture.

V

With this surrender, the state's strategy changed. 'Rough' culture was no longer to be harassed on a broad front, but was to be offered more effective, state-sponsored competition in the form of rational recreation. The mid- and late 1930s witnessed key legislative initiatives which were to define this new strategy.

In 1938, Parliament passed the Holidays with Pay Act, ending two decades of trades–union industrial action, and giving to nearly all paid workers rights to have at least one week's holiday (three days for agricultural workers) with pay.[63] In the late 1930s, the Scottish Office agreed that the Scottish hills should be liberated for the people to walk and climb in; St Andrews House files show it was willing, even keen, to include Scotland in the English and Welsh Access to Mountains Act of 1939, but reluctantly agreed to exclude it because of the opposition of those who felt that legislation would limit, not increase, rights to roam under Scots law.[64]

Another major area in the promotion of rational recreation to emerge in the mid-1930s was the field of community services and sports. Various Scottish government committees, notably that on Juvenile Delinquency, had been pressing since the early 1920s for a government policy of promoting social and community centres in working-class areas. This started to emerge in the mid-1930s in the new housing schemes, as councils, education authorities and charitable bodies co-ordinated pioneering schemes, leading to the provisions in the Education (Scotland) Act of 1936, superseded by the Physical Training and Recreation Act of 1937. Walter Elliot, Secretary of State for Scotland, announced in a radio broadcast that a quarter of a million pounds would be spent over three years: 'We want to avoid any suggestion of compulsion about physical training and sport. We want our young folks to take healthy exercise and play games for the fun of the thing.'[65] Progress was greatly delayed by World War II, but in 1946 a section of the Scottish Education Department was set up to co-ordinate government support for sports and community facilities, with the Education (Scotland) Act of 1945 allowing the establishment of state 'camps, holiday classes, playing fields, play centres, gymnasiums, swimming baths, and other establishments ... for recreation'.[66] Community centres were envisaged in the short term 'to provide for relaxation and relief from the fatigue and stress which war conditions have imposed'. But a whole new philosophy on leisure was starting to evolve in government circles. The Scottish Education Department (SED) concurred with a circular from the Ministry of Education in 1944 which stated:

> Already it is clear that there is little tradition of leisure amongst large
> classes of those to whom it has come, and the increase of leisure
> confronts us with a new social problem. Experience has shown that
> men and women do not as a rule make the best use of their leisure
> if the only facilities available outside the home are those provided by
> commercial enterprise. ... [W]e are of opinion that the provision
> of communal facilities for the rational and enjoyable use of leisure,

wherever this may be needed, is a necessary part of the country's
educational system.[67]

Encouraging voluntary organisations was the first priority, and especially
those serving new housing estates and rural villages. In housing estates, the
'social vacuum' was to be filled by community associations funded to build
centres and to employ wardens who 'should combine the qualities of a
parson, teacher, salesman and administrator'. A circular from the SED in
1946 spoke of community centres being of 'paramount importance if past
mistakes which have led to juvenile delinquency and other social weaknesses are to be avoided'.[68]

Progress remained slow. Though local youth and community services
emerged, notably in Ayrshire and Lanarkshire in 1943–4, the sole training
course for youth and community leaders in Scotland was suspended
between 1950 and 1960. By 1958, provision was extremely patchy
throughout the country: there were 11 leaders for the whole of Glasgow,
but 8 for the much less populous Ross and Cromarty.[69] It was after 1966
that central the local government started to invest significant amounts in
youth and community work – £7.5 million between 1966 and 1972. The
key was the emerging awareness of the problems of peripheral housing
schemes, notably due to the much publicised Frankie Vaughn initiative
among Easterhouse gangs. The Alexander Committee on Adult Education
in Scotland in 1974 led to wider training of youth and community professionals, and the establishment of centres and services. By the 1980s, the
Sports Council (which supplanted the less pro-active Scottish Council
for Physical Recreation), the SED and the Countryside Commission for
Scotland formed a broad integrated policy for promoting sports, recreation
and leisure.[70]

The final aspect of the work of the Scottish Office has been the preven-
tion of voluntary-sector collapse. In 1918–19, state intervention started in
this field with the Board of Agriculture in Scotland establishing the Scottish Women's Rural Institutes 'for the spread of interest in all branches of
Agriculture, in domestic economics, and the deepening sense of the needs
of the sisterhood in our midst' – all in an attempt to improve the quality
and structure of rural life to reduce rural depopulation; the same was done
nationally at the same time by the establishment of the Miners' Welfare
Institutes in an attempt to reduce miners' radicalism.[71] Whilst the 1937
Recreation Act led to increased provision of facilities, direct financial support on a wide basis emerged first as part of the wartime emergency in the
1940s and only subsequently as a permanent policy; by 1959, £21,570 was

being distributed to youth organisations alone (the largest amounts going to women's and girls' organisations). The level of funding increased markedly in the late 1960s, with cash funding for youth, community and sports organisations exceeding a million pounds per year (excluding provision of halls, playing fields, camps, offices and training courses). The effect was that by the late twentieth century, few voluntary organisations in the field of sport, recreation or youth failed to benefit from state support and subsidy.

VI

During the course of the century, the state was increasingly drawn into what it perceived as the potential vacuum in rational recreation created by the fragility of the voluntary sector. From attempting to suppress 'rough' culture in the first three decades, local and national government moved after 1935 to the encouragement of healthy, rational recreations in their attempt to compete with an increasingly commercialised and legitimised 'rough' culture. The nature of 'acceptable' leisure constantly shifted and is still dong so. When ice-cream shops first proved troublesome in the early 1900s, the state's instinct was to control and suppress. But ice-cream shops became tolerable in comparison to billiard rooms, and both became tolerable alternatives to even worse forms of youth culture later on, leading to state support of billiards and snooker in youth clubs. Voluntary was better than commercial, but commercial was better than illegal and 'rough'. If an activity could not be suppressed, it was taken out of its 'rough' context and placed in a 'rational' context of community centre, youth group or voluntary organisation; failing that, a 'respectable' commerce was allowed to take over.

What constituted 'rational' in twentieth-century recreation became a shifting sand. Indeed, the state played a major part in changing the cultural meanings of activities like betting, buying ice-cream, using slot machines and playing billiards. With time, it sought to change the meanings of other activities too – like breaching the Sabbath for sport (which some councils started to allow in the late 1940s), cinema-going (permitted for non-clubs from the late 1960s), shopping (from the mid-1970s), and pub-going (which it liberalised on all days of the week with the Licensing Act of 1976). But working-class culture constantly re-invented itself. In the last quarter of the century, the popular culture of the street came under greater, not less, pressure, with criminalisation of new forms: 'raves', 'new age' travellers, and the use of new 'soft' drugs such as Ecstasy. High unemployment, rising homelessness and new idealised lifestyles (eco-warriors, the M77 motorway encampment, alternative trading systems, animal activists) have lacerated the skin-deep sheen of any social ubiquity that television and silicon-chip technology might appear to have created. 'Mass culture' never became a reality. Social class, as well as ethnicity, gender and age, have continued to permit ideology and culture to interact, leaving recreations persisting as reflections of very different 'moral preferences' and 'principles of life'.

NOTES AND REFERENCES

1. P. Burke, 'Popular culture between history and ethnology', *Ethnologia Europaea*, 14 (1984), p. 12.
2. J. Walvin, *Leisure and Society 1830–1950* (London, 1978), p. 134.
3. T.C. Smout, 'Patterns of culture' in T. Dickson and J.H. Treble (eds), *People and Society in Scotland, vol. III, 1914–1990* (Edinburgh, 1992), pp. 261–81.
4. R. Johnson, 'Three problematics: elements of a theory of working-class culture' in J. Clarke, C. Critcher and R. Johnson (eds), *Working-class Culture: Studies in History and Theory* (London, 1979), p. 234.
5. W.H. Fraser, 'Developments in leisure' in W.H. Fraser and R.J. Morris (eds), *People and Society in Scotland, vol. II, 1830–1914* (Edinburgh, 1990), pp. 236–64; C. Harvie and G. Walker, 'Community and culture' in ibid., pp. 336–57.
6. T.C. Smout, 'Patterns of culture', p. 273.
7. A. Davies, *Leisure, Gender and Poverty: Working-class Culture in Salford and Manchester, 1900–1939* (Buckingham, 1992); M. Clapson, *A Bit of a Flutter: Popular Gambling and English Society, c.1823–1961* (Manchester, 1992); S. Jones, *Workers at Play: A Social and Economic History of Leisure 1918–1939* (Manchester, 1986), esp. pp. 66–7.
8. See for instance W.H. Fraser, 'Developments in leisure'; H. Cunningham, 'The metropolitan fair: a case study in the social control of leisure' in A.P. Donajgrodski (ed.), *Social Control in Nineteenth Century Britain* (London, 1977), pp. 163–84.
9. D. Higgins, 'Music hall as popular entertainment in Glasgow 1850–1914', unpublished B.A. dissertation, Department of History, University of Strathclyde, 1993, p. 37. *The Glasgow Programme*, 7 March 1904; I am grateful to Paul Maloney for the latter reference.
10. *North British Daily Mail*, 6 January 1900.
11. E. Perrett, *The Magic of the Gorbals: How We Lived, Loved and Laughed 1914–60* (Glasgow, 1990), p. 63.
12. *Stirling Observer*, 1 December 1900; J. Wilson, 'The history of the cinema, 1915–65, with special reference to Glasgow', unpublished B.A. dissertation, Department of History, University of Strathclyde, 1993, pp. 36–7; I am grateful to Paul Maloney for the Hubner material.
13. H.K. Clarkson, *A Survey of the Leisure Time of West Lothian School Children* (Edinburgh, 1938), pp. 8–12.
14. Cf. data cited by Christopher Harvie, quoted in Wilson, 'The history of the cinema', pp. 16, 23, 26, 31, 41.
15. T. Mason, *Association Football and English Society 1863–1915* (London, 1980), pp. 155–7.
16. M. Atkinson, *Local Government in Scotland* (Edinburgh, 1904), p. 50; *Clydebank and Renfrew Press*, 8 April 1938.
17. *North British Daily Mail*, 6 January 1900.
18. Clarkson, *Leisure Time*, 10.
19. T. Johnston, *Memories* (London, 1952), pp. 22–3.
20. H. Tomney, 'Dancing Daft: Glasgow's dance halls c.1920–c.1960', unpublished B.A. dissertation, Department of History, University of Strathclyde, 1994, p. 11.
21. T. Ferguson and J. Cunnison, *In Their Early Twenties: A Study of Glasgow Youth* (London, 1956), p. 47.
22. Tomney, 'Dancing Daft', p. 11; *The Glasgow Herald*, 26 January 1955.

23. R.J. Holt, 'Football and the urban way of life in nineteenth-century Britain' in J.A. Mangan (ed.), *Pleasure, Profit, Proselytism: British Culture and Sport at Home and Abroad 1700–1914* (London, 1988), p. 70; J. Robertson, *Uppies & Doonies: The Story of the Kirkwall Ba' Game* (Aberdeen, 1967), p.6.

24. H.F. Moorhouse, 'Shooting stars: footballers and working-class culture in twentieth-century Scotland' in R. Holt (ed.), *Sport and the Working Class in Modern Britain* (Manchester, 1990), pp. 179–97.

25. B. Murray, *The Old Firm: Sectarianism, Sport and Society in Scotland* (Edinburgh, 1984); G. Walker, '"There's not a team like the Glasgow Rangers": football and religious identity in Scotland' in G. Walker and T. Gallagher (eds), *Sermons and Battle Hymns: Protestant Popular Culture in Modern Scotland* (Edinburgh, 1990).

26. H.F. Moorhouse, 'Repressed nationalism and professional football: Scotland versus England', in J.A. Mangon and R.B. Small (eds), *Sport, Culture, Society* (London, 1986); see also A. Bairner, 'Football and the idea of Scotland' in G. Jarvie and G. Walker (eds), *Scottish Sport in the Making of the Nation: Ninety Minute Patriots?* (Leicester, 1994).

27. J.M. Bradley, *Ethnic and Religious Identity in Modern Scotland* (Aldershot, 1995), pp. 47–8.

28. R.H. Holt, *Sport and the British: A Modern History* (Oxford, 1989), pp. 257–8.

29. Curiously, football was one of the few areas where state regulation was slow to develop in any depth. Not until the Safety of Sports Grounds Act 1975 and the Safety of Places of Sport Act 1987 were demands for structural improvement and crowd control imposed on sports (mainly football) grounds on a par with those imposed from the start of the century upon music halls, cinemas and dance halls.

30. I. MacLaren, *Church Folks* (London, 1901), pp. 33, 41.

31. C.G. Brown, *The Social History of Religion in Scotland since 1733* (London and New York, 1987), pp. 169–208; S. Yeo, *Religion and Voluntary Organisations in Crisis* (London, 1976), esp. pp. 163–84.

32. Figures calculated from R. Currie, A. Gilbert and L. Horsley, *Churches and Churchgoers: Church Growth in the British Isles since 1700* (Oxford, 1977), pp. 169, 172; and C.G. Brown, *Social History of Religion*, p. 85.

33. The plebiscites were enabled under the Temperance (Scotland) Act 1913. See B. Aspinwall, *Portable Utopia: Glasgow and the United States 1820–1920* (Aberdeen, 1984), pp. 106–50; and E. King, *Scotland Sober and Free: The Temperance Movement 1829–1979* (Glasgow, 1979).

34. Quoted in C.G. Brown and J.D. Stephenson, '"Sprouting wings?" Working-class women and religion in Scotland, 1850–1950' in E. Gordon and E. Breitenbach (eds), *Out of Bounds: Women and Society in the Nineteenth and Twentieth Centuries* (Edinburgh, 1990).

35. P. Bilsborough, 'The development of sport in Glasgow, 1850–1914', unpublished M.Litt. thesis, University of Stirling, 1983, pp. 144–9.

36. Figures based on data in J. Springhall, *Youth, Empire and Society: British Youth Movements, 1883–1940* (London, 1977), p. 31; B.M. Fraser, 'The Origins and Early History of the Boys' Brigade', unpublished Ph.D. thesis, University of Strathclyde, 1980, pp. 350, 504; and *Scottish Sports Council: Survey of Youth Organisations: School-aged Sport Working Paper No. 7* (Edinburgh, 1988), p. 21.

37. B.M. Fraser, 'The Boys' Brigade', p.488.

38. *Glasgow Battalion Annual Report*, 1914, quoted in Bilsborough, 'Sport in Glasgow', p. 147.

39. *Scottish Sports Council: Survey of Youth*, p. 10.

40. Scottish Records Office [SRO], ED27/369, Standing Consultative Council on Youth Services in Scotland.

41. Figures calculated from data in SRO ED27/369.

42. Burgh Police (Scotland) Act 1892; Burgh Police (Scotland) Act 1903; Burgh Police (Scotland) Amended Act 1911.

43. SRO, DD5/1247 Billiard and Bagatelle Rooms.

44. SRO, DD5/1049 Bylaws – Public billiard and Bagatelle Rooms. See also the many files on burghs adopting these powers at DD5/1247–1894.

45. Clarkson, *Leisure Time*, pp. 11–13.

46. See for instance SRO, DD5/1196, Stirling Children's Playgrounds 1924. Some 2.3 per cent of convictions before Stirling Police Court in 1950 were for playing football in the streets (under

s. 381(26) of the 1892 Act). Penalties were ten-shilling fines or seven days in gaol. Central Regional Archive [CRA], SB2/1/1, Police Court Stirling, Ledger of fines Imposed 1950–67.

47. *Stirling Observer*, 26 December 1906.

48. ibid., 7 October 1908.

49. B. Smith, 'Temperance, Up Helly Aa, socialism and ice cream in Lerwick 1890–1914', unpublished lecture to Shetland Civic Society, 1984. I am grateful to the author for permission to use this material.

50. CRA, DO2.3.1, Doune Town Council Minutes, 11 July 1921.

51. SRO, HH1/1841, Mechanical Games in Use at Fairgrounds.

52. SRO, HH1/1843, Automatic Gaming Machines; HH1/1848, Royal Commission on Betting.

53. SRO, HH1/1843.

54. SRO, HH1/1842, Betting (Child Messenger) Bill.

55. SRO, HH1/1838, Betting Offices in Glasgow.

56. *Royal Commission on Lotteries and Betting, Minutes of Evidence, Fourteenth Day*, 1932.

57. *Royal Commission on Lotteries and Betting, Interim report*, 1933, Cmnd 4234, pp.21–2.

58. R. McKibbin, 'Working-class gambling in Britain 1880–1939', *Past and Present*, 82 (1979), p. 152.

59. J. Prendergast, *'Edge Up': Memoirs of a Glasgow Street Bookmaker* (Glasgow, 1992), p. 84.

60. SRO, HH1/1849, Royal Commission on Betting.

61. Prendergast, *'Edge Up'*, pp. 212–42; *Edinburgh Evening News*, 28 January 1955.

62. In Glasgow between 1934 and 1953 there were ten dance halls licensed to the Ancient Order of Hibernians, ten to Masonic Lodges and nine to Orange Lodges; Tomney, 'Dancing Daft', appendix A.

63. Jones, *Workers at Play*, pp. 17–20.

64. SRO, HH1/1102–1105, Access to Mountains Bill.

65. SRO, ED14/328, Physical Training and Recreation Bill.

66. SRO, ED14/460, Education Scotland Bill.

67. *Ministry of Education, Community Centres* (1944), pp. 3–4, 16.

68. *Scottish Education Department, Circular No. 5*, 8 February 1946.

69. Calculated from data in SRO, ED27/369.

70. *Countryside Commission for Scotland, Planning for Sport, Outdoor Recreation and Tourism: I. Strategic Issues* (c.1976).

71. CRA, PD97/1/1, Kippen W.R.I., Minutes, 23 September 1919.

The author thanks Professor T.M. Devine of the Research Centre for Scottish History, University of Strathclyde, for financial assistance in undertaking research for this chapter.

12. LIBERATION OR CONTROL: WHAT ARE THE SCOTTISH EDUCATION TRADITIONS OF THE TWENTIETH CENTURY?

Lindsay Paterson

Here are two well-known twentieth-century views of the Scottish educational tradition. The first was written in 1921 by John Struthers, the secretary of the Scottish Education Department:

> The force of public opinion is strong enough to ensure the maintenance of the immemorial Scottish tradition that, subject to the over-riding condition of intellectual fitness, no child, whatever his home circumstances, shall be debarred access to the Secondary School and the University by lack of opportunity.[1]

The second comes from Scotland's foremost social historian, T.C. Smout:

> It is in the history of the school more than in any other aspect of recent social history that the key lies to some of the more depressing aspects of modern Scotland. If there are in this country too many people who fear what is new, believe the difficult to be impossible, draw back from responsibility, and afford established authority and tradition an exaggerated respect, we can reasonably look for an explanation in the institutions that moulded them.[2]

Smout's version is now dominant. Since the 1960s, Scottish education has been seen as being characterised by competitive individualism, authoritarianism, and palliatives that masquerade as reforms, and these educational features are believed to be at the roots of some of the main social ills of Scotland. At its most extreme, the critique asserts that institutional education has poisoned the minds of successive generations of Scots, stultifying even the informal education that people might organise with each other in their homes or other venues. This pernicious legacy is allegedly made worse by the accompanying myth that the Struthers version of history is actually true:

'the level of veneration of tradition and complacency about our education system is staggering'.[3]

This view did not emerge merely as an accident of intellectual enquiry. it has occurred at a time when a whole range of Scottish social institutions and their governing élites are being challenged, not only by writers but also in the arena of Scottish politics. The ruling groups that managed the Welfare State also managed Scotland's constitutional place in the United Kingdom for most of this century. Questioning the Union – as has happened with increasing intensity since the 1970s – has therefore entailed questioning the role of these élites too.

This chapter offers a third view of Scottish education. It argues that there is no dominant Scottish 'tradition', and that each of the multiple 'traditions' has been available for political use throughout the century. This account owes a great debt to the works of A. McPherson, R.D. Anderson and R.E. Bell. If this is an 'Edinburgh school' in contrast to writers such as Walter Humes and H.M. Paterson from Glasgow, then an implicit further point might be that one source of multiple traditions is Scotland's geographical diversity.[4]

The thrust of the recent criticism of the Scottish system has nevertheless had to deal with the undoubted fact of educational expansion and change. Before looking at the critical accounts in more detail, we should first set out a map of what happened in this expansion. Primary education remained largely unchanged until the 1960s, when the significant event was the introduction of the so-called 'progressive' ideas which will be discussed fully later. The main changes occurred in secondary education.

In secondary education, there have been three main phases of reform.[5] The first lasted from before the beginning of the century until the 1930s, and involved the extension of secondary education to most of the eligible age group. The legacy from the nineteenth century was universal elementary education (enshrined in the 1872 Act), and an assortment of provision for later years organised in essentially three forms – the old academies, offering a full five years of secondary education, the new Higher Grade schools, which were intended to provide a form of intermediate education that was successful in countries such as Germany, and the advanced divisions of elementary schools, which provided fairly uninspiring work for pupils who had to stay in school until they were aged 14 but who had been judged academically unable to cope with one of the other two types. The Education Act of 1918 sought to simplify this by asserting the principle of free secondary education for all, in schools of a common type. In the same spirit of inclusiveness, it also brought the schools that had been run by the

Roman Catholic Church into the national system, while allowing the church to retain influence on the curriculum and on staff appointments. The principles of this Act were not implemented straightforwardly, and the Scottish Education Department (SED) itself attempted to maintain a bipartite system consisting of full secondary education for what it regarded as the naturally small group of intellectually able pupils and lower-level vocational work for the majority.[6] Allocation between these two was supposed to be decided on the results of a test of ability given at age twelve, and this separation was rigid. But the assertion of inclusiveness was itself important, representing a point of reference for the next generation of reformers.[7]

The second phase lasted from the 1930s until the 1960s, and involved less institutional change than incremental growth. The bipartite system was mostly in place by the 1930s, and the 1945 Education Act merely confirmed what was already there (unlike the analogous Act for England and Wales in 1944). With the minimum leaving age raised to fifteen in 1947, the secondary structure in the 1940s and 1950s consisted of five-year senior secondaries and three-year junior secondaries, the former providing the only route to university. This institutional stability, however, masked growth in the size of the senior-secondary population, from around thirty per cent in the late 1930s to over forty per cent in the late 1950s.[8] The intellectual minority was not so naturally small after all.

The final phase of expansion has lasted from 1965, with the abolition of selection for different types of secondary school. The resulting comprehensive secondary schools were in place throughout the public sector by the late 1970s (approximately six per cent of secondary pupils continuing to be educated in private selective schools which charged fees). This reform not only represented an expansion in itself, especially when the leaving age was raised to sixteen in 1973, but it also stimulated further expansion, most notably by encouraging pupils to stay on in school beyond that age. The evolution of comprehensive education is discussed more fully below, because it provides a key test of whether the system really has been as pernicious as its critics allege.

Higher education, too, expanded, although not significantly until the 1960s. Since then, there have been three important changes. The first was with the founding of four new universities in the mid-1960s (alongside the four ancient ones), and with that the reinforcement of the separation between two branches of higher education: these eight universities on the one hand, and on the other the colleges of technology, art, education, and so on. This change accompanied a doubling in the proportion of the age group who entered higher education, from about nine per cent in the early

1960s to about seventeen per cent in 1979. The second phase of expansion lasted from the late 1970s until the late 1980s, by which time the proportion entering higher education had increased to around twenty-five per cent. But this growth was largely in the non-university colleges. The last phase has lasted until the present: the participation rate reached thirty-eight per cent in 1993. This very rapid growth in only a few years was speeded by the abolition of the distinction between universities and colleges in 1993, the re-designation of five of the latter as universities, and the absorption of most of the remainder into one of the thirteen universities. These institutional changes followed the transfer of responsibility for the whole sector to the Scottish Office (the eight older universities having previously been funded by the University Grants Committee, based in London).

In the face of these expansions, why have commentators continued to be sceptical? The evidence that is cited for this view usually takes one of four forms. The first form refers to a timeless pathology, mirroring that aspect of the traditional myth that refers to timeless democracy. We have already seen some of this type of critique in the quotations at the beginning. Another example is from H.M. Paterson, who starts his 1983 essay with the assertion that Scottish education, and culture more generally, have been shaped 'for many centuries' by poverty, which has been alleviated only for historic moments.[9] He goes on: 'the massive determination of this material fact has *permanently* marked the culture, the social structure and the psyche of Scotland'.[10] This produces, he alleges, the 'co-existence of solidarity and division' – and the education system has been dominated by division: 'if Scottish schools were ever democratic, they were democratic in a particular way which emphasised social division, competitive liberalism, and individual achievement at the expense of others'.[11] This view of eternal deficiencies is particularly popular among educational dissidents – people who have worked within the system to change it, and have encountered overwhelming opposition. An example is the noted radical educator R.F. Mackenzie, who taught in several schools in Scotland and England between the 1940s and 1970s, and who eventually was forced to resign in 1974 from his post as head-teacher of Summerhill Academy in Aberdeen after a stormy conflict with the city's education authority. He attributed his failure to achieve the kind of education system he would have liked to see to the 'traditional Scottish academic education' which was, he believed, too ingrained in parents' minds ever to allow change.[12]

It is difficult to deny, however, that there have been attempts at reform, and so timelessness is not a wholly convincing argument. So a more persuasive body of evidence for the negative view relates to the failure of reform. The more cynical version of this doubts that the reforms were well-intentioned in the first place. H.M. Paterson claims that what was called 'secondary education for all' between the 1920s and 1940s was merely a relabelling of the previously invidious post-elementary schooling that was available in working-class areas. Invoking again the timelessness of peculiarly Scottish characteristics, but now applying it to explain the failure of reformers, he argues that the bipartite system:

> represents a particularly Scottish solution of the problems involved
> in sieving a nation, by the device of mass schooling, so as to recruit
> talent to the leader class whilst, at the same time, placating and
> controlling the many who could never reach such heights.[13]

Even the attempts at reform that went beyond the immediately achievable were, in this view, illusions. For example, the Advisory Council on Education in Scotland published a report on secondary education in 1947 which, in important respects, anticipated comprehensive education by two decades (the radicalism of this report is discussed further below). A recent critic has described it, however, as much more conservative: it sought to 'utilise education as a civilising instrument, an exercise of welfaring paternalism rather than an open invitation towards personal development'.[14] On another apparently progressive document – the Primary Memorandum of 1965, which inaugurated a revolution in the styles of teaching in primaries – the claim has been made that the liberal rhetoric conceals the true purpose in which 'education [is] an instrument for promoting the value-system of a reified society'.[15] Thus the recurrent theme in this critique is that apparent reform is merely a confidence trick by the middle class – a way of keeping the working class under control.

The less cynical view of the failure of reform does not doubt the good intentions of some of the reformers, but questions whether real educational change can be achieved in a conservative society. For example, we find R.F. Mackenzie, like other radicals, claiming that the reforming ideals of the Welfare State have been disappointed:

> those of us who had imagined that the Labour Party would
> make fundamental changes in our society, and particularly in
> our educational system, now see their efforts overborne like
> an irrelevant eddy in a stream.[16]

Referring to the introduction of comprehensive education he argues further that:

the story of an attempt to carry out this policy shows what happens when a revolutionary new idea has to be realised by people who have had a severely traditional education.[17]

One of his main criticisms was that the new comprehensives were still dominated by academic competition – still based on the principle of meritocracy, according to which pupils are given educational opportunities in proportion to their performance in public examinations.[18] Although this might have been an improvement on selection by, say, inherited wealth, it still vitiated any attempt to develop schools into communities of learning.

Similar points have been made about adult education. It too has been accused of surrender to the state: the old ideals of an independent working-class education have sold out to the meliorist and state-sponsored classes of the Workers' Educational Association, the university extra-mural departments, or the vocationally-oriented certificates of the further-education colleges.[19] The tradition that people might educate themselves is believed to have suffered from the decline of the educative and socialising aspects of the labour movement, and from the growth in a tendency to watch allegedly unenlightening television.

Higher education, too, has been castigated for evading radical change. The distinction between the eight universities funded from London and the colleges funded by the Scottish Office partly corresponded to a hierarchy of social status and academic purpose: the universities, it was claimed, turned their backs on Scottish society, and the colleges of education allegedly grew to resemble the community colleges of the USA. In this caricature, the betrayal by the universities and the lack of vision in the colleges of education helped to stultify the educational system as a whole: the colleges offered an unchallenging programme mainly for working-class young women intending to enter primary teaching and for unimaginative university graduates of both sexes who drifted into secondary teaching because they could think of nothing better to do. In this process, the ancient Scottish unity of higher learning was broken, thereby fatally undermining the core principle of the 'democratic intellect', in which the purpose of learning was to serve society.[20]

These views from within the system do find some support from social scientists and even from policymakers – in Scotland as elsewhere. Thus one of the main conclusions from the research that has been done on the effects of the successive waves of secondary-education expansion is that the reduction in relative social-class inequalities in access to school and post-school education has been slight.[21] The absolute class differences have narrowed, in the sense that they have been legislated away. Thus, obviously, there are now no social-class differences in staying on to age sixteen because everyone is compelled to do so. But there remain such differences in staying on beyond that compulsory point.[22]

The legislators who inaugurated these expansions were not naive enough to suppose that education could be reformed in the absence of social reform generally. After all, the post-1945 Welfare State was imagined as a whole, a goal that is evident in a statement from the secretary of the SED in 1946, John Mackay Thomson, writing about the ostensibly non-educational topic of providing meals and milk for school-age children: 'the service is inseparably bound up with the life and organisation of the schools themselves'.[23] The problem was not, then, one of the motives of reformers – even of the relatively conservative officials in the department – but rather of the scale of reform that was required.

From the perspective of a later period in politics, the Welfare State has been so paternalistic and centralised that it could not possibly have developed an education system that would be truly liberating. Scottish society, and in particular the teaching profession, has been too conservative to act on the more radical possibilities inherent in the reforms. So there is a paradox that the ideal of education for all at a particular stage of education defeats its own purpose, because as soon as reformers attempt to give to everyone an education that was previously confined to an élite, that education is inevitably diluted and made rigid by bureaucracy. For example, McPherson (usually an optimist) argues that 'a convincing body of alternative experience cannot be accumulated about ideas or forms that are not practised or whose practice has been forgotten'.[24]

Lying behind these critiques is a set of ideals which relate in some way or another to the alternative tradition of radical educational thought. This started as an international movement stemming immediately from the child-centred pedagogy of the US educationalist John Dewey, but deriving also from Pestalozzi, Froebel, Kilpatrick, and ultimately Rousseau. As John Darling says in his lucid account of it, there is no definitive statement of child-centred education, but the key elements are:

- an appreciation of children as individuals
- an awareness of children's growth and development: childhood is to be celebrated in its own right, and should not be thought of as a defective version of adulthood
- it is in the nature of the child to be active: children are naturally geared towards learning

- diversity among children is welcomed
- the teacher is a 'facilitator', allowing children to learn for them-selves[25]

The progressive educationalists insist on the ideals even in the face of grave practical difficulties. If, in practice, children are less than naturally enthu-siastic learners, then this is either because of the passivity induced by traditional authoritarian schooling, or because the school curriculum bears little relevance to what children want to know.

The educational ideals implied by this list could hardly be more differ-ent from the Scottish system as characterised by its critics; that is as suffer-ing from dull uniformity, from distrust of children's creativity, from a tendency to see education as being primarily about preparation for adult work, and from placing the teacher at the centre of the educational process.

The main vehicle for expounding these ideas in the first half of the twentieth century was the New Education Fellowship.[26] It attracted to its membership many prominent educationalists in the 1920s and 1930s, including R.H. Tawney, Karl Mannheim, and A.S. Neill, who was judged widely to be the main representative of the new education in Britain. Neill's membership shows that Scots were among the advocates of the new education as far back as the early years of the century.[27] Indeed, the first national section of the Fellowship was in Scotland in 1924. Neill, like many other Scottish supporters, reacted against the traditional Scottish approach to education. Eventually he left, and in 1924 established his famous experi-mental school, Summerhill, at Lyme Regis on the south coast of England, but others, such as R.F. Mackenzie, stayed. (Summerhill moved in 1927 to Leiston in Suffolk.)

Similar ideals were expressed by other Scottish thinkers, even those opposed to Dewey. For example, the philosopher John Anderson argued in the middle of the century against a utilitarian view of education. Education was not *for* anything at all, contrary to the dominant Scottish view.[28] It was its own purpose, and indeed the purpose of human beings was to lead an educated life.[29] Similarly, a recurrent strand in thinking about university education was that it should have this freedom from the constraints of social usefulness.[30]

So there have been radical Scottish dissidents even as the state has spon-sored recurrent phases of expansion. This should make us re-phrase the claim that the Scottish tradition is oppressive and so on; there is at least another tradition. But the fact that some of the prominent supporters of that alternative tradition were dissidents does mean that the negative view of the development of Scottish education has always had contemporary supporters, some of whom, such as Neill and Anderson, abandoned the country altogether. It also means that, looking back, current exponents of this negative view have been able to point to the radical dissidents as proof that the reforms had failed. But the problem with this way of looking at it is that it is anachronistic and unhistorical. The simple fact is that progressive ideals were also firmly in the mainstream, whatever the dissidents may have claimed.

The first group of influential radicals were people who, although not part of the educational establishment, nevertheless had a significant influence on educational practice. Prominent among these was William Boyd.[31] He was founder of the Glasgow University Education Department in 1907, where he remained until his retiral in 1945. He was a firm believer in the ideas of the new education, was a member of the New Education Fellowship, and wrote a history of it.[32] At the same time, he was also an important figure in mainstream education in Scotland through his teaching on the Ed.B. classes in the university; the largest group of students on these courses consisted of teachers in schools. He was also influential in the Educational Institute of Scotland (the teachers' trade union), where he encouraged an interest in research. He was a pioneer of guidance (later, as we will see, to become a way in which the child-centred approach entered the system), and he established the first child-guidance clinic in Glasgow. He also conducted social work among the unemployed of Clydebank (for which he earned the inaccurate reputation of being a Marxist). In that sense he was a dissident, because it probably cost him the chair of education in the university, but it was a dissidence that placed him firmly in the main political tradition of west-central Scotland. From the same political allegiance came his advocacy of 'education for all', somewhat before Tawney published his book of that name in 1922.[33] So Boyd is one figure who was a firm believer in the new education and who also had an influential role in the mainstream of Scottish education.

Other examples of such influential semi-outsiders abound. For example, there is A.D. Lindsay, who was associated with the New Education Fellowship and was a pioneer of adult education for the working class.[34] His most famous educational experiment was the founding of Keele University in north-west England, in the 1950s, which he explicitly modelled on Scottish practices of curricular breadth and social openness. A similar point can be made about Jennie Lee, the Labour MP, who had at least as good a claim as Harold Wilson to be the political driving force behind the founding of The Open University. She chaired the advisory committee set up by the 1960s Labour government to put the idea into practice.[35] Her ideas on open access to education came from her socialist upbringing in south Fife, where she inherited a belief that education should be open to everyone, and should be liberating, not oppressive.[36] The Open University has now become a part of the educational mainstream, and so represents another route by which radical thinking with a strong Scottish input has influenced educational practice. A final example of an influential Scottish semi-outsider is the artist William Johnstone, who developed from the 1920s to the 1960s a programme of child-centred art education which would allow art to be linked to the rest of the curriculum. There are links between these ideas and the art curriculum that has been developed for children aged five to fourteen in Scottish schools in the 1990s.[37]

It could be retorted that some of these radical Scots practised their ideas mainly outside Scotland. But their decision to move south was not like Neill's; they did not imagine themselves to be in a sort of educational exile. Lindsay continued to have sufficient faith in the Scottish tradition to cite it frequently as an admirable model. Lee – in common with other labour politicians of her generation – believed she could best serve the interests of the working people of one part of Scotland by gaining power in Westminster. Johnstone, although based mainly in London, remained a close associate of the poet Hugh MacDiarmid and of other members of the 'Scots Renaissance'. These people's radicalism indicates something about the potential of Scottish educational culture. They have as great a claim to being considered Scottish as, say, the novelist Lewis Grassic Gibbon (another person who moved to London). Far from being timelessly pathological, Scottish education actually has inspired some very progressive thinkers indeed.

The opposition between progressivism and what happened in the mainstream has, in any case, never been as stark as the negative view of Scottish education has claimed. A good example here is Sir James Robertson, who was an influential member of the Advisory Council on Education in Scotland and was author of most of its report on secondary education in 1947. Later he became Principal of Aberdeen College of Education, and chaired the Scottish Council for the Training of Teachers. The Advisory Council document addressed the question of what form of education was required for democracy.[38] The Secretary of State for Scotland, Tom Johnston, who had established the Council, had asked it to look at the issue of education for citizenship in the new democratic era. The report's recommendations were radical in two notable respects. It proposed that the omnibus school of rural Scotland be erected into a national system; these schools were the closest that the country had to comprehensives in the nineteenth and early twentieth centuries, because they educated all the pupils in the community (although they differentiated them by measured intelligence once they arrived). So this proposal, if implemented, would have contributed to making true the traditional Scottish 'myth' about education by forcing the relative social openness of the rural secondaries to be extended to the national system. This part of the report's recommendations stood as a radical point of reference for critics of selective schooling – throughout Britain – in the 1950s.[39] The other radical aspect of the recommendations was the proposal to abolish external examinations, in an attempt to reduce the extent to which examinations dominated school life. Again this was a key component of progressive education.

A. McPherson and C.D. Raab described the report as having 'blended progressive educational thought from England, America, and elsewhere, with the rhetoric and practice of Scottish democracy'.[40] We could add to this that, with people like Boyd, progressivism can be said to have had Scottish roots too. The report was, of course, of its time: it retained a paternalism in much of its moral outlook, which has led some of its critics half a century later to question whether it was progressive at all.[41] But the main point is that the report was remarkably radical for its time, and was not the product of outsiders or dissidents. It placed itself in the mainstream of the Scottish tradition, it inspired radical critics of that tradition for a generation, and it became an official part of the tradition when some of these critics came to power with the Labour government of the 1960s, and inaugurated comprehensive schooling.

Furthermore, until the 1960s, the most influential way in which educational radicalism entered the mainstream was through some of the very people whom modern-day radicals despise as authoritarian and reactionary. This is where the greatest dangers of anachronism lie. One example is the highly influential Godfrey Thomson, who was Head of the Department of Education in Edinburgh University between 1925 and 1951, and was also Principal of Moray House College of Education at the same time.[42] His influence was largely through his intelligence tests, which he advocated as the basis of selection for secondary education. This has made him a demon for some modern critics.[43] There is no doubt that he was a more conservative thinker than Boyd, but we must be careful not to forget the force that meritocratic selection seemed to have in the 1920s, even in politically radical circles (including the Labour Party). Selection by measured intelligence seemed a fairer way than selection by birth as was practised in the nineteenth century even in the somewhat meritocratic Scotland. People like

Thomson justified selection by measured intelligence on grounds of equal opportunities. He was in fact a believer in comprehensive education – the omnibus school – for social reasons. There would, however, be internal differentiation on meritocratic grounds (as indeed happened at least until the 1970s). To allocate to wholly different schools, he believed, would be unfair, because it would prevent children transferring between tracks. And it would be socially divisive.

This concern with equal opportunities earned him the admiration of many political radicals, such as Jennie Lee.[44] He was influential also on reformers in other areas of social policy. For example, his tests were used by the psychologist James Drever of Edinburgh University to help with adoption placements, attempting to match children with intellectually suitable parents.[45] This may now seem bizarrely paternalistic, but at the time it could be regarded as a real liberation from the nineteenth-century practice of placing children in families according to vague judgements of the moral character of prospective parents.

Thomson was not an isolated eccentric. Other educational radicals were equally firm in their belief in testing. An example is William McLelland, who was principal of Dundee College of Education, Executive Officer of the Scottish Council for the Training of Teachers, and author of the astonishingly influential *Selection for Secondary Education* (1942).[46] He was thoroughly convinced that selection could be made to be fair, and could be used to further the ideals of the New Education Fellowship, of which he was a member. Far from being obsessed with testing for its own sake, he was in fact the author of that part of the 1947 Advisory Council Report on secondary education which advocated the abolition of external examinations.[47]

The radical potential of intelligence tests was doubted increasingly in the 1950s, and was officially abandoned in 1965 in the move to comprehensive education. The prevalent understanding of 'reform' and of 'equal opportunities' had changed. When people lump together the proponents of intelligence tests in the period from 1920 to 1950 with the proponents of them in the period since the 1960s they are missing a crucial historical shift.

A further point can be made about comprehensive reform: it was seen by many as embodying the ideals of the new education. Indeed the 1960s marked a significant stage in the incorporation of progressive ideas into mainstream thought. The comprehensive idea had its origins firmly in the most radical parts of the progressive movement.[48] It had been influenced by the progressives' scepticism about unnecessary testing. Inspired by a socialist concern with social justice, it drew on the idealism of the 1947 Advisory

Council Report: as a matter of fact, the results of intelligence tests corre-
lated highly with social class, the best results being achieved by children of
middle-class homes, despite the rhetoric of Thomson and others that the
purpose of the tests was to allow talent to be found in all classes. The comprehensive ideal grounded itself in Scottish educational culture by being
associated with a growing belief that the Scottish democratic tradition
should be interpreted in an egalitarian way rather than competitively.

The immediate origin in doubts about selection explains the most salient
feature of the new system that emerged: the abolition of selection for
secondary school. This did have some effect in the way intended – a small
reduction in social-class differences in attainment. It had a very sharp effect
on gender differences. And all this happened in a context of rising attainment that was probably itself a result of the move towards comprehensive
education.[49] The abolition of selection also extended citizenship by giving
access to the same type of school. This can be seen as fulfilling the Advisory
Council's proposal in 1947 to set up omnibus schools as an answer to Tom
Johnston's question about education for democracy. But including pupils of
different social origins in the same type of institution has a longer history
than that, extending at least to the incorporation of the Catholic schools
into the public system in 1918.

In the long term, the most radical effect of comprehensive education has
not been in these overtly political changes but in the slow revolution it has
brought about in the educational aspirations of the whole community. The
first generation of parents from comprehensive schools are now measurably
contributing to their children's education. That is why the most long-
lasting way of bringing about a change in the quality of non-institutional
education in a community is to change the institutions.[50] Public sponsorship of institutions has produced rising levels of education. That has
improved the capacity of today's parents to provide educational opportunities for their children.[51] And that, in turn, creates rising demand by the
community for better public provision. The most obvious way in which
this is manifest in the 1990s is in demand for higher education.

A more speculative effect of comprehensive education is a reduction in
social hierarchies and in the readiness to accept authority unquestioningly
– despite T.C. Smout's apparent belief (in the passage quoted at the beginning) that Scottish culture continues to be excessively deferential. Most
obviously, the social inclusiveness of comprehensive schools has accompanied, and may have influenced, the revolution in women's aspirations to
equal citizenship.[52] It has legitimised a rhetoric of equal opportunities to
which subsequent reformers can appeal, for example, in asserting the rights

of people from minority ethnic groups. There has also been a slow extension of the rights of children themselves, and in this context it is relevant that the New Education Fellowship was influential in the founding of UNESCO (the United Nations agency that has sought to improve children's welfare).[53]

So the single act of abolishing selection has been a real victory for progressive educational thought. Moreover, during the ensuing three decades, a succession of other reforms has followed, all of which have involved importing into mainstream education the ideas that the progressives evolved in the 1920s and earlier.[54] The most immediate of these reforms has been the reduction of internal selection within schools, so that children of all abilities are taught in the same class. This relates also to the revolution in primary education which took place alongside the comprehensive reforms of secondaries, a revolution embodied in the 1965 Primary Memorandum. Both these changes drew on the standard beliefs of child-centred education (as outlined earlier).

Having placed all secondary pupils in the same school, having begun to educate them in the same classes, and having also raised the minimum age at which they could leave school to sixteen, the system needed a fundamental reform in what was taught and learnt. The goal here was another fairly standard item in the progressive programme of the early twentieth century – that there should be a common curriculum, so that the stratification of knowledge could not become a source of social stratification. The outcome was the report of the Munn committee (1977), the slow implementation of which has given pupils access to a broader curriculum than ever before.[55] The committee consciously rooted its recommendations in the Scottish tradition of curricular breadth, and in the ideals of the 1947 Advisory Council.

Along with that reform of the curriculum there was an extension of assessment at age sixteen: that part of the radical agenda which opposes assessment has not been achieved. But, as with the intelligence testing for children aged twelve in the earlier part of the century, this assessment for all was advocated on the grounds of citizenship. So long as society at large judges people by the examinations they have passed, access to certificates is a necessary part of being a full citizen. The same questions about universal certification are now confronting the next stage of education, at ages sixteen to eighteen, and the key debate is about how to ensure that all students should have access to the same type of certificate, and therefore potentially to the same social status.[56]

If assessment has grown in a way that some of the early progressives would have found distasteful, they probably would have thoroughly approved of the growth of the guidance movement.[57] The language of guidance, as embodied even in official documents, would be congenial to Boyd or even Mackenzie: 'the belief that all people have value in their own right, and that their feelings, opinions and actions are important, whether or not they correspond to those of others'.[58] That official line has produced increasing satisfaction with schooling among pupils and among the community at large.[59] All of this shows that the ideas of the progressives have indeed had an impact, in either a direct or a diffuse way. One commentator has summed it up in relation to R.F. Mackenzie: 'he indicated long ago many of the directions in which schools have now actually begun to go'.[60]

One of the most substantial achievements of comprehensive education was that it whetted people's appetite for more. The main reason why higher education has expanded rapidly since the early 1980s is that the parents of today's school leavers benefited from the first wave of secondary-school reform in the 1960s. They have passed on this generally good experience of education to their children as raised expectations. In one sense, therefore, the democratic intellect could hardly be in better shape. With nearly forty per cent of young people entering higher education, it could be argued that Scotland is closer now than it has ever been to opening its universities to the mass of the people; in particular, participation by women has gone through a revolution, not only insofar as they now enter at a higher rate than men, but also in that they are even taking part in some areas that traditionally have been male preserves (such as science, although not yet technology). If the universities did turn their backs on Scotland in the 1960s, they have been forced to rethink their national Scottish role since 1979. The 1970s scepticism about control from the Scottish Office (and even from a prospective Scottish parliament) has dwindled. There has been a flourishing of scholarship on Scottish topics, right across the arts and social sciences: indeed, if Scottish culture in general has partly reinvented itself in the last thirty years, then a large debt is owed to Scottish academics.

Whenever someone points to any achievements of Scottish education, as in this account of the radical tradition, they run the risk these days of being accused of complacency, or of returning to the old celebratory accounts. That is not the intention of this chapter. No truly radical agenda is ever completed, if only because the terms are constantly reinterpreted. We saw that in the changing attitudes to selection for secondary school; we see it again in the doubts about universal certification. The point is to understand the process historically. It is not enough even to say that there are several Scottish traditions in education, because that kind of statement rests on a version of the same inadequate image of timelessness that we found earlier in both the celebratory and the condemnatory accounts. In the timeless view, the traditions hang on the museum wall, as it were, ready for use by whoever wants to take them down. The problem, when time enters, is to understand who uses them, and when.

One way of making sense of this is by referring to three interests which Raymond Williams found to have influenced educational reform in Britain.[61] The radical visions came from the 'popular educators', which in Scotland as elsewhere would include the members of the New Education Fellowship. But they achieved what they did because they could find allies among the believers in economic efficiency, the people who would support secondary education for all, or comprehensive education, or – now – expanded higher education on the grounds that the nation could not afford to miss any pocket of talent. A third element in the alliance was, in Williams's terms, the group of 'old humanists', people whose philosophical inclination was that education should be universal, but who did not share the full social radicalism of the political left. In Scotland, the paternalism of officials in the SED who were interviewed by McPherson and Raab would fit this picture.[62] Their early upbringing in the omnibus schools of small-town rural Scotland gave them a benignly optimistic vision of the national culture, even while being deeply suspicious of the sources of socialist militancy in the industrial west. What they must have made of some of Willie Ross's political associates when he was Secretary of State is not recorded, but the important political point is that he and they could become allies. Critics of the radicals get mixed up here between these three lines of argument. Williams's point is that the coincidence of interests does not make the radical victories any less real. Nor does the fact that the Labour Party contained many supporters of all three camps make the Labour Party radicals any less sincere. Scottish society has been sufficiently pluralist to allow this kind of coalition to happen. It has also been sufficiently autonomous from England to allow the terms of the coalitions to be set differently, and so to allow the progressive ideals to be absorbed as a modification of a putatively unchanging Scottish democracy.[63] But in the process of getting their ideas into the mainstream by means of such alliances, the radicals have, of course, had to modify their goals. So the critics of the system can always point to the failures.

Finally, then, why have the critiques of Scottish education recently been so prolific, and the celebrations so sparse? There are two parts to an answer, and they point to what might happen in the future. The first is that the coalition for expanding public education has held together in Scotland long after it fell apart in England. There has been nothing like the collapse in the influence of reformers which Stephen Ball traces in England.[64] The reasons for this are a complex mixture of educational reality and nationalism. Probably the 1960s reforms really were more effective in Scotland, and that kept the national-efficiency people in the coalition. Thus all sorts of semi-establishment bodies in the 1980s were in favour of more expansion (for example, the Standing Commission on the Scottish Economy and the Scottish Council (Development and Industry)). Popular attitudes were supportive of public education, as we have seen, and thus picked off the congenial bits of the Thatcherite education policies without subscribing to the intended ideological justification. For example, the right of parents to choose a school for their child, inaugurated in 1981 by the Conservative government, has been highly popular, but has been received as simply a -natural further step in the same direction as comprehensive education, both being about extending individual choice. It seems likely that the same government's devolution of some power to individual schools will be similarly popular, allowing some of the experimentation which – as we saw earlier – the radical critics have claimed is not possible in a nationally unified system. Certainly the opportunities to experiment offered by the Technical and Vocational Education Initiative in the mid-1980s were seized upon enthusiastically by schools, pursuing lines of educational development which the more conservative proponents of a greater attention to vocational education can hardly have welcomed.[65]

Attempts to reverse the 1960s reforms from the governments of Margaret Thatcher and John Major have provoked that instinctive nationalism which runs right through the Scottish educational system. So the reforming coalition has held together, at least defensively, on nationalist grounds too. That nationalism brings us to the second explanation of the growth of the radical critique. Scottish nationalism of the period since the 1960s has been as much a critique of the élites which have ruled Scotland in the Union since 1945 as of the current constitutional framework of Scottish government.[66] The élites have, as it were, been accused of collaboration. This dissatisfaction with the current governing system probably owes something to the same social forces that gave Thatcher's governments their strengths in England in the 1980s – the frustration with paternalistic conservatism and interest-group bargaining. So the plethora of critiques of Scottish education that have appeared recently are a foretaste of political battles to come. The defensive coalition has lasted as the only vehicle for maintaining public education within the present terms of the Union. A despairing perception of the unsatisfactory compromises this involves might be the reason why so many of the recent accounts of Scottish education are so bitter. But if a Scottish parliament is secured, that defensive rationale would be demolished overnight. Scottish education would then be faced with a newly stark choice between maintaining what exists, and reinventing a radical agenda. That there would indeed be such an agenda is evidenced by the severity and extent of the critiques that we have seen. But, in the debate that might then emerge, it would be important not to lose sight of the achievements of radical educationalists this century. It is their relative success which allows us to hope that radical reform is worth pursuing at all.

NOTES AND REFERENCES

1. Quoted in A. McPherson and C.D. Raab, *Governing Education* (Edinburgh, 1988), p. 408.
2. T.C. Smout, *A Century of the Scottish People, 1830–1950* (London, 1986), p. 229.
3. L. Hills, 'The Senga syndrome: reflections on 21 years in education' in F.M.S. Paterson and J. Fewell (eds), *Girls in Their Prime* (Edinburgh, 1990), pp. 148–66.
4. R.D. Anderson, *Education and Opportunity in Victorian Scotland* (Edinburgh, 1983); R.D. Anderson, 'Education and society in modern Scotland', *History of Education Quarterly*, 2 (1985), pp. 459–81; R.D. Anderson, *Education and the Scottish People, 1750–1918* (Oxford, 1995); R.E. Bell, 'Godfrey Thomson and Scottish Education', (unpublished manuscript, 1975) and R.E. Bell, 'The Education Departments in the Scottish Universities' in W. Humes and H. Paterson (eds), *Scottish Culture and Scottish Education, 1800–1980* (Edinburgh, 1983), pp. 151–74.
5. A. McPherson, 'Schooling' in A. Dickson and J.H. Treble (eds), *People and Society, vol. III 1914–1990* (Edinburgh, 1993), pp. 80–107; J. Gray, A. McPherson and D. Raffe, *Reconstructions of Secondary Education: Theory, Myth and Practice since the War* (1983); McPherson and Raab, *Governing Education*, J. Scotland, *The History of Scottish Education, vol. II* (1969) and G.S. Osborne, *Change in Scottish Education* (1968).
6. J. Stocks, 'The people versus the department: the case of circular 44', *Scottish Educational Review*, 27 (1995), pp. 48–60.
7. McPherson, 'Schooling'.
8. G.S. Osborne, *Scottish and English Schools* (1966), p. 217.
9. H.M. Paterson, 'Incubus and Ideology: the development of secondary schools in Scotland, 1900–1939' in Humes and Paterson (eds), *Scottish Culture and Scottish Education*, pp. 197–215.
10. ibid., p. 198 (my emphasis).
11. ibid., p. 205.
12. R.F. Mackenzie, *State School* (1970), p. 17.
13. H.M. Paterson, 'Incubus and Ideology', p. 200.
14. D. Northcroft, '"Secondary Education" and the rhetoric of change', *Scottish Educational Review*, 24 (1992), pp. 76–92.
15. F.J. McEnroe, 'Freudianism, bureaucracy and Scottish primary education' in Humes and Paterson (eds), *Scottish Culture and Scottish Education*, pp. 244–66.
16. Mackenzie, *State School*, p. 67
17. ibid., p. 136.
18. J. Darling, 'Merit, equality and educational opportunity', *Scottish Educational Review*, 8 (1976), pp. 19–23.
19. A. Alexander, 'The education of adults in Scotland: democracy and curriculum', *Studies in the Education of Adults*, 26 (1994), pp. 31–49.
20. G.E. Davie, *The Crisis of the Democratic Intellect: the Problem of Generalism and Specialisation in Twentieth Century Scotland* (Edinburgh, 1986) and W. Humes, *The Leadership Class in Scottish Education* (Edinburgh, 1986), pp. 141–7.

21. Gray, McPherson and Raffe, *Reconstructions of Secondary Education*, pp. 197–268, and C. Benn and B. Simon, *Half Way There* (London, 1970).

22. L. Paterson and D. Raffe, '"Staying-on" in full-time education in Scotland, 1985–1991', *Oxford Review of Education*, 21 (1995), pp. 3–23.

23. J. Lloyd, 'Education and welfare during the Second World War', *Scottish Educational Review*, 23 (1991), pp. 93–103.

24. McPherson, 'An Angle on the Geist' in Humes and Paterson (eds), *Scottish Culture and Scottish Education*, p. 236.

25. J. Darling, *Child-Centred Education and its Critics* (1994), pp. 2–5 and H. Entwhistle, *Child Centred Education* (London, 1977).

26. W. Boyd and W. Rawson, *The Story of the New Education* (London, 1965).

27. J. Croall, *Neill of Summerhill* (London, 1983).

28. Osborne, *Change in Scottish Education*.

29. J. Anderson, *Education and Enquiry* (ed.) D.Z. Phillips (Oxford, 1980).

30. G.E. Davie, *The Democratic Intellect: Scotland and her Universities in the Nineteenth Century* (Edinburgh, 1961) and *The Crisis of the Democratic Intellect* (Edinburgh, 1986).

31. Darling, *Child Centred Education*; Bell, *Godfrey Thomson* and Bell 'The Education Departments'.

32. Boyd and Rawson, *The Story of the New Education*.

33. Stocks, 'The people versus the department'.

34. D. Scott, *A.D. Lindsay: a Biography* (Oxford, 1971) and S. Maxwell, 'The secular pulpit: presbyterian democracy in the twentieth century' in H.M. Drucker and N. Drucker (eds), *Scottish Government Yearbook 1982* (Edinburgh, 1982), pp. 181–98.

35. G. Rumble, *The Open University of the United Kingdom* (Milton Keynes, 1982).

36. J. Lee, *This Great Journey: A Volume of Autobiography, 1904–1945* (1963).

37. S.W. MacDonald, 'A moment in time – the Scottish contribution to progressivism in art and education. The work of William Johnstone artist and art educator', *Scottish Educational Review*, 27 (1995), pp. 72–6.

38. J. Lloyd, 'Tom Johnston's parliament on education: the birth of the sixth Advisory Council on Education in Scotland', *Scottish Educational Review*, 16 (1984), pp. 104–15.

39. Benn and Simon, *Half-Way There*, J. Robertson, 'Impressions and Comments' in J. Nisbet and G. Kirk (eds), *Scottish Education Looks Ahead* (Edinburgh, 1969), pp. 220–9.

40. McPherson and Raab, *Governing Education*, p. 48.

41. Northcroft, '"Secondary Education"'.

42. Bell, *Godfrey Thomson*; S.A. Sharp, 'Godfrey Thomson and the concept of intelligence' in J.V. Smith and D. Hamilton (eds), *The Meritocratic Intellect: Studies in the History of Educational Research* (Aberdeen, 1980), pp. 67–78 and G. Thomson, *A Modern Philosophy of Education* (1929).

43. H.M. Paterson, 'Godfrey Thomson and the Development of Psychometrics in Scotland' (unpublished manuscript, 1975).

44. Bell, *Godfrey Thomson*, p. 1.

45. V. Cree, *From Public Streets to Private Lives* (Aldershot, 1995).

46. Paterson, *Godfrey Thomson*.

47. J. Duffield, 'Advice and educational policy making: Scotland and New South Wales, 1942–61', *Scottish Educational Review*, 27 (1995), pp. 37–47.

48. Boyd and Rawson, *The Story of the New Education*; I.G.K. Fenwick, *The Comprehensive School, 1944–1970* (1976) and D. Gordon, 'The legacy of R.F. Mckenzie', *Scottish Educational Review*, 20 (1988), pp. 32–41.

49. A. MacPherson and J.D. Wilmns, 'Equalisation and improvement: some effects of comprehensive reorganisation in Scotland', *Sociology*, 21 (1987), pp. 509–39.

50. A. MacPherson, 'How good is Scottish education, and how good is the case for change?' in A. Brown and R. Parry (eds), *Scottish Government Yearbook 1990* (Edinburgh, 1990), pp. 153–67.

51. P. Burnhill, V. Garner and A. MacPherson, 'Social change, school attainment, and entry to higher education, 1976–86' in D. Raffe (ed.), *Education and the Youth Labour Market* (Lewes, 1988), pp. 66–99 and L. Paterson, 'Socio-economic status and educational attainment: a multidimensional and multi-level study', *Evaluation and Research in Education*, 5 (1991), pp. 97–121.

52. P. Burnhill and A. MacPherson, 'Careers and gender: the expectations of able Scottish school

leavers in 1971 and 1981' in S. Acker and D. Warren (eds), *Is Higher Education Fair to Women?* (1984), pp. 83–114.

53. S. Asquith, 'Scotland's children: getting our act together', *Scottish Affairs*, 5 (1993), pp. 5–21 and A. Cleland, 'Legal solutions for children: comparing Scotland with other jurisdictions', *Scottish Affairs*, 10 (1995), pp. 6–24.

54. L. Paterson, 'The achievements of comprehensive education in Scotland' in *The Threat to Comprehensive Education in Scotland*, Educational Institute of Scotland (Edinburgh, 1994), pp. 6–14.

55. L. Croxford, 'Equal opportunities in the secondary school curriculum in Scotland', *British Educational Research Journal*, 20 (1994), pp. 371–91.

56. A. McPherson, 'The Howie committee on post-compulsory schooling' in L. Paterson and D. McCrone, *Scottish Government Yearbook 1992* (Edinburgh, 1992), pp. 114–30.

57. A. Fletcher, *Guidance in Schools* (Aberdeen, 1980).

58. Scottish Central Committee on Guidance, *More than Feelings of Concern: Guidance in Scottish Secondary Schools* (Edinburgh, 1985).

59. Paterson and Raffe, 'Staying on'; J. Macbeath, *Talking About Schools: Surveys of Parents' Views on School Education in Scotland* (Edinburgh, 1989) and M. Arnott, 'Thatcherism in Scotland: an Exploration of Educational Policy in the Secondary Sector', unpublished Ph.D. thesis, University of Strathclyde, 1993, pp. 39–40.

60. D. Gordon, 'The legacy of R.F. Mackenzie'.

61. R. Williams, *The Long Revolution* (1961).

62. McPherson and Raab, *Governing Education*.

63. L. Paterson, *The Autonomy of Modern Scotland* (Edinburgh, 1994).

64. S. Ball, *Politics and Policy Making in Education* (1992).

65. ibid., and L. Paterson, 'Local variation in the Scottish pilot projects of the Technical and Vocational Education Initiative', *Research Papers in Education*, 8 (1993), pp. 47–71.

66. T. Nairn, 'Tartan Power' in S. Hall and M. Jacques (eds), *New Times* (1989), pp. 243–53 and Paterson, *The Autonomy of Modern Scotland*.

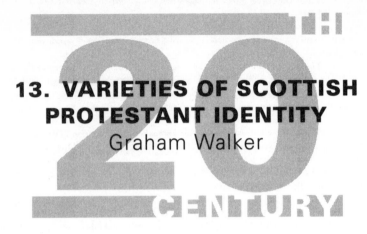

13. VARIETIES OF SCOTTISH PROTESTANT IDENTITY
Graham Walker

This chapter will investigate the ways in which Protestantism, either in the form of a conscious expression of religious faith or as a social and cultural badge of identity, has been a significant feature of Scottish life this century. It will be concerned with religious institutions, particularly the Church of Scotland, and its relationship to the nation's political, social and cultural life. The way the term 'Protestant' has been attached to facets of Scottish life ranging from popular stereotypes to leisure pursuits will be examined, as well as reactions against perceived Protestant values and influences in literature and popular culture. In short, this chapter will provide a commentary on the role of Protestant identity in twentieth-century Scotland, and perceptions of that role, both appreciative and critical.

I

In ecclesiastical terms the century opened notably with the Union of the Free Kirk and the United Presbyterian Church. These two churches had been the main standard-bearers of Presbyterian dissent in Scotland since the religious upheavals of the 1840s;[1] during the nineteenth century they had warred with the Church of Scotland over the issue of disestablishment. Nevertheless, the formation of the United Free Church out of the two dissenting churches actually proved to be a step towards re-unification with the Church of Scotland. Talks between the two bodies began in the early years of the century and culminated in the Union of 1929, an episode considered below.

In the Edwardian era there was still a marked expansiveness about Scottish Protestantism. As historians are coming more fully to recognise, Protestantism - in effect Presbyterianism - was a driving force behind an imperial identity which viewed the Empire as a means of showcasing and

enhancing Scottish national talents and virtues. Presbyterianism was central
to a moral outlook which galvanised Scots to meet the challenges of empire
building, missionary work, wealth creation and governance. Scotland's
partnership with England in this imperial mission did not, in the view of
the Scots, attenuate Scottish nationality; rather they considered their Scottishness to be complemented by the wider British imperial identification.
This outlook confidently prevailed until at least World War I.[2]

Empire was viewed as a force for moral and social progress. For most
Scottish Protestants imperial benefits were linked to the possibilities of
social reform, an outlook perhaps best epitomised by the august figure of
Lord Rosebery: Liberal Imperialist (and prime minister 1894-5), self-styled
spokesman for Scottish interests, and devout churchgoer.[3] Both the Church
of Scotland and the United Free Church possessed a social-reforming sense
of mission at home in the early twentieth century, and the 'Christian social
progressivism' of the late Victorian period in some cases mutated into a
more critical disposition towards economic orthodoxies.[4] Undoubtedly,
this was more a characteristic of the United Free Church than of the
Church of Scotland. Protestant church adherence in Scotland peaked in
1905,[5] and it is perhaps true to say that its simultaneous influence over high
and low echelons of Scottish society was also never more pronounced.

Presbyterianism in the early twentieth century continued to hold local
government responsibilities, particularly in the realms of education and
welfare provision. This was to cease in 1929 with the reorganisation of the
local government system and the abolition of the old parish councils. However, well beyond that date the identification of the Kirk with a broad,
enabling form of educational provision, has remained a staple of Scottish
folklore. What has also persisted is an accompanying perception that such
a religiously driven educational system, offering equality of opportunity
to all, has equipped the 'lads o' pairts' to 'get on' in their chosen careers,
particularly *outside* Scotland. An important part of the Scottish Protestant
self-image, especially in the early years of the century, was the pride in the
Scot-in-exile, most commonly in England, rising to the top of his profession or career ladder. Personifying this was the Free Church minister from
Aberdeen, William Robertson Nicoll, who became editor of the influential *British Weekly*, a non-conformist Liberal Imperialist journal.[6] In early
1914 the Scottish Conservative and Unionist Party circulated a memorandum in which it urged the latter to counter the Scottish Home Rule lobby
with the argument that Home Rule would close off avenues of advance-
ment in England to enterprising and educated Scots.[7]

The importance of education to the Protestant view of its own

contribution to Scottish development ensured that it would be an issue surrounded by religious disputation in the twentieth century. Protestant
polemicists argued that Presbyterianism had liberated the Scottish mind and
given the nation a muscular intellectual temper.[8] Much of this kind of
polemic was in the form of an attempt to contrast Protestantism favourably
with Catholicism and pejorative notions about Catholic education leading
to intellectual 'enslavement' died hard in the Protestant community.
The persistence of such attitudes, combined with the endurance of a view
of Scottish education as symbolic of a kind of Protestant virtue, help to
explain the intensity of the periodic outbursts of educational controversy
in public life this century. The Presbyterian churches have consistently
viewed themselves as the carriers of a vital educational heritage which
is felt to be the key to the national genius. Pride in Scottish inventors, in
scientific and technological achievement as well as, more ambiguously
literature and the arts, has not significantly dimmed in the course of the
twentieth century, and it often still carries overtones of Protestant self-
congratulation.

World War I was a profound shock to the generally prevalent sense of
Protestant well-being in Scotland. The churches' backing for the war effort
was fervent; they were among the major agents of the British patriotic
clamour which attended the outbreak of hostilities. Ministers joined up as
combatants as well as chaplains, divinity students volunteered eagerly, and
by 1915 it was reckoned that some ninety per cent of the 'sons of the manse'
had enlisted.[9] The Church of Scotland magazine *Life and Work* carried
encomiums to the Presbyterian commander of the troops, Earl Haig, and
the loyalist verse of its readers at the front: 'God make us less unworthy/to
call that flag [Union Jack] our own'.[10]

The impact of the tragic losses incurred in the war left the churches
stunned, and more prepared than ever to bridge intra-Presbyterian divisions. This was reflected in the Church of Scotland's desire, realised in
parliamentary legislation in 1921, for clarification of its position in relation
to the state. The Declaratory Articles, as they were called, upheld the
Church's spiritual freedom from state control, while at the same time recognised the Church as the National Scottish Church. This was to be of crucial
importance in smoothing the way to complete union with the United Free
Kirk, so long of course at odds with the Church of Scotland over matters
of state control and state patronage.

In a wider cultural sense the Presbyterian churches contributed as
notably to the process of commemoration and remembrance of the war as
they had to the patriotic campaign at its beginning. They felt their losses

as acutely as any other segment of British society. As R.D. Kernohan has written:

> Tens of thousands of the Kirk's young people were among the Scottish dead; a note in *Life and Work* added the more precise statistics that among them were fifty-four ministers and probationers of the Scottish Presbyterian churches, sixteen of whom had been chaplains, and fifty-two divinity students. The bugle's last, sad notes were slow to fade.[11]

The churches filled with war memorials; the dead were honoured with both solemnity and pulpit oratory which suggested an eagerness to banish any doubts about the necessity of their sacrifice. Sermons preached at unveilings of war memorials connected the deeds of World War I with displays of martial valour in Scottish history dating back to Bannockburn.[12] World War I, indeed, marked the apotheosis of the cult of heroism and courage around Scottish regiments, and an association between military prowess and distinctively Scottish qualities.

In this process the Presbyterian churches played a significant part. In 1926 in an address at the Laying up of the Colours of the Royal Scots, the Reverend Charles Warr of St Giles in Edinburgh delivered the following eulogy to his military audience:

> This regiment whose honour is in your keeping has represented much that typifies the peculiar character of the Scottish people. Let it be your aim to preserve this tradition. Without arrogance or contempt of others, but with quiet determination, endeavour to maintain the distinctive genius of Scotland. By your example counter each influence that would tend to weaken those qualities of sturdy self-reliance, robust fidelity, and dogged perseverance in the loyal execution of work and duty which have both been your country's pride. To none more than to those who serve and have served beneath the colours of a Scottish regiment do we look as trusty guardians of the best in our nation's history.[13]

Of the popular Protestant imagery of twentieth-century Scotland, military honour takes its place along with educational excellence as the virtues apparently most valued by the Church of Scotland, notwithstanding the significant increase in pacifist sentiment in the Kirk from the 1930s down to the present.[14]

The union of 1929 was designed to bolster the church's role in Scottish life, to repair the damage done by divisions and to restore the spiritual authority which many of its clergy felt had been eroded. These churchmen were aware that allegiance to the church was weak in what were called 'the great centres of congested industrialism'.[15] Presbyterian divisions had resulted in an ineffective ecclesiastical means of addressing such problems. The 'social vision' of the churches was by the late 1920s rather compromised by the emergence of a generation of leaders whose desire to see social reform was somewhat tempered by their anxiety about left-wing politics. The leading Church of Scotland figure from the 1920s through to the 1940s, the Reverend John White of the Barony Parish in Glasgow, typified this outlook.[16] White was a Conservative in politics and concerned about Church union as a means of restoring traditional forms of authority which had been severely undermined by the impact of war and its aftermath of social and labour unrest. In 1929 the Presbyterian churches appear to have been engaged in a symbolic event designed to boost Protestant morale: it was an assertion of Protestantism as the guardian of the nation's welfare and identity in the face of a range of perceived threats which included secularisation trends, a growth in communist and socialist politics, and, most far-reachingly, the presence of a sizeable Catholic community of Irish origin which was considered 'alien'.[17] This latter question will be returned to.

In addition, Scottish Protestant self-confidence in the post-World War I era was dented by the dramatic upsurge in emigration. Between 1921 and 1931 the emigrant total numbered 392,000.[18] Such a haemorrhage of population caused widespread anxiety in Scottish establishment circles and something of a crisis among intellectuals who feared the erosion of the Scottish character and the much-vaunted tradition of excellence in education, the law, religion and public life in general.[19] The campaign against Irish Catholic immigration, in the inter-war era, to which the Presbyterian churches contributed with arguments of a racist nature, should be viewed in this context of perceived crisis about the future of the nation and of the values with which Protestants identified. By 1929 the Presbyterian churches interpreted as a decline in their position and influence their loss of responsibility to the state of functions they had exercised in local parishes; they then contrasted this balefully with a perception of the Catholic Church increasing its strength on the basis of its control over the Catholic sector of state-subsidised schooling. Education, it must be remembered, had a totemic significance; the Presbyterian churches felt that Catholic control of education, guaranteed by the 1918 Eduction Act, rubbed salt in the wound of their loss of educational influence.

The Union of the Presbyterian churches was solemnised in October 1929. For a week Edinburgh hosted the churches' deliberations and cere-

monial occasions; thousands were in attendance and psalms were sung in
the streets as ministers walked in procession. It appeared at the time to
strengthen the Church's position as membership stood at 1,300,000, some
27 per cent of the total population, and about twice the Roman Catholic
figure. The Union embraced around 90 per cent of Presbyterians, with only
small congregations of dissenters stubbornly continuing to pursue their
own independent line.

The series of ceremonies and celebratory events surrounding the Union
repay investigation. On these occasions much was said about the Church's
role in Scottish history and contemporary life, and much was asserted in an
effort to reclaim the ground which was felt to have been lost. Important
insights into Presbyterian perceptions of Scottishness can be discerned.

The Moderator of the United Free Church, Principal Alexander Martin,
struck a populist note in his estimation of the Church's contribution to
Scotland's historical progress. He was reported as saying that:

> No one who knew their Scottish history would deny that the
> Church had fulfilled many a notable public service in the past.
> It had been on the floor of the General Assemblies rather than in
> the corrupt estates or Privy Council that the battle of the Scottish
> people for freedom had been fought and won. The burden of the
> poor was borne for centuries by the Church unaided and in her
> system of education she laid during the past ages the foundation
> of a democracy in which all barriers were down, and the way was
> open and free for all.[20]

Thus Presbyterianism was asserted as the faith of the people, as the church
on the side of the people, stressing the virtues of democracy and distrusting
the privileged and the powerful in the state – a truly dissenting perspective.

The Moderator-Designate of the re-united Church of Scotland, the Very
Reverend John White, chose to invoke the illustrious canon of Burns, Scott
and Carlyle in an apparent attempt to identify the Kirk with literary greatness, but also to argue that Scott and Carlyle (Burns was dropped in this
respect) helped to 'deepen the spirit of reverence' in Scotland.[21] *The Scotsman*, rejoicing over the event, editorialised as follows:

> Scotland alone can fully understand the inwardness of this Union.
> Many an exiled Scot will break through the crust of his usual calm
> to explain to his neighbour the meaning of the events of this week
> but with only a modest success. The alien will be left with his
> perplexity plus a certain unspoken tribute to the subtlety of the

Scottish mind. To the exile himself, with whom love of country
and respect for the Kirk are almost synonymous terms, the tidings
of this week will be as water to a thirsty sod.[22]

Quite apart from the equation of love of country and respect for the
Kirk, this editorial is interesting for its choice of the theme of the exiled
Scot on which to lead. This may have reflected the extent to which emigration weighed heavily on Scottish opinion-formers' minds, and the sense
of pride in the Scot abroad mentioned earlier, still evident here, may have
been tempered by anxiety about the effects of depopulation. The editorial
also went on to credit the Church with instilling intellectual qualities, a
moral earnestness and 'a keen discernment of the deeper issues of life'.[23]

Finally, there appeared an article in *The Scotsman*'s 'Church Union
Supplement' by Professor Archibald Main on the Scottish Church's place
in the nation's history. In perhaps its most revealing passage Main stated:

Our country was not a nation, in any strict sense of the word,
before the Reformation, and the most efficient instrument in the
making of lowland Scotland was the reformed religion. The
refashioning of the medieval Church accomplished more for the
unity of the Scottish race than the victory at Bannockburn or the
defeat at Flodden. After the year 1560 the ordinary man gained
what the extraordinary cleric had lost, no more was the layman a
humble puppet of the Mother Church – he could voice his views
in Kirk-sessions or General Assembly, he could take part in the
election of his minister, he had the opportunity of influencing
public opinion.[24]

Main added that after the Reformation the General Assembly became the
most representative institution in Scotland, a view still echoed in more
recent years by Scottish Church leaders even in the face of drastic decline
in Church membership. It is clear from this passage that he viewed the
Church as a vital instrument of nation-formation; and he seems also to be
equating the modern Scottish nation with lowland Scotland – a Whiggish
view which elided the jagged edges of the troubled episodes in modern
Scottish history represented by the Highland clearances and the transformation of a whole way of life. Moreover Main, in common with the other
commentators on this historic occasion, made no reference to the rigid
Calvinism of much of the remaining population of the West Highlands and
Islands. The 'Wee Frees' have always co-existed awkwardly with mainstream Presbyterian churches in the context of Scottish Protestantism:

culturally, socially, and politically, as well as religiously, they have formed a very distinctive community, and much liberal Presbyterian opinion in recent decades has distanced itself even further from their doctrinaire views. It might also be said that there has been a tendency among such liberal Protestants towards rather complacent cultural assumptions about this community.[25]

One of the arguments used by the small minority of dissenters against the Union of 1929 was that, following Presbyterian unity the Church leaders would pursue unity with the other major branch of British Protestantism, namely the episcopal tradition as represented by the Anglican Church in England and the small Scottish Episcopal Church. The prospects of such a union were seriously, if vaguely, discussed in the early 1930s.[26] This led to popular opposition which drew on a deep-rooted antipathy to notions of privilege which surrounded the heavily aristocratic Scottish Episcopal Church and the Anglican Church. The emotion aroused also fed off the durable appeal of covenanting legends from the 'killing times' of the seventeenth century.[27]

This issue of 'bishops in the kirk' was to resurface in the 1950s and 60s when it became the subject of a hostile campaign by the *Scottish Daily Express*.[28] The response to the campaign might be said to have indicated that even among those whose allegiance to the Church had lapsed or who possessed no such allegiance, there was a sense of pride in 'thrawn Presbyterian principle', especially when it was counter-pointed to notions of privilege. In relation to the Episcopacy question, there was a popular equation of 'true' Presbyterianism with a democratic stand and a parallel equation of Episcopacy with Englishness, snobbery and feudal privilege. Ironically, given its Jacobite pedigree, the Scottish Episcopal Church was caught in the sweep of this popular reaction as an extension of the 'English Church'. Again, the Covenanters were invoked to stir up memories of heroic Scottish national resistance. In such episodes Presbyterianism, in its store of myths and in the popular resonance of some of its distinctive features, became a force for the expression of Scottish national indignation.

Politically, the Church of Scotland was for the most part willing to appoint itself the 'voice of the nation' in the quest for home rule in the late 1940s and 1970s.[29] Even in the 1980s and 1990s the Church's influence on the campaign for a Scottish Assembly, most notably through the Constitutional Convention,[30] has been out of proportion to its strength in Scottish society. While Unionist feeling in the Church of Scotland has always been strong, and outright separatism a small minority taste, the level of support accorded by the Church to home rule has underscored its importance as a symbol of Scottish national identity and its willingness to act as such.

The re-united Church of Scotland's attempts to strengthen its position among the working class of the cities made little headway during the economically depressed 1930s. Mention should, however, be made of the Reverend George MacLeod's social evangelism in the Govan district of Glasgow; this community-based movement evolved into the Iona Community, a strand of the Church which, since the 1930s, has attempted to connect the Reformed tradition most closely to early Scottish Christianity.

During World War II social concerns were highlighted by the work of the Baillie Commission, whose deliberations constituted one of the Church's most substantial contributions to public policy debate in the twentieth century. Other notable interventions have been made through the Church and Nation Committee, for example on Central Africa in the late 1950s and early 1960s, on the effect of North Sea oil in the early 1970s, and on matters of Scottish nationality and constitutional proposals.[31] The Church and Nation Committee reports have consistently formed the most publicised event of the General Assembly, which tends to be regarded by Church members and a sizeable proportion of the public as the most representative Scottish national forum in the absence of a Scottish legislature. However, this notion would seem increasingly difficult to sustain in regard to the question of how representative the attenders of the Assembly are of wider Scottish society in its contemporary multi-ethnic and religious mix.[32]

In the decade following World War II the Church enjoyed a boom in membership, something that appears to have been aided by the evangelical campaigns of the time, both native and imported.[33] This increase peaked in 1956, and from around 1963 the Church entered a period of 'membership catastrophe' from which it has yet to emerge.[34] From the early 1960s secular forces pushed Scotland more firmly into line with England; only the Western Isles and smaller rural communities defied the trends. The huge demographic changes affecting the cities in the 1960s and 1970s played havoc with Church organisation. The Church's responsiveness to social questions – the Reverend Geoff Shaw became a legendary figure among the poor of the Gorbals in the 1970s – did not stem the decline in adherents; neither did liberal-left political stances on questions such as nuclear weapons and women's issues – the Church began ordaining women ministers in the 1960s.

II

There have been a variety of Protestant identities expressed through politics in twentieth century Scotland. These expressions are most clearly discernible in the first half of the century, after which the connections between Protestantism and political allegiance gradually loosened. However, this is not to say that religious variables have ceased to influence political behaviour, as recent political controversies show.

In the early part of the century Protestant influences can be traced to all the main political parties in Scotland. In their passionate support for monarch, constitution and Empire, the Conservatives stood for an image of Britain which was fundamentally Protestant and viewed Scotland as a loyal segment of the British national mosaic. The Conservatives suffered in Scotland from their aristocratic associations and had trailed behind the Liberals for the greater part of the nineteenth century. By the twentieth century they had in effect joined forces – although the Union was not officially cemented until 1912 – with those Liberals who had split from their party over the issue of Irish home rule from 1886 onwards. These Liberal Unionists were largely urban-based and represented the industrial and commercial bourgeoisie and a sizeable number of manual workers. The Irish issue motivated them above all and they identified firmly with the stance taken by the Irish Unionists against home rule.

As the Irish controversy wore on through three successive Home Rule bills between 1886 and 1912, the most determined opposition came from the Protestant Unionist population concentrated in Ulster. In Scotland the issue divided the Irish immigrant community along parallel Protestant-Catholic lines. Catholic Irish numbers in Scotland were about three to four times that of the Protestant Irish, but both were organised politically: the Catholic Irish through the United Irish League which supported the Liberals in their attempts to pass Home Rule, and the Protestant Irish through the Orange Order which supported the Conservative and Liberal Unionist opposition to it. The Orange Order, an overwhelmingly proletarian organisation with strong roots in Glasgow and the industrial west of Scotland, was the most obvious organisational expression of the Irish Protestant cultural influence in Scotland, and it was to maintain this influence throughout the twentieth century.[35] Translated into political terms, the Orange message was of an Irish 'zero-sum' nature: that when Catholics seemed to improve their position, it had to be at the expense of Protestants. As will be shown, this mentality came to shape aspects of Scottish politics, particularly in the inter-war years.

The merger of the Conservative and Liberal Unionists resulted in the party being known simply as 'the Unionists' in Scotland, a situation that lasted till 1965. The Union strictly speaking was that between Britain and Ireland, but in practice it also meant the integrity of the whole UK. At the point of merger in 1912, the West of Scotland Liberal Unionist Association records include the following very typical declaration of their political 'raison d'être':

> The finest population in Ireland (the Ulster Unionists) are being driven to extremes, and are imploring our help. They believe that their rights as British citizens, the peace of their homes, the prosperity of their businesses, their religious freedom itself, are all involved in the struggle. No Scotsman could read without deep emotion the narrative of a vast and loyal population, closely united to us by ties of race and religion, flocking to their Churches to implore the Most High to avert the threatened danger and we in the West of Scotland, of all in the British Isles, should hold out a strong hand to them in their hour of distress.[36]

The Unionists therefore became a party which appealed in the industrial west of Scotland at least, to Protestant voters on the basis of a loyalist message very reminiscent of Ulster. It fused the appeals of Empire, religion, Ulster, and a definition of Scottishness which derived to a large extent from Presbyterian mythology discussed earlier. In the inter-war years some of the party's Scottish MPs were Orange Order members; indeed, Sir John Gilmour, Secretary of State for Scotland at different points in the 1920s and 1930s, was an Orangeman. Glasgow Unionist Association records contain many indications of anti-Irish Catholic sentiment and illustrate the degree to which the Unionists shared in the Scottish Churches' scapegoating campaign against the Irish Catholic community in the inter-war era. In August 1927, for example, there was an association discussion of the emigration problem and the recorded comment was that the field was being left to the Irish 'whose desire it was to gain this country for Roman Catholicism'.[37]

The Unionist Party, especially in the inter-war period, gave overt political expression to the fears and prejudices of many Protestant Scots. Anti-Catholicism functioned as an important, if negative, expression of Protestant identity. The Churches' expressions of anti-Catholicism had their roots mainly in a desire to see the Protestant faith prosper in Scotland and Presbyterian traditions and values upheld. They believed that the large Catholic community of Irish extraction was unassimilable, and was having a detrimental effect on the national character. This view was shared by prominent Scottish Nationalists of the period, such as Andrew Dewar Gibb and George Malcolm Thomson; in the 1930s the Scottish National Party sought Scottish Home Rule within the Empire and repudiated Irish nationalism.[38]

The Unionists, while taking the same positions on the supposed Catholic

Irish threat to Scottish nationhood, gave the whole matter an Ulster type of twist. They made use of an essentially Irish political rhetoric – the language of loyalism – which held that loyalty to the state (and the crown) should be rewarded with jobs and favours, and that 'disloyalty' in this regard should not be rewarded. What was 'un-Scottish' for the Unionists was also depicted as 'un-British'. It was only by using such a language that the Unionists could continue to appeal in a populist fashion and face up to the political threat of Protestant extremist organisations such as the Scottish Protestant League (SPL) and Protestant Action (PA), both of which made significant gains in local government politics in the 1930s, in Glasgow and Edinburgh respectively.[39]

However, as Steve Bruce has pointed out, the Unionists in Scotland, in contrast to the Unionists in Northern Ireland, had no substantial 'pork barrel' with which to reward working-class supporters, and ultimately were part of a political party whose wider (British) agenda offered little scope for religious sectarianism.[40] The Unionist hold on the Protestant working class was nowhere near as tight as in Northern Ireland. Two important issues on which the Orange Order campaigned for decades in Scotland – namely the 1918 Education Act and mixed marriages – did not break down into neat and tidy political terms. It was a Conservative-dominated coalition government which passed the 1918 Act providing for full state support for Catholic schools, and it was a Conservative government in 1926 which passed the Catholic Relief Act which allowed the Orange Order to claim that the state was strengthening the position of the Catholic Church while the Church attempted to undermine the law of the land with its stance on mixed marriages: the Catholic Church in a decree issued in 1908 held that mixed marriages not sanctified by the rites of their Church were invalid. In addition, it is somewhat ironic that the campaign for legislation to halt Irish immigration into Scotland received no assistance from Orangeman Sir John Gilmour when he was Secretary of State.[41]

There were limitations to the Unionists' ability to secure Protestant working-class support. From World War I onwards, the Labour movement in Scotland enjoyed some success in bringing Protestant and Catholic workers together around a politics of class interest. To a large extent Labour inherited the skilled-worker (and predominantly Protestant) vote which had gone to the Liberals in large measure from the time of the franchise extensions of the late nineteenth century. Indeed, the formative influences in the Scottish Labour movement, with its stress on ethical questions and enthusiasm for temperance and educational opportunities, appropriated a great deal of the Presbyterian moral righteousness which characterised the

Scottish Liberals. Well into the twentieth century certain Scottish Labour leaders periodically sounded definitively Protestant (and Presbyterian) notes – Thomas Johnston (editor of the ILP paper, *Forward*) occasionally took inspiration from the Covenanters and what he called 'the grand moments of the democratic theocracy'[42] – and the psalm-singing send-off for the Clydeside MPs to Westminster in 1922 has been part of Scottish socialist folklore ever since. Notions of 'Presbyterian democracy' have been an integral part of socially radical politics in Scotland in the nineteenth and twentieth centuries. Labour could, and did, exploit deteriorating worker-employer relations in some workplaces to take votes, on a class basis, from workers who continued to hold deeply sectarian views. Neither did sectarianism prevent the steady rise of trades unionism in Scotland.

The Unionists, over the period 1918–60, were the most successful of the Scottish political parties; their ability to draw on substantial pan-class Protestant support was demonstrated in their Scottish electoral zenith in 1955, and in surveys of political behaviour in relation to religious affiliation in the early 1960s.[43] On the other hand, Scottish Protestants have shown a far greater tendency to distribute their votes among the Scottish parties than their Catholic counterparts. This was evident in the overwhelmingly Protestant nature of the SNP support in the party's 1970s high tide in con-trast to the remarkably solid Catholic Labour vote in the same period.[44] In the 1980s and 1990s there have been indications of a Catholic shift from Labour to the Nationalists, but it is still slight and does not alter the general political picture of a Catholic-Labour alliance co-existing with a fairly even Protestant split between the Conservatives, Labour, and the SNP.[45]

Since the 1960s the Unionists (Conservatives after 1965) found that pre-viously successful formulas no longer reaped the same electoral dividends among the Protestant working class. Many were beginning to question the benefit of Britishness, especially with the decline of Empire. It might also be argued that the paternalistic dimension of Scottish Unionism which bound worker and employer in some industries and businesses, declined along with those industries themselves. After 1945 there was no equivalent generation of industrialists such as Lithgow, Weir, Colville, Craig and Cargill.[46] Powerful élites in the business world after 1945 did not epitomise the wider cultural identity, of special appeal to Protestant Scots, which these industrial figures of the pre-1945 period were able to do. The post-war era saw a decline in associations which brought employer and privileged worker together. The records of one such, the West of Scotland Association of Foremen Engineers, conveys the flavour of paternalism most vividly. At this association's Burns Supper in 1916 John Ure-Primrose, flour-mill owner, Freemason, Liberal Unionist, ex-Lord Provost of Glasgow and Chairman of Rangers Football Club, delivered a eulogy on Burns and said that it was remarkable that 'while Scotland had great soldiers, preachers, statesmen, pioneers, investors and captains of industry, it was at the shrine of a poor and in many ways unfortunate poet that she worshipped annually'.[47] Besides Ure-Primrose, other members of the West of Scotland industrial and business élite who patronised this association included Lord Weir, Sir Archibald Denny and Sir William Beardmore. A certain Protestant loyalist identity was cultivated in such organisations, and the Unionists lost an important means of political influence when they declined; and they did so in proportion largely to the increase in the role played by the trade unions, particularly during World War II and after. Furthermore, nationalised industry and multinationals after 1945 tended to pursue non-sectarian employment practices which broke the Protestant monopoly of skilled labour. Finally, a combination of secularisation, an increase in mixed marriages, and a Catholic community whose Scottish identity came to eclipse its Irish one, took much of the force out of religious differences as a matter of political division.[48]

Nevertheless, the recent controversy over the allegations of corruption and sectarian discrimination levelled at Monklands District Council is reason enough to caution against conclusive statements about religious identity ceasing to be a factor in Scottish politics. Many commentators who had come to such a conclusion were abruptly disabused by the experience of the Monklands by-election of June 1994 which seemed in some ways to have let loose a host of religiously-based grievances which had been bubbling under the surface of Scottish politics for some time, particularly in relation to local government practices. The by-election suggested that rival sets of fears and suspicions about religious influence and motivations were alive and well, at least in areas like Lanarkshire. In relation to matters of Protestant identity and anti-Catholic feeling, Monklands reflected the durability of baleful perceptions of a cohesive Catholic community pursuing its own interest purposefully. The same attitudes have also been apparent in recurring controversies over the funding of separate Catholic schools. For many poorer Protestants there has arguably taken root in recent years a sense of being marginalised and denied a voice; in contrast to this they perceive Catholics to be looked after and spoken for by the Labour Party in particular.

III

Overall, religious identity has been expressed ambiguously, and usually faintly, through the medium of politics in Scotland since the 1960s.

However, this has rather belied the continuing strength of religious feelings, albeit of a rather 'secularised' and residual nature, in the popular culture of the nation.

Until at least the 1960s the churches were major providers of outlets for social and leisure activities. During the period of membership growth in the Church of Scotland from around 1945–56, Sunday School enrolment rose by 41 per cent.[49] Membership of an organisation like this, or of Church youth clubs and the Boys' Brigade, was a feature of the average Protestant Scot's upbringing until very recently. Even if parents did not attend church, they tended to send their children to such organisations. If the churches claimed much less of the adults' time and energies as the century progressed, notice should still be taken of the range of social activities such as debating circles, guilds, and sports which the churches provided.

Outside the Church certain organisations either actively promoted, or were popularly associated with, a Protestant identity. The Orange Order was the most robust of these, although its political influence through the Unionists, which had always been limited and conditional in nature, was increasingly eclipsed by its social and cultural role as the century wore on. In the areas of its original nineteenth-century growth, in the mining towns of Lanarkshire and Ayrshire and the once-thriving textile communities of Renfrewshire, as well as in working-class Glasgow, it maintained itself as a communal focus. Through its annual raucous celebrations of the Battle of the Boyne it impinged on the consciousness of lowland Scotland and bequeathed an essentially Irish set of images and repertoire of songs, tunes, and slogans which have shaped profoundly the idiom in which religious allegiance has been asserted and defined in twentieth-century Scotland. From Orangeism derives part of the popular sentiment around the monarchy, crude popular stereotypes about Catholics and Catholicism, and the Protestant tribalist content of Scottish football culture. For many of their huge army of followers through the years, Rangers Football Club has stood for a Protestant 'cause' which has encompassed both the Irish political situation and home-grown rivalries with Catholics.

Orangeism has bred a defensive, defiant mentality. It has attracted much middle-class disdain, and as a result has been a rather incongruous vehicle of both sectarian sentiments and class consciousness.[50] It is often bracketed with Freemasonry in the minds of those who perceive both secret societies to be operating an agenda in favour of Protestants at the expense of Catholics. It is believed that such an agenda has operated in the past, and still obtains, in relation especially to matters of employment. While there is an overlap in membership, Freemasonry has a substantially larger number of adherents, is much more socially heterogeneous than the Orange Order, and claims also to be religiously mixed. Given its wealthier patrons and more venerable standing in British life it seems fair to conclude that it has exercised a lot more influence than the Orange Order over the securing of jobs and favours, although the extent to which this has been so can only be a matter for speculation.[51] What has been established fairly clearly is the Masonic character of many skilled trades in the heavy industrial sectors of employment, particularly engineering and shipbuilding, sectors dominated for many years by Protestants.[52]

In Scottish literature many of these cultural forms of Protestant community identity have been portrayed memorably, particularly by Alan Spence in his novel *The Magic Flute* and his collection of short stories, *Its Colours They Are Fine*. In the novel, set in Govan, his protagonists are exposed to a typical range of urban West of Scotland working-class Protestant experiences and influences: Sunday School, the Boys' Brigade, Rangers matches at Ibrox, and Orange marches. Some of them go on to work in the shipyards, join the masons, and stick fast to the identity shaped for them by their environment. Spence's is an intimate perspective at once critical and sympathetic. Earlier novels by George Blake (*The Shipbuilders*) and Gordon Williams (*From Scenes Like These*) also tellingly capture this world. Wider-ranging explorations of the Scottish Protestant mentality, lowlands-based in their settings, are a feature of the work of novelist Robin Jenkins.[53]

On the other hand, there are many examples in literature and the arts generally in Scotland of uncompromising reaction against Protestant cultural forces. This is particularly marked among writers of a Highland background who have generally taken a jaundiced view of the effects of Calvinism on the creative energies and abilities of their people. Novelists like Fionn MacColla[54] (who converted to Catholicism) and Iain Crichton Smith[55] have tackled this theme in their work, and the indictment against Calvinist Presbyterianism as suppressive of artistic achievement has been orthodoxy in cultural nationalist circles throughout the century.

The dour, ascetic, joyless Calvinist has indeed become a popular stereotype – nowhere more so than in the television comic creation the Reverend I.M. Jolly, played by Rikki Fulton. It is a stereotype lampooned exhaustively, and in many ways cultivated lovingly and exported for consumption to England and beyond. An essentially Protestant form of Scottishness has become the staple of the rather masochistic way in which Scots choose to present themselves in popular cultural terms.

Yet the very prevalence of such lampooning and parodying should caution against too sweeping a summation of Protestantism in relation to popular culture and entertainment. Much work of a comic and lively nature has adopted a loosely Protestant cultural guise, from 'bluenose' comedians like Lex MacLean and popular entertainers like Andy Stewart to the sabbatarians of the folk-rock band Runrig. The *Sunday Post* has been couthy and folksy in the extreme but hardly dour. Of course, such phenomena as the *Post*, and indeed the Harry Lauder school of entertainment, have been accused by Nationalist intellectuals such as Tom Nairn of 'deforming' Scottish culture, but this once deeply influential argument has itself come under attack recently from, it might be said, a post-modernist perspective.[56]

The intellectual reputation of Scottish Protestantism this century has suffered from the condemnation of its effects on the arts. The days are long gone when it could be routinely claimed that workers argued with each other in factories over fine theological points.[57] Yet, George Elder Davie's stress on the importance of Presbyterianism to the development of Scotland's distinctive philosophical and educational traditions has been echoed in a recent scholarly appraisal.[58] The kind of boasts made by churchmen and Protestant polemicists early in the century about the beneficial moral seriousness of Presbyterianism, the intellectual training it afforded, and the culture of healthy dissent it engendered, have continued to find endorsement among Scottish thinkers.

It has been argued that Protestantism has been a signal feature of twentieth century Scotland and that varieties of Protestant identity have shaped the life of the nation in spheres such as politics, education, work, the military, and high and low culture. In terms of religious faith Protestantism has largely lost its position of relative dominance in Scottish society. As Scotland becomes at once more religiously and culturally pluralist *and* more secular, it remains to be seen if Protestantism can rediscover the dynamic qualities of its past to justify itself as a vital creed for the challenges of the new century, and to essay a positive vision rather than functioning as a rather nominal token of identity for a mass of people with whom it has lost touch.

NOTES AND REFERENCES

1. See S.J. Brown and M. Fry (eds), *Scotland in the Age of the Disruption* (Edinburgh, 1993).
2. For discussion of this point see, for example, R.J. Finlay, 'Controlling the Past: Modern Scotland and Scottish Historiography' in *Scottish Affairs*, No. 6 (Spring 1994), pp. 127–42; G. Walker, 'Religion, Empire and Nationality in Scotland and Ulster before the First World War' in I.S. Wood (ed.), *Scotland and Ulster* (Edinburgh, 1994); and D.W. Bebbington, 'Religion and National Feeling in Nineteenth Century Scotland and Wales' in S. Mews (ed.), *Religion and National Identity: Studies in Church History*, Vol. 18 (Oxford, 1982).

3. See R.D. Kernohan, *Scotland's Life and Work* (Edinburgh, 1979), p. 144; I. McLeod, 'Scotland and the Liberal Party 1880–1900' (M. Litt. thesis, University of Glasgow, 1978).

4. See S.J. Brown, 'Reform, Reconstruction, Reaction: The Social Vision of Scottish Presbyterianism c.1830–1930', *Scottish Journal of Theology*, Vol. 44 (1991), pp. 489–517.

5. C. Brown, 'Religion and Secularisation' in A. Dickson and J.H. Treble (eds), *People and Society in Scotland, vol. III, 1914–1990* (Edinburgh, 1992).

6. See T.H. Darlow, *William Robertson Nicoll* (London, 1925), especially discussion in ch. 29.

7. Bonar Law Papers, House of Lords Records Office, 32/3/30. See also NLS Acc. 10424/63.

8. For example, Hector MacPherson, *Scotland's Debt to Protestantism* (Edinburgh and London, 1912).

9. Kernohan, *Scotland's Life and Work*, p. 96.

10. ibid., p. 97.

11. ibid., p. 109.

12. See 'Address at the Opening of the Scottish National War Memorial' in C.L. Warr, *Scottish Sermons and Addresses* (London, 1930).

13. 'Address at the Laying of the Colours of the Royal Scots' in Warr, *Scottish Sermons*.

14. The pacifist strain in the church was identified most strongly with the Reverend George MacLeod.

15. 'The Union of the Scottish Churches' in Warr, *Scottish Sermons*.

16. See Brown, 'Reform, Reconstruction, Reaction'.

17. The most notable contributions to this topic include: T. Gallagher, *Glasgow: The Uneasy Peace* (Manchester, 1987); S.J. Brown, ' "Outside the Covenant": The Scottish Presbyterian Churches and Irish Immigration 1922–38', *Innes Review*, XLII, No. 1 (Spring 1991), pp. 19–45; and R.J. Finlay, 'Nationalism, Race, Religion and the Irish Question in Inter-War Scotland', *Innes Review*, XLII, No. 1 (Spring 1991), pp. 46–67.

18. Scottish Records Office [SRO] 37110/1, Scottish Office Report on the Irish in Scotland.

19. See R.J. Finlay, 'National Identity in Crisis: Politicians, Intellectuals, and the End of Scotland, 1920–1939', *History* (Summer 1994).

20. *The Scotsman*, 1 October 1929.

21. ibid.

22. ibid., 2 October 1929.

23. ibid.

24. *Church Union Supplement*, 2 October 1929.

25. For contemporary polemics on this issue see John MacLeod, *No Great Mischief if They Fall* (Edinburgh, 1993).

26. A. Muir, *John White* (London, 1958), p. 297.

27. See C. Harvie, 'The Covenanting Tradition' in G. Walker and T. Gallagher (eds), *Sermons and Battle Hymns* (Edinburgh, 1990).

28. T. Gallagher, 'The press and Protestant popular culture' in Walker and Gallagher, *Sermons and Battle Hymns*.

29. See J.H. Proctor, 'The Church of Scotland and the Struggle for a Scottish Assembly', *Journal of Church and State*, Vol. 25, No. 3 (1983), pp. 523–43.

30. See 'Church and Nation Committee 1989 Report on the Government of Scotland', in J. Stein (ed.), *Scottish Self-Government: Some Christian Viewpoints* (Edinburgh, 1989). This report offers some distinctively Scottish theological perspectives on the sovereignty question.

31. See D. Forrester, 'The Church of Scotland and public policy', *Scottish Affairs*, No. 4 (Summer 1993), pp. 67–82.

32. See comments of W.S. Johnston in 'Church and State in Scotland Today', in A. Elliott and D. Forrester (eds), *The Scottish Churches and the Political Process Today* (Edinburgh, 1986); but also the view of Joyce McMillan in *The Guardian*, 25 May 1995.

33. The Rev. Tom Allan's 'Tell Scotland' campaign of the 1940s; Billy Graham's visits in the 1950s.

34. See Brown, 'Religion and Secularisation'.

35. E. McFarland, *Protestants First!* (Edinburgh, 1991); G. Walker, 'The Orange Order in Scotland Between the Wars', *International Review of Social History*, XXXVII, No. 2 (1992), pp. 177–206.

36. West of Scotland Liberal Unionist Association, Secretary's Report, 5 December 1912, National Library of Scotland [NLS] Acc. 10424/22.

37. Glasgow Unionist Association Minutes, 29 August 1927, NLS Acc. 10424/73.
38. See Gallagher, *Glasgow*, ch. 4; Finlay, 'Race, Religion, Empire and the Irish Question'; '"Outside the Covenant"'.
39. See Gallagher, *Glasgow*, ch. 4; also T. Gallagher, *Edinburgh Divided* (Edinburgh, 1987), passim.
40. S. Bruce, 'Sectarianism in Scotland: A Contemporary Assessment and Explanation', *Scottish Government Yearbook* (1988), pp. 150–65.
41. See Brown, '"Outside the Covenant"'; Walker, 'Orange Order'.
42. *Forward*, 3 June 1911, and 24 June 1911.
43. See Walker, 'Orange Order' for fuller discussion.
44. I. Budge and D. Urwin, *Scottish Political Behaviour* (London, 1966), pp. 60–5, 68–71.
45. J. Brand, *The National Movement in Scotland* (London, 1978), pp. 150–4.
46. Statistical evidence in J. Mitchell, 'Religion and Politics in Scotland' (Paper presented to seminar on Religion and Scottish Politics, University of Edinburgh, 4 December 1992).
47. See D. McCrone, 'Towards a Principal Elite: Scottish Elites in the twentieth Century' in Dickson and Treble (eds), *People and Society*.
48. Strathclyde Regional Archives, TD 1115/1/3.
49. See D. McCrone, *Understanding Scotland* (London, 1992), pp. 155–9.
50. Brown, 'Religion and Sectarianism'.
51. See G.P.T. Finn, 'In the Grip? A psychological and historical exploration of the social significance of freemasonry in Scotland' in Walker and Gallagher, *Sermons and Battle Hymns*.
52. See J. Foster, 'A Century of Scottish Labour', *Labour History Review*, Vol. 55 (Spring 1990), pp. 64–8.
53. See discussion of Jenkins by Glenda Norquay in C. Craig (ed.), *The History of Scottish Literature*, Vol. 4 (Aberdeen, 1987). ch. 17.
54. See discussion by Isobel Murray in Craig op. cit., ch. 7.
55. See discussion by Roderick Watson in Craig, *History of Scottish Literature*, ch. 20.
56. See T. Nairn, 'The Three Dreams of Scottish Nationalism' in K. Miller (ed.), *Memoirs of a Modern Scotland* (London, 1970); D. McCrone, *Understanding Scotland*, ch. 7.
57. See Ian Jack's autobiographical essay, 'Finished with Engines' in his *When the Oil Ran Out* (London, 1987).
58. G.E. Davie, *The Democratic Intellect* (Edinburgh, 1981), especially introduction and ch. I; C. Beveridge and R. Turnbull, *The Eclipse of Scottish Culture* (Edinburgh, 1989).

Research for this chapter was assisted by a grant from the Nuffield Foundation.

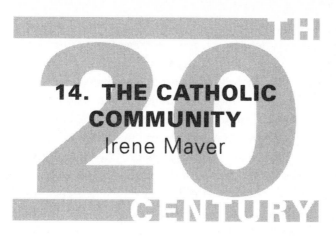

14. THE CATHOLIC COMMUNITY
Irene Maver

I

The Catholic community in twentieth-century Scotland has proved to be remarkably resilient, despite the challenge of secularisation and lingering preconceptions of the faith as alien and subversive. By the 1990s the Church was claiming over 800,000 adherents, a figure which some suggested has edged out the Church of Scotland as the nation's single largest denomination, depending on definitions of membership.[1] Whatever the precise quantification in contemporary terms, and recent fluctuations in membership fortunes, the Catholic Church has been able to consolidate its position from the 1900s, helped to a large extent by the relative homogeneity of the community which it serves. While the profile of the four million adherents in England and Wales is characterised as more diverse, cosmopolitan and ethnically complex, Scotland's Catholics have tended to be concentrated in the specific geographical area of the industrial west, and are largely the product of sustained Irish immigration during the nineteenth century.[2] Because of its origins and territorial base, the community north of the border has coalesced more readily; a phenomenon which has worked both in its favour and to its detriment. Thus, although the Church constructed a considerable organisational infrastructure, the self-contained nature of Scottish Catholicism also fuelled perceptions of insularity, which in turn heightened sectarian tensions in a predominantly Protestant society.

The focus on the sectarian dimension has been a preoccupation of historians in recent years, particularly with reference to the charged economic climate of the inter-war period, when overt manifestations of anti-Catholicism were common.[3] And there is a profound irony in such attempts to disentangle the rhetoric from the reality, given that in 1934 one eminent Scottish historian starkly commented that 'The vast majority of the

607,000 Roman Catholics in the country are of Irish descent, and their presence constitutes the main sociological problem of modern Scotland'.[4] Certainly, the Catholic presence in the community cannot be fully understood without appreciating the degree of antagonism which it evoked, and which even by the 1990s could resurface, as with the bitter controversy over alleged preferential treatment of Catholics by Monklands District Council. The strand of sectarianism in Scotland may not be consistent, but has had disconcerting continuity, despite the optimistic assessment that it is now reduced to the trappings of tribalism; that is, 'the Orange parades, Republican marches and Old Firm football matches ... [which] ... are no longer the tip of the sectarian iceberg; they are all of the iceberg that remains'.[5] Even so, the sheer volume of research on the subject reveals its importance in Scottish history, and particularly the relevance of the debate to the degree of sectarian influence since the 1900s, and the extent to which the Catholic community has been wholly accepted and assimilated.

However, there is a real danger of an historiographical imbalance by such close scrutiny of sectarianism, as it forms only part of the complex Catholic experience in twentieth-century Scotland. This is not to suggest that Scottish historians have been narrow or obsessive in their approach, as the post-1918 period has not generally been deemed significant for research until very recently. In this context, the focus on sectarianism can be seen as pioneering. Nor is the patchy response to Catholic history unique to Scotland. Leslie Woodcock Tentler, in a detailed assessment of the state of American Catholic history, has written persuasively of its continuing marginality to the academic mainstream, despite the Church having been the single largest denomination since the mid-nineteenth century.[6] There are uncanny echoes of Scotland in his identification of the gaps in research, especially the impact of women, both in religious orders and as part of the laity. Similarly, preconceptions about the seemingly sinister influence of clerical control have tended to colour analyses of American working-class history, with the implication that Catholics eschewed radical politics and industrial militancy. Yet recent case studies of communities across the Atlantic are unravelling the much more intricate interactions between the priesthood and their parishioners, and the conflicts within the Church over matters of ideology and morality. Catholic history can therefore say much about the contradictions inherent in religion, as well as giving broader insights into the workings of a definable community, and the shifting power-structure therein.

This chapter is, of necessity, a selective overview of the Catholic community in Scotland, and although chronological in structure, focuses mainly on the earlier rather than the later period. Despite the obstacles, the first half of the century was characterised by growing Catholic assertiveness, particularly as political and educational opportunities became more widely available. In this connection, 1918 was pivotal, first because of the introduction of manhood suffrage and the limited female franchise, second because Catholic schools became part of the state system, albeit retaining their own religious character. These developments allowed for greater Catholic participation in Scottish public life, although the process was by no means immediate, but generational. Indeed, despite the easing of institutional constraints from the end of World War I, less tangible barriers still remained, and for all that Catholics became more active in the Scottish political mainstream, this was not translated into significant Westminster representation until after the 1960s.[7] It should also be cautioned that the Catholic experience was not uniform throughout Scotland during the twentieth century, even though the community remained comparatively homogeneous. This analysis has tended to focus on the territory where the Catholic population was most densely concentrated, and where previous research has proved to be most prolific; that is, the industrial west. Yet it is perhaps too easy to generalise about Scottish Catholicism from one geographical perspective. As has been previously suggested, the community was not a monolith, and only further delving by researchers can disentangle the complexities.

II

What characterised the Catholic community in Scotland at the turn of the nineteenth century? In terms of numbers, it has been estimated as ten per cent of the total population (446,400 out of 4.5 million), concentrated overwhelmingly in the west of Scotland.[8] Nearly 70 per cent was accounted for in the separate dioceses of Glasgow, Motherwell and Paisley, indicating a predominantly urban and industrial focus. However, outwith this territorial orbit, both Dundee and Edinburgh had significant Catholic enclaves, which – as in much of the Lowlands – derived from relatively recent Irish settlement. Not that the indigenous Catholic presence in northern Scotland was insubstantial, particularly in such traditional areas of strength as the north-east (Aberdeenshire and Banffshire) and the Gaidhealtachd (almost wholly within the bounds of Inverness county). Moreover, while Irish immigration was steadily slowing down from its mid-nineteenth-century peak, overseas incomers were boosting Scotland's Catholic population qualitatively, if not quantatively. At this time, Italians numbered some 3,000 in Glasgow, making it the third largest community in the United Kingdom after London and Manchester; in comparison, Edinburgh's Italians comprised almost 1,000.[9] Poles and Lithuanians, too, fleeing from 'Russification' imposed by the Tsarist regime from the 1870s, found their way predominantly to the Lanarkshire coal fields, establishing a community at least on a numerical par with the Italians.[10]

There was thus a multi-faceted ethnic and cultural dimension to Scotland's Catholic profile by the 1900s, although the Irish origins of the majority overwhelmed the community's collective identity up to the 1920s and beyond. Indeed, it became difficult for contemporaries to disentangle the designations 'Catholic' from 'Irish', despite the influx of Europeans to Scotland and even though there was an increasingly wide generation gap separating the Irish antecedents of many Scottish-born Catholics. Undoubtedly, the proportion of Scotland's Irish-born population remained consistently higher than that of England and Wales; however, this included a substantial number of Protestants, given the geographical proximity of Ulster.[11]

The propensity for ethnic stereotyping shrouded a clearer understanding of the Catholic community during the early twentieth century; perceptions rather than reality all too readily fuelled conventional wisdom, especially in the urban context, where evidence of the immigrant lifestyle was most visible. The problem of definition was partly attributable to the seemingly contradictory nature of Catholicism, which could appear to those outside the faith as both subversive and conservative, exotic and forbidding. And, as Tom Gallagher has pointed out with reference to the Catholic Irish, the Scots' sense of insecurity about their own national identity at a time of unprecedented social change exacerbated fears bout the perceived alien presence in their midst.[12] Ironically, in view of the often observed Catholic defensiveness over their minority status in Scotland, it was the defensiveness of the majority which helped to shape the image.

Notwithstanding these broader Scottish sensibilities, much of the Catholic experience during the opening decades of the twentieth century has been depicted in terms of the 'siege mentality', especially in relation to the industrialised communities. Such self-protective attitudes were nurtured in the wake of the 1845 potato famine, which was described by one recent commentator as 'the most important event in the development of the Catholic Church in Scotland', because of the unprecedented incursion of adherents from Ireland.[13] Yet for all that Irish incomers were not representative of Scottish Catholics generally by the 1900s, suspicion of the host community remained deeply engrained among Catholics of Irish descent, because of the legacy of predatory and exploitative behaviour. The grim realism of Patrick MacGill, the Donegal-born novelist, captured the sense of Catholic Irish ambivalence towards Scotland prior to 1914, not least because of the community's continuing concentration in relatively lowly positions in the labour market.[14] During the 1900s, it was unequivocally stated in evidence to the Royal Commission on the Poor Law that the Irish comprised 'the great body of unskilled casual labour in Glasgow'.[15] That the self-proclaimed Second City of the Empire was so dependent on this group became glaringly apparent in 1902, when a strike of municipal street sweepers and refuse collectors resulted in victory for the workers, because of public concern over the rapidly deteriorating urban fabric. One journal made great play of the pugnacious Irish predilections of Glasgow's corps of 'scavengers', and their indulgence in ''sthrikin' an' foightin'' to remedy their grievances.[16] It was patronising and theatrical imagery, but expressed much about contemporary perceptions, and the compartmentalisation of Scottish society along ethnic and religious lines.

Such assertiveness, in the face of formidable obstacles, reveals the extent to which the years up to the 1920s were pivotal for Scotland's Catholics. Although the old defensiveness could still show through, especially in matters relating to the preservation of religious identity, the steady development of an integrated social infrastructure based on the parish unit had become a source of considerable strength. The Church itself had been able to carve out a clearer profile following the restoration of the hierarchy in 1878; material evidence was demonstrated in the number of schools and chapels which were constructed, especially in the industrial areas.[17] In Glasgow, where the Catholic population had risen by over 100,000 during the last 30 years of the nineteenth century, the number of priests servicing the territory of the archdiocese increased from 74 to 234.[18] This framework was further consolidated with the establishment of organisations like the Catholic Union in 1885, which – with some success – aimed to open out Catholic membership of representative bodies like School Boards and Town Councils.[19] This necessarily entailed a growing emphasis on political involvement, whether in the immediate realm of party activity, or via trade union affairs. Politics came to be a crucial area of contact between Catholics and non-Catholics, and has been acknowledged as one of the primary routes for assimilation into Scottish society during the twentieth century.[20] Mutual identification of interests could clearly submerge previous sectarian antagonisms, although this process was often piecemeal and slow-moving, especially prior to 1922, when the Irish nationalist agenda directed political energies among a significant section of the Catholic population.

In the context of greater Catholic assimilation, much has been made of the increasing orientation of adherents towards the Labour Party, even prior to the massive franchise extension in 1918. Most notably, the efforts of the charismatic figure of John Wheatley in the west of Scotland have been perceived as of paramount importance in muting the hostility of the Catholic Church towards socialism and realigning political loyalties. As Sheridan Gilley has demonstrated, Wheatley's struggle with clerical opposition to his ideological viewpoint was not so clear-cut as has hitherto been presupposed; the priests were by no means neanderthal in their approach to social reform, and far from being a sign that the faith was backward-looking, the debate on socialism showed how far such issues could be openly discussed.[21] Moreover, the evolutionary socialism represented by the Independent Labour Party was qualitatively different from the secularist tradition espoused in continental Europe, which the 1891 papal encyclical *Rerum Novarum* had been promulgated specifically to undermine. Labour and Catholicism – at least in Scotland – were by no means incompatible, and Wheatley's preparedness to come to terms with both demonstrated how far influential Catholics by the 1900s were looking beyond the confines of their own community, while at the same time retaining their religious identity – not, it should be added, that the Labour Party's relationship with the Catholic Church was harmonious, or that there was ready support from within the Catholic community. Indeed, with reference to Dundee, William Walker has illustrated how far the Catholic Irish were actively discouraged from Labour movement participation until after World War I.[22]

However, the growing appeal of the Labour Party as a possible political alternative for Catholics during the 1900s was symptomatic at a deeper level of the increasingly ambiguous and uneasy identification of Scotland's Catholics with Liberalism. For all that the Liberal Party represented much that Catholics could identify with, in terms of Irish Home Rule, social welfare and electoral reform, many Catholics did not wholly trust Liberal intentions. Certainly, in the west of Scotland, they detected a strong whiff of paternalism behind Liberal pronouncements, not least because of the influence of evangelical Presbyterians within the higher echelons of the party. Although this influence was beginning to erode, as Liberalism itself became increasingly defensive in the squeeze between Labour and Unionism, Catholics remained acutely sensitive to the sometimes subtle sectarianism behind Liberal pronouncements. The temperance issue was one very obvious example of this, given the disproportionately high percentage of Catholic Irish publicans in working-class communities. Patrick O'Hare, an Irish-born wine and spirit merchant, who in 1903 had the distinction

of becoming Glasgow Corporation's first Catholic bailie since the Reformation, severed his connection with the Liberal Party because of teetotal
pressure against him.[23] In this context, stricter temperance legislation
for Scotland – which was one of the achievements of the Liberal government in 1913 – was bitterly resented as thinly disguised social control. It is
scarcely surprising that from this time the Labour Party began to mute its
previously assertive pro-temperance stance in order not to alienate potential Catholic support.

The uneasiness about Liberal motivations was, of course, not solely the
preserve of Catholics, although it went a long way towards explaining
Catholic defensiveness at the time. The community was very much aware
that the carrot as well as the stick approach could be used to undermine
Catholic integrity. Even the support of Scottish Liberals for Irish Home
Rule was ambiguous, because evangelical Presbyterians – in a direct line of
thought from the theologian Thomas Chalmers – believed that the missionary impulse would overwhelm a revitalised, self-governing Ireland and
'truth', in the form of Protestantism, would suddenly triumph in the previously oppressed and demoralised nation.[24] Such missionary sentiments
had also underpinned evangelical efforts during the nineteenth century to
proselytise Catholics in Scotland, especially the young. Along with the
fear of secularism, this constituted a major reason why Catholic schools
remained doggedly outwith the state system after the implementation of
the 1872 Education Act. However, by the early twentieth century this
commitment to principle was proving expensive for the Catholic community to sustain, which was why it eventually opted for state control in 1918,
albeit with specific safeguards for preserving religious character.[25] This
unique compromise, as far as a predominantly Protestant society was
concerned, undoubtedly boosted Catholic social mobility by expanding
opportunities for post-elementary education. Notwithstanding the perpetuation of separate spheres of schooling, the 1918 legislation has
been identified as another milestone on the route to Catholic assimilation,
because it allowed for greater equalisation of Scottish educational
standards.[26]

III

The generous concession to Catholic identity inherent in the 1918 Education Act was an acknowledgement of the community's growing importance, especially in the electoral context. It was evidence, too, of the
traditional Liberal eschewal of confrontation, and use of the subtle approach
to hold on to the reins of power. This strategy had worked remarkably well

up to World War I, as was testified by the muted reception in Glasgow for the Ulster hero, Sir Edward Carson, during the Home Rule crisis of 1912.[27] However, the bitter experience of the war finally cut across Liberal aspirations in Scotland. The anti–Irish – and, implicitly, anti–Catholic – rhetoric which began to be articulated forcefully after 1922 has to be viewed in this context, given the power-vacuum that was created with the demise of Liberalism as an electorally meaningful political force. Rather than the Catholic community being on the defensive, it was a substantial segment of the Scottish Protestant establishment which closed ranks to fend off perceived challenges from the hitherto 'submerged' population, be it Catholic, Irish, socialist, or all three combined. Of course, wider influences were at work to create this turnaround, and the blighting impact of economic depression was a formidable catalyst in shaping attitudes. As Scotland's global status seemed to decline inexorably, with unprecedented levels of overseas emigration, the image of the industrial wasteland began to permeate the public consciousness, helped in no small measure by a coterie of influential propagandists.[28] Thus, according to Andrew Dewar Gibb, Regius Professor of Private Law at Glasgow University:

> in the heart of a dwindling though virile and intelligent race there is growing up another people, immeasurably inferior in every way, but cohesive and solid, refusing obstinately, at the behest of obscurantist magic-men, to mingle with the people whose land they are usurping; unaware, or if aware, disloyal to all the finest ideals and ambitions of the Scottish race.[29]

Gibb's rhetoric directly echoed the infamous report to the 1923 General Assembly of the Church of Scotland which, in a blatant appeal to native sentiment, identified the Catholic presence as both subverting and corroding the Scottish national identity. As Stewart J. Brown has shown, the ensuing campaign of the Church in defence of Protestant integrity constituted a new departure, which shifted the emphasis from the subtle, proselytising approach of the pre-war period to that of aggressively isolating Scotland's Catholic community, derived as it largely was from Irish immigrants.[30] There were political overtones to the anxieties within the national Church, as Catholic support for the Labour Party was believed to have contributed substantially to electoral successes from 1922, even though the Catholic presence among Scottish Labour leaders was in fact disproportionately small.[31] Nevertheless, perceptions rather than reality continued to colour the debate, with Church pronouncements adding legitimacy to the anti-Catholic crusade, which reached ugly proportions during the 1930s. In

Edinburgh, where Catholics made up less than nine per cent of the population, John Cormack's populist Protestant Action gained widespread following, which led to significant victories in the 1935 and 1936 municipal elections.[32] The movement also left a trail of violence in its wake, most notably at the Catholic Eucharist Congress held in June of that year. It should be added that the onset of war in 1939 and the new climate of solidarity and social reconciliation effectively ended the rise to stardom of such men as Cormack, although the Catholic journalist, Colm Brogan, could still obliquely refer to 'The Problem' as bedevilling community relations in the post-war period.[33]

However, outside perceptions of the Catholic community during the inter-war years could be far from negative. In his travel book *Scottish Journey* (1935), Edwin Muir was lyrical in his evocation of the Grotto at Carfin, a place of Catholic pilgrimage in the heart of industrial Lanarkshire, which he considered to be 'the only palpable assertion of humanity that I came across in the midst of that blasted region'.[34] Indeed, Carfin proved to be a symbol of regeneration for Scotland's Catholics in several ways. From 1916 a colourful Corpus Christi procession had annually taken place there, which impressed itself on more than just the Catholic consciousness. As the *Motherwell Times* reported of the 1923 ceremonial:

> There was no fear of trouble in the upland miners' village. It has a majority of Catholics, some of whom are of Scottish descent, some of Lithuanian, most of Irish stock, but all of whom are on the best of terms with the Presbyterian minority – on such good terms that two years ago the County Council authorities permitted the Carfin congregation to do as their brethren in foreign lands, and not merely confine the procession to the presbytery grounds.[35]

Yet ironically, by opening out the procession, the authorities had inadvertently breached the terms of the 1829 Catholic Emancipation Act, which still rendered it illegal for priests to parade in public wearing formal vestments. And, by a further irony, it was the 1924 minority Labour government which was accused of over-zealousness in interpreting the law, by effectively banning the ceremonial. That partisan pressure had been brought to bear on the Secretary for Scotland, William Adamson, eventually became clear, and steps were immediately taken from all sides of the House of Commons to rescind the proscriptions. However, with the typical slowness of parliamentary procedure, this was not implemented until 1926, under the terms of the Roman Catholic Relief Act.[36]

Despite the controversy over Carfin, the Labour Party generally reaped the electoral rewards from the 1920s as far as many working–class Catholics were concerned. However, this support derived from a mutual coalescence of interests rather than the appeal of Labour *per se*, and Catholic identification with a professedly socialist party could still remain ambiguous. Communism represented a particularly potent challenge to Catholicism, perhaps because they both shared a global vision of social change and the way in which power should be exercised. Moreover, as with many denominations at the time, there were obsessive fears about 'leakage' of Church membership, and the siren call of alternative faiths, into which category Communism fell. The Church therefore responded to the challenge by ensuring that its voice was forcefully heard in the crusade against Communism. This stance tested many Catholic loyalties, especially during the highly-charged political climate of the Spanish Civil War, when there was outrage over the perceived partisan stance of the Church in favour of Franco's Nationalists.[37] This in turn prompted John Wheatley's successor as MP for Glasgow Shettleston, John McGovern, to embark on a pugnacious whirlwind campaign of anti-clericalism. It needed the skill of a seasoned campaigner like Patrick Dollan, the great inter-war Labour Party organiser and alleged creator of the Labour municipal machine in Glasgow, to restore the delicate balance and retain wavering Catholic support.

The fact that Catholics were increasingly identifying with the Labour Party, and that politicians like Dollan and McGovern came from a Catholic background (albeit lapsed) revealed that credibility was steadily being consolidated in public life. Significantly, in 1939 Dollan became Lord Provost of Glasgow; a considerable achievement, given the long pedigree of committed Presbyterian incumbents to the post. This upward mobility was reflected generally during the inter-war period; a feature which had by no means been absent from the nineteenth and early twentieth centuries, but which tended to be linked with only a few occupational areas, notably (and notoriously) the drinks' trade.[38] The broadening of educational opportunity was an important catalyst for this shifting profile of the Catholic community. Teachers were accorded particular status at the time, forming 'the evident backbone of the growing Catholic middle-class', even though the professions generally were still not wholly receptive to Catholic aspirants.[39] Nevertheless, an important citadel was breached in 1931 when the writer Compton Mackenzie was elected rector of Glasgow University, despite a co-ordinated sectarian smear campaign against him.[40] There was an irony in this success, as Mackenzie had stood as a Scottish nationalist, at a time when anti-Catholic rhetoric within the movement was mounting. The aforementioned Andrew Dewar Gibb was one of the spearheads of the movement, and his views on Scottish racial purity – with strong eugenics overtones – were one reason why Catholics came to hold such distaste for artificial birth control. Indeed, it was partly to offset the more extreme statements of men like Gibb that the Catholic Truth Society began to make a positive appeal to Catholics and non-Catholics alike, in order to give better information on questions of Church doctrine.

IV

Scotland's Catholics during the first half of the twentieth century demonstrated what Steve Bruce has described as 'cultural defence and cultural transition', in an effort to retain community identity and adapt to a rapidly changing social environment.[41] However, the perpetuation of this self-preservation mechanism even in the post-1945 period indicated that their position was far from secure. The brief resurgence of Scottish nationalism arising from the Covenant movement in the late 1940s had double-edged implications for Catholics, with Andrew Dewar Gibb still disdainfully describing the majority of adherents as a 'foreign element'.[42] On the other hand, Moray Maclaren – writer, broadcaster and nationalist sympathiser – took issue with this equation, suggesting that indigenous Catholics were truer Scots because they had not renounced the 'Old Religion'.[43] Charles Oakley's popular history of Glasgow, *The Second City*, which first appeared in 1946, stated unequivocally that there was no issue on which contemporary commentators were less willing to dwell than on the Irish in Scotland, and, implicitly, the anti-Catholicism that this could evoke.[44] The pioneering work of historian James Handley during the 1940s has to be viewed in this context, given the hitherto circumspect or hostile attitude towards the Irish or 'Scoto-Irish' presence.[45] And leading on from this, Colm Brogan – himself the descendant of Donegal immigrants – wrote in 1952 of changing times in Glasgow:

> Controversy is now idle. The Catholic population of Glasgow is bedded down. It is there, it is large, it is growing, and it cannot be got rid of by any method short of those favoured by Herr Himmler.[46]

The fortunes of other sections of the Catholic community fluctuated in the years leading up to the 1950s. With reference to those resident in the Gaidhealtachd, there was much concern about the threat of unemployment and depopulation, and the consequent erosion of their distinctive cultural identity.[47] On the other hand, Terri Colpi has described the Italian experience as having been 'golden', at least during the inter-war period.[48] By concentrating their energies on catering, in an area which the native population tended to avoid, this comparatively small group made an important niche for itself in Scottish society. Certainly, just about every town had at least one Italian family who supplied ice-creams or fish teas. Yet there was a severe jolt to the confidence of the community when Italy entered the war in 1940, triggering anti-Italian riots throughout mainland Britain. There were particularly violent incidents in Scottish urban centres, which have been attributed partly to anti-Catholic sentiments.[49] However, the war also had the effect of adding to the Catholic presence north of the border, with the incursion of thousands of Poles fleeing first German occupation, then Soviet domination. The statelessness of the Poles aroused some hostility in Scottish mining communities, where there was fear that they would compete unfairly in the job market. Yet ironically, the government had actively encouraged Polish resettlement, in the belief that the dislocation of war would create a domestic labour shortage, especially for its ambitious programme of reconstruction.[50]

In the west of Scotland, particularly, the post-1945 period was characterised by major slum clearance and housing projects. Within 30 years, Glasgow's spatial profile had altered dramatically, with the creation of peripheral housing estates and the transfer of some 200,000 inhabitants to overspill areas and new towns.[51] A community like the Gorbals, which had a substantial Catholic population, was thus dislocated, with major implications for parochial life. For its part, the Catholic Church was prepared to confront the issue, with the restructuring of the massive Archdiocese of Glasgow in 1948 to more manageable proportions. Additional parishes were created to cope with the new demographic trends, and a total of 102 emerged between 1945 and 1970 in the west of Scotland alone.[52] This was the period when a 'serene and confident image' was presented by the Church hierarchy, although the reality was often more turbulent, with recurring tensions over, for instance, the nature of Catholic outreach work.[53] Moreover, membership losses became far more pronounced during the third quarter of the twentieth century, with an estimated 120,000 adherents drifting away from the Church.[54] In comparative terms, however, the Church responded far more positively than the Church of Scotland in its efforts to check declining membership, and, in particular, to retain the loyalties of the young. However, it has been suggested that this was the inevitable price to be paid for assimilation. As the ties of the Church were loosened, cultural identity no longer equated with Catholic identity.[55]

The process of Catholic upward mobility certainly became more pronounced after World War II. During the 1940s James Handley had referred

to the limited opportunities for Catholics in the professions; by the 1970s
the position had altered substantially.[56] Between 1956 and 1972 the number of Catholic students attending Glasgow University almost trebled, and
the city was eventually reckoned to have one of the largest Catholic student
bodies in the United Kingdom.[57] The blatant bias manifested in the job
market during the early and mid-twentieth century also gave way to a more
open and competitive environment, with the rise of the public service and
decline of the industrial sector contributing largely towards this. The craft-
orientated industries of the west of Scotland, notably engineering and shipbuilding, had been notoriously difficult for Catholics to enter; however, the
political domination of Scottish local government by the Labour Party from
the 1970s provided something of a counterpoint to this, with Catholics
taking much of the initiative, both as employers and employees.[58] The
pioneering exploits of Patrick Dollan on Glasgow Corporation during the
inter-war period thus bore fruit, and were emulated by Catholics throughout Scotland. Indeed, this was allegedly taken to extremes by Monklands
District Council, which served the Lanarkshire communities of Airdrie and
Coatbridge. In 1995, following an independent investigation by Professor
Robert Black of Edinburgh University, accusations were made of discrimination in favour of Catholics, with especial emphasis on the secretive
role of the Knights of St Columba, a group of Catholic businessmen often
compared with the Freemasons.[59] The issue remains controversial. If the
socio-economic status of Scotland's Catholics altered significantly during
the second half of the twentieth century, with the gradual erosion of the
old enclave mentality, the Church's profile came much more to the fore-
front of Scottish religious life. An important symbol of this changing status
came in 1969, when Archbishop Gordon Joseph Gray became Scotland's
first resident Cardinal since the Reformation. Gray, born in Leith, represented the traditional, native Scots strand in the Church's leadership, which
had long held a position of ascendancy, despite the predominant immigrant
orientation of Catholic adherence in the west of Scotland. Indeed, well into
the twentieth century there could be tensions between these two components of Scottish Catholicism, with class and cultural differences muddying
priorities and creating separate territorial spheres of influence. However,
from the 1960s Catholics became less identified with specific ethnic communities. The global Church took on new directions, too, in the aftermath
of the Second Vatican Council (1962–5), which opened up debate over the
role of the priesthood and laity, and the need for liturgical change. In comparative terms, there was little organised opposition in Scotland to the disappearance of traditional Catholic devotions, particularly in the Tridentine

Latin mass.[60] Energies were more likely to be channelled into such controversial areas as the pro-life movement, in the wake of the 1967 Abortion Act, and in defence of denominational education. Indeed, during the mid-1970s, Archbishop Thomas Joseph Winning made an outspoken plea for the preservation of distinctive Catholic schooling, arguing that 'to be open to the world does not mean to conform to the world'.[61] The debate was still going strong some twenty years later.

By the late twentieth century the Church of Scotland was still defending what it perceived as Catholic integrity, although from the 1960s, under the influence of Pope John XXIII, it was also committed to ecumenicalism. While there could still be occasional setbacks in relations with the Church of Scotland, in 1975 Archbishop Winning became the first Catholic to address the General Assembly, where he spoke of the need to 'replace the climate of sterile polemics with an atmosphere of genuine brotherly love'.[62]

The links became even stronger in May 1982, when Pope John Paul II undertook his historic visit to Scotland, and met with the Moderator of the Church of Scotland, Professor John Macintyre, under the statue of John Knox outside the Assembly Hall.[63] On both occasions small groups of die-hard Protestants mounted vociferous 'No Popery' demonstrations, but their presence was perceived as something of an anachronism, and not representative of either the Church of Scotland or popular opinion. In the context of the 1923 General Assembly, and the debate over the 'menace of Romanism' which triggered the subsequent anti-Catholic crusade, the two gestures towards denominational reconciliation were symbolic. The subsequent rally held in Glasgow's Bellahouston Park, where over 250,000 people turned out to greet the pope, was also a very public display of Catholic resilience and confidence. This is not to suggest that sectarianism was vanquished as a result of the papal visit; however, as numerous commentators at the time remarked, the event seemed to constitute a rite of passage for the Church, and its previously marginalised adherents in Scotland.

NOTES AND REFERENCES

1. M. Linklater and R. Dennistoun (eds), *The Anatomy of Scotland: How Scotland Works* (Edinburgh, 1992), p. 93; see also C. Brown, *The Social History of Religion in Scotland since 1730* (London, 1987), p. 44.
2. V.A. McClelland, 'Great Britain and Ireland' in A. Hastings (ed.), *Modern Catholicism: Vatican II and After* (Oxford, 1991), p. 365.
3. The historiography of sectarianism in Scotland is discussed in C. Brown, *The People in the Pews: Religion and Society in Scotland since 1780* (Glasgow, 1993), pp. 34–7.

4. C.S. Pryde, *Social Life in Scotland Since 1707* (London, 1934), p. 29.
5. S. Bruce, 'Out of the ghetto; the ironies of acceptance', *Innes Review*, XLIII (1992), pp. 147–8.
6. L. Woodcock Tentler, 'On the margins: the state of American Catholic history', *American Quarterly*, 45 (1993), pp. 104–27.
7. T. Gallagher, *Glasgow, the Uneasy Peace: Religious Tension in Modern Scotland* (Manchester, 1987), pp. 268–70.
8. J. Darragh, 'The Catholic population of Scotland, 1878–1977' in D. McRoberts (ed.), *Modern Scottish Catholicism* (Glasgow, 1979), p. 232.
9. T. Colpi, 'The Scottish Italian community: senza un campanile?', *Innes Review*, XLVI (1993), p. 161. For the wider context, see her detailed study, *The Italian Factor: the Italian Community in Great Britain* (Edinburgh, 1991), esp. pp. 47–69.
10. K. Lunn, 'Reactions and responses: Lithuanian and Polish immigrants in the Lanarkshire coalfield, 1880–1914' in *The Journal of the Scottish Labour History Society* (1978), pp. 23–38: M. Rodgers, 'The Lithuanians', *History Today* (July 1985), pp. 16–20.
11. J. McCaffrey, 'Roman Catholics in Scotland in the 19th and 20th centuries' in *Records of the Scottish Church History Society*, XXI (1983), pp. 276–7. In 1901, there were 205,000 Irish-born in Scotland, or 4.5 per cent of the total population.
12. T. Gallagher, 'The Catholic Irish in Scotland; in search of identity', in T.M. Devine (ed.), *Irish Immigrants and Scottish Society in the Nineteenth and Twentieth Centuries* (Edinburgh, 1991), p. 20.
13. P. Reilly, 'The mirror of literature; the development of Catholicism in Scotland since 1845', *Scottish Affairs*, 8 (1994), p. 89.
14. P. Reilly, 'Catholics and Scottish literature, 1878–1978' in McRoberts (ed.), *Modern Scottish Catholicism*, pp. 185–7.
15. Quoted in J.H. Treble, 'The market for unskilled male labour in Glasgow, 1891–1914' in Ian MacDougall (ed.), *Essays in Scottish Labour History* (Edinburgh, 1979), p. 122.
16. 'Misther McGurk's reflections on the scavengers' strike', *The Bailie*, 26 February 1902.
17. A. Ross, 'The development of the Scottish Catholic community, 1878–1978' in McRoberts (ed.), *Modern Scottish Catholicism*, p. 38.
18. P.F. Anson, *The Catholic Church in Modern Scotland, 1560–1937* (London, 1937), p. 187.
19. J. McCaffrey, 'Irish issues in the nineteenth and twentieth century; radicalism in a Scottish context?' in T.M. Devine (ed.), *Irish immigrants*, pp. 131–4.
20. McCaffrey, 'Roman Catholics in Scotland in the 19th and 20th centuries', pp. 293–7.
21. S. Gilley, 'Catholics and socialists in Scotland, 1900–1930' in R. Swift and S. Gilley (eds), *The Irish in Britain, 1815–1939* (London, 1989), pp. 212–38.
22. W.M. Walker, 'Irish immigrants in Scotland: their priests, politics and parochial life', *Historical Journal*, XV (1972), pp. 663–4.
23. For O'Hare's background, see *The Scottish Guardian*, 15 August 1902, and his obituary in *The Glasgow Herald*, 10 November 1917. O'Hare was briefly Irish Nationalist MP for Monaghan between 1906 and 1907.
24. Chalmers' views on Catholic emancipation are quoted in D. Keir, *The House of Collins: the Story of a Scottish Family of Publishers from 1789 to the Present Day* (Glasgow, 1952), pp. 28–9.
25. Rev. Brother Kenneth, FMS, 'The Education (Scotland) Act, 1918, in the making', *Innes Review*, XIX (1968), pp. 91–128.
26. McCaffrey, 'Roman Catholics in Scotland in the 19th and 20th centuries', pp. 297–9.
27. Gallagher, *Glasgow, the Uneasy Peace*, p. 72.
28. R.J. Finlay, 'National identity in crisis: politicians, intellectuals and the "end of Scotland", 1920–1939', *History* (1994), pp. 242–59.
29. A.D. Gibb, *Scotland in Eclipse* (London, 1930), p. 56.
30. S.J.Brown, '"Outside the Covenant": the Scottish Presbyterian Churches and Irish immigration', *Innes Review*, XLII (1991), pp. 25–7.
31. See the introduction to W. Knox (ed.), *Scottish Labour Leaders, 1918–1939* (Edinburgh, 1984), p. 30.
32. For the background to Cormack's success in Edinburgh, see T. Gallagher, *Edinburgh Divided: John Cormack and No Popery in the 1930s* (Edinburgh, 1987), and Gallagher, 'Protestant extremism in urban Scotland, 1930–1939: its growth and contraction', *Scottish Historical Review*, LXIV (1985), pp. 143–67.

33. C. Brogan, *The Glasgow Story* (London, 1952), pp. 179–96.

34. E. Muir, *Scottish Journey* (Edinburgh, 1979 edn; first published 1935), p. 170.

35. Quoted in S. McGhee, 'Carfin and the Roman Catholic Relief Act of 1926', *Innes Review*, XVI (1965), p. 60.

36. ibid., pp. 75–7.

37. T. Gallagher, 'Scottish Catholics and the British Left, 1918–1939', *Innes Review*, XXXIV (1983), pp. 36–8.

38. See, for instance, B. Aspinwall, 'The Catholic Irish and wealth in Glasgow', in Devine (ed.), *Irish Immigrants*, pp. 91–115, and Aspinwall, 'Children of the dead end: the formation of the modern Archdiocese of Glasgow, 1815–1914', *Innes Review*, XLIII (1992), pp. 119–44.

39. Ross, 'Development of the Catholic Community', p. 43.

40. J.M. MacCormick, *The Flag in the Wind: the Story of the Nationalist Movement in Scotland*, p. 51.

41. Bruce, 'Out of the ghetto', p. 146.

42. A.D. Gibb, *Scotland Resurgent* (Stirling, 1950), p. 83.

43. M. Maclaren, *The Scots* (Harmondsworth, 1951), pp. 220–2.

44. C.A. Oakley, *The Second City* (London, 1946), p. 70.

45. See J.E. Handley, *The Irish In Scotland* (Glasgow, 1964), which is an amalgam of two earlier works published in 1943 and 1947 respectively.

46. Brogan, *The Glasgow Story*, p. 195.

47. R. Macdonald, 'The Catholic Gaidhealtachd' in McRoberts (ed.), *Modern Scottish Catholicism*, pp. 71–2.

48. Colpi, *The Italian Factor*, pp. 71–97.

49. ibid., pp. 105.

50. C. Holmes, *John Bull's Island: Immigration and British Society, 1871–1971* (London, 1988), pp. 211–12.

51. T.A. Markus, 'Comprehensive development and housing, 1945–75', P. Reed (ed.), *Glasgow: the Forming of the City* (Edinburgh, 1993), pp. 147–65.

52. Brown, *Social History of Religion in Scotland*, p. 224.

53. Gallagher, *Glasgow, the Uneasy Peace*, p. 236.

54. ibid., pp. 238–9.

55. Bruce, 'Out of the ghetto', p. 153.

56. Handley, *The Irish in Scotland*, p. 357.

57. Gallagher, *Glasgow, the Uneasy Peace*, p. 240.

58. For an account of anti-Catholic bias in the industrial sector, see H. McShane and J. Smith, *No Mean Fighter* (London, 1978), pp. 19–20.

59. *The Scotsman*, 20 June 1995.

60. J. Cooney, *Scotland and the Papacy: Pope John Paul II's Visit in Perspective* (Edinburgh, 1982), p. 94.

61. Archbishop Winning, 'The positive value of Catholic education' in M.G. Clarke and H.M. Drucker (eds), *Our Changing Scotland: A Yearbook of Scottish Government, 1976–77* (Edinburgh, 1976), p. 40.

62. *The Glasgow Herald*, 22 May 1975.

63. ibid., 1 June 1982.

15. MAPS OF DESIRE: SCOTTISH LITERATURE IN THE TWENTIETH CENTURY
Roderick Watson

In another context I wrote recently that 'the main state left to a stateless nation may well be its state of mind, and in that territory it is literature which maps the land'.[1] But the 'map' metaphor is a tricky one, for in the world of literature, the landscape changes with time as new features emerge – a situation more like politics, perhaps, than geography. And if a week is a long time in politics, a decade is a very long time in literature. ...

This is because literary maps are made by critics rather than by theodolites. No one can deny that Ben Nevis is the highest mountain in Britain, but not everyone would agree that Hugh MacDiarmid is the greatest British poet of our century. Literary reputations rise and fall, and the significance of writers in the landscape of their times is liable to change as the years roll by and new features come into view. A brief example will suffice.

When Alasdair Gray's *Lanark* was published in 1981 it 'rearranged', so to speak, some of the features of the landscape which had gone before. From the twin peaks of *Lanark* and *1982, Janine* (1984), books once out of sight over the horizon came back into view – such as David Lindsay's *Voyage to Arcturus* (1920), James Thomson's *City of Dreadful Night* (1880), George MacDonald's *Lilith* (1895) and *Phantastes* (1858), Carlyle's *Sartor Resartus* (1836), Hogg's *Three Perils of Man: War Women and Witchcraft* (1822) and *Confessions of a Justified Sinner* (1824); Byron's *The Vision of Judgement* (1823), William Tennant's *Anster Fair* and *Papistry Storm'd* (1812, 1827), Henry Mackenzie's *The Man of Feeling* (1771) and even Sir Thomas Urquhart's *Rabelais* (1653), and the other David Lindsay's *Ane Satyre of the Thrie Estaitis* (1552).

Lanark allowed us to reassess the Scottish penchant for dealing with other realms, mixing metaphysical questions and fantastic inner experience with terror, black bawdry and political satire, all expressed with an extraordinary textual energy. And from this point of view later arrivals on the scene, such as Frederick Lindsay's *Brond* (1983) and Iain Banks's *Wasp Factory* (1984) and *The Bridge* (1986), could now be placed within a clearly defined tradition.

This is how the literary landscape can be seen to shift, depending on where you stand. And where you stand is, of course, the key questions, as any historian knows. If this chapter were to attempt to give an account of all the Scottish writers who have produced work in, or concerning, Scotland during the last 95 years, there would be little room for more than their names. Yet 'history' – and especially 'literary history' – is not just a matter of biographies and bibliographies (although they have a part to play) for it must acknowledge, too, those shifts in the cultural imagination which govern *how* we see things every bit as much as *what* we see. Ideology is inescapable, and in culture criticism the mythologies which we construct – the stories we tell ourselves about ourselves – guide us or control us just as much as do the material conditions of production. This chapter will discuss these mythologies by making critique of what seem to me to be the leading imaginative tendencies in Scottish writing during the first three-quarters of the twentieth century. If many excellent writers are not discussed by name, it may still be possible to locate them on this cultural map.

Over and above my categorisation into 'radical' and 'conservative' literature, I am going to propose a slow shift in the critical and popular attention paid to Scottish literary identity, away from what was an essentially symbolic or 'metaphysical' way of responding to the world, towards (on the surface at least) more 'realistic' modes. This move might be expressed, for example, by the shift in popular acclaim away from the works of Neil Gunn towards those of James Kelman. But then there is Alasdair Gray who seems to inhabit both camps.

SCOTTISH 'RENAISSANCES': THE FIRST GENERATION

It is widely supposed that 'The Modern Scottish Renaissance' began with Hugh MacDiarmid's espousal of the cause in the early 1920s, and that the phrase itself was taken from an influential article entitled 'Le groupe de "la Renaissance Écossaise"' written by the French critic Denis Saurat for the *Revue Anglo-Américaine*, in April 1924. (Saurat had been a lecturer in French at Glasgow University, where he became friends with the composer F.G. Scott, and it was Scott who brought Saurat into contact with MacDiarmid (Grieve) and the Scottish literary revival.)

In fact, however, the phrase 'Scots Renascence' (sic) was first used nearly thirty years earlier, as part of the Celtic revival associated with publications from Patrick Geddes's Outlook Tower in Edinburgh at the turn of the century. As a biologist turned sociologist, a city planner and a socio-geographical visionary, Geddes wanted to create a new and vital rapproche-ment between the industries and cities of the new century and the tra-ditional values of craft and community which belonged to pre-industrial times ('Work': 'Place': 'Folk'). He also aimed 'to arrest the tremendous centralising power of the metropolis of London'[2] by bringing Scotland into touch with small cultures everywhere, especially in Europe, in what he saw as a 'cosmopolitan' concept of diversity rather than a narrowly nationalist spirit. In an article for the first edition of his new review, *The Evergreen*,[3] Geddes outlined his plans for the 'reunion of Democracy with Culture', not so much in the 'parliamentary and abstract sense, but in the civic and concrete one. ...'[4] As part of this aim he wanted to promote the creative arts in his 'Celtic Library', which published a number of books by the Scot-tish writer William Sharp, or rather by 'Fiona Macleod', not so much a pen name as a fully fledged alter ego, the secret of whose non-existence was kept almost until the author's death.

Fiona Macleod belongs to the movement that has come to be associated with the 'Celtic twilight', and indeed 'she' corresponded with W.B. Yeats in Ireland whose collection of stories in 1893 had first given that phrase to the world at large. The movement, and Macleod's writing, took a particu-lar interest in mystical experience, in the spirituality of the Gael, and tended to be suffused with a melancholy sense of loss. As part of this programme Fiona Macleod wrote an essay called 'Celtic', published in the *Contemporary Review* for 1900, in which she proposed that a love of the land was central to the Celtic experience:

> But it is also true that we love vaguely another land, a rainbow-land, and that our most desired country is not the real Ireland, the real Scotland, the real Brittany, but the vague Land of Youth, the shadowy land of Heart's Desire. And it is also true, that deep in the songs we love above all over songs is a lamentation for what has gone away from the world ...[5]

We have to understand the attraction of the 'Celtic Twilight' in Ireland and Scotland (and in England, too, of course) as a genuine longing for spiritual value and national identity, both of which were felt to be under threat from capitalism, mass society and an increasingly industrial world. On the other hand, for Fiona Macleod such values were always and only to be found in dreams and songs and stories, for in 1901 she dismissed 'the dream of an outward independence' as 'a perilous illusion', preferring to

think that 'what is left of the Celtic races, of the Celtic genius, may permeate the greater race of which we are a vital part'.[6]

That 'greater race' was the 'British' race, of course, and it is interesting
to reflect on the way in which the marginalised areas of the United Kingdom came to be seen as the repositories for a lost conscience, that 'vital
part' of the body politic which could be evoked and enjoyed and visited,
but never fully lived or emancipated. If Walter Scott had invented the
Highlands for his times in terms of primitive valour, action and doomed
romance, then the Celtic Revival replayed the same tune at the turn of the
century in more ethereal and spiritual terms.

Nevertheless, despite Fiona Macleod's 'winged destiny' (which amounted
to little more than cultural submergence), the Gael's desire for 'outward
independence' (however 'perilous') was soon to appear in Ireland and to
make itself very forcibly felt indeed. And in the political and economic
aftermath of the Great War – ostensibly fought for the rights of 'poor little
Belgium' – even the lowlands of Scotland began to consider questions
of identity, nationalism and independence. Yet the literary productions of
modern Scotland continued to be haunted, and are so even to this day, by
Celtic projections of another place, 'the shadowy Land of Heart's Desire',
replete with everything that has somehow 'gone away from the world'.

This sense of exile and lost virtue, what I term a mythopoeic or Edenic
vision of Scotland, seems to lie at the heart of Edwin Muir's poetry; Muir's
successors in this vision would include George Mackay Brown's account of
Orkney (Brown was a pupil of Muir's at Newbattle Abbey from 1950 to
1951), Neil Gunn's Sutherland and Caithness, aspects of Grassic Gibbon's
Kinraddie, Derick Thomson's Lewis and Christopher Rush's East Neuk of
Fife. The preface to Rush's *A Twelvemonth and a Day* (1985), for example,
speaks of:

> the last great days of the Scottish herring fishing and steam drifters,
> a lament for their passing, and more positively, a celebration of their
> vanished values. Perhaps not entirely vanished – for the book is also
> about growing up; and all of us have been children ...[7]

In these lines Rush makes quite explicit the Edenic connection by which
childhood can recapture that pastoral past – if only for a few magical years
– before time moves on. The literary model for this point of view, by which
children trail 'clouds of glory' from some primal state of absolute whole-
ness, was early established by William Wordsworth, whose autobiographical poem *The Prelude* was such a marked influence on Neil Gunn's own
autobiography, *The Atom of Delight* (1956).

The passage of time is central to such visions, for childhood is seen as a primal, timeless, and even a static state, as in Muir's depiction of Orkney, where a young boy lies forever on a 'sunny hill,/To his father's house below securely bound',[8] looking out to the 'unseen straits' of the world beyond. Gibbon's *Sunset Song* evokes the same sense of an endless past and a suspended present when he writes about Chris Guthrie's childhood in a landscape marked by ancient standing stones and mythologised by tales of how Cospatric killed a gryphon in the Den of Kinraddie.

Yet these mythologies are not quite so easily dismissed as sentimentalisations of the past as we might suppose. The early twentieth century was a time of rapid and radical change, and Scotland was then (as it still is to some extent) a country in which the deepest rural experience could be lost or rediscovered within only a few miles of the darkest urban deprivation. Loch Lomond is not so far, after all, from Drumchapel. Or consider the history of those thousands of immigrants from traditional peasant communities who crossed the Irish sea to work in the factories of the West of Scotland: a Celtic twilight of a different kind.

It is Edwin Muir who gave this sense of expulsion its most poignant expression in the first version of his autobiography, which he called (tellingly) *The Story and the Fable* (1940):

> I was born before the Industrial revolution, and am now about two
> hundred years old. But I have skipped a hundred and fifty of them.
> I was really born in 1737, and till I was fourteen no time accidents
> happened to me. Then in 1751 I set out from Orkney for Glasgow.
> When I arrived I found that it was not 1751, but 1901, and that a
> hundred and fifty years had been burned up in my two days'
> journey. But I myself was still in 1751, and remained there for a
> long time. All my life since I have been trying to overhaul that
> invisible leeway. No wonder I am obsessed with time.[9]

One cannot deny the almost literal truth of this experience, and we should remember that within four years of the move to Glasgow both Muir's parents died, as did two of his brothers (one from TB and the other from a tumour of the brain). Such a history certainly explains why Muir found so much to fear and despise in the modern world (and his native country), from McClintock's bone factory in Fairport, to the interrogations and anxious border crossings which he witnessed in his post-war travels in Czechoslovakia under Communist rule. It is a particular irony of fate that made Muir and his wife Willa the first translators of Kafka into English, and it is difficult to imagine what it must have been like to find oneself with

'One Foot in Eden', and the other in Kafka's surreal novel, *The Castle*.

The same evocation of traditional values (in this case 'Celtic' or 'Gaelic' ones) against the horrors of the modern world can be found in Neil Gunn's work, and most pointedly in his novel *The Green Isle of the Great Deep*, published in 1944, which is haunted by the premonition of Auschwitz, and by reports of show trials and brainwashing in Stalin's Russia, hitherto held by many writers of the Left (including Gunn himself) to be the model for a better society.

It was Naomi Mitchison who seems to have indirectly persuaded Gunn to tackle the harsher face of contemporary events in this novel, for her socialist ideals laid more stress on communal commitment and the world of politics than the more interior journeys which characterise Gunn's novels. Nevertheless, many of Mitchison's novels, most especially *The Corn King and the Spring Queen* (1931), have also dealt with a mythopoeic past, albeit one in which women managed to find a creative and sexual emancipation still being fought for by Mitchison's generation.

Gunn took up the challenge and in *Green Isle* young Art and old Hector (who first appeared in a novel of that name two years earlier) are transported to the utopia of Tir nan Og, only to find it in the hands of faceless administrators and managers. Art's anarchic boyish spirit and the shy, stubborn wisdom of Old Hector eventually win through in a subtle work that bears comparison with *Brave New World* or *1984*, and reads like a precursor to South American 'magic realism'. Nevertheless, if the moral of the book is that the 'fable' can save us by re-entering the 'story' of history, one has, perhaps, to ask whether 'magic' is enough in the face of the corporate state.

On a less fictive level, in 1928 Gunn claimed that the Celtic connection possessed a 'hidden heart' – much needed by the modern world – and these claims echo a strongly-felt element in Scottish nationalism and the early literary renaissance at large:

> History is not an affair of one's yesterday and today; its waves and recessions are slow and august. The dissatisfied Scot may be feeling back for a potency greater, more imperatively needed by humanity at large, than he knows of. His stirring to a sense of receding nationality may also be an instinctive reaction against a world-wide gathering of mechanistic forces, his Celtic unconscious rebelling against the tyranny of the iron wheel.[10]

Hugh MacDiarmid's case for 'the Gaelic idea' had very similar roots, evoking the 'potency' of instinct and the unconscious as symbolised by 'Deirdre of the Sorrows' and 'Audh the deep-minded' in the poetry and

propaganda he was writing in the 1930s and 1940s, in which Celtic spirituality found parallels in the visionary poems of Alexander Blok and aspects
of the Russian Orthodox Church. MacDiarmid associated this spirituality
specifically with the feminine – just as William Sharp had done over thirty
years earlier when he wrote 'we are all seeking the Fountain of Youth, the
Golden Isles, Avalon, Woman'.[11]

Indeed, this Celtic resurgence became part of MacDiarmid's vision of an
'East-West synthesis' by which Russia and Scotland would come together
in an extraordinary amalgam of radical democratic socialism along communist lines, with what would seem to be a much more conservative attraction to 'L'Esprit Celtique'. MacDiarmid declared his political model to be
'Scottish Worker's Republicanism *à la* John Maclean', in keeping with 'the
practice of the Soviet Union in regard to minority elements'.

> We too in Scotland must have an autonomous republic and equal
> freedom and facilitation for our Scots Gaelic and Scots Vernacular
> languages. Our minimal demand is to have Scotland on the same
> footing in all these respects as one of the autonomous republics of
> the U.S.S.R.[12]

So we can see where the Celtic spirit fits in, but, writing this in 1936,
MacDiarmid was tragically misinformed (or wilfully blind) about the real
fate of ethnic and cultural minorities in Stalin's Russia. In his wilder
moments he seems to have wanted to claim Stalin, from Georgia, as a kind
of Scot:

> 'Stalin the Georgian,' I have said. We are Georgians all,
> We Gaels.
> The name *Karthweli* by which the Georgians themselves call
> Their race and their country is none other
> Than our Scottish Argyll – the Georgian equivalent
> of *Ard-Gael* (High Gael).
>
>   … Now let the fingers clench back
> To come to rest in the palm of the sun's hand again,
> The reconcentrated power of the human race.
> So let the first conceivers and builders of civilisation give now
> (Since the other have poisoned the wells and perverted
> The noble impulse that originated with our fathers)
> The sign of the Clenched Fist – the Communist salute,
> For the Gaelic refluence, and the re-emergence
> Of the Gaelic spirit at the Future's strongest and deepest root![13]

MacDiarmid's radical intentions may be plain, but the trouble is that these deepest roots, along with a search for origins (the noble impulses of 'our fathers') come from a whole vocabulary of race mythology, invoked since the early nineteenth century to justify the superiority of the British, or the Northern European races, or (eventually) Aryan supremacy – all with the specific aim of legitimising nation states, imperial expansion and the exploitation of 'lesser' breeds.

In this respect it is rather alarming to recognise that conceptions such as the 'other-worldly' spirituality of the Gael, so central to the Celtic Revival and so attractive as a counterbalance to the alienation of industrial capitalism, could be applied with equal conviction to programmes of either pluralism of unification, to further the ends, in other words, of either international socialism or fascism.

Thus it can be seen that the fabric of Scottish identity, as woven by the early writers of the modern Literary Renaissance, contains a curious amalgam of radical and conservative elements, neither of which can be entirely separated from each other. Poetry is poetry, of course, and history is history and the twain need never meet, but it is difficult not to feel at times that Muir's poetic vision (replete with dream images and Jungian symbols) has not been translated into a kind of pseudo history by his successors. Hence, for example, from the vantage point of a timeless Orkney, mythopoeticised and ritualised by acts of baking bread, brewing beer and catching fish, George Mackay Brown regards both the Reformation and the industrial revolution as terrible wrong turnings, offering the goddess of material plenty and 'Progress' in place of the old ways,[14] while the closing pages of Christopher Rush's *A Twelvemonth and a Day* are a sustained elegy to childhood and a lost past, both equally idealised and coloured by a deeply conservative distaste for contemporary life:

> I go back, I smell tar and tangle, I try to catch these old ghosts
> of the fishing that flutter in the meshes of the new nylon nets and
> linger in the smartly coloured lobster creels, where rubber and
> plastic piping take the place of the boughs my grandfather cut so
> carefully. The Common Market lives, the cod-end of the net bursts
> like an obscene sausage on the deck of the trawler, now a floating
> factory, and the life of the sea spills out brutally and without
> discrimination. The old fishing ways and the men who followed
> them are pale shadows of the past.
>
> It has all broken up – their community, their art of the story,
> their feeling for the sea. The faces in the firelight have faded into

the garish light of the TV screen and of what is sometimes called progress. The folk culture is now embalmed in the Anstruther Fisheries Museum, the saddest place in the East Neuk. ... They are all gone then – the days and the people, and their language and their ways, and the stories they told me.[15]

The book ends with a list of deaths and exits, somehow symptomatic of the passing of value and virtue from the world, yet one would have to point out that people have always died, or married and left town, and note, too, that the nature of these deaths (grandmother's asthma, old George's stroke and grandfather's drowning) are not unrelated to the harsh and difficult conditions of a time that Rush insists on seeing, for the most part, as days of departed 'glory'. Now living in a nearby city, the writer feels 'exiled' from this vision and reflects that 'fifty miles might well be fifty million, and the years that intervene between childhood and today be fifty million light years. Or more.'[16] He was writing this in 1985.

The inheritance of the Celtic twilight could not have a more eloquent spokesperson, and in this evocation of traditional culture as a lost Eden, it becomes quite clear that 'our most desired country' in the words of Fiona Macleod, is not the 'real Scotland', but indeed 'the vague Land of Youth, the shadowy land of Heart's Desire'.

Hugh MacDiarmid's version of the old stories and the old songs started with a much more radical edge. His case for the revival of the Scots language in the early 1920s was deliberately iconoclastic:

> We confess to having been discouraged when thinking of the Vernacular Movement by the fact that the seal of its approval is so largely set upon the traditional and the conventional. ... If all that the Movement is to achieve is to preserve specimens of Braid Scots, archaic, imitative, belonging to a type of life that has passed and cannot return, in a sort of museum department of our consciousness – set apart from our vital preoccupations – it is a movement which not only cannot claim our support but compels our opposition. The rooms of thought are choc-a-bloc with far too much dingy old rubbish as it is.[17]

The 'Theory of Scots Letters' which MacDiarmid promoted in 1923 (from which this extract comes) dedicated itself to 'the newest and truest tendencies of human thought', claiming that 'only in so far as the vernacular has unused resources ... has it possibilities of literary value', adding that 'our interest, therefore, should centre not so much in what has been done in the Doric as in what has not but may be done in it. No literature can rest on its laurels.'[18]

MacDiarmid's whole case for small nations and for the value of supposedly 'minority' or 'marginal' cultures rested on the possibility that they could contribute elements of unique and radical value to the world at large and to what he called 'the expressive resource of modern life'. This position lies at the heart of MacDiarmid's cultural, political and linguistic separatism and nationalism, and it seems to me to remain an admirable credo. Indeed the essence of this case was to be repeated by other writers in the years to come, on behalf of working-class experience and demotic language, and then (most notably by Janice Galloway and Agnes Owen) on behalf of working-class women.

In the first instance, what MacDiarmid brought to poetry in Scots is characterised by an extraordinary expressionistic energy. Indeed, the conceptual and technical force of the early lyrics and of *A Drunk Man Looks at the Thistle* (1926) have specific elements in common with German Expressionist literature and painting of the years just before and after World War I. In a different context the avant-garde nature of MacDiarmid's project can clearly be demonstrated by reference to the extraordinary prose writing to be found in *Annals of the Five Senses*, one of his earliest books, published under the name of C.M. Grieve in 1923, but written at least three years earlier.[19]

Time and again I find expressionistic speed and radical compression in MacDiarmid's use of Scots, and indeed his lyrics have some claim to be more successful examples of early modern 'Imagism' than many of the poems written ten years earlier by Pound, Joyce, T.E. Hulme, Hilda Doolittle ('H.D.') or William Carlos Williams. The connection is all the more striking when one recognises that many of MacDiarmid's most striking tropes have been derived (or sometimes directly borrowed as Kenneth Buthlay has pointed out) from vernacular terms or sayings which he found in Jamieson's *Dictionary of the Scottish Language*, the very book which led him to describe the vernacular as 'an inchoate Marcel Proust – a Dostoevskian [sic] debris of ideas – an inexhaustible quarry of subtle and significant sound'.[20]

Consider the following lines from his poem 'Thunderstorm' for example, in which the phrase 'I'se warran ye're rawn for the yirdin' is given by Jamieson as an idiomatic example of the use of the word 'rawn' to mean 'afraid': ' "I'se warren ye're *rawn* for the yirdin," i.e. "I can pledge myself for it that you are afraid on account of the thunder".'[21]

> I'se warran' ye're rawn for the yirdin'
> An no' muckle wunner,
> When the lift's like a revelled hesp
> I' the han's o the thunner.[22]

Look up 'hesp' ('a hank of yarn') in Jamieson, and you will find '*To make a revell'd hesp*, to put a thing in confusion.'[23]

At this point the reader might be forgiven for thinking that it was the Reverend Dr Jamieson (or at least his folk sources) who wrote at least half of the verse in question, and not the poet at all. On closer examination, however, we should realise that MacDiarmid's contribution was far from trivial. What he did was to make the *sky* like a revell'd hesp, and to put it in the *hands* of the thunder, so that the yarn-winding imagery of a familiar fireside domestic activity is translated to a cosmic arena to become something terrifyingly strange: both homely and unhomely at the same time (which was Freud's definition of 'the uncanny'). The concatenation of 'sky/yarn: hands/thunder' is crucial, and the unlikeliness of the combination, and yet its startling fitness, is repeated again and again in hundreds of images throughout MacDiarmid's Scots poetry.

Far from being evidence of an unseemly debt (or even plagiarism), this marriage between a traditional ethos and the violent collision of images which characterised avant-garde and expressionist art of the period, is exactly what validates MacDiarmid's claim that 'the Scots Vernacular is a vast storehouse of just the very peculiar subtle effects which modern European literature in general is assiduously seeking'.[24] This is as good an example of the 'radical' use of 'traditional' material as one could hope for.

Consider too, the following lines from 'In the Pantry': 'Knedeuch land / And a loppert sea / And a lift like a blue-douped / Mawkin'-flee',[25] in which the first two adjectives deal with 'A peculiar taste or smell; chiefly applied to old meat or musty bread' (which must have conjured up that maggot 'maukin'-flee') and the condition of coagulated ('loppert') milk. However powerful the folk-elements here, the brilliance of the poem is made by the extraordinary imaginative leap by which the poet (or perhaps God) looking at the beautiful earth, is likened to a hungry man raiding the pantry, and finding its colours the colours of mould, and nothing fit to eat. Nothing could be further from the songs of 'lamentation for what has gone away from the world', and yet, as we have seen, MacDiarmid's 'Gaelic Idea' did later come to be touched by a vision of Scotland which owed something to that Celtic twilight.

The same combination of the radical and the magical can be found in the work of Lewis Grassic Gibbon (James Leslie Mitchell). He was fiercely dedicated to communist ideals, yet his best-known character – Chris Guthrie of *A Scots Quair* – personifies an archetypal relationship with the land, the seasons and with the changelessness of change itself, which comes to seem increasingly mystical as the trilogy progresses.

At one level of course, Grassic Gibbon's novel is very clearly rooted in history, telling us about the last of the old tenant farmers whose 'sunset song' is brought about by the social and economic changes of World War I and the rise of large-scale agriculture. In the next two volumes we read about the tribulations of the spinners in the linen mills of Segget, and the industrial struggles of the factory workers in Duncairn. But Chris's relationship to the land is more than a matter of social history, for Grassic Gibbon's trilogy constructs her as a person uniquely in touch with other ways of being at a dark and intuitive level, partly to do with her sex, and partly to do with her sense of the land as something timeless and primal. To such a sensibility, the political, social and religious ideals of men (specifically men) come to seem no more than ephemeral:

> clouds by day to darken men's minds – loyalty and fealty, patriotism, love, the mumbling chants of the dead old gods that once were worshipped in the circles of stones, christianity, socialism, nationalism – all – Clouds that swept through the Howe of the world, with men that took them for gods: just clouds, they passed and finished, dissolved and were done ...[26]

So it is that Grassic Gibbon's trilogy ends in a curious impasse, with Chris returning to the land both literally and symbolically as she fades away into the twilight and the rain and the stones of an ancient Pictish hill fort, while her son, the young radical Ewan, sets off on a Labour march to London. The future may well belong to Ewan in Grassic Gibbon's eyes, but he paints it as an ugly picture of *realpolitik* on Ewan's part, and of police brutality on the part of the state, while the true heart of the trilogy remains with Chris in what I believe is yet another version of that land of heart's desire.

Even so, this division does mark a kind of watershed in my symbolic map of how modern writers have plotted Scottish identity, for the next thirty years will see a slow move towards Ewan's world, a world of literary realism dealing more directly with urban deprivation and political analysis, away from the 'rainbow land' of a mythic past. Nevertheless, versions of that past can still be found in contemporary texts from George Mackay Brown, Christopher Rush and others, while retellings of it in newly mythopoeic terms – this time charged with a feminist critique of modern society – can be identified in the Celtic symbols and the 'magic realism' of writers such as Sian Hayton's 'dark-age' trilogy (*Cells of Knowledge*, 1989, *Hidden Daughters*, 1991, and *The Last Flight*, 1993), Ellen Galford's *Queendom Come* (1990), and Margaret Elphinstone's *An Apple from a Tree* (1991).

THE 'SECOND GENERATION'

The so-called second generation of the 'Modern Literary Renaissance' is particularly notable for the quality and the variety of its poetry. Every one of these poets explored, to some extent or another, questions of Scottish identity and community. Alex Scott and Tom Scott committed themselves to writing in Scots, while George Bruce used a pared-down English to meditate on his own and his family's roots in Fraserburgh and the hard life of fishing communities on the north-east coast. Iain Crichton Smith's early collections were particularly marked by his love-hate relationship with the Free Kirk on Lewis and how that Calvinistic outlook coloured his own sense of the existential bareness to be found in the world at large. Derick Thomson's account of his own roots in the same community is suffused with a gentler and much more elegiac sense of loss and exile, closer to the Gaelic experience (he writes only in Gaelic) of so many folk who found that they had to leave the islands of their youth to pursue their careers in the cities to the south. George Campbell Hay's poetry, on the other hand, embraces all three of Scotland's languages, and the experience of war-time in the desert which so shook his stability in later years also brought him a sense of affinity with the Arabs he met there, as fellow members of despised 'minority' cultures sharing particularly austere religions.

In a metaphorical sense, and almost literally too, George Mackay Brown did not leave the Orkney Islands, and his work has regularly constructed island life as an outpost of traditional values and mythic force in a world in which 'Word and name are drained of their ancient power. Number, statistic, graph are everything.'[27] The finest expression of this point of view, and one that has struck a particular chord with environmentalists everywhere, is his novel *Greenvoe* (1972). Sorley Maclean's Gaelic poetry makes a very powerful balance between his roots on Skye, where he finds a landscape whose smallest feature is alive with genealogy and an oral history going back hundreds of years, and modern Europe where his socialist commitment can see nothing but the ills of capitalism, conflict and exploitation. Somehow Maclean's poetry manages to hold the two worlds of Chris and Ewan together in a completely unsentimental way, but the cost is a kind of suspended anguish and an austere poetic voice.

By comparison, Norman MacCaig moved much more easily between

Edinburgh and Inverkirkaig, yet the true point of balance for him remains, I think, in the communities and landscapes of the north west, and his love for the place and its people imparts an added sense of irony and proportion to his already dry and witty way of looking at the world. On the other hand, the modern experience, however terrible, has never been ironised or underplayed in the work of Edwin Morgan, whose enthusiasm for the changing surface of things makes him one of the few poets writing in English today who has resolutely embraced the shock of the new, and taken up the challenge to live wholly and fully (and with a proper conscience) in the 'present' of urban experience and contemporary technology. This makes him a rare and valuable cultural asset. And yet his work still explores crucial questions of Scottish identity and community experience, especially associated with his native Glasgow, and perhaps this exploration is sparked by an added sense of poignancy prompted by his homosexuality, which has given him much experience of being someone (until more recent years at least) likely to be regarded as beyond the pale of conventional society.

There are many forms of difference and exclusion, and some of them have been based on the grounds of language itself, and then of class. William Soutar was among the earliest poets of this generation to take up MacDiarmid's challenge to write in Scots, but his decision to stay with lyrics, song forms and the whigmaleeries of rhymes for children, means that his Scots poetry does not in itself break out from the special generic enclave (somewhere between a playpen, an Edinburgh drawing room and a sheep-fank) which work in Scots had been allowed to inhabit since the mid-nineteenth century. Sydney Goodsir Smith's work looked back to the larger-than-life sociability and the goliardic and 'unrespectable' energy of eighteenth century Edinburgh, but this apparently 'historical' cast (seen in a consciously polysyllabic and 'literary' Scots) is qualified by a wide breadth of reference and a sense of free structure and many-voiced discourse not unlike some of Ezra Pound's work. In this sense, Smith is an 'early modernist' in the same vein as the MacDiarmid of *A Drunk Man Looks at the Thistle*, and the successors to this tendency can be seen today in the young writers whom Duncan Glen refers to as the 'nouveau academics', most notably Robert Crawford, W.N. Herbert and David Kinloch who write a dense and deliberately estranged Scots – a kind of linguistic cubism – which in some cases goes straight back to the practice of extracting passages verbatim from Jamieson's Dictionary.

In contrast, Robert Garioch's Scots was taken from the Edinburgh streets, using what he called the 'artisan Scots' of the ordinary man in Leith (or maybe sitting in Princes Street Gardens), often disaffected, sometimes retired or unemployed, whose sceptical view of the great and the good in his native city speaks for the thousands of folk who will never get the chance to shake hands with Timothy Clifford.

In terms of our literary map, this particularly urban direction in the use of the Scots voice was to be the road ahead for many subsequent writers. Robert Garioch, and Ian Hamilton Finlay's little book with the long title, *Glasgow Beasts, an a Burd, aw an a Fush, haw, an Inseks* (1961), paved the way for Tom Leonard's much more political engagement to make 'art' from the speech of those who have been denied a voice in the literary canon. The modern Scots poet must speak, in Leonard's words, for all those 'thit / hi bilonged / tay a / class uv / people / thit hid / hid thir / langwij / sneered / it /since hi / wuz born', suffering 'thi / violence uv / people in / positions / uv / power telln / him his / culture wuz / a sign / of his / inferiority.'[28]

In the same vein, but less overtly political, I would place the colloquial wit and energy of Liz Lochhead's poetry, as well as her drama and monologues, and notably also the work of the poet Kathleen Jamie whose collection, *The Queen of Sheba*, uses Scots and speaks for the experience of schoolgirls, housewives, girlfriends, housing estates and shopping centres. A feminist perspective on Jamie and Lochhead would see their writing as an empowerment in the same cause as the linguistic empowerment sought by Leonard and Kelman in their work, however 'masculinist' their outlook might be. Certainly an overtly feminist perspective plays a part in the writing of poets such as Jackie Kay and Angela McSeveney, although their register is closer to a more regular form of English.

If I had to make a historical link between the second generation of the 'Scottish Renaissance' and some of the contemporary writers mentioned above (many of whom would deny all connection to the Renaissance movement per se) then I would point to the experience of the Glasgow Unity Theatre in the 1940s. In tracing a cultural shift, which I have characterised as a move away from Chris Guthrie and the land, towards the cities and the more actively political concerns of Ewan Tavendale, I think that the Unity programme, by creating a specifically political agenda to deal with working-class life and accents, can be seen as an event whose significance is much greater in retrospect than its relatively short-lived critical success would seem to have warranted at the time.

The Unity Theatre's aim to perform Scottish working-class plays to match O'Casey and Gorky (both of whom were also featured by them) produced works such as Robert McLeish's *The Gorbals Story* (1946), Ena Lamont Stewart's *Men Should Weep* (1947), George Munro's *Gold in His*

Boots (1947) and James Barke's *Major Operation* (1941), and the link to more
contemporary writing for the Scottish stage could not be made more
clearly than by pointing out that Roddy McMillan, author of *All in Good
Faith* (1958) and *The Bevellers* (1973), was an actor (along with Russell
Hunter) in the original production of *The Gorbals Story* in 1946. It was to
take another thirty years, but the resurgence of working-class drama in the
1970s makes us reassess the significance of The Unity Theatre group.[29]
There are dozens of these later productions which one could mention, but
among the most notable have been the output of the 7:84 Theatre Company, especially their debut play, John McGrath's *The Cheviot, the Stag and
the Black Black Oil* (1973); then there was Hector Macmillan's *The Sash*
(1973) and *The Gay Gorbals* (1976), and Roddy McMillan's *The Bevellers*
(1973) along with John Byrne's *Slab Boys* trilogy (1978, 1979, 1982).

Bill Bryden's productions – *Willie Rough* (1972) and *Benny Lynch* (1974),
and then *Civilians* (1981) and ultimately *The Ship* (1993) and *The Big Picnic*
(1994) – come from the same territory, but seem less challenging, somehow, having settled for familiar sentiment and large-scale theatrical spec-
tacle. The most striking developments in this genre have moved over to
what are, in effect, films for television (rather than 'the television play'),
with the work of Peter McDougall, and the brilliant productions of *Tutti
Frutti* and *Your Cheatin' Heart* from John Byrne, whose stage plays were
positively filmic in their pace and technique from the very start.

Whether these plays are 'working-class drama' or not the fact remains
that in the mid-1970s, Scottish culture was resounding to the vitality and
the liberating violence of urban demotic speech, heard in theatres, wholly
uncensored, for the first time. I stress the dates, because it is against this
background that we must place the final literary movement discussed in this
chapter, namely the rise of west of Scotland urban realism in poetry (already
mentioned) and also in the prose of writers such as William McIlvanney,
James Kelman and a whole host of younger authors, such as Gordon Legge,
Duncan McLean and Irvine Welsh who are in danger of being known
collectively (though not accurately) as successors of Kelman.

UNTO THE THIRD GENERATION

It is tempting to see these writers as 'realists', pure and simple, as if there
were no philosophical implications to their position, but this would not be
accurate. 'Realism' has its own symbolic burden, its own sentimentalities,
and it can carry a subtle political agenda just as well as the more mythopoeic writing with which we began. (If you doubt that there is more than

one kind of 'realism', compare the writing of Carl MacDougall, Alan Spence and Irvine Welsh.)

William McIlvanney's work is haunted by class loyalty and the possibility of community just as much as are the novels of Neil Gunn, but McIlvanney's community has been gravely damaged by the industrial work ethic, first in *Docherty* (1975) set in about 1906, and then by the collapse of that ethic 80 years later, in *The Big Man* (1985). In either case, these novels tend to pit one man against a system which is always portrayed as being somehow impersonal, unapproachable, predetermined and even unchangeable. The lack of a labour history among the coal miners in *Docherty*, for example, is a very striking textual absence: which is to say that the author's eye is directed elsewhere than politics. In fact, McIlvanney's ethic is essentially that of existential tragedy, and his characters tend to live by the premise that if a man can't be free, he can at least be independent.

It is the old spinster lady, Miss Gilfillan, who defines this concern with 'independence' at the very beginning of *Docherty*:

> She felt it was a ridiculous word in this place, for what claim could
> anyone who lived here have to independence? They were all slaves
> to something, the pit, the factory, the families that grew up
> immuring the parents' lives, the drink that, seeming to promise
> escape, was the most ruthlessly confining of all. Whatever hireling
> they served, owed its authority to a common master: money, the
> power of which came from the lack of it. Poverty was what had
> brought herself to this room. It defined the area of their lives like a
> fence. Still, in that area Mr Docherty moved as if he were there by
> choice, like someone unaware of the shackles he wore and who
> hadn't noticed that he was bleeding.[30]

Here is the quintessential McIlvanney protagonist. We are all slaves to some system or other, and if it is not capitalism, then it is mortality itself, and all we can do is get through our allotted span with as much pride and decency as we can muster. The opening pages of *Docherty* are replete with images of the High Street, and the society that created it, as if it were some entirely deterministic laboratory of human behaviour and breakdown. (The same dark vision was later offered in 1981 from a different genre and in deceptively genial mode by Alasdair Gray's account of 'the Institute' and 'the Creature' in *Lanark*.)

In fact, neither Tam Docherty, Dan Scoular nor Jack Laidlaw are entirely unaware of their position, and much of the inward power of McIlvanney's writing stems from the pain of this knowledge, as when he describes

Docherty's inadequacy – despite his physical strength, work skills and male pride – in the face of the situation in which he finds himself: 'He was like a gunfighter, practised to perfection, unafraid, heroically hard, and pitted against germ warfare.'[31]

The gunfighter ethos is not dissimilar to Raymond Chandler's famous description of the private eye as a knight in rusty armour (which became a model for the books about Jack Laidlaw the police detective), but it reaches its apotheosis in Dan Scoular's capacity for bare-knuckle fighting in *The Big Man*. Yet Scoular learns the hollowness of such prowess and out of this most intensely masculinist value system he even manages to come to a reconciliation with his wife Betty whose freedom he has found so perplexing in the past. Nevertheless, in re-dedicating herself to Dan, Betty is giving herself back to 'renewed risk' in place of the materialistic banalities of her lover's world which now seem 'like package deals in a brochure'[32] and this seems to validate the gunfighter ethos. And the book ends with the same affirmation of risk, with Dan drinking in his local pub, comforted by the inarticulate male camaraderie around him, and certain of only one thing, which is that some day, some time, Matt Mason or his men will come for revenge, symbolising nothing less than the immanence of mortality itself: 'He felt the joy of being here, whatever the terms. Tonight or tomorrow it might come. He wasn't unique in that. It was what his father had faced, and countless others.'[33]

This is Ewan Tavendale's world indeed. One might be forgiven for wishing that in *Docherty* and *The Big Man* some creative and fulfilling equivalent could be found for Chris Guthrie's engagement with the land. Some sense of the 'feminine' or the Other – however disturbingly impersonal it might be – would be a welcome relief for these lonely men, essentially sealed-off (even from their lovers), given to physical action, but held rigid by the male ethos and a sense of socio-political futility in an existential realm of pain and courage, and masochistic or homo-erotic martyrdom. Viewed in this light, I think the 'realism' of McIlvanney's novels can be seen to be a brilliant but wholly idiosyncratic (and essentially tragic) vision of the human condition, or more accurately the male condition, which is every bit as symbolic or as 'poetic' as Grassic Gibbon's account of Diffusionism or the changelessness of change. Kelman occupies the same territory – a territory of terrible defeat – made tolerable by existential heroism, if at a rather more minimal level, and made brilliant by the speed and the poetry of his language. Consider Sammy Samuels, for example, the protagonist of *How Late It Was, How Late* (1994) as another version – only a little more damaged – of the McIlvanney hero.

The most recent Scottish writing in the vein of demotic realism, by Irvine Welsh, Duncan McLean and Gordon Legge is much more challenging. Welsh's *Trainspotting* (1993) and *Marabou Stork Nightmares* (1995), McLean's *Bucket of Tongues* (1992) and Gordon Legge's *In Between Talking About the Football* (1991) offer little space for the existential hero, and almost no sense of community in a world of decaying council-housing estates, drug addiction, disaffected youth, football casuals and the electric thrills of random violence.

We seem to have come a long way, from Deirdre of the Sorrows to Kelman's Busconductor Hines. But I wonder if this is as great a change as it seems, at least in terms of the fact that both these figures are attempts to construct an identity which makes sense out of being 'Scottish', and to find some value there. Is this not the same process in action – once defined as 'Celtic', but now constructing itself as 'working class', by which we seek our 'lost conscience' or a 'vital part' of the body politic? I am worried by the awful fixity of Kelman's characters, and while I admire their capacity to survive, or even to embrace their condition, they seem to me to be trapped, in the end, in the way that Vladimir and Estragon are trapped in *Waiting for Godot*: 'Vladimir: "Well? Shall we go?" / Estragon: "Yes, let's go." / *They do not move.*' The perception that there is 'nothing to be done' is acceptable and undeniable, I think, in absolute metaphysical terms, but it is disturbing (as Kelman means it to be) in a genre which presents itself as realism. If the 'realism' of McIlvanney can be revealed as essentially heroic and tragic, then Kelman's vision is deeply existential and even, finally, metaphysical.

The case of Welsh, McLean and Legge is more problematic in that the world they depict is an even more striking challenge, not only to the bourgeois values of conventional utterance and conventional society, but also to all those mythopoeic constructions of 'Scottish' (or 'Gaelic' or 'Celtic') identity which offered some special value (however humble) to the world at large. Nor can these texts be easily assimilated into 'working-class' literature with its emphasis on political awareness and group solidarity, for the world of drugs and gratuitous violence lacks all such insight. On the other hand, the very vividness with which this world is described, does become a kind of political statement – as an act of truth-telling about areas of social experience which rarely feature in literature and are shown by the media only to be demonised. It is true that some very real critical problems are raised by the deliberately shocking aspects of this writing (graphic descriptions of rape feature in *Marabou Stork Nightmares* and in Duncan McLean's *Bunker Man*) but in their quieter moments there is a remarkable energy to be found here too and, especially in Gordon Legge's writing, a zany good humour which reaffirms the indestructibility of the human spirit, however marginalised or reduced its circumstances.

If I have reservations about what I take to be the tragically closed and monologically masculine social worlds shown to us by McIlvanney and Kelman, or about the violent nihilism of boys on housing estates or football terraces as described by these younger writers, I have no reservations about their narrative brilliance. I have a particular admiration for Kelman's capacity to write creative prose which manages both narrative and dialogue within the parameters of working-class realism, and yet achieves, too, a speed and a wit which remains true to that milieu and, more importantly, true to the value and the thrill of all inner experience, regardless of class, accent or education. If there is a sense of optimism or real freedom to be found in Kelman's fictional world, it is in the quality of his writing. It is this that validates the plea he made at the Booker Prize ceremony on behalf of 'a literary tradition to which I hope my own work belongs, I see it as part of a much wider process, or movement, towards decolonisation and self determination.'[34]

That process has indeed been a continuing exploration on the part of Scottish writers this century, and they have come up with a number of different models, as I have shown, in the quest to articulate a sense of themselves and to find something of value in their cultures, languages and communities. I have drawn fairly broad contours on the map, focusing on parameters which I have described as radical and conservative, mythopoeic and realistic, and I hope I have shown that these lines may not be as far apart as they seem. And if I had to cite examples of how some contemporary writers seem to me to manage to build a bridge between 'metaphysical' and 'realistic' modes, I would point first and foremost to the work of Alasdair Gray whose imaginative realms manage to be deeply political and whose pessimism never dismisses our capacity for love and our desperate need to learn how to love. In more 'realistic' genres (although no strangers to symbolism), the same redeeming spirit can be found in the work of Nan Shepherd, Catherine Carswell and Naomi Mitchison and, in more recent years in the prose of Dilys Rose, A. Kennedy, Janice Galloway, Andrew Greig, Ron Butlin, Brian McCabe, Bernard McLaverty and Alan Spence. But this is to start on another journey dealing with the many other excellent writers I have not mentioned, which would be another map – less bold in its features perhaps – but with finer details along the way.

NOTES AND REFERENCES

1. R. Watson, *The Poetry of Scotland* (Edinburgh, 1995).

2. Quoted in E.A. Sharp, *William Sharp (Fiona Macleod) A Memoir*, vol. II (London, 1912, 2nd ed.), p. 49.

3. The title paid deliberate homage to Allan Ramsay's anthology *The Ever Green*, which heralded the Scottish vernacular revival in 1724.

4. P. Geddes, 'The Scots Renascence' in *The Evergreen: A Northern Seasonal*, Vol. 1, 'Spring' (1895).

5. 'Celtic', collected in F. Macleod, *The Winged Destiny: Studies in the Spiritual History of the Gael* (London, 1927), p. 198.

6. 'Prelude' in *Winged Destiny*, p. 178.

7. C. Rush, *A Twelvemonth and a Day* (Edinburgh, 1994), p. vi.

8. E. Muir, 'Childhood', *Collected Poems* (London, 1960), p. 19.

9. Appendix II, in E. Muir, *An Autobiography*, ed. P. Butter (Edinburgh, 1993), p. 289.

10. N. Gunn, 'The Hidden Heart', *The Scots Magazine*, 9, 5 (August 1928), reprinted in *Gairfish*, 1 (1990) p. 19.

11. W. Sharp, *Ecce Puella and Other Prose Imaginings* (London, 1896), p. 19.

12. H. MacDiarmid, *Lucky Poet* (London, 1972), p. 145.

13. H. MacDiarmid, 'The Fingers of Baal Contract in the Communist Salute', from *Poems of the East-West Synthesis* (1946) in *The Complete Poems of Hugh MacDiarmid*, Vol. 1 (London, 1978), pp. 679–80. See also *Lucky Poet*, p. 321.

14. See 'Islands and People' in G. Mackay Brown, *An Orkney Tapestry* (London, 1973), especially pp. 20–3.

15. C. Rush, *A Twelvemonth and a Day*, pp. 306–7.

16. ibid., p. 301.

17. C.M. Grieve, 'A Theory of Scots Letters', *The Scottish Chapbook*, I, 7 (February 1923), p. 182.

18. ibid., p. 183.

19. We know that MacDiarmid was aware of contemporary European movements at this time because some Scots lyrics in *Sangschaw*, *Penny Wheep* and *A Drunk Man* are clearly derived from English translations made by Babette Deutsch in 1923 in her collections *Contemporary German Poetry* and *Modern Russian Poetry*.

20. Grieve, 'A Theory of Scots Letters', p. 210. See also Kenneth Buthlay's essay, 'Some Hints for Source Hunters', *Scottish Literary Journal*, 5, 2 (December, 1978).

21. In *Jamieson's Dictionary of the Scottish Language* (Edinburgh, 1877), p. 425.

22. 'Thunderstorm', in *Complete Poems*, p. 51.

23. ibid., p. 269.

24. 'A Theory of Scots Letters', p. 210.

25. 'In the Pantry', *Complete Poems*, p. 33.

26. L. Grassic Gibbon, *Cloud Howe* (Edinburgh, 1989), p. 142.

27. G. Mackay Brown, *An Orkney Tapestry*, p. 21.

28. T. Leonard, 'Unrelated Incidents (7)', *Intimate Voices* (Newcastle upon Tyne, 1984), p. 93.

29. See, for example, D. Hutchison, 'Scottish Drama 1900–1950' in *The History of Scottish Literature, Vol. 4, Twentieth Century*, ed. C. Craig (Aberdeen, 1987).

30. W. McIlvanney, *Docherty* (Sevenoaks, 1987), p. 15.

31. ibid., p. 211.

32. W. McIlvanney, *The Big Man* (Sevenoaks, 1989), p. 253.

33. ibid., pp. 270–1.

34. James Kelman's Booker Prize acceptance speech, October 1994. Kelman went on to assert the right to defend 'the validity of indigenous culture' in the face of attack, and if that seems a little excessive, we might like to reflect on Simon Jenkins' article for *The Times* which proposed that 'political correctness' rewarded Kelman as 'a white European male, acceptable only because he was acting the part of an illiterate savage. Booker contrived both to insult literature and patronise the savage.'

INDEX

Moray House College of Education, 240
Morgan, Edwin, 298
Mosspark, 11
Muir, Edwin, 277, 288–9
multinationals, 26–8
municipal elections, 277
municipal housing, 139
municipal socialism, 47, 124, 147
Munn committee (1977), 243
Munro, George, 299
myth, 104, 114–15, 240, 286, 289, 292

Nairn, Tom, 266
National Covenant, 6
National Farmers' Union, 175
National Government, 52, 78–9
National Health Service, 93
national identity, 215, 258, 272
national insurance, 89
National Party of Scotland, 6, 77, 91
National Planning, 95
National Trust for Scotland, 6
nationalised industry and multinationals, 263
nationalism, 5, 46, 87, 105, 246
neighbourhoods, 11
Neill, A. S., 237
New Education Fellowship, 237–8, 241, 245
new industries, 20
'new' liberalism, 69
New Town, 26, 58–9, 61, 93, 134, 280
Nicoll, William Robertson, 251
No Mean City, 214
North of Scotland Hydro Electric Board, 5, 162, 164
North Sea oil, 4, 8, 22, 29–33, 96–7, 117, 258
Northern Ireland, 261
nurses, 198

Objective One, 159, 165–6
oil industry, 154
Old Firm football, 270
Open University, 238–9
Orange Order, 259, 261, 265, 270
Orr, John Boyd, 179
overspill policies, 144
Owen, Agnes, 294

Paisley, 14
parental choice in school placements, 8
Parliament, 88
part-time workers, 197, 199, 202
patriotism, 65
Penny Concerts, 213
per capita income, 20, 23
physical education, 217
pig production, 184
Pirie, D. V., 70
planning technology, 10
ploughmen, 171, 182
poetry, 294–5
Poles, 272, 280
poll tax, 8, 99

Pope John Paul II, 282
popular culture, 12, 210–11, 250
population, 124, 175
potatoes, 179, 183
poultry production, 184
poverty, 67
prayer meetings, 210
Presbyterianism, 250, 257, 275
primary education, 231
private ownership, 11
productivity, 183
Protestantism, 12, 71, 117, 215, 250, 252, 256, 259, 261, 277,
public expenditure, 5, 47
public health, 123
Public Health (Scotland) Act (1897), 173
public house, 211, 213, 219
public ownership, 11
public-sector housing, 4, 46, 138
public service, 8, 124, 146, 281

radio, 90, 210, 217
railways, 170
Rangers Football Club, 215, 264
rational recreation, 210–11, 226
Ravenscraig strip mill, 22–3, 54–6, 98
rearmament, 19
reconstruction, 280
Red Clydeside, 59, 75, 102
referendum (1 March 1979), 97
Reform Act (1918), 73
Reformation, 256, 292
Regional Grant assistance, 5
regional planning, 93, 144
Regional Policy scheme, 55
religion, 113, 270, 273
Rent Strike (1915), 148
Republican marches, 270
republicanism, 79
Rosebery, Lord, 251
Ross, Willie, 54, 96, 245
Royal Commission on Scottish Affairs, 94
Royal Commission on the Constitution, 96
Royal Scots, 253
rugby, 214
Runrig, 266
rural, 154, 289
rural electrification, 162
rural society, 9
rural, 154, 289
Rush, Christopher, 288, 292

Sabbath, 226
Saltire Society, 6, 123
Sandys, Duncan, 87
Saurat, Denis, 286
savings, 36
scientific, 183, 252
Scotland Act (1978), 97
Scotland Bill (1979), 8
Scotland's class structure, 110
Scots Renaissance, 239